CIVILIANS IN WAR

A project of the International Peace Academy

CIVILIANS IN WAR

EDITED BY
Simon Chesterman

LYNNE
RIENNER
PUBLISHERS

BOULDER
LONDON

Published in the United States of America in 2001 by
Lynne Rienner Publishers, Inc.
1800 30th Street, Boulder, Colorado 80301
www.rienner.com

and in the United Kingdom by
Lynne Rienner Publishers, Inc.
3 Henrietta Street, Covent Garden, London WC2E 8LU

Library of Congress Cataloging-in-Publication Data
Civilians in war / edited by Simon Chesterman.
    p.   cm.
  Included bibliographical references and index.
  ISBN 1-55587-988-8 (alk. paper) — ISBN 1-55587-965-9 (pbk. : alk. paper)
  1. War casualties.   2. Combatants and noncombatants (International law)   3. Military
history, Modern—20th century.   4. War—Moral and ethical aspects.   5. Civil-military
relations.   I. Chesterman, Simon.

U21.2.C517   2001
172'.42—dc21
                                                                              00-045980

British Cataloguing in Publication Data
A Cataloguing in Publication record for this book
is available from the British Library.

Printed and bound in the United States of America

∞   The paper used in this publication meets the requirements
    of the American National Standard for Permanence of
    Paper for Printed Library Materials Z39.48-1984.

  5   4   3   2   1

Contents

Foreword

Vartan Gregorian

In an obscure corner of the International Court of Arbitration in the Hague "Peace Palace" hangs the portrait of the long-dead Nicholas II, the variously revered and reviled czar of the Russian empire who was the inspiration behind the first Hague International Peace Conference in 1899. Tour guides at the Peace Palace report that few contemporary visitors can identify the visage of the man whose motives in calling for an international conference to both curtail the resort to war and to mitigate its most inhumane effects have long been questioned. Some argue that the czar promoted the conference because he was painfully aware of his nation's inability to compete in a global arms race. Others, more charitably, point to an influential meeting between the thirty-year-old czar and the Polish railway magnate Ivan Bliokh, who published a six-volume work in 1898 that graphically quantified the horrendous casualty rates and other havoc that would result from a future war.[1]

Just as Robert Frost once maintained that a poet can take credit for anything a reader may find in one of his poems, even if unintended, modern observers can look back at Czar Nicholas's inspiration regarding the Hague International Peace Conference as transcending his motives, whatever they might have been. The czar's recent canonization by the Russian Orthodox Church, decidedly not for his irresolute, inept, and autocratic record as monarch but rather for his death as a "martyr for faith" at the hands of the Bolsheviks in July 1918, only underscores the deep ambiguity that continues to haunt his legacy. It is an ambiguity that still haunts the Peace Conference more than one hundred years after it was convened.

The letter of invitation to The Hague sent by the Russian foreign minister, Count Mikhail Mouravieff, on behalf of the czar proclaimed that "this conference should be, by the help of God, a happy presage for the century which is about to open. It would converge in one powerful focus the efforts of all States which are sincerely seeking to make the great idea of universal peace triumph over the elements of trouble and discord."[2] As this volume documents, all the well-intentioned platitudes and solemn pronouncements against war and its consequences that emanated from the conference did not prevent the ensuing century from being the most sanguinary and violent in human history. Indeed, even as the participating nations in the conference accepted their invitations, the major powers of the day were already laying the groundwork for the conflagration that would engulf Europe and the world in fifteen short years. And yet, as I will propose at the conclusion of this brief foreword, despite some of the grim evidence to the contrary there remains reason to believe that what was wrought at the first Hague Conference, and the second that took place in 1907, remains very much a work in progress.

Andrew Carnegie, the visionary and beneficent industrialist and philanthropist whose foundation I currently have the honor of serving as president, was, as is well known, an ardent champion of the Hague Peace Conference. His personal acquaintance with and even affection for some of the leading statesmen and potentates of the day (including Nicholas II) only reinforced his conviction that reason and sound policy would triumph over bellicosity, "the foulest fiend ever vomited forth from the mouth of Hell."[3] Schooled in the optimistic worldview of such eminent international pacifists as Nobel laureate Norman Angell, Baron d'Estournelles de Constant, Baroness Bertha von Suttner, and U.S. merchant and career diplomat Oscar Strauss, as well as his own deep and wide reading of history and philosophy, Carnegie was a firm believer in the power of international treaties and agreements to triumph over war. He—like the seventeenth-century father of modern international law, Hugo Grotius, whom he revered—believed that nations are bound by natural law, independent of God, and based on humankind's own fundamentally pacific nature. It was, in Carnegie's view, the responsibility of the civilized and enlightened nations of the world to weave a dense web of legal instruments and institutions to codify this natural impulse and thus enable the new century to be free from the scourge of war.

In his outstanding biography of Carnegie, Joseph Frazier Wall recounts the philanthropist's abiding faith in the mastery of civilization over barbarism and his hope for a pacific future as expressed in an address he made in 1905 to inaugurate his second term as rector of St. Andrews University:

> It is possible to point to many bright rays, piercing the dark cloud, which encourage us. . . . Non-combatants are now spared, women and children are no longer massacred, quarter is given, and prisoners are well cared for. . . . There is great cause for congratulations. If man has not been busily striking at the heart of the monster War, he has at least been busily engaged drawing in some of its poisonous fangs. . . . Thus even in the savage reign of man-slaying, we see the blessed law of evolution increasingly at work performing

its divine, making that which is better than that which has been and ever leading us on to perfection.[4]

Carnegie backed up his evocative, if naïvely optimistic, words with the carefully cultivated fruits of his vast personal fortune. With the persistent encouragement of Frederick Holls, secretary of the U.S. delegation to the Hague Conference, and Andrew White, then U.S. ambassador to Germany, Carnegie was persuaded to finance the building of a Peace Palace in The Hague that would house an International Court of Arbitration and a legal library, the largest of three peace monuments that he would build to advance the cause that had become his life's work (the others were the Pan American Union Building in Washington, D.C., and the Central American Court of Justice in Cartago, Costa Rica). The cornerstone of the magnificent building was laid in the summer of 1907 at the opening of the Second Hague International Peace Conference. It would finally be completed, with much fanfare, six years later.

Just as the bricklayers and engineers were erecting the physical edifice that would serve to symbolize the quest for peace, so, too, was Carnegie constructing the institutional edifice that would represent his principal legacy to his deeply held beliefs. From 1903 to 1914, in addition to the three Peace Palaces he constructed, Carnegie established and endowed four U.S.-based foundations dedicated to the cause of peace, including the policy research center, the Carnegie Endowment for International Peace in 1910, and the philanthropic Carnegie Corporation of New York in 1911.

Tragically, it would not take very long for the more bellicose impulses of nations to overwhelm, yet again, the pacifism that Carnegie so fervently championed. By 1905, the Russo-Japanese War had demonstrated to the world the potency of a Japan that had eschewed the mobilization of a narrow professional army in favor of a nationwide effort to create a "total war machine"—a lesson that was not lost on the other great powers of the day, whose rhetoric in the cause of peace was belied by their methodical preparations for war.

However, it was a later series of small but exceedingly vicious wars—the object of one of the Carnegie Endowment's first international inquiries—that served as both a grim precursor of the wider violence looming on the horizon and a poignant disavowal of the Panglossian perspective voiced by Carnegie at St. Andrews. The 1913 endowment-sponsored "Report of the International Commission to Inquire in to the Causes and Conduct of the Balkan Wars" catalogued such brutalities and depredations visited upon both combatants and civilians alike in this beleaguered corner of the once powerful Ottoman empire that it shocked the adherents of European and North American peace movements, including Carnegie himself. The report highlighted a malevolent force to which neither Carnegie nor his pacifist brethren had given proper due, a force that disregarded the strictures of international norms and law with reckless and violent abandon. As the authors of the commission report described, it was the "megalomania of the national ideal"[5] that served to both ignite and sustain the barbarity that characterized the two Balkan Wars of 1912 and 1913 (to say nothing of its contemporary manifestations) and would provide the impetus for World War I, which would soon follow.

Even as the storm clouds gathered in the years before the "Great" War, Carnegie persisted in his efforts to avert conflict through his personal appeals to the monarchs of Europe, particularly Kaiser Wilhelm of Germany. Although an earlier plan orchestrated by Carnegie to promote a "league of peace" through a meeting involving the kaiser, King Edward VII of England, and former U.S. President Theodore Roosevelt had foundered in the wake of King Edward's death, Carnegie remained a preternatural optimist even as the guns of August blazed in 1914. But such optimism could not be sustained in the face of the grim reports from the front and the harrowing accounts of German atrocities and the genocide against the Armenians in the Ottoman empire in 1915. An exasperated Carnegie, the man whose lifelong motto was "All is well since all grows better," had decided by 1917 that "Germany [was] beyond reason"[6] and that the only hope for world peace was for the United States to enter the war to help defeat Germany and its allies. Thus it was that a man devoted to the cause of peace found himself a defender of "the foulest fiend ever vomited forth by Hell," albeit in the name of a "war to end all wars." Carnegie died in 1919, spared the indignity and pain of seeing the League of Nations rejected by the United States Senate and with it the hopes of yet another generation of disappointed pacifists.

What then of the legacy of Carnegie's Peace Palace, the Hague Conference, and the dreams that inspired them? Pessimists have ample reason to point to the bloody and tumultuous history of the past century, punctuated as it was by a seemingly unremitting stream of brutality against civilians, including the massacre of the Assyrians, the Armenian genocide, the Spanish Civil War, the Italian assault on Ethiopia, the Japanese "Rape of Nanking," the unspeakable horrors of the Holocaust, and the atomic bombings of Hiroshima and Nagasaki. What is more, the past fifty years have seen no diminution in the scope and intensity of such barbarity, even as modernity marches confidently forward. From the killing fields of Cambodia and the mass graves of El Salvador to, more recently, the genocide in Rwanda and the massacres in Bosnia, human beings do not seem to have learned anything from these collective obscenities except how best to murder one another. Technological advancements, although amply enlisted in the cause of such malevolence, have not even been necessary to further its prosecution—as the machetes and pick axes of Sierra Leone so gruesomely give testament.

As a historian, I am compelled by training and temperament to take the long view. In many ways, the violence perpetrated during the twentieth century was no more intense and deadly to civilians than that of the Romans laying waste to Carthage (or the Vandals and Visigoths sacking Rome centuries later), the decimation wrought by Genghis Khan and his hordes, or the religion-fueled massacres of the Thirty Years War. The absolute number of violent deaths in the twentieth century was clearly unprecedented, but in relative terms, the long march of history is abundantly littered with the corpses of men, women, and children who were victims of war.

And yet, something did change in the past century. The concept of total war first pioneered by Napoleon in his mass mobilization of "the people" reached its apogee in the twentieth century during World Wars I and II when "the people" became, more than ever, both an instrument and a target of combatants. But along with this increase in the victimization of civilians and the blurring of lines between combatant and noncombatant also came a revived recognition of the need to rein in the dogs of war, particularly as they threatened the lives of the innocent and the vulnerable. And so, in spite of—and perhaps more accurately, in response to—the depredations of the past century came the body of international humanitarian and human rights law, given early voice at the Hague International Peace Conference in 1899 (and detailed in this volume) that offered a normative and legal rationale for mitigating the worst impulses of the human condition.

It was not so much that Andrew Carnegie overstated his case at St. Andrews in 1905 when he heralded "the many bright rays, piercing the dark cloud, which encourage us," but that his judgment was premature. It would take the bitter crucible of the total wars that were waged with increasing lethality during the ensuing decades to shake humanity out of its dangerous stupor and to "draw in some of the poisonous fangs" of war. The record of the past one hundred years, to say nothing of the past ten, is a distressing reminder that the world still has far to go to realize the enlightened vision of the first Hague Conference. But the legal and institutional scaffolding first erected at that conference has allowed latter-day proponents of peace to contribute the intellectual bricks and mortar to the construction of an even more lasting and glorious monument, as yet unfinished, than Carnegie's heralded Peace Palace. Thus, although Czar Nicholas's portrait may hang in relative obscurity in a darkened corner of that palace, and contemporary Russians may debate his checkered legacy, his compelling *cri de paix* first uttered on the eve of the twentieth century still echoes in the untrammeled recesses of a new and hope-filled millennium, along with the abiding promise of Carnegie's optimistic dictum that "all is well since all grows better."

Notes

Vartan Gregorian is president of the Carnegie Corporation of New York.

1. Michael L. Nash, "A Century of Arbitration: The International Court of Justice," *Contemporary Review* (May 1999), pp. 1, 5. "Ivan Bliokh" is the Russian spelling of the Polish-born "Jan Bloch."

2. Avalon Peace Project of the Yale Law School, "The Hague Peace Conference," p. 7, available on the Internet at www.yale.edu/lawyerweb/avalon/lawofwar/hague99/ hag/99-01.

3. Joseph Frazier Wall, *Andrew Carnegie* (Pittsburgh: University of Pittsburgh Press, 1989), p. 916.

4. Ibid.

5. *The Other Balkan Wars: A 1913 Carnegie Endowment Inquiry in Retrospect with a New Introduction and Reflections on the Present Conflict by George F. Kennan* (Carnegie Endowment for International Peace, 1993), p. 11.

6. Wall, *Andrew Carnegie*, p. 1033.

Acknowledgments

This volume had its genesis in the conference Civilians in War: 100 Years After the Hague Peace Conference, held in New York in September 1999. The conference was generously sponsored by the Carnegie Corporation of New York, whose president, Vartan Gregorian, cochaired the event with Rita E. Hauser, Esq., chair of the Board of the International Peace Academy (IPA), and David M. Malone, president of IPA. Elizabeth M. Cousens, also from IPA, designed the original project, which was ably brought to fruition with the assistance of Charles K. Cater.

The involvement of the Carnegie Corporation of New York went well beyond the role of sponsor. In addition to the critical and much appreciated role of David C. Speedie in conceiving the project and Stephen J. Del Rosso Jr. in encouraging the transformation from conference to edited volume, Dr. Gregorian has helped shape the agenda in this important emerging field of international concern and action. To him and all the staff at the Carnegie Corporation, warmest thanks.

Most of the contributors to this volume have built upon papers presented at the conference. Their work was enriched by the interventions of the many able and eminent persons who attended. It is not possible to list all these interventions, but special mention should be made of the keynote address by Canadian Minister for Foreign Affairs Lloyd Axworthy and the address by U.S. Assistant Secretary of State for Democracy, Human Rights, and Labor Harold H. Koh. Building upon the discussion that took place at the conference (both on- and off-the-record), further chapters were solicited. It has been a rewarding experience to work with all these authors in the final development of their contributions.

At the production stage, Karin Wermester at IPA provided invaluable assistance that made it possible to edit the volume from Belgrade, a hurdle lowered still further by the efficiency and professionalism of our publisher, Lynne Rienner, and her team.

—Simon Chesterman

CIVILIANS IN WAR

Introduction: Global Norms, Local Contexts

Simon Chesterman

The origins of modern international humanitarian law, the problematic body of rules designed to limit suffering in time of war, can be traced back to the Austro-Italian War of 1859. Jean-Henri Dunant, a Swiss businessman, happened to arrive in Castiglione della Pieve on the same day that the Battle of Solférino was fought nearby—a "mere tourist," as he wrote in the memoir of what he witnessed. The brutality of the battle was not untypical of its time, but Dunant's depiction of the human misery was graphic and pointed. In particular, he focused on the aftermath of battle, the wounded men whose numbers overwhelmed the army medical services and began to fill the town:

> Men of all nations lay side by side on the flagstone floors of the churches of Castiglione—Frenchmen and Arabs, Germans and Slavs. Ranged for the time being close together inside the chapels, they no longer had the strength to move, or if they had there was no room for them to do so. Oaths, curses and cries such as no words can describe resounded from the vaulting of the sacred buildings.[1]

Dunant called for the establishment of "relief societies for the purpose of having care given to the wounded in wartime" and "international principles" to serve as the basis and support for these societies—precursors to the International Committee of the Red Cross (ICRC) and international humanitarian law. This set the stage for the more formal convention on the laws and customs of war adopted at the Hague International Peace Conferences of 1899 and 1907.

A century later, what is striking about these conventions is the near absence of provisions for the protection of civilians. This reflected the nature of wars in Europe at the time, dominated by set-piece battles between professional standing armies. At the same time, one concern of negotiators at The Hague was to limit the application of the new laws of war to such professional soldiers—excluding, for example, the population of an occupied territory who might rise up against their new rulers.

War, of course, has changed. In World War I only 5 percent of all casualties were civilian; in World War II that number was 50 percent; and in conflicts through the 1990s, civilians constituted up to 90 percent or more of those killed, with a high proportion being women and children.[2] The adoption of the Fourth Geneva Convention on the Protection of Civilians in 1949 was a recognition of the changing face of war, but it does not appear to have reversed the trend. Fifty years after the Nuremberg Trials, Europe once again convened a war-crimes tribunal to examine atrocities in the former Yugoslavia, while a parallel institution was established to look at the still more bloody events in Rwanda.

Clearly, more than reliance on rules is needed. This book seeks to expand the tools available to national and international actors to protect civilians in times of war. It brings together the work of academics, policymakers, and field practitioners from the legal, security, and humanitarian fields. Part 1 provides a normative framework for the volume, situating international humanitarian law in its historical and political context. Part 2 then looks at the question of how humanitarian actors can and should engage with belligerents to encourage respect for these norms. In situations where this fails, Part 3 examines legal and military options available to the international community to compel compliance. Finally, Part 4 proposes a reevaluation of protection strategies, drawing strategic and analytical conclusions from the preceding chapters. The focus is not on the development of new norms or institutions but on making better use of what is currently available. Much of the present volume, therefore, concerns case studies of conflicts, with a particular emphasis on the intrastate conflicts that characterized the late twentieth century. Understanding why international humanitarian law is disregarded in many armed conflicts, and the successful methods that have been used to induce or compel belligerents to respect the law, are important steps toward limiting suffering in future battles.

Part 1 begins with a chapter by Karma Nabulsi on the legal and historical development of the category "civilian." There is a widespread misconception that international humanitarian law was developed in large part to protect the civilian population in times of war. In fact, the category of civilian was originally defined in order to *exclude* such persons from protection that was accorded to belligerents. Nabulsi argues that the changing status of this term reflects competing ideologies underlying efforts to regularize or mitigate war. The continuing relevance of these debates can be seen in the many intrastate conflicts of the present period. In a conflict where the criterion of distinction between armies is ethnicity, who is a civilian and who is a belligerent?

In Chapter 2, Guy Lamb explores the question of why belligerents violate the rules of international humanitarian law, using the examples of the war of liberation in Namibia (1960–1989) and the ongoing conflict in Angola. He examines violations by both state and rebel forces in these two conflicts, noting the particular circumstances that explain some abuses against civilians and establishing two sets of common themes. The first set concerns the possibility of observation, with abuses being more likely to take place in geographically isolated environments. Lamb also establishes a correlation between lack of monitoring and continued abuses: the media and human rights groups are typically prevented from gaining access to areas in which civilians are alleged to have been targeted, reinforcing the isolation. This leads to the second set of themes: lack of accountability. Punishment for abuses in the cases he considers was rare—in fact, there is evidence that certain human rights abuses were actually encouraged. In other cases, the absence of accountability had structural origins, particularly in rebel movements with autocratic tendencies.

This last point is expanded upon in Part 2. A central dilemma facing international organizations concerned with the protection of civilians is whether and how to conduct relations with nonstate belligerent groups. In Chapter 3, Marie-Joëlle Zahar draws on interviews conducted with militias in Lebanon and Bosnia and Herzegovina to develop a typology of civil-militia relations. By examining such factors as the extent to which a militia identifies with the civilian population and the economic relations between the two groups, she establishes an analytical framework for evaluating the prospects of engaging with a militia on humanitarian issues concerning the civilian population. Her work also suggests the importance of understanding the economic agendas of parties to a conflict.

Chapter 4 turns to an in-depth case study of the activities of the International Committee of the Red Cross in Colombia, including its efforts to engage the various parties to the conflicts that have troubled that country over the past decades. Pierre Gassmann held the position of ICRC head of mission in Colombia from 1996 to 1999, and he provides a unique perspective on the history of those conflicts and the efforts to protect civilians. The ICRC now operates out of seventeen offices throughout that country, having established working relations with no less than 150 different guerrilla fronts. One reason for its success in engaging with belligerents, Gassmann argues, is the ICRC's policy of discreet and confidential persuasion, limiting its public condemnation of breaches of international humanitarian law to statements of principle. Such quiet diplomacy, encouraging belligerents to internalize the norms protecting civilians, may sometimes achieve far more than ostentatious condemnations of violations.

In Chapter 5, William O'Neill evaluates the mechanisms available to the United Nations for securing compliance with international humanitarian law. After reviewing the traditional mechanisms—the Commission on Human Rights, special rapporteurs and working groups, the various treaty bodies, and the High Commissioner for Human Rights—he focuses on the relatively recent emergence of the human rights field operation. The first such operation was a 1991 mission to El Salvador, where civilians were sent to monitor compliance with human rights and international humanitarian law by both the state security forces and the Farabundo Martí National Liberation Front (FMLN) guerrillas. Other missions soon followed, including the International Civilian Mission in Haiti (MICIVIH), which is examined as a case study. O'Neill concludes by addressing the often-overlooked question of how to measure the success of such operations.

Chapter 6 also addresses engagement with local actors: children, and how to protect them from the consequences of war. Alcinda Honwana draws on interviews conducted in Angola and Mozambique to convey the experiences of children directly and indirectly involved in armed conflict. These experiences range from children who serve as soldiers, to the victims of sexual abuse. By examining local practices of "war cleansing," by which children who have fought in war are reintegrated into society, she argues for greater emphasis on community participation in the dissemination of international humanitarian law, particularly as it applies to children.

Whereas Part 2 concentrates on inducing belligerents to comply with international humanitarian law, Part 3 addresses the question of compelling them to do so, by legal and military means. Chapter 7 by Simon Chesterman considers the use of international criminal law in dealing with atrocities. Colored by the legacy of the Nuremberg Trials, international criminal prosecution is too often understood in ideal terms, and as the only alternative to blanket amnesties. This idealism is reflected in the jurisprudence of the two ad hoc tribunals established for the former Yugoslavia and Rwanda in 1993 and 1994, each dealing with distinct situations quite unlike the position of the Allies following the unconditional surrender of Germany. In fact, international criminal law is only one of a range of mechanisms that are available in postconflict situations—the choice of the appropriate remedy must ultimately depend upon the country within which the atrocities have taken place.

In Chapter 8, Navanethem Pillay, president of the International Criminal Tribunal for Rwanda, discusses the particular question of how international criminal law deals with sexual violence in times of conflict. Long considered to be an inevitable and unavoidable concomitant of war, rape was often overlooked in criminal proceedings such as the Nuremberg Trials. In recent years, the Rwandan Tribunal has produced some of the most significant jurisprudence on rape as an international crime; Pillay presents this jurisprudence in its proper national and international context.

The chapter by Adam Roberts critically reviews the use of "humanitarian" issues as triggers for military action, usually—though not always—under the auspices of the UN Security Council. Roberts first examines the extent to which the identification of humanitarian concerns has become the touchstone for the initiation of military action, and the overlapping (and sometimes contradictory) purposes that may contribute to such action being carried out. He then considers the different attitudes to the use of humanitarian issues as a trigger for military action in the laws of war, in humanitarian organizations, in the ICRC (considered a "special case"), and in certain UN documents, the quality of which has been uneven. A central problem with the emerging regime, he concludes, is that it is difficult to combine humanitarian ends with well-defined political goals and effective military means. Uses of force to stop war crimes, protect threatened civilians, and ensure the safety of humanitarian workers need to be serious, sustained, planned properly, and led effectively. Difficulties in using force for at least partly humanitarian ends are particularly acute when, as so often happens, the progression to the use of force is halting and ambivalent.

Ambivalence is the subject of Edward Luck's chapter, with an analysis of the political side of economic or military intervention to enforce humanitarian norms. Such action is often halting and inconsistent, presenting mixed messages on the commitment of the international community to enforce international humanitarian law. Luck addresses the politics of ambivalence from three perspectives: the political culture of the United Nations, the structural asymmetries of an international order made up of sovereign states, and the ambiguous nature of the conflicts themselves. This critique leads to a warning against the current fashion of "ad hockery"—flexible responses that may in fact undermine the international rule of law.

Part 4 provides a practical and analytical synthesis to the themes that run throughout this book and maps out new territory for protection of civilians in the twenty-first century. In Chapter 11, Claude Bruderlein argues for a critical reappraisal of the international community's approach toward humanitarian crises. First, the role of nonstate actors must be given greater prominence. This includes nonstate armed groups as well as corporations, whose economic stake in conflict areas may be a key leverage point for humanitarian actors. Second, Bruderlein identifies a disturbing trend toward the relativization of the category "civilian," by reference to differing scales of "innocence." Such a development would undermine fundamental principles of international humanitarian law, which should instead be *re*asserted and supported by stronger and more effective action under existing mechanisms. Such mechanisms can also be reinforced by expanding the scope of humanitarian protection to include the provision of durable solutions for the victims of war, diversifying the agents and implementation strategies of such protection, and developing field strategies that actively include local structures.

Bruce Jones and Charles Cater conclude by drawing together four levels of politics and policy that are explicit or implicit in the preceding eleven chapters. The protection of civilians in and from war requires making effective connections between these four levels: universal norms, international and regional organizations, strategies for protection, and the specific local context in which an armed conflict takes place. Jones and Cater's analysis leads to recommendations in the area of specific research agendas, organizational development, and a reassessment of the political engagement necessary to achieve effective action in this area. Crucially, they argue that the search for a more effective and consistent implementation of international norms and laws to protect civilians in war begins with more consistent and effective engagement in domestic politics, both at the local level at which conflict takes place and in the capitals of those states that possess the resources and capacity, though often lack the will, to act.

Henri Dunant concluded his memoir of Solférino with the observation that although the new and frightful weapons of destruction available to soldiers seemed likely to abridge the duration of future wars, it nevertheless appeared likely that future battles would only become more and more murderous. In fact, the murderousness of armed conflict often depends on only the most basic of weapons. The challenge for the international community, then, is not so much to develop new international norms and new regimes but to make those global norms relevant to local contexts.

Notes

1. Henri Dunant, *Un souvenir de Solférino* (Geneva: Jules-Guillaume Fick, 1862), available in French and English at www.icrc.org.

2. See Geraldine van Bueren, "The International Legal Protection of Children in Armed Conflicts," *International and Comparative Law Quarterly* 43 (1994), p. 809.

PART 1

International Humanitarian Law in Context

1

Evolving Conceptions of Civilians and Belligerents: One Hundred Years After the Hague Peace Conferences

Karma Nabulsi

There is today a broad consensus on the purposes of international humanitarian law (IHL). It is seen as a set of rules to mitigate the excesses of war and as the correct means of introducing humanitarian protection for civilians caught up in its devastation. "Civilians" and "belligerents" are the two most commonly used categories in this normative order, yet what these terms meant in the past, when the laws were originally created, is still poorly understood. Of these categories the term *civilians* has, without question, a stronger and more urgent contemporary resonance. For those who seek to mitigate the effects of violent conflict, the primary difficulty is still how best to protect civilians. Lawyers, members of humanitarian relief organizations and international agencies, policymakers, and the public broadly agree that the protection of noncombatants is the most pressing concern.

These norms have a long history, but war itself continues to change shape; new ideologies and technologies challenge common understandings and agreements, even as the deaths of hundreds of thousands of people through political violence continue to claim our sympathy and our concern. It is therefore legitimate to ask what need there is to provide historical and conceptual foundations for these two categories of actors in IHL. Why should we attempt to understand the particular historical wars that inspired their creation, rather than the ones that concern us today? Wars of empire and of conquest do not adequately capture the current state of conflict today: ethnic, national, and civil wars; wars fueled by drug trade; wars involving

9

strange and terrible chemicals that not only kill whole societies but pollute their lands for generations after; and, most tragically, wars where children are not only the objects of violence but also its agents. Surely, then, the search for rules that attempt to respond to these realities must have a greater claim upon us.

In this chapter I argue that the historical development of IHL continues to have contemporary relevance. Beyond the simple but central fact that both the Hague Regulations of 1899 and 1907 and the four Geneva Conventions of 1949 remain the basic legal framework that continues to apply to conflicts, many of the concerns of the twentieth century have echoes and antecedents in the wars of nineteenth-century Europe. Moreover, the concerns of the nineteenth century have shaped the particular way in which these laws were formed. This background can provide an informed understanding of the present shortcomings and complexities of IHL in the twenty-first century. And, finally, the difficulties that emerged in the course of attempts to define civilians and combatants (and the distinction between them) one hundred years ago are proving equally divisive today.

Before looking at the particular context in which the concepts of civilians and combatants were developed, it is important to note that IHL as it was developed in The Hague a century ago differed greatly in scope from the way it applies today. Most obviously, at the Hague Conventions, lawyers and diplomats were engaged exclusively with mitigating the practices of wars in Europe—European conflicts on European territory between European peoples.[1] It is clear that both the theory and practice of these earlier wars are distinct from the types of wars that are our present concern. Historical contingency is always relevant when looking at the universal application (and especially the creation) of laws. Even the Geneva Conventions clearly reflect the realities and the concerns of war in Europe—specifically those of World War II—rather than the wars then being fought in Africa, the Middle East, and Asia. It was not until the 1970s that such wars had a significant impact on the development of IHL, with the addition of the 1977 Protocols Additional to the Geneva Conventions.

An historical and ideological context is therefore crucial for understanding the conceptual categories of both civilians and belligerents in modern IHL. Belligerents and civilians are distinct concepts, and their evolutions follow different historical paths. The rule that provided the basic conceptual separation of belligerents from civilians—the distinction between combatant and noncombatant—was first codified one hundred years ago at The Hague. But another anniversary should be noted when marking the first time that civilians truly became a real concern of the lawmakers: fifty years ago, when the Fourth Geneva Convention on the Protection of Civilians was adopted in 1949. The next section explores this historical context.

Evolving Notions of Civilians: The Historical Context of the Fourth Geneva Convention

In order to provide both the guidelines and the legal mandate for the protection of civilians, most of us turn to the Geneva Conventions, in particular the Fourth Geneva Convention of 1949—the "Civilians Convention"—rather than the Hague Regulations. It is a commonplace in the literature that the catastrophic results of "total war" were the primary factor behind the introduction of this new convention, which was designed better to protect civilians in wartime. The character of war, it was argued, had radically changed from the "traditional" conflict between two professional armies in the field; as a new set of norms had been created between 1939 and 1945, a new set of laws was needed to reflect them. The jurist William Ford represented the views at the time as follows:

> Hardly a century ago war was a matter involving but small numbers of people. The situation changed when national consciousness and democracy began to develop. Since then the number of people affected by war has constantly increased, so the important dividing line between combatants and non-combatants laid down in the law of war has gradually become blurred. . . . Wars are developing into struggles between the masses. Sir Winston Churchill said, "When democracy forced itself upon the battlefield, war ceased to be a gentleman's game."[2]

Two factors were seen to be key to the advent of total war and the subsequent international legislation at Geneva in 1949: first was the methods used by the Axis armies of occupation, in particular those of the Nazi regime. Gerald Draper summarized this common interpretation of the origins of the Civilians Convention as reflecting "in a particularly vivid manner the experience of the Second World War. One lesson from this experience was that war crimes caused more loss of life than military operations."[3] Another factor in the origins of the Civilians Conventions was the emergence of large-scale resistance as a new feature of war. As the historian Philippe Masson has noted, in the years before, during, and after World War I, military strategists did not concern themselves with methods of guerrilla warfare, either at the military academies or in military literature.[4]

Vibrant doctrines of conquest and occupation already existed in the nineteenth century and were themselves competing with equally powerful ideologies of resistance.[5] Indeed, by looking at the nineteenth century, one cannot agree with the claims advanced at Geneva by some jurists that the Civilians Convention was created merely to reflect a particular modern reality. Rather, it is necessary to look back further, to return to the political arguments and legal debates at The Hague, to find the source of these doctrines.

Evolving Notions of Belligerents: The Historical Context of the Hague Conventions

In the second half of the nineteenth century some progress had been made on the regulation of war. By 1899, the European powers had obtained agreement at two international conventions. The first was the 1864 Geneva Convention on Prisoners of War, inspired by Henri Dunant's eyewitness account of the extreme suffering endured by wounded soldiers in the field during the Austro-Italian war, *Un souvenir de Solférino* (and his subsequent lobbying of the Swiss government).[6] The second was the St. Petersburg Declaration of 1868.[7] Still unresolved were the lawful practices of armies on land and the difficulties these caused, notably the distinction between combatant and noncombatant and the rights and duties of occupying powers and occupied inhabitants.[8] The one existing national codification, the Lieber Code, introduced a set of legal guidelines at the time of the Civil War in the United States.[9] The Hague Convention was formally negotiated at a diplomatic conference over the summer of 1899 and was the first international treaty to deal with the laws and customs of war in a convention.

The problems of introducing laws into the processes of war were perceived in far different terms and were intended to serve far different purposes than protecting civilians. The problems went deeper than the content of the laws—they went directly to an ideological conflict over the meaning of war itself. The central problem engaging the lawmakers at The Hague was most emphatically *not* the protection of civilians but defining what types of combatants the laws were to cover. The debate was so centrally concerned with this issue that it had the effect of restricting the debate to that class of individual. Who was a legitimate belligerent? Diametrically opposed to the manner in which the debate is constructed today—how best to protect civilians— the legal controversies were driven by the problem of how to legitimate particular claims of combatants. Although this was the first time the international community sought to incorporate these experiences into the regulation of warfare, it was not the first time that such legal concepts had been advanced. The Hague Regulations both conspicuously and consciously ignored this issue. Indeed, the real centenary on the issue of belligerents was precisely one hundred years before work on the Additional Protocols began in 1974, with the failed attempt to introduce notions of legitimate guerrilla war into wars of national self-defense at the Brussels Conference of 1874.[10]

One can identify at least three conflicting claims on the question of civilian resistance advanced at The Hague. The first attempted to protect and enhance the status of professional standing armies of the state. The second sought to grant such uprisings belligerent status, a position held notably by small states that relied on national civilian militia, together with *levée en masse* and guerrilla warfare as the central methods of defense. A third position resisted the introduction of the laws into the arena of war entirely. This view was argued by those states with large armies, which sought to maintain total freedom of action in wartime. This challenge of formulating the distinction between combatant and noncombatant drove most aspects of the legal controversy at conferences between 1874 and 1949.

The Legal Controversy over Belligerency Status

The first problem was the definition of "occupation," which hinged on the precise conditions necessary for its legal commencement. For an invading army, the sooner an overrun territory was declared occupied, the more rapidly that army was recognized as the occupying power.[11] In one view, the simple act of tacking a poster to a tree was sufficient to declare that a military occupation had begun in that area, and it was the only condition needed to require the complete passivity of the population.[12] Others, however, argued that a large number of conditions had to be met: not only did the local population first have to be completely subdued but also, for an occupation to continue, it needed to be maintained by force. The object of stipulating such exacting conditions was tactical: the longer a state of occupation could be delayed, the longer citizens had a right to bear arms in defense of their country.[13]

The second problem concerned the question of legitimate combatants. In the traditional laws of war, only professional soldiers were granted belligerent status. The historical privilege was created to serve what Michael Howard describes as "the parasitic warrior-aristocracy."[14] Accordingly, all civilians who participated in hostilities were considered outlaws and, in the chilling words of the draft Russian text at the Brussels Conference in 1874, were to be "delivered to justice."[15] Those contesting this legal norm argued that all citizens who bore arms for the nation were legitimate combatants.

Equally controversial was the issue of prisoners of war. Small countries sought to have all armed defenders protected from reprisals if captured (as professional soldiers already were).[16] A further debate centered on the concept of the *levée en masse*. As one observant jurist remarked,

> All that can be learnt from the precedents of Napoleon's wars is that each belligerent, when invaded, appealed to the peasantry to rise and expel the invader, without caring how much they suffered, provided they did some harm to the enemy; but whenever the same nation became in its turn an invader it did not scruple to treat the enemy's peasants as brigands.[17]

The larger powers sought to have the conditions for a legitimate uprising restricted in several ways, above all by requiring its necessary organization under military command. It was also to be limited both temporally and spatially, in that it was to be launched only at the moment of an invasion and occur only in territories not yet subjected to occupation.[18]

The final set of legal issues centered on the question of permitted army methods in occupied territories, such as reprisals, levies, and requisitions.[19] The first of these, reprisals, was used by armies to punish illegal acts by the inhabitants of occupied territories.[20] Those who argued for the rights of armies wanted to maintain and consolidate the practice of reprisals; those who campaigned for the rights of resistance advocated its complete abolition; and finally, those who saw themselves as introducing a degree of "humanity in warfare" desired to mitigate the practice. Occupying armies typically used levies and requisitions as further methods of punishment, and opinion was deeply divided over their appropriate use. As might have been expected, armies and occupying states insisted on a free hand in their application whereas representatives of nations likely to be invaded argued that they should be used more sparingly.[21] The Hague Conference, in what was seen at the time as a positive step, succeeded in achieving a consensus by omitting the majority of troublesome issues that had wrecked the Brussels Conference of 1874. The problems, although somewhat in abeyance during World War I, returned with a vengeance in 1939. Finally, an attempt was made to resolve these legal controversies over the definition of combatants in the Additional Protocols, where the complex question of the rights of national liberation movements in war received substantial attention—notably in developing a more accurate and detailed definition of the term *guerrilla*.[22]

But from where, precisely, did this ideological conflict emerge? What was the purpose of the laws of war at the time they were introduced into international treaty law in 1899 at The Hague? The legal debates all emerged from the way in which the laws were structured in the late nineteenth century.

Political Principles Underlying the Hague Regulations of 1899

International law in the nineteenth century, both in its structure and practitioners, was broadly liberal in its political assumptions and underpinnings in its attachment to law, order, political stability, hierarchy, continuity, and tempered progress. Yet there is much evidence that the early founders of the laws of war—those who created the Hague Regulations, rather than international lawyers in general—held strongly conservative, even reactionary, views. The Grotian international legal tradition (named after the seventeenth-century Dutch jurist Hugo Grotius) developed during the late nineteenth and early twentieth centuries in the context of framing of the laws of war. The ideas of certain key individuals played a crucial role in constructing the modern *jus in bello* (the law relating to conduct in war), notably in defining the distinction between combatant and noncombatant on which that body of rules relied.

Central to their position was a desire to limit the rights of belligerency to a particular class of participant—the soldier—and to exclude all others from the right to become actively involved in war.

The Grotian approach was only one of many traditions of thought and practice on war and the laws of war. Two other main patterns of thought about the laws of war in Europe at that time represented the views of participants in war. The first was the republican tradition. This tradition of customary practices of war emerged as a direct result of the quest for independence and political autonomy from empire in the late eighteenth and nineteenth centuries; it developed subsequently into a distinctive doctrine of patriotism. The main tenets of this ideology were that civilian defense militias were valued and that wars of conquest were considered illegal. Resistance by civilians or civil militias to any foreign invasion was not only permissible but both a citizen's right and duty. The other main current of practice was expansive militarism (also known as martialism), which was also widespread in nineteenth-century Europe. This doctrine was in direct opposition to the republican one, given that it supported the rights of armies and perceived the attempt to regulate war through laws as both impossible and undesirable. Militarists believed an army had the right to conduct war as it saw fit, and that all civilian involvement in wartime of any type, political or military, was criminal. These two traditions, along with the Grotian tradition, were central to custom and thought on war when the laws of war were being framed at The Hague. They had all emerged from the types of wars that developed in Europe in the course of the nineteenth century: wars of empire, invasion, occupation, and national liberation.

The Legal Norms at The Hague

Five basic norms constituted the laws of war as understood at the end of the nineteenth century. The first, codified at The Hague, was the primacy of law. Within this principle was a cluster of equally significant beliefs: war, it was held, could only be mitigated and not abolished; this mitigation could not come from political action, public pressure, or human nature but only from the introduction of specific laws. Accordingly, the codification of war itself was seen as a primary goal by international jurists, and the creation of international legal conventions covering the practices of war was considered an undeniable (and exclusive) duty of states. Finally, principles of "just" war were not allowed to enter the discussion of the codification of the laws of war; such concepts were perceived to have a destabilizing effect on the entire legal order of *jus in bello*.

The second norm was the introduction of the parity of rights. Keeping the concept of *jus ad bellum* theoretically separate from that of *jus in bello* made it easier to establish and maintain a legal parity between belligerent parties.

This second normative principle was essentially a pragmatic concession to the reality of war:

> International law has no alternative but to accept war, independently of the justice of its origin, as a relation which the parties to it may set up if they choose, and to busy itself only in regulating the effects of the relation. Hence both parties to every war are regarded as being in an identical legal position, and consequently possessed of equal rights.[23]

This formal equality between belligerents could, however, be vulnerable to charges of partiality in practice. The class of person that could represent a belligerent party at war was restricted to the professional soldier by the lawyers at The Hague. This meant that, whether invading or defending, only armies could be included within the law, and they could be judged only by their professional conduct during that war. The president of the Brussels Conference, Baron Jomini, argued consistently for the maintenance of a pragmatic symmetry between the position of conqueror and that of the invaded. Unfortunately, this had the unpleasant effect of granting a moral asymmetry to the parties, and it favored the invading army, given that it was usually far larger than the army of the invaded country, who needed to rely on civilian defense. Yet this "parity" of rights did not extend to resisting civilians.[24]

The third norm was the distinction between combatant and noncombatant. A key principle underpinning the entire system of the laws of war was the distinction between lawful and unlawful combatant. This norm criminalized civilian participation (political or military) in resistance to military occupation. The distinction was introduced as a *via media* norm, which was to advance the notion of moderation in war. Making the rights of civilians conditional upon their remaining "innocent" served two interconnected purposes.[25] First, this legal abstraction was created to address the interests of invading armies (who, it was then hoped, would find the principle serviceable enough to adopt). However, the custom and practice of a distinction between lawful and unlawful combatant had emerged from a different historical source than that asserted by this group of lawyers: the ancient privileges of soldiers. Indeed, the legal norm claimed as its purpose (and its customary antecedents) the protection of civilians from the brunt of the battle. Yet it connected the privileges that accrued to the protection of civilians with a correlative duty of passivity on their part:

> The right of the non-combatant population to protection for their persons and property, the limits and extent of which right we have hitherto been discussing, necessarily involves on the part of those who have obtained this protection on the faith of their being non-combatant a corresponding duty of abstaining from all further hostilities against the invaders.[26]

To underscore this normative conception of civilian passivity, several jurists attempted to assert that certain historic forms of resistance by civilians were imaginary. Some of the most active publicists of the laws of war in the nineteenth century, while denying the existence of the *levée en masse*, added moral condemnation of those civilians who crossed the "sacred line" between combatant and noncombatant:

> That which is called patriotic insurrections or irregular uprisings by the entire population to harass a legitimate army should always be condemned, without bothering to distinguish between methods used.[27]

In this scheme of things, therefore, the only spirit in which to address the challenge of introducing humanity in warfare was to posit a clear distinction between lawful and unlawful combatants; any other position not only muddied the legal waters but was also an act of supreme moral irresponsibility.

The fourth norm was obedience to a "reasonable" occupier. This norm significantly linked the rights of noncombatants to humanity and protection with the duty of obedience by the occupied civilian population to a "reasonable" occupying power. The accepted norm was that civilians owed obedience to the military occupier: exactly how much and to what type of occupier were the issues over which there was some minor dissension.[28]

For example, one U.S. legal publicist argued that the duty of obedience existed only if the occupant adhered to his own responsibility of preserving order and public safety; if he "promoted his own aims," the inhabitants could disregard his orders.[29] However, as a later jurist noted of this particular legal norm, "it is not the right of the citizen in occupied territory to judge the legality of an occupant's order, and in the event of an adverse personal decision, to claim a right of disobedience."[30] General H. W. Halleck of the United States recommended that if the occupant imposed an "unusual, unnecessary, and unmerited harshness," the inhabitants were released from their obligation of nonresistance and "restored to the rights enjoyed by a belligerent in war"; yet what could be considered "unusual, unnecessary, and unmerited harshness" remained undefined.[31] The extent of the disobedience allowed by civilians was also a matter variously assessed by different jurists of the period.[32] The customary laws of war (accepted as legitimate practice) considered many political yet nonviolent activities by an occupier to be disobedience.[33]

The final norm of this code was an attempt to balance the twin principles of military necessity and humanity. This proved the most synthetic and abstract position espoused by the jurists, given that the two principles were polar opposites and, arguably, essentially irreconcilable. Yet these principles were perceived as embodying the two structural pillars necessary to provide a middle path for the laws of war; accordingly, both principles were inseparable and equally necessary. The maintenance of a theory based on dialectical opposites was a particularly "Grotian" contribution to IHL. The only variation was the particular emphasis on one or the other principle, depending on an individual's ideological grounding and political preference. Some of the more conservative lawyers (influential at The Hague) believed that in order to conform with military necessity, the instrument of reprisals was to be commended as the surest means of upholding the rule of law:

> This terrible right has forever been employed against an enemy who did not respect the laws and customs of war or who took recourse to means forbidden by the *droit des gens*. It will never disappear, because the laws of war are laws of necessity, and it will always be necessary to repress acts of treason, bad faith, and vengeance.[34]

As we shall see in the following section, mid-twentieth-century jurists, in particular jurists of the International Committee of the Red Cross at Geneva in 1949, had a far different view of the matter. Indeed, they believed that humanity ranked much higher than military necessity and that reprisals had to be restricted, with certain methods even banned.[35] Although they continued to recognize the doctrine of military necessity, they found most of its methods inappropriate and were successful in ranking the rights of humanity over those of military necessity in many cases.

The New Conception of Civilians
at Geneva in 1949

The evolving legal culture that sought to introduce mitigation and regulation into war relied, then, on certain basic understandings. These laws were created in Europe to tackle the problems of war in Europe; in the nineteenth century, these problems concerned conquest and occupation. By the end of World War II, these norms had changed. In particular, it was recognized that civilians should be protected from the actions of aggressor states. The republican paradigm of war became increasingly powerful, due to the increasing legitimation of the participation of civilians in war as agents rather than passive victims. The myth as well as the actual practice of resistance relied on a more popular notion of citizenship, patriotism, and participation in defense of the country. The transformations in the international order confirmed this postwar era as the beginning of "international humanitarian law" rather than that of "the laws and customs of war," as at The Hague.

In this respect, several changes in the legal approach to the negotiations in 1949 were significant. The first was the creation of the Civilians Convention, marking a radical shift from the emphasis on *jus in bello* and confirming the more democratic principle that laws came before war. Many particular methods of reprisals were banned at Geneva. For example, there was wide-spread support for forbidding absolutely such practices as deportations, taking of hostages, collective punishments, inhumane internment, torture, and the resettling of a belligerent's population on occupied territory.[36] Nevertheless, the principle of military necessity remained a central tenet of this new doctrine. Balancing the demands of war against humanitarian concerns continued to be the basic principle for mitigating the excesses of armed conflict, with the two principles wedded into a single axiom of law. As one ICRC delegate at Geneva said,

> If the protection of civilians is to be effective, the wording of the provisions on which it is based must take account of the requisites of war. Otherwise they run the risk of remaining a dead letter. If our work is to be of value, we must always keep realities in view, and avoid laying down rules that cannot be applied.[37]

Yet the same convention reflected the modern notion that law was made not only for states but for their citizens as well. Civilians were now seen as a distinct category under international law, whereas previously the laws of war had been directed solely at states' interests rather than those of civilian populations. Individuals were therefore granted rights and protections under international law. Also, the understanding that resistance by civilians was a real custom of war began to be accepted in discussions about the distinction between lawful and unlawful combatants. A new legal interpretation, which considered resistance to be a crime not against international but only martial law, gained growing support. By 1949 some countries reinterpreted their domestic law so as to enshrine such a duty. At Dutch trials in 1946, a judge ruled that the Hague Conventions did not create legal obligations in conscience binding on the inhabitants. The Dutch Court of Cassation, examining war crimes that occurred during German occupation, ruled that resistance was a "permissible weapon to use against the occupant." The norm was explicitly included in Yugoslavia's postwar constitution, which prohibited the acceptance of foreign occupation by officials or the population. Belgium, by contrast, legislated preemptively to cede the occupier a range of rights only under local or "municipal" law; the occupier therefore derived neither sovereign nor international rights over the inhabitants, merely what rights the occupied government had granted it.[38] Also marking a new departure for the notion and treatment of civilians at Geneva was the introduction of the concept of proportionality in the punishments that could be used under martial law to punish civilian hostilities under occupation.[39] But the most significant development in Geneva, quite distinct from those of the nineteenth-century lawyers who constructed the Hague Regulations, was the outright banning of most of the traditional tools used by occupying armies to punish civilian resistance, and the denunciation of many established army practices as "grave breaches" of this body of law.[40]

Conclusion

I have argued that an understanding of both time and place is crucial for an appreciation of the nature of certain problems that are associated with the application of "neutral" and "universal" laws. The world in which these laws were constructed was clearly not neutral but both ideologically driven and value-laden. By showing the evolving norms concerning civilians and belligerents, the claim here has not been to dismiss law as merely a reflection of power politics but to demand a more serious appreciation of the context of international humanitarian law, of its strengths and its weaknesses.

The Grotian tradition, from which the more rarefied tradition of the laws of war emerged, contains both strengths and weaknesses as an ideological construct. Its strengths suggest ways of making IHL more relevant to conflicts of the twenty-first century. One of its greatest assets was its sheer discursive power, its capacity to articulate the proper frontiers of legitimate discourse in the field and, in so doing, to represent the political interests of the hegemonic powers. Grotian ideology performed this function with notable skill and consummate elegance. This sensitivity was also apparent in the tradition's flexibility and adaptability, ensuring that its principles were always attuned to the needs of the times (at least as defined by the dominant powers).

This last strength leads us to a paradigm that would serve our needs far better than the one proposed by that particular group of lawyers in 1899. The views of the dominant powers of today's international system parallel, in both norms and practices, the republican paradigm of the laws of war. This position, although now hegemonic, had been advanced by rather more marginalized legal experts of The Hague period, such as the French legal scholar Charles Lucas of the International Institute of Law. He fought almost singlehandedly for the mitigation of war rather than simply its regularization, and he argued progressive ideals and legal norms with persuasive and consistent skill. While most progressive jurists of this period sought to realize republican goals in the arena of domestic law, with extraordinary commitment Lucas engaged in the more lonely battle to introduce norms of democracy and justice in the international realm. More than a century ago he was advancing norms now accepted as customary law in the international system: aggressive war as illegal, the outright banning of most severe types of army reprisals in occupied territories, the introduction of legal restraints on all combatants—be they civil militias or standing armies.[41] Although the lawyers of empire such as Bluntschli and de Martens are today celebrated, and Charles Lucas entirely forgotten, it is his vision of the system of the laws of war in the nineteenth century that we would unquestioningly adhere to in the twenty-first.

Notes

1. In 1899 sixteen Latin American countries attended as well as Siam, China, Mexico, and Japan, together with the influential presence of the United States; although the concern was strictly with European wars, the Hague Conferences were not restricted to European participants (unlike its predecessor in Brussels in 1874). See William Hulls, *The Two Hague Conferences and Their Contributions to International Law* (Boston: Ginn, 1908), pp. 10–17.

2. William Ford, "Resistance Movements and International Law," *International Review of the Red Cross* (Oct. 1967), p. 43.

3. G.I.A.D. Draper, *The Red Cross Conventions* (London: Stevens, 1958), p. 26.

4. P. Masson, *Une guerre totale 1939–1945: Stratégies, moyens, controverses* (Paris: Pluriel, 1990), pp. 314–315.

5. "Introduction and Legal Commentary," in Jéan Pictet, *The Geneva Conventions of 12 August 1949: Commentary* (Geneva: ICRC, 1960), vol. 4, p. 4. For an analysis of the legal difficulties outstanding after the Geneva Conventions were negotiated, see Richard R. Baxter, "So-Called 'Unprivileged Belligerency': Spies, Guerrillas, and Saboteurs," *British Yearbook of International Law* 28 (1951), pp. 323–345.

6. Henri Dunant, *Un souvenir de Solférino* (Geneva: Jules-Guillaume Fick, 1862), available in French and English at www.icrc.org.

7. The St. Petersburg Declaration was directed at "[r]enouncing the use, in time of war, of explosive projectiles under 400 grammes in weight"; it contains the famous statement of principle, "the only legitimate object which States should endeavor to accomplish during war is to weaken the forces of the enemy state." "Declaration Renouncing the Use, in Time of War, of Certain Explosive Projectiles, done at St. Petersburg, Dec. 11, 1868," in Adam Roberts and Richard Guelff, *Documents on the Laws of War*, 2d ed. (Oxford: Clarendon Press, 1989), pp. 30–31.

8. Doris Graber, *The Development of the Law of Belligerent Occupation 1863–1914: A Historical Survey* (New York: Columbia University Press, 1949), pp. 13–36.

9. Instructions for the Government Armies in the Field, issued as General Orders No. 100 of Apr. 24, 1863. For more details on the Lieber Code see Richard R. Baxter, "Le Premier effort moderne de codification du droit de la guerre: Francis Lieber et l'Ordonnance no. 100," *Revue internationale de la Croix Rouge* (Apr.–May 1963).

10. See T. E. Holland, "A Lecture on the Brussels Conference of 1874, and Other Diplomatic Attempts to Mitigate the Rigors of Warfare," in *Lectures 1874–84* (Oxford: Oxford University Press, 1876), pp. 5–7.

11. Graham Bower, "The Nation in Arms: Combatants and Non-Combatants," *Transactions of the Grotius Society* 4 (1919), p. 75.

12. The Dana edition of Wheaton's *International Law* asserted that occupation actually changed the "political status" of the inhabitants (London: G. G. Wilson, 1889), p. 469; likewise Birkhimer declared that once people lived under the occupying power's rule and received the "benefits" of its law, they owed it a duty of obedience termed allegiance: W. Birkhimer, *Military Government and Martial Law* (Washington, DC, 1892), p. 3.

13. An in-depth legal debate on the accepted conditions for military occupation can be found in *Revue de droit international et législation comparée* 8 (1875–1876), in which jurists of the Institute of International Law attempted to address the flaws in the Brussels Draft through an extensive questionnaire. On contemporary typologies of military occupation, see Adam Roberts, "What Is a Military Occupation?" *British Yearbook of International Law* 55 (1984), pp. 249–305.

14. Michael Howard, "Temperamenta Belli: Can War Be Controlled?" in *Restraints on War* (Oxford: Oxford University Press, 1979).

15. "Actes de la Conférence réunie à Bruxelles, du 27 juillet au 27 août 1874, pour régler les lois et coutumes de la guerre," *Nouveau recueil général de traités* 4 (1879–1880), pp. 223–224, and appendix, p. 302.

16. See M. Clarke, T. Glynn, and A. Rogers, "Combatants and Prisoner of War Status," in M. Meyer (ed.), *Armed Conflict and the New Law: Aspects of the 1977 Geneva Protocols and the 1981 Weapons Convention* (London: British Institute of International and Comparative Law, 1989), p. 111; see also C. Rousseau, *Le Droit de conflit armé* (Paris: A. Pedone, 1983), p. 72; A. Rosas, *The Legal Status of Prisoners of War: A Study in International Humanitarian Law Applicable in Armed Conflicts* (Helsinki: Helsinki Academia Scientiarum Fernica, 1976).

17. This example was used by Droop to argue for an international conference to regulate the laws of war. H. Droop, "On the Relations Between an Invading Army and the Inhabitants, and the Conditions Under Which Irregular Troops Are Entitled to the Same Treatment as Regular Soldiers," *Transactions of the Grotius Society* (London: Wildy, 1871), p. 722.

18. H. Meyrowitz, "Le Statut des saboteurs dans le droit de la guerre," *Revue de droit pénal et droit de la guerre* 5 (1966), p. 144.

19. For a broad survey of these methods in the nineteenth century, see J. Bray, *L'Occupation militaire en temps de guerre* (Paris: A. Rousseau, 1900), pp. 154, 181–183, 191; see also F. Morgenstern, "The Validity of the Acts of the Belligerent Occupant," *British Yearbook of International Law* 28 (1951), pp. 291–322.

20. For an overview of nineteenth- and early twentieth-century practices, see the comprehensive work by Fritz Kalshoven, *Belligerent Reprisals* (Leyden: Sijthoff, 1971).

21. E. Stowell, "Military Reprisals and the Sanctions of the Laws of War," *American Journal of International Law* 36 (1942), pp. 642–644.

22. See M. Veuthey, *Guerrillas et droit humanitaire* (Geneva: ICRC, 1976), especially p. 193.

23. William Edward Hall, *A Treatise on International Law*, 8th ed. (Oxford: Clarendon Press, 1924), p. 82.

24. "Actes de la Conférence," p. 72.

25. The term *innocent* was used by humanitarian lawyers when espousing the case for the protection of civilians. For an interesting modern debate that examines some (but not all) of the philosophical shortcomings of conflating "innocence" with noncombatant immunity, see G. Mavrodes, "Conventions and the Morality of War," *Philosophy and Public Affairs* 4, 2 (1975), pp. 117–131, and two replies to this article, R. Fullinwider, "War and Innocence," *Philosophy and Public Affairs* 5, 1 (1975), pp. 90–97, and L. Alexander, "Self-defense and the Killing of Non-combatants: A Reply to Fullinwider," *Philosophy and Public Affairs* 5, 4 (1976), pp. 408–415.

26. Droop, "Relations Between an Invading Army and the Inhabitants," p. 713.

27. Rolin-Jacquemyns, "Second essai sur la Guerre Franco-Allemande dans ses rapports avec le droit international," *Revue de droit international et législation comparée* 3 (1874), pp. 26–27.

28. J.H.W. Verzijl, *International Law in Historical Perspective* (Leyden: Sijthoff, 1976), p. 151. See also E. Nys, *Le Droit International: Les Principes, les théories, les faits* (Bruxelles: A. Castaigne, 1906), vol. 3, p. 223.

29. Bray also believed that if an occupant instituted an arbitrary, violent regime, the inhabitants should no longer obey and could either fight or flee from the region: Bray, *L'Occupation militaire*, pp. 181–183.

30. Gerhard Von Glahn, *The Occupation of Enemy Territory: A Commentary on the Law and Practice of Belligerent Occupation* (Minneapolis: University of Minnesota Press, 1957), p. 47.

31. General Henry Wager Halleck, *International Law, or, Rules Regulating the Intercourse of States in Peace and War* (San Francisco: Watson, 1861), p. 795. This position is also adopted in Dana's edition of *Wheaton's Elements of International Law*, p. 437.

32. Richard Baxter cites five types: "First, the duty of obedience based on allegiance . . . secondly, a position of temporary allegiance, one favored in Anglo-American law. Thirdly, a duty of obedience created by international law. This legal theory was preferred by writers on the continent, and inferred a concomitant designation of those that disobeyed as 'war traitors' or 'war rebels'. Fourth, the duty of obedience imposed by municipal law. . . . And finally, a duty of obedience based exclusively on the power of the occupant, a position that held great currency in all the legal schools of thought, Anglo-Saxon, Germanic, and Continental": Richard R. Baxter, "The Duty of Obedience to the Belligerent Occupant," *British Yearbook of International Law* 27 (1950), pp. 235–236.

33. Under this interpretation, the Allied armies entering and occupying Sicily in 1943 determined that a host of activities were punishable by death. These included possessing a wireless radio, concealing or assisting escaping prisoners of war, being found in a forbidden area, and leading a demonstration or assembly against the occupation: "Military Order No. 1 of 1943," cited in Glahn, *The Occupation of Enemy Territory*, appendix.

34. General T. Brialmont, *Angleterre et les petits états* (Brussels: C. Muquardt, Librairie Militaire, 1875), p. 63.

35. See, e.g., Pictet, *The Geneva Conventions*, vol. 4.

36. Paul de la Pradelle, *La Conférence diplomatique et les nouvelles conventions de Genève du 12 août 1949* (Paris: Editions Internationales, 1951), p. 34.

37. Max Petitpierre, federal counsellor of the Swiss government, at the opening ceremony of the diplomatic conference, April 1949. See *The Final Record of the Diplomatic Conference of Geneva of 1949* (Berne: Federal Political Department, 1949), vol. 2A, p. 10.

38. *In re Contractor Worp*, and *In re Van Huis*, cited in W. B. Cowles, "Trials of War Criminals (Non Nuremberg)," *American Journal of International Law* 42 (1948), p. 312; *In re Rauter*, *War Crimes Reports* 14 (1948), pp. 127–129.

39. Morgenstern, "Validity of the Acts of the Belligerent Occupant."

40. G. Cahen-Salvador, "Protéger les civils," *Hommes et mondes* 67 (Feb. 1952); de la Pradelle, *La Conférence diplomatique*, p. 57.

41. Some examples of his work on the laws of war are: *Civilisation de la guerre, observations sur les lois de la guerre et l'arbitrage international* (Paris: Cotillon, 1881); *Les Actes de la Conférence de Bruxelles considérés au double point de vue de la civilisation de la guerre et de la codification graduelle du droit des gens* (Orléans: E. Colas, 1875); *La Conférence internationale de Bruxelles sur les lois et coutumes de guerre* (Paris: A. Durand, 1874); *Rapport verbal de M. Charles Lucas sur "Le Droit*

de la guerre" de M. Der Beer Poortugael (Orléans: E. Colas, c. 1876); *Rapport verbal de M. Charles Lucas sur "Le Précis des lois de la guerre sur terre" par M. le capitaine Guelle* (Orléans: E. Colas, c. 1881); *Compte-rendu sur le "Traité de droit international public, Européen et Américain, suivant les progrès de la science et de la pratique contemporaines" par M. Pradier-Fodéré* (Orléans: Girardot, 1881).

2

Putting Belligerents in Context: The Cases of Namibia and Angola

Guy Lamb

Efforts to limit war are as old as war itself. Historical records of early battles indicate that warriors have always been concerned about moral considerations, especially in terms of protecting noncombatants. With the onset of modern warfare, formal rules emerged—commonly referred to as the laws of war or international humanitarian law—seeking to impose restrictions on the methods of warfare. One of the central tenets of this body of rules is the distinction between combatants and noncombatants. The latter, by definition outside the conflict, are not supposed to be the target of attack. The reality of war, however, is that noncombatants routinely endure severe hardships or are systematically targeted by belligerents. Such violations of the laws of war are usually condemned by the international community. Nevertheless, few attempts have been made to provide a clearer understanding of *why* violations of the laws of war take place.

In this chapter I seek to fill that gap, using the examples of the war of liberation in Namibia (1960–1989) and the ongoing conflict in Angola. In protracted conflicts such as these, the distinction between combatant and noncombatant may become blurred. I examine the issue of compliance with this basic rule from the perspective of the belligerents and the context within which they operate. Such understanding is the first step toward prevention.

Namibia

Namibia (formerly South West Africa) has a violent history, one of exploitation, gross human rights violations, and genocide. The period of German colonial rule (from the late 1800s to 1915) was the most brutal; in 1904 the colonial administration actively sought to exterminate the Herero and Nama people following an armed rebellion. Approximately 74,000 Herero and Namas were killed as a result.

Following its invasion of the German-held territory during World War I, South Africa became Namibia's next colonial master. Under South African rule, the indigenous population continued to be oppressed as the new rulers implemented racially discriminatory policies. In 1960, organized resistance to South African rule emerged in the form of the South West Africa People's Organization (SWAPO). In 1966, SWAPO launched an armed struggle in which its armed wing, the People's Liberation Army of Namibia (PLAN), mounted a guerrilla campaign against the South African occupation regime. In response, the South African Defense Force (SADF) and the South African Police (SAP) employed counterinsurgency strategies against SWAPO and its alleged supporters. In 1988, after almost three decades of war, South Africa agreed to withdraw from Namibia as part of the Angolan peace settlement, paving the way for Namibia's independence in March 1990.

Between 1966 and 1988, the period under consideration, the laws of war concerning the status of civilians were routinely ignored by both sides. This section presents an overview of these violations and analyzes the circumstances that contributed to this state of affairs.

Actions by the South African Security Forces

The pattern of human rights violations committed by the South African security forces against civilians varied over the period 1966–1989. These violations were mainly dependent on the nature and level of SWAPO's resistance to the South African occupation, particularly PLAN's military effectiveness. Typically, high-profile SWAPO members and alleged insurgents within Namibia were targeted. Many of these individuals were imprisoned under harsh conditions; torture was frequently used. Two instances of gross human rights violations committed by members of the South African security forces stand out, however: the SADF's raid on SWAPO's camp at Cassinga in Angola, and the actions of Koevoet, a SAP counterinsurgency unit.

Cassinga. In May 1978, the SADF launched an aerial assault on Cassinga, a SWAPO camp located 250 kilometers north of the Namibian/Angolan border. This operation involved the dropping of three hundred Alpha bombs and seven 400-kilogram fragmentation bombs by the South African Air Force followed by the deployment of 370 paratroopers. The SADF believed Cassinga to be the planning headquarters of SWAPO's armed wing. However, the Cassinga camp, despite having a significant military dimension, also housed a large civilian refugee population. During the attack approximately six hundred South West Africans were killed by the SADF.[1] According to the South African Truth and

Reconciliation Commission, the raid on Cassinga was "the single most controversial external operation of the Commission's mandate period."[2] The Truth and Reconciliation Commission's report reveals that the SADF generals strongly believed that Cassinga was a key military target that had to be incapacitated in order to prevent SWAPO from building up its military capacity.[3]

By failing to take adequate steps to protect the lives of civilians during its assault on Cassinga, the SADF violated the laws of war. Under this doctrine, the right of parties in a conflict to adopt means of injuring the enemy is not unlimited: a distinction must at all times be made between persons taking part in hostilities and civilians, with the latter being spared from hostilities as much as possible.

Koevoet. In January 1979, the South African government established a highly mobile, elite police counterinsurgency unit, which became known as Koevoet, meaning "crowbar." According to Louis le Grange, the South African minister of law and order at the time, Koevoet was "the crowbar which prizes terrorists out of the bushveld like nails from rotten wood." Initially, Koevoet's primary directive was to gather intelligence. Communication difficulties with the SADF, the physical environment, and time constraints tended to render the information it gathered useless, however. As a result, it soon acquired combat capabilities.[4] By 1984 its functions centered on search-and-destroy missions. At its peak Koevoet consisted of 250 white officers and 750–800 black special constables.[5]

In operational terms, Koevoet was a highly effective unit and claimed responsibility for at least 70 percent of SWAPO military losses. As an incentive, members of Koevoet received monetary rewards for killings, captures, and the discovery of arms on a graduated scale. Koevoet members were paid R2000 for every SWAPO insurgent that they captured or killed.[6]

Koevoet members were involved in numerous human rights violations apart from killings. These violations included physical beatings, the destruction of property, sexual assault (including rape), and various forms of torture (such as solitary confinement, electric shock, submersion in water, mock burials, mock executions, roasting over fire, and sleep, food, and water deprivation) as a means of coercion, intimidation, and the extraction of information. In addition, corpses of alleged SWAPO insurgents were displayed on Koevoet's armed personnel carriers for purposes of spreading terror and intimidating villagers.[7] There is insufficient evidence to suggest that these actions were encouraged by senior police officials, but as no Koevoet member was reprimanded for these terror tactics it can be assumed that these actions were at least condoned by the leadership of the SAP.

Among other acts, Koevoet is alleged to have assassinated approximately fifty prominent SWAPO sympathizers within Namibia and blown up an Anglican seminary at Oniipa and the printing press of the Evangelical Ovambo-

Kavango Church, which produced one of the few indigenous-language news-papers in Namibia. The SADF blamed these actions on SWAPO, however.[8]

Actions by the South West Africa People's Organization (SWAPO)

SWAPO also violated the laws of war when it came to the treatment of civilians. During the three decades of liberation struggle, two major crises within the ranks of SWAPO saw the organization's leadership turn on segments of its own members and accuse them of being treasonous. Many of these individuals became the target of human rights violations.

The Zambian crisis. The first crisis took place in 1974, when the SWAPO Youth League (SYL) openly criticized the SWAPO leadership over a lack of accountability, transparency, and representativeness. The SYL demanded that a SWAPO congress, which was long overdue, be held. Similar criticisms emerged from within the ranks of SWAPO's armed wing, PLAN. Since the early 1970s, many PLAN cadres, including senior military officers, had become increasingly dissatisfied with the SWAPO executive and had begun to express a lack of confidence in the political leadership's ability to direct the liberation struggle. This was inspired by PLAN's lack of representation on the executive, and the management of the armed wing's logistics (there were severe shortages of food, clothing, medicine, arms, and ammunition).[9] This dissatisfaction was also linked to rumors that senior SWAPO officials were misappropriating funds and equipment that had been allocated to the liberation struggle.[10] The SWAPO executive's inability to address PLAN's grievances led to the emergence of a group of several hundred cadres known as the "anticorruption fighters." They called for an organizational overhaul of PLAN and a party congress to be held.

In March 1976, representatives of the anticorruption group traveled to Lusaka and met with the SWAPO vice-president, Mishake Muyongo (the rest of the SWAPO executive refused to meet with the group), the African Liberation Committee of the Organization of African Unity (OAU), and representatives of the Zambian government. The PLAN delegates expressed their lack of confidence in PLAN commanders and Peter Nanyemba, the secretary of defense. Mishake Muyongo assured the PLAN delegation that steps would be taken to restructure the current command structure, although neither the PLAN leadership nor the incumbent commanders were a party to this decision.[11]

In the absence of action on their demands by the SWAPO executive, the anticorruption group seized control of PLAN's central base and a few satellite camps. The SYL was also involved in this uprising. The Zambian government, at the request of the SWAPO leadership and fearing that this unrest could intensify, sent in several battalions of Zambian soldiers. The dissidents were forced to surrender, and forty-eight anticorruption fighters were arrested.[12] At the same time, the president of SWAPO, Sam Nujoma, and other SWAPO leaders convinced the Zambian authorities to arrest the dissident SYL leaders and their sympathizers within the SWAPO leadership circle. High-profile dissidents were sent to Tanzanian jails in order to avoid a writ of *habeas corpus* that had been secured in Zambian courts. Following international pressure, they were eventually freed in 1978. Over a thousand rank-and-file dissidents were sent to concentration camps in Mboromba in Zambia.

The detainees at the Mboromba camp had to endure extreme hardships, including starvation and disease.[13] In April 1977, two detainees managed to escape to Nairobi. A press release was drafted in which the plight of the cadres at Mboromba was described in detail, drawing considerable international attention.[14] Faced with a potentially embarrassing situation, the Zambian authorities intervened and gave the detainees the choice of either accepting the protection of the United Nations High Commissioner for Refugees (UNHCR) or returning to SWAPO for rehabilitation. Approximately three hundred chose to leave SWAPO and were taken to the UNHCR refugee camp in northwestern Zambia, where they stayed until 1989. The remainder, approximately 1,300, opted for rehabilitation by SWAPO. It has been alleged that those who led the anticorruption campaign were put to death, though this has never been confirmed.

The spy drama. In 1981, at a time of intense organizational paranoia, the SWAPO Military Security (Intelligence) Organization was established under the leadership of Deputy Army Commander Solomon Hawala, answerable only to Nujoma. The Security Organization consisted of 250 personnel, the majority of whom had received security training in the Soviet Union or East Germany. Its sole aim was to identify potential spies and arrest and interrogate them. It had wide-ranging powers of arrest and could even recall SWAPO cadres who were studying abroad to Angola for questioning. After a relatively short period, this security agency became an institution of organized terror that embarked on an apparently irrational witch-hunt for spies within SWAPO. The Security Organization did not discriminate in terms of whom it targeted: individuals from all parts of SWAPO were arrested. Those who were to be detained were recalled to Luanda and taken into custody, then transported to Lubango, an Angolan town 250 kilometers north of the Namibian border and home to SWAPO's military headquarters.

Throughout this period, the Security Organization's mode of operation remained relatively consistent. Detainees who refused to admit to being "sent"—that is, by the South African authorities—were tortured until they confessed to various crimes that their captors wanted to hear and gave the names of "coconspirators." The techniques of torture included various forms of beatings (with sticks and rubber strips, or while prisoners were suspended by poles) as well as mock live burials and executions. Detainees were neither charged with specific acts of espionage nor presented with evidence that they had spied for the South African government. It was understood that any person implicated by three such "confessions" might in turn be detained, with these confessions being the sole "evidence" against the detainees.[15] Detainees were confined to pits in the ground, which were covered with poles, leaves, tarpaulins, sand, and sheet metal. They had to endure harsh conditions, including poor food and sanitation, as well as inadequate medical care. Disease, particularly beri-beri and malaria, was rampant in the "dugouts" and camps. A number of detainees died as a result.[16]

With many SWAPO members being arrested on what appeared to be an arbitrary basis, and in the absence of accurate information, intense paranoia began to take root. As the arrests became more frequent and irrational, members of the Central Committee attempted to intervene, but they were rebuffed by Hawala. By the late 1980s the situation reached a crisis point. Nearly one thousand SWAPO members had been arrested and taken to Lubango. Nujoma's wife was interrogated in 1988, and his brother-in-law, Aaron Muchimba, who was also a Central Committee member, was arrested the following year.[17]

In 1988, a diplomatic agreement was reached among South Africa, Angola, and Cuba, paving the way for the implementation of UN Security Council resolution 435 (1978), which provided for Namibia's independence. This ultimately prevented the security clique from taking complete control of SWAPO, which probably would have brought about the movement's demise. The formal end of the war saw the release of the detainees.

When SWAPO was questioned by its patrons and the international community over the alleged human rights violations, the response of its leadership was that the detainees were spies and hence needed to be disciplined. However, as a Human Rights Watch report pointed out, even persons accused of espionage activities are entitled to certain rights under customary international law. Article 3 common to the Geneva Conventions requires that those who are not in combat or no longer in combat must be "treated humanely."[18]

Due to mounting pressure from civil society groups during the transition period, the United Nations established a commission of inquiry to investigate the detainee issue and associated human rights abuses. After a series of investigations in which members of the commission interviewed former detainees and visited SWAPO camps in Angola, a report was released. According to this report, at least 914 individuals were imprisoned in Lubango by the SWAPO security services. The commission reported that 484 detainees were released and/or repatriated, 115 died in the prison camps, and the status of 315 was unknown and required further investigation. Groups like the Parents Committee, an organization comprised of the parents of detainees, criticized the accuracy of the findings of the UN report, claiming the figure of 914 was too low.

The number of people who were imprisoned by the SWAPO Security Organization or died in detention remains unknown; given the current political landscape in Namibia, this situation appears unlikely to change.

Explaining the Lack of Compliance with the Laws of War and Human Rights Abuses

Cassinga and Koevoet. The SADF's decision to attack Cassinga was influenced by three factors. First, at the time, South Africa was an international outcast, notorious for its racist attitude toward its black population and its system of apartheid. Wide-scale human rights abuses were typical of the late 1970s in South Africa. Given this context, an aerial bombardment of a SWAPO camp that was believed to be a significant military target was not entirely out of character with government policies.

Second, the SADF had major concerns about PLAN and its expansion. From 1977, by using Angola as a springboard, PLAN had begun to intensify its military operations. In 1978 PLAN was operating with larger guerrilla units than it had before, and it was able to move about with relative ease in northern Namibia. Certain areas even became "no-go" areas for the South African security services. PLAN also engaged in acts of sabotage in Windhoek, Keepmanshoop, and Swakopmund, Namibia's urban centers.[19] Consequently, the SADF sought to launch a preemptive strike against SWAPO to prevent it from enhancing its military capabilities.

Third, the attack on the Cassinga camp coincided with a significant breakthrough in the negotiations over Namibia's future. In April 1978, the South African government had accepted proposals that would lead to Namibian independence, although the conditions were not as attractive as South Africa would have liked. Notably, the South African government did not want a strong SWAPO presence in Namibia. Hence the SADF sought to weaken SWAPO's military standing through a series of cross-border interventions into Angola.[20] The raid on Cassinga might have been an attempt to undermine the agreement for Namibia's independence if the South African administration felt that it could attain a better bargaining position under a new set of negotiations.

Turning to Koevoet, the unconventional nature of the Namibian conflict meant that it was inevitable that the South African government would launch a counterinsurgency strategy of some sort. Koevoet was given wide-ranging powers but with minimal oversight of its activities. There were, therefore, no effective mechanisms in place to minimize brutality against civilians and extrajudicial killings of alleged SWAPO insurgents. In fact, through the bounty system, such actions were encouraged. The South African Truth and Reconciliation Commission has found that this bounty policy served as a positive inducement for the commission of gross human rights violations, including killings.[21] Koevoet's actions were rarely questioned by the South African government; indeed, the counterinsurgency unit was perceived to be highly efficient. A culture of impunity took root within Koevoet.

In both Cassinga and Koevoet, the world's media and human rights monitors did not have access to the relevant areas; any human rights violations could therefore be hidden from public scrutiny. Cassinga is far from any urban center, and at the time of the SADF attack it lay in contested territory between the Angolan government forces and the National Union for the Total Independence of Angola (UNITA) rebels.[22] The area in which Koevoet operated was known as the "police zone" and was off-limits to foreigners. A partial explanation of the human rights abuses might therefore be that they took place because the parties in question could get away with them.

The Zambian crisis and the spy drama. The various human rights abuses committed by SWAPO against its own members are more complex. Leaders of liberation movements who are forced to conduct protracted wars from exile tend to become arrogant, despotic, and paranoid. This was the case with the SWAPO executive during the Zambian period. As time progressed, the executive became increasingly self-righteous and intolerant of criticism. The SWAPO executive believed that it instinctively knew what was in the best interests of the liberation movement. Any challenge or criticism of the leadership from within SWAPO was seen as treasonous.

In the aftermath of the Zambian crisis, SWAPO authorities declared that the arrest and imprisonment of the dissidents were undertaken to prevent chaos and an implosion of the liberation movement. In protracted liberation wars, human lives often become secondary to the cause for which the movement is fighting. Under these conditions, the sacrifice of large numbers of cadres might have been seen as acceptable. A more plausible explanation is that these actions were undertaken to prevent a change in leadership and to consolidate power. Accusing one's detractors of spying is a convenient way of discrediting them: such allegations may be virtually impossible to disprove. Given the level of paranoia within the SWAPO executive, however, its members possibly believed that some SWAPO members were spies for the South African security forces.

With the onset of the spy drama, the conditions under which the SWAPO leadership operated deteriorated. Decisionmaking procedures were increasingly opaque and unaccountable; in the wake of military setbacks, intense paranoia set in. Under the security-centric influence of the Angolan government's armed forces, strongmen from the Security Organization took control. The Security Organization became obsessed with rooting out spies and informers, effectively enjoying a free reign within SWAPO. This set the stage for the human rights violations that ensued.

In both cases, SWAPO camps were off-limits to the media and human rights monitors, with the result that human rights abuses largely went unreported. In addition, SWAPO's actions were either condoned or ignored by its host countries, Zambia and Angola. The international community turned a blind eye to human rights abuses, viewing the goal of Namibian independence as of greater importance. In particular, SWAPO had to be seen as morally superior to the South African security forces. This contributed to an environment in which human rights violators continued to act with impunity.

Angola

Angola has been in a state of war for almost four decades. What began in the 1960s as an armed struggle between various liberation movements against Portuguese colonial occupation later mutated, following independence in 1975, into a protracted civil war between the Popular Movement for the Liberation of Angola (MPLA) government and the National Union for the Total Independence of Angola (UNITA) rebel movement. This prolonged state of war has been briefly disrupted by two failed peace agreements, the Bicesse Accords of 1991 and the Lusaka Protocol of 1994. At present, a resolution to the conflict appears unlikely in the short term.

The focus of this section is the period since the demise of the Lusaka Protocol in the latter part of 1998 and the return to fighting by the MPLA and UNITA. This period has seen the continuation of Angola's long and shocking history of violations of the laws of war, particularly human rights abuses of noncombatants. According to Human Rights Watch, human rights violations by both the Angolan government and UNITA were a major factor in undermining the Lusaka peace process.[23]

After the signing of the Lusaka Protocol, there were numerous violations of the cease-fire arrangement by both UNITA and Angolan government security forces, such as small-scale attacks, ambushes, and looting. These violations began to increase in 1997, with UNITA repeatedly stalling on the disarmament and demobilization of its armed forces and on handing over key territories (as provided for in the Lusaka Protocol). In light of these actions, the UN Security Council imposed sanctions prohibiting the purchase of diamonds from UNITA or from UNITA-controlled areas. Previously, the UN had imposed two sets of sanctions against UNITA. The first set (1993) concerned arms, military equipment, and fuel and was imposed after UNITA refused to accept the 1992 election results. The second set of sanctions was imposed in 1997, when UNITA failed to comply with its obligations under the Lusaka Protocol. These sanctions involved the freezing of UNITA bank accounts, prohibiting travel by senior UNITA officials, and the closing of UNITA's foreign offices.

Fighting resumed between UNITA and the government forces in the latter part of 1998. Armed conflicts between the government security forces and UNITA intensified from March 1999 in the north of Angola and in the diamond areas in the northeast and central highlands. As a consequence of these military confrontations, several hundred civilians died and thousands were displaced. In July, clashes between government forces and UNITA intensified in the provinces of Bié, Malange, and Huambo. The Angolan air force bombed UNITA's headquarters in the central highlands, and UNITA forces indiscriminately shelled the cities of Kuito and Malanje. Hundreds of civilians were killed as a result, and more than 200,000 were displaced.[24] In addition, the Angolan Armed Forces (FAA) launched counterinsurgency operations against UNITA, with FAA soldiers being implicated in numerous serious human rights abuses.[25]

Human Rights Abuses by the Angolan (MPLA) Government

Human rights nongovernmental organizations (NGOs) allege that the Angolan security forces have committed gross human rights violations. These include the torture and physical abuse of civilians while in custody; disappearances of alleged UNITA sympathizers while in custody; and summary extrajudicial killings of civilians, particularly in areas formerly held by UNITA. Prison conditions are said to be "life-threatening" due to inadequate food, medicine, and sanitation. Many prisoners are believed to have died as a result of these conditions.[26]

During military campaigns, there have been allegations that the FAA has been responsible for the indiscriminate killing of civilians and pillaging. In addition, civilians have been subjected to arbitrary forced conscription into the military, and antipersonnel land mines have been used extensively.[27]

Human Rights Abuses by UNITA

It has also been alleged that UNITA has been involved in numerous human rights abuses, particularly against civilians. According to Human Rights Watch, Amnesty International, and the U.S. State Department, UNITA soldiers have been involved in extrajudicial executions of civilians, notably of traditional leaders. In addition, certain detainees have "disappeared" while in UNITA custody; torture and physical abuse of captives have also been rife. UNITA forces have been accused of rape, mutilations, and abduction of civilians (including slavery) as well as maintaining cruel and inhuman prison conditions. UNITA has allegedly recruited child soldiers and forced many civilians in its occupied territories into military service.[28]

During its military campaigns, UNITA forces indiscriminately shelled besieged cities and towns, in particular Malanje and Kuito, where over seven hundred civilians were killed. UNITA also makes extensive use of antipersonnel land mines, with the result that vast tracts of land have become depopulated. Its members are alleged to have killed a number of noncombatants during attacks on civilian traffic (both in Angola and, more recently, in Namibia), which the U.S. State Department believes were designed to disrupt transportation and commerce, isolate populations, and maintain a climate of insecurity.[29]

Explaining Violations of the Laws of War in the Current Angolan Conflict

The conflict in Angola has a significant economic dimension. Angola has rich oil and diamond resources for which both the government and UNITA compete. Indeed, profits from oil and diamonds seem to keep the Angolan war alive. The Angolan government, for example, generated $900 million from oil revenues, a significant portion of which has allegedly been used to finance its war effort.[30] However, as the destination of profits from the government's oil dealings is shrouded in secrecy, an accurate figure is difficult to establish. UNITA, for its part, is estimated to have earned $3.7 billion from diamond sales between 1992 and 1997. Claims have been made that senior military officers from both the Angolan armed forces and UNITA have enriched themselves from their involvement in the diamond and oil businesses.[31] It has been argued, furthermore, that the belligerent parties in the Angolan war might have sought to perpetuate the civil war in order to protect their economic interests.

After forty years of war, a culture of human rights abuse among the major players has become entrenched. Angolan citizens are mere pawns in the struggle over who controls the Angolan territory and its vast mineral resources. There is little respect for the sanctity of human life. This is evident in the extensive use of land mines by both UNITA and the government forces. According to Human Rights Watch, out of a population of nine million people, Angola has 70,000 amputees—one person in every 470.[32]

Other reasons for the violations that take place are specific to the two parties.

Angolan government. In general, since the demise of the Lusaka peace process, government security force members appear to have acted with impunity. Human rights abuses of civilians by the security forces go unpunished. The Angolan government does not officially prohibit independent investigations of its human rights record, but it fails to cooperate and often uses security conditions as a pretext to deny access to affected areas.[33] The Angolan government has failed to equip, pay, or feed members of its security forces, with the result that these individuals have resorted to extortion and theft. It has been reported that security force members regularly confiscate food, including relief food aid, livestock, and vehicles.[34]

Within Angola, the government has instituted a ban on media coverage of the civil war. Journalists have been harassed on numerous occasions, with some being detained and imprisoned by the police.[35] In addition journalists are prevented from visiting sensitive areas. Even though the international media has been able to provide the outside world with information on events in Angola, the media censorship has created conditions under which human rights abuses can be easily concealed.

UNITA. Since 1998, UNITA and its leader Jonas Savimbi have been increasingly marginalized, due largely to their noncompliance with the conditions set out in the Lusaka Protocol. Wide-ranging sanctions have been imposed on UNITA, and it has been forced to close down all of its foreign offices. Savimbi has been branded "an international war criminal and an international terrorist" by the Angolan government. At the Southern African Development Community (SADC) Summit held in Mauritius in September 1998, the SADC heads of state, in a joint statement, also referred to Savimbi as a war criminal who is "incapable of leading his party on to the road of peace in Angola."[36]

The Angolan president has called for Savimbi to be put on trial in the Angolan courts. There have also been reports that Savimbi could be indicted for murder in the United States: he allegedly ordered the shooting down of a UN aircraft in which various personnel, including a U.S. citizen, were killed.[37] In the absence of any viable alternative, UNITA's only feasible option for survival is to continue fighting.

Savimbi has led the UNITA movement since its inception in 1966 without interruption. Over time he has taken on a godlike status among many UNITA supporters. This state of affairs has contributed to an abuse of power by the UNITA leadership. It is alleged, for example, that Savimbi ordered the assassination of senior UNITA officials that either defected to the MPLA or broke away from UNITA and established a rival party, UNITA-Renovada. Large-scale human rights abuses can also be attributed to the abuse of power and lack of accountability within the UNITA movement.

In terms of monitoring alleged human rights abuses, it is almost impossible for the media and human rights monitoring groups to get access to UNITA-held areas. When access is granted, UNITA officials closely supervise the movements of these organizations. Access to sensitive areas is prohibited.

Conclusion

As the conflicts in Namibia and Angola indicate, limiting the consequences of war remains a Sisyphean task. This chapter has examined the contextual factors and motivations that lead to abuses such as those that have characterized the conflicts in Namibia and Angola. Both cases point to some particular circumstances explaining abuses against civilians, but there are also some striking commonalities. These may be divided into four categories.

First, physical geography played a significant role in contributing to violations. Cassinga, Lubango, and other territories in Angola's interior are relatively isolated. This allowed the human rights abuses and other atrocities to take place in the absence of public scrutiny and to be easily concealed.

A second and related point concerns the lack of monitoring. In both case studies, the media and human rights monitoring groups were prevented from gaining access to areas in which civilians had allegedly been subjected to numerous human rights abuses. This contributed to the ease with which such abuses were hidden. The absence of a human rights culture can facilitate a situation where human rights abuses become more the rule than the exception. In addition, false perceptions of the moral standing of the belligerent group are perpetuated in the international arena.

Third, individuals that committed violations tended to do so with impunity. Punishment for these abuses was rarely dispensed. This laid the ground for further human rights abuses. In certain situations, human rights abuses were rewarded—especially if these abuses succeeded in defeating the enemy, acquiring territory, and bringing sections of the civilian population under control. Those directly responsible for human rights abuses often found themselves elevated within the belligerent's organizational structure, as was the case in SWAPO's "spy drama."

Fourth, and particularly applicable to the rebel movements UNITA and SWAPO, there was a distinct lack of accountability on the part of the leadership. These movements were elite-dominated and had autocratic tendencies. This state of affairs facilitated the emergence of greed, corruption, and a lack of concern for the well-being of the rank-and-file members and noncombatants among the rebel leadership.

Methods and mechanisms to encourage or oblige belligerent groups to comply with the laws of war—in particular, to respect the human rights of noncombatants—are in short supply. Rebel groups are secretive and distrustful of outsiders and international pressures. Governments, as in the case of the apartheid and MPLA regimes, are often international pariahs. The only room for maneuver lies with the belligerent's foreign backers, who can make compliance with the laws of war a condition for financial and material support. In many instances, however, foreign backers have questionable human rights records and/or lack the requisite political will to do so. In addition, a critical factor is that belligerent groups often employ terror tactics, including murders of civilians to mobilize and control civilian populations.

In short, the brutal truth is that the laws of war are often violated simply because they achieve a particular objective, such as depopulating areas rich in valuable natural resources or preventing communities from siding with opposition, and because the perpetrators can get away with it.

Notes

1. Annette Seegers, *The Military in the Making of Modern South Africa* (London: I. B. Tauris, 1996), p. 224.

2. Truth and Reconciliation Commission, *Truth and Reconciliation Commission of South Africa Report* (Cape Town: Truth and Reconciliation, 1998), vol. 2, p. 46 [hereafter, TRC Report].

3. Ibid., p. 47.

4. Seegers, *The Military,* p. 225.

5. TRC Report, vol. 2, p. 74.

6. Eugene de Kock, *A Long Night's Damage: Working for the Apartheid State* (Saxonwold: Contra, 1998), p. 82.

7. TRC Report, vol. 2, p. 75.

8. Gavin Cawthra, *Brutal Force: The Apartheid War Machine* (London, International Defence and Aid Fund for Southern Africa, 1986), pp. 123–124.

9. Lionel Cliffe, *The Transition to Independence in Namibia* (Boulder, CO: Lynne Rienner, 1994), p. 22.

10. Colin Leys and John Saul, "Liberation Without Democracy? The SWAPO Crisis of 1976," *Journal of Southern African Studies* 20, 1 (1994), p. 134.

11. Guy Lamb, "Civil Supremacy of the Military in Namibia: An Evolutionary Perspective," master's thesis, University of Cape Town (1999), pp. 106–108.

12. Leys and Saul, "Liberation Without Democracy?" pp. 137–138.

13. Siegfried Groth, *Namibia: The Wall of Silence—The Dark Days of the Liberation Struggle* (Wuppertal: Peter Hammer, 1995), pp. 55–66.

14. Leys and Saul, "Liberation Without Democracy?" pp. 139–140.

15. Human Rights Watch, *Accountability in Namibia: Human Rights and the Transition to Democracy* (New York: Human Rights Watch, 1992), p. 72.

16. John Saul and Colin Leys, "SWAPO: The Politics of Exile," in Colin Leys and John Saul (eds.), *Namibia the Two-Edged Sword* (London: James Currey, 1995), pp. 56–57.

17. Ibid., p. 56.

18. Human Rights Watch, *Accountability in Namibia,* p. 71.

19. Susan Brown, "Diplomacy by Other Means—SWAPO's Liberation War," in Leys and Saul, *Namibia, p.* 29; Peter H. Katjavivi, *A History of Resistance in Namibia* (London: James Currey, 1988), p. 87.

20. Seegers, *The Military,* pp. 223–224.

21. TRC Report, vol. 2, p. 77.

22. Annemarie Heywood, "The Cassinga Event: An Investigation of the Records" (Windhoek: Archeia 18, 1994), p. 6.

23. Human Rights Watch, *Angola Unravels: The Rise and Fall of the Lusaka Peace Process* (New York: Human Rights Watch, 1999), p. 2.

24. Ibid., p. 3; Amnesty International, "Angola," Annual Report 1999 (Apr. 12, 2000), available at www.amnesty.org/ailib/aireport/ar99/arf12.htm.

25. U.S. Department of State, "Angola," *1999 Country Reports on Human Rights Practices,* Feb. 25, 2000, available at www.state.gov/www/global/human_rights/1999_hrp_report/angola.html.

26. Ibid.; Human Rights Watch, *Angola Unravels,* p. 3; Amnesty International, "Angola."

27. Amnesty International, "Angola."

28. Human Rights Watch, *Angola Unravels,* p. 3; Amnesty International, "Angola"; U.S. Department of State, "Angola."

29. U.S. Department of State, "Angola."

30. Alex Vines, *Peace Postponed: Angola Since the Lusaka Protocol* (London: CIIR, 1998); Colin McClelland, "Oil Giants Rejoin Fight for Angola Prize," *Mail and Guardian,* Feb. 7, 2000; Global Witness, *A Rough Trade: The Role of Companies and Governments in the Angolan Conflict* (London: Global Witness, 1998).

31. Global Witness, *A Crude Awakening: The Role of the Oil and Banking Industries in Angola's Civil War and the Plunder of State Assets* (London: Global Witness, 1999); Global Witness, *A Rough Trade.*

32. Human Rights Watch Arms Project, *Still Killing: Landmines in Southern Africa* (New York: Human Rights Watch, 1997), p. 5.

33. U.S. Department of State, "Angola."

34. Ibid.

35. "Angola: Journalist Convicted," *Integrated Regional Information Network News Briefs,* Apr. 3, 2000, available at www.reliefweb.int/IRIN/sa/countrystories/angola/20000403.htm.

36. Chris Gordon, "No More Talking to Savimbi," *Mail and Guardian,* Sept. 18, 1998.

37. Victoria Brittain, "UN Moves to Close Net on UNITA Leader," *Mail and Guardian,* Mar. 14, 2000.

PART 2

Inducing Compliance

3

Protégés, Clients, Cannon Fodder: Civil-Militia Relations in Internal Conflicts

Marie-Joëlle Zahar

At least two dozen civil wars are currently raging around the world. These conflicts, like most other internal conflicts in the past decade, are characterized by extremely high numbers of civilian casualties. Whereas international law often plays at least some role in shielding civilian populations during interstate wars, one or more combatants in most internal conflicts are usually not party to the treaties that regulate the conduct of hostilities. At the same time, a striking feature of contemporary civil wars is the use of noncombatants as instruments and objectives of warfare.

The absence of clear guidelines on how and when to intervene in internal conflicts creates a particular set of challenges for international organizations concerned with humanitarian assistance and protection of civilian populations. First, most of the content of international humanitarian law (IHL) has been elaborated in the context of interstate conflicts. This means that international organizations have little or no leverage on combatants to compel respect for minimum standards. Second, internal conflicts typically pit a state against part or parts of its society. This limits the access of international organizations, either because state authorities resist what they see as external interference in an internal matter or because the nonstate actors block access to areas under their control. Third, if international organizations do manage to secure access, the absence of specific guidelines may hamper negotiations to obtain access to civilian populations and improvement in their living conditions.

The result is that international organizations often face a dilemma. In circumstances where they reach agreements with combatants on access to civilians, they may become or be seen as "complicit" in the cause of one or more armed factions. In such cases, humanitarian organizations have been accused of giving in to blackmail. Critics note that international humanitarian assistance allows combatants to shirk their responsibilities toward civilians. At most, however, this assistance will be as an unwilling collaborator in the actions of combatants.[1] Dialogue with belligerent groups may also give legitimacy to such actors, with the related danger that humanitarian assistance may be diverted to other aims and allow combatants to prolong the conflict.

In spite of this growing concern over the fate of civilian populations, there has been little systematic research on the crucial topic of civil-militia relations. In particular, the incentives for belligerents to respect the rights of civilians are little understood. What factors shape relations between these two groups? Can these factors point to ways of alleviating a humanitarian crisis and encouraging militias to abide by legal and customary obligations toward civilians in war? Do they provide the international community with tools that improve access to civilian populations?

In this chapter I first elaborate a working definition of the term *militia*. I then discuss the factors that affect the nature of civil-militia relations. In a third section, I develop these factors into a typology of civil-militia relations, ranking belligerent groups from most to least challenging in terms of their expected compliance with the letter and the spirit of IHL. Finally, I draw practical implications from the typology to improve the fate of civilian populations in times of internal conflict.

The horrors of ethnic cleansing and other violence targeted at civilians frequently overshadow other aspects of civil-militia relations; they obscure the fact that these relations are complex and nuanced. In particular, they vary depending on the nature of the groups involved, they change over time, and they can be—if not molded—at least influenced by the actions of the international community.[2]

A Working Definition of Militias

I use the term *militia* as a generic label that includes all nonstate actors who resort to violence in order to achieve their objectives. Though there are obvious differences between, for example, the Irish Republican Army (IRA), the Sendero Luminoso, and the Kosovo Liberation Army (KLA/UCK), these groups all share core characteristics that allow them to be grouped under the label *militia* for the purposes of this analysis.

In recent times, *militia* has been used loosely to describe the private armies of pro-regime strongmen and the paramilitary formations that organize in defense of the political order in a given country.[3] In Togo, for example, Emmanuel Eyadema, one of President Eyadema's three sons, established his militia in Lomé in the early 1990s. Likewise, in Rwanda, the Interahamwe were intimately connected to the regime of President Habyarimana. The word has also been used in connection with states where the central authority has been considerably weakened to describe the formations established by war-lords, tribal or regional strongmen, drug lords, and the like. In Lebanon and Bosnia, for example, paramilitaries were often referred to as militias.

The word *militia* is used here in lieu of, and in reference to, the follow-ing terms: guerrillas, revolutionary armies, insurgents, state proxies fighting on behalf (but not at the behest) of the state, ethnic armed formations, and warlord movements. At the most fundamental level, militias are armed fac-tions resorting to violence to attain their objectives. Though they may hold de facto authority in the political landscape of the countries in which they oper-ate, or be connected to established and recognized political forces, militias are usually considered to be "illegitimate."

As I have defined it, *militia* applies to groups that vary in terms of their military structure, connection to the central authorities, and membership cri-teria. There are not only similarities but also differences between a revolu-tionary army, an insurgent group, and an ethnic militia. These differences are of interest because they affect civil-militia relations.

Military structure. Though guerrillas and revolutionary armies are defined as militias, they differ widely in terms of military structure. Guerrilla warfare refers to hit-and-run operations carried out by small bands of irregulars. Guer-rilla tactics usually involve raids and sabotage operations.[4] They have been used in the fight against enemy occupation, as illustrated by Tito's partisans in Yugoslavia during World War II. Guerrilla warfare has also been the cen-terpiece of a number of internal wars, such as the conflicts in Angola and Mozambique. Whereas some groups adopt guerrilla tactics and remain small and loosely structured, others develop along the lines of conventional armies. The term *revolutionary army* brings China and Vietnam to mind. In both instances, Communist insurgents engaged in regular army operations as well as in guerrilla warfare.[5]

Connection to the central authorities. Militias are not necessarily opposi-tion forces. Insurgents use violence to challenge the power of the state. In Northern Ireland, for example, this is the main difference between the IRA and the Ulster Defense Forces. Yet there have been numerous instances in which states cultivated militias as adjuncts of state power, the paradigmatic case being the Interahamwe in Rwanda. It is, however, important to distin-guish between state proxies fighting on its behalf, and state proxies fighting at the behest of the state. This distinction is important because many regimes (such as the Duvaliers in Haiti and the Somozas in Nicaragua) are highly per-sonalized but still do not qualify as militias.

Membership criteria. The dividing line between states on the one hand and insurgents, guerrillas, and revolutionary armies on the other tends to be ideological. Insurgents typically espouse different political objectives than the states that they oppose. The term *guerrilla* has often been used to refer to insurgents espousing left-leaning ideologies, especially in Latin America. But militias can also form along ethnic divides. This type of militia has become increasingly common with, though not exclusively connected to, the resurgence of ethnonational conflict in the former Soviet Union and Eastern Europe. The Bosnian Serbs fall under this category. So do Chechen, Abkhaz, and other ethnic groups currently engaged in civil wars in the Caucasus and Central Asia. Finally, militias can regroup individuals sharing a particular private interest such as the attempt to establish monopoly over the production and trade of a specific commodity, be it diamonds or drugs. The absence of collective, versus private, interest is said to be "a major distinguishing feature of warlord politics."[6] Warlords may mobilize followers along tribal or family lines, as was the case in Somalia. However, narco-terrorist warlords in Colombia and Southeast Asia operate differently, usually attempting to control peasant/rural populations in their areas of operations.

Dimensions of Civil-Militia Relations

Civil-militia relations are typically analyzed in terms of identification or control. There is a general assumption that where a militia identifies with a population, it will treat civilians well. Where no such identification exists between the militia and civilians, the modus operandi of civil-militia relations will be control. This explanation may be superficially attractive, but it is simplistic and often incorrect. Both identification and control are complex factors, and it is erroneous to think of them as polar opposites. Identification with a civilian population does not automatically imply that a militia will refrain from attempting to control a group or community. Control, for its part, should not be thought of in a purely military sense. There are less obvious ways in which a militia can control civilian populations, such as the creation of civilian dependence on the militia for security, sustenance, and economic relations. This section presents the dimensions of identification and control that are relevant to a typology of civil-militia relations.

Defining Membership: "In-Groups" and "Out-Groups"

In terms of civil-militia identification, the first and most obvious consideration is the difference between the treatment of one's "in-group" and the treatment reserved for "out-groups." Identification of in-groups and out-groups may be depend on social constructs, such as ethnicity, religion, language, tribe, or clan. In Somalia, membership of the various militias was a function of one's clan lineage. In Bosnia, nationality often determined membership, though this was linked to ethnic and religious identification (Serb-Orthodox, Croat-Catholic, "Bosniac"-Muslim). Identification can also be economic, where civilians identify with the economic grievances of the combatants, or political, where they share a common ideological creed. An example of economic identification would be the support that inhabitants of Chiapas, Mexico, provided for the Zapatista National Liberation Army (EZLN).

Whereas militias may routinely violate the human rights of noncombatants on the opposite side (members of the out-group, however defined), these same militias are often involved in the protection and promotion of the rights of their own civilian populations (in-group members). The militias that practice ethnic cleansing and engage in kidnapping, torture, and indiscriminate shelling of noncombatant populations will simultaneously claim that their actions are in defense of the rights of their "aggrieved" communities. A cynic might dismiss these arguments as convenient justifications, but extensive interviews with militiamen in Republika Srpska in Bosnia and Lebanon suggest that many believe that they are or were fighting for a "just cause."[7]

Lebanon's Hizballah (Party of God) provides a striking example of this dichotomy. Hizballah is committed to forcing the Israel Defense Forces out of occupied South Lebanon and to the implementation of UN Security Council resolution 425 (1978). The militia (turned party in 1990) has resorted to guerrilla methods, including the shelling of civilians within Israel. Hizballah has also been involved in the abduction of civilians, the use of booby-trapped cars, and other actions clearly contravening IHL. At the same time, however, it has upheld a tradition of providing social services to the poorest strata of the Shi`a community of Lebanon. Its efficient and responsive organization has earned it wide social support mainly in the Biqa` Valley and in southern Lebanon. Hizballah's extensive range of services includes medical care, schooling, community centers, and food banks.[8] In the words of one Lebanese political analyst, Hizballah is seen there "primarily as a social movement, a defender of the poor."[9]

Another example of this in-group/out-group dichotomy is the attitude of the Lebanese Forces, the main Christian militia in Lebanon's civil conflict. The Lebanese Forces drove Palestinians from the enclave under their control. They entered the Palestinian camps of Sabra and Shatila on the heels of the Israel Defense Forces' invasion of Lebanon in 1982, massacring the entire civilian population of the camps. The same militia treated Christian civilians differently. It sought to "provide citizens living in the free zones (Christians) with a decent livelihood";[10] a full gamut of social services (health, education, economic assistance) were initially offered through the Popular Committees and later regrouped under the aegis of the Social Solidarity Foundation.

Membership is thus an important factor in improving access to civilian populations in internal conflicts. The wider the "constituency" of a militia, the more it will be responsive to arguments about the need to improve the fate of civilians. The narrower a militia's constituency, the less likely this group will be to exhibit concerns for the civilian population at large.

This is not to say that militias will necessarily treat in-groups well. It is important to bear in mind that social identification with a militia does not automatically imply that civilians share its economic or political objectives. Indeed, there may be economic or political differences between members of the same ethnic or religious group. Members of the same class may also split over ethnic tensions. Social, economic, and political cleavages are not always reinforcing; they can be crosscutting. For example, contrary to popular opinion, not all Bosnian Serbs agreed with the extremist views of the leadership in Pale—in spite of their shared "ethnicity." Similarly, economic civil-militia cohesion may be torn asunder by ethnic tensions or political differences that emerge at a later point in a given conflict.

Factionalism among the various branches of the Sudan People's Liberation Army (SPLA) is a good case in point. In general, southern Sudanese of all stripes agreed on their opposition to the political, economic, and developmental preeminence of the North. However, this opposition did not prevent serious factionalism from developing within the southern resistance movement along linguistic, tribal, and other lines. Such factionalism has been considered one of the most important keys to understanding the SPLA.[11]

The Economic Dimension of Civil-Militia Relations

Militias often depend on civilian populations for two essential resources: fighters and revenue. Both are necessary to sustain the military effort. Militias may also find independent sources of revenue through external patrons or the sale of commodities on the international market. The various forms of economic relations affect the incentives for militias to uphold international norms of conduct vis-à-vis civilians.

Some militias try to induce populations under their control to provide resources willingly; others force populations to sustain their needs. Civil-militia relations in such situations range from the parasitic to the symbiotic. Parasitic fund-raising refers to the steady yielding of income through extortion, theft of international aid, licensing fees, or "revolutionary taxation." Symbiotic fund-raising denotes efforts to promote certain types of activities in exchange for a share in the outcome. In the latter situation, the economic development of the area and the economic well-being of the population may be dependent on the provision of security and infrastructure.[12] Similarly, the militia's income may depend on the population's ability to conduct economic exchanges without fear of extortion. The more dependent the militia is on the civilians over whom it has control, the more likely it will be to avoid harming them. Moreover, militia dependence on the population provides a space for civilians to negotiate the terms of militia conduct vis-à-vis noncombatants.

Sources of militia revenue. Sustained military conflicts require militias to seek revenue. This may come from a variety of sources, domestic or external.

A common source of combatant revenue in civil wars is extortion. Armed men take advantage of their weaponry to engage in theft, looting, and other forms of property acquisition; the fear and helplessness of the population make them relatively easy prey. Extortion can generate substantial amounts of revenue, but the supply side is limited.

When they control territorial enclaves, militias often impose fees on entry to and exit from their zones of control, sometimes known as "licensing fees." These fees apply equally to individuals and merchandise. In Republika Srpska, a substantial amount of revenue was thus generated by issuing "exit visas" to Bosnian Muslims who sought official assurances that they would be allowed to leave the Bosnian Serb areas safely. "Taxation" can be imposed on aid recipients, whether at distribution sites or at the source. In the latter case, aid convoys may be hijacked and their contents sold, or a protection cost may be imposed to secure the delivery of the aid to its intended recipients. Though a common feature in civil wars, the role of aid in conflict dynamics was a particular feature in commentary on Somalia.[13]

An independent resource base usually involves some form of "revolutionary taxation." As early as 1976, barely one year into the Lebanese conflict, the Lebanese Forces established the "national treasury," a highly organized financial department responsible for generating revenue for the war effort. More recently, the KLA established an international fund ("Homeland Calls") as an essential element of its effort to secure independence for Kosovo from Serbia.

But independent resource bases can also be established by taking a more active role in the economy of the territories under militia control. Peru's Sendero Luminoso typically altered the economic base of areas under its control, establishing cooperative forms of agriculture. In the Philippines, the New People's Army has implemented land reform and attempted to replace capitalism with a cooperative parallel economy.[14] Militias, not unlike states, can also provide security and infrastructure to underpin normal economic exchanges. In return, they receive a part of the population's income. In Lebanon's Christian enclave, the Lebanese Forces established an elaborate infrastructure to regulate the conduct of commerce and other economic activities. This involved customs duties, harbor facilities, a price control commission, and a body of lawlike regulations on the conduct of business, as well as the provision of internal security within the militia's zone of control. This infrastructure was instrumental in allowing the population to conduct business and continue relatively normal economic activities. In return, the Lebanese Forces collected taxes and excise duty on goods and services.

In some cases, the involvement of militias in the economy is so diversified and complex that it becomes difficult to separate the gray economy from the legal market economy. The militias not only replace the state in the provision of a framework for the conduct of economic exchanges, they also form business empires, often with connections to international markets. This is most evident in the case of narco-terrorist militias.

Finally, militias also turn for support to external actors who sympathize with their cause. In the early days of the IRA, for example, much of its support came from the United States, where about fifteen million Americans are of Irish descent. The New York–based Irish Northern Aid Committee (Noraid) became the largest external source of cash. In addition, machine guns, rifles, pistols, grenades, and ammunition were sent to help the underground fighters.[15] Militias also seek external patrons willing to finance the war effort because of shared ideology or for strategic reasons. The Lebanese Forces turned to Israel for assistance; Belgrade extended lines of supply and financial support to the Bosnian Serbs.

Types of civil-militia economic relations. Not only do the sources of militia revenue differ; the types of economic relations that tie these groups to the population also vary accordingly. I distinguish four types of civil-militia economic relations: predatory, parasitic, symbiotic, and independent.

Predatory economic relations: In the case of predatory economic relations, militias that rule through fear do not care much for the population's evaluation of their performance. In Lebanon, from 1975 until the early 1990s, militias were estimated to have raised as much as $500 million from ransoms alone.

In Republika Srspka, the Bosnian Serb leadership took the real and movable property of Muslims. The so-called bureaus for population exchange carried out systematic harassment of Muslim populations. Terrorized Muslims would sign "official" documents, "willingly" giving up their material property in return for the right to leave—itself often made official by the "purchase" of a departure "visa."[16]

Parasitic economic relations: In the case of parasitic militias, civil-militia relations are similar to the relations of protection rackets with prospective "protégés." The militias essentially undertake to ensure civilians' "security" in return for a financial contribution. In Lebanon, for example, militias on all sides of the conflict imposed direct and indirect taxes on citizens, commercial establishments, and industries as well as at public facilities, harbors, and customs.[17]

In Republika Srpska, the real property of Muslims was awarded to the "war municipality" or "crisis committee" of the particular town. Close associates of the local leaders got first pick; state officials used the remainder to control the Serb population. In Bijeljina, for example, one of the officials in charge of the cleansing campaign soon got involved in the business of security and real estate. He would "[shake] down local businessmen and [offer] incoming Serb refugees their pick of 'abandoned' homes, provided that they could come up with the requisite sweetener." In Prijedor, Simo Drljaca, the police chief who played a leading role in setting up the notorious Serb concentration camp in the area "managed to retain control over the resulting purified *opstina* or district. Locally, he was known as Mr. Ten Per Cent, because of the kickbacks and extortion payments he squeezed from almost every enterprise in town."[18]

Though this type of economic relations is similar to predatory relations in that it is based on the use of coercion, the difference lies in the fact that civilians get limited benefits (housing, security) from parasitic relations while they get none from predatory relations.

Symbiotic economic relations: Not all civil-militia economic relations are parasitic or predatory, however. There are many situations where militias have, for a variety of reasons, sought to reshape economic relations in their areas of control. While some have totally transformed the mode of production from capitalism to socialism, others have interfered in the economy in a different way—providing security, infrastructure, and the rule of law necessary for the orderly conduct of economic exchanges in return for a percentage of the profit made by the population. Apart from reorganizing the relations of production in the areas under their control, militias have often been known to provide a full array of social contract services to local populations.[19] Interestingly, in several cases the civilian populations have come to perceive the combatants as governments.

There is much evidence that insurgents in Cuba, Venezuela, Colombia, and Guatemala, among others, also sought to provide civilian populations with social contract services. Norman Gall quotes a Venezuelan peasant who summarized this situation by distinguishing the guerrillas' *gobierno de arriba*, or government up in the hills, from the *gobierno de abajo*, the "normal" government down in the towns.[20]

In Ethiopia, the Eritrean People's Liberation Front (EPLF) sought to apply its Maoist message of social transformation. The EPLF wanted to gain the support of rural populations, which was necessary to ensure freedom of movement and as a source of recruits, sustenance for armed guerrillas, and intelligence. In Sahel, for example, where the Ethiopian state was absent, one nomadic clan leader referred to the EPLF in 1977 as a *hukuma*, the Arabic word for government.

It is important to note that civil-militia economic relations can change over time. In Republika Srpska and Lebanon, early parasitic relations developed into (and sometimes coexisted with) the provision of collective goods, a centerpiece of the relations between the militia and the population. In Republika Srpska, the Bosnian Serb leadership controlled imports and exports, delivering licenses to traders, providing a "legal" framework for the conduct of business, and receiving payment in return. This infrastructure remained one of the main sources of Bosnian Serb revenue, especially as the imposition of economic sanctions by the international community provided an opportunity for enrichment through sanction busting. The Bosnian Serbs also put in place "war municipalities" that provided, among other things, relocation and gainful employment to displaced Serbs. The Lebanese Forces' financial needs grew with the collapse of state structures and with the militia's increasing responsibility for the population on whose support it depended. As a result, the militia took a number of steps to institutionalize revenue generation beyond revolutionary taxation. In 1982, the Lebanese Forces founded the Gamma Group, an organization working on "short and long-term projects to salvage the Lebanese infrastructure and plan for the reconstruction of Lebanon via a 'Marshall Plan' of sorts."[21] The Gamma Group's studies transformed the economic relationship between the Forces and the population. The militia diversified its involvement in the economy of the enclave by setting up a number of legitimate businesses and buying shares in others. Lebanese Forces businesses ranged from maritime transportation to the management of parking lots. The interface between the parallel economy and the legal economy was such that it approximated that of a corporatist state.[22] At the same time, the Lebanese Forces established sophisticated institutions to deal with socioeconomic issues; the National Solidarity Foundation addressed all the needs of the population, providing employment, low-cost housing, medical care, schooling assistance, and the like.

Independent sources of militia revenue: Some militias obtain most of their revenue from external sources. Economic relations with the civilian population in such circumstances are commonly lopsided. Although civilians may need to work for the militia to earn their livelihood, the militia itself is not really dependent on its workforce but on its connections to the global markets where its products (such as precious stones and drugs) are sold.

In Liberia, Charles Taylor's power continues to rely on independent connections to global markets and regional nonstate actors. The resources of Taylor's National Patriotic Front of Liberia (NPFL) derive from its control of diamond smuggling, logging,[23] rubber production, and iron-ore mining.[24] In Angola, UNITA initially used the illicit sale of ivory and rhino horn abroad as a means of financing its military acquisitions. By 1993, the movement controlled an estimated $1 billion in annual earnings from gemstone exports.[25] UNITA's stake in Angola's diamond industry is estimated at between $300 million and $1.5 billion in annual revenues.

It is important to note that civil-militia relations are not merely relations between an agent (the militia) and its target (civilian populations). Civilian populations have agency in shaping these relations as well. When militias depend on the civilian population for logistical support, manpower, and/or funding, civilians have some means at their disposal to renegotiate the terms of their relations to the combatants. The relationship between combatants and host societies may also be one of common interest, whereby the population supports the insurgency, which, in turn, represents popular aspirations.[26] However, such instances are better dealt with on a case-by-case basis.

The Nature of Militias and Its Impact on Civil-Militia Relations

Apart from issues of identification and economics, militia-specific factors such as objectives and structure also play a role in shaping civil-militia relations.

Militia objectives. The calculus of belligerents should be understood in the larger context of their objectives. A group seeking international legitimization will approach civil-militia relations differently from a more radical organization. A group seeking separation will also evaluate the costs and benefits of transgressing human rights norms differently from one that seeks inclusion in the political system.

Whether they seek to secede or to renegotiate the role of their "in-group" in the future polity, militia leaders typically want their voices to be heard.[27] Facing an authoritarian regime, a militia may seek to attract international attention to its plight in an attempt to modify an unfavorable internal balance of power—the KLA is a case in point. But what starts as a tactical move often turns into a central objective. The need to attract international support is a direct consequence of the nature of the international order, in which the primacy of states makes the resolution of civil conflicts particularly difficult.[28] International actors tend to privilege "legitimate interlocutors"—that legitimacy is usually associated with statehood.

In practice, this often means that states will play on the illegitimacy of insurgent movements to exclude them from peace negotiations. In the Bosnian war, for example, the international community chose to negotiate with Slobodan Milosevic, the president of the Federal Republic of Yugoslavia, rather than deal with the Bosnian Serbs. This phenomenon is not restricted to militias. Even regimes that are not considered "legitimate" will often be discounted as negotiating partners. In the Shaba crisis, for instance, the inability of the United States to treat Angola's MPLA (Popular Movement for the Liberation of Angola) regime as more than a Soviet puppet caused the failure of negotiations in 1977.[29]

Militias thus face a conundrum. They may become de facto authorities with which local and international actors are forced to deal, but this will not in itself secure their legitimization or their inclusion in future negotiations. When such nonstate actors become more visible and draw more support, they risk being portrayed as "mavericks threatening international legitimacy." Hence, militias are particularly concerned with the issue of being "heard, perceived, and recognized by nation-states and international organizations."[30] This predicament has a direct impact on militia development. Whether or not militias intend to establish a separate state, it is not uncommon for them to look increasingly like quasi-states or to develop governments-in-waiting. The adoption of such proto-state characteristics may become an end in itself, as a militia appropriates the forms and procedures of a state to achieve the ultimate objective of gaining legitimacy and recognition.

The Palestine Liberation Organization's (PLO) struggle for recognition is illustrative of this conundrum and of its dynamics. In an effort to mount a successful guerrilla war against Israel and to gain autonomy from often-constraining allies, the PLO underwent a process of institutionalization. This did not automatically enhance the legitimacy of the group, however. Although the Arab League recognized the PLO as the sole legitimate representative of the Palestinian people, this legitimization was neither universal nor unproblematic. Instead, the PLO's growing capacity and visibility were instrumental in heightening the threat perceived not only by Israel but also by its allies, Jordan and Lebanon. In both countries, embattled regimes saw the increasingly complex and powerful organization as a threat to their stability and acted militarily to contain this threat. The PLO continued to be viewed as a terrorist group—and a more dangerous group in view of its growing capabilities—by the United States and Israel. It was not until the negotiations leading to the 1993 Oslo Accords that the United States and Israel extended official recognition to the PLO and included it in peace talks. This recognition followed a number of signals indicating that the PLO would behave in a "statelike" manner—including but not limited to a public renunciation of terrorism. This shift toward moderation in the PLO can be traced back to 1974, but it took until 1993 for the PLO to be accepted as an interlocutor in peace talks.

Objectives can also shape militia incentives to respect the human rights of civilians in a more direct manner. A group with a universal message of solidarity will act differently toward civilians than a group with ethnically based objectives; a group seeking secession may evaluate its relations with civilians through the prism of its need for territory.

In Bosnia, control over territory was central to the Bosnian Serbs. Without condoning the process, even "population transfers" were carried out with this in mind: "to consolidate ethnically pure territories that would vote correctly in a referendum on sovereignty and in future elections and to justify government administration by their national group."[31] Bosnian Serbs knew from experience that a majority could easily ignore a minority's objections in a referendum. Their own wishes to remain within Yugoslavia had been brushed aside by Bosnian Muslim and Croat parliamentarians in early 1992. It was therefore not sufficient to have military control over territory—one had to ensure that its inhabitants would vote "correctly" in any upcoming referendum. In this instance, the critical need to gain control of territory shaped Bosnian Serb attitudes toward non-Serb civilian populations. The perceived need to drive these populations out of Srpska gave rise to the policy of ethnic cleansing that turned the Bosnian war into such a humanitarian and moral nightmare.[32] Ethnic cleansing was the instrument through which Republika Srpska acquired its territorial definition and through which the Serbs achieved their objective of controlling territory.[33]

In summary, militia objectives can affect civil-militia relations directly, by determining the militia's position vis-à-vis the population under its control, or indirectly, by shaping the way combatants seek to be perceived by the international community. The need to shape perception of the militia may be reflected in its organizational form and development.

Militia structure. The various militias considered here differ in their organizational complexity and coherence. Whereas some groups are loosely structured, others are highly organized along military lines (revolutionary armies, for example). Still others have developed beyond the military realm and established social and economic divisions, earning, in the process, the label of quasi-states or de facto states. The structure of these groups is important because it may impede or assist in the development of norms of conduct toward civilians.

For example, one would expect that the more structured a group, the easier it would be to determine the chain of command and control and therefore to attribute responsibility and accountability for violations of the rights of civilian populations. In Bosnia, responsibility for ethnic cleansing undertaken between 1992 and early 1993 was more diffuse than after that period, when the Srpska Demokratska Stranka (Serb Democratic Party of Radovan Karadzic) unified the small bands of irregulars under the banner of the Vojska Republike Srpske (Serb Army). This process of unification was highly instrumental in the identification of the political and military leaders of the Bosnian Serbs and the subsequent indictment of Radovan Karadzic and Ratko Mladic as war criminals.

Where a group is loosely structured, where the membership is fluid and norms of conduct underdeveloped, it becomes more difficult for outsiders and leaders alike to enforce standards of conduct and to develop enforcement mechanisms. In the Sudan, the growth of the SPLA Civil Administration was instrumental in the development of institutions to regulate civil-militia relations. In 1983, the SPLA enacted its Penal Code, a disciplinary code confined to the military. The code prescribed the death penalty for a number of crimes committed by military personnel, including looting and rape. In 1984, the Penal Code was amended to include a disciplinary law for the army, a general penal code, and a code of procedures. The 1984 laws recognized the application of customary law in each community within SPLA-controlled territory, and they established three tiers of military courts. However, the application of these norms and procedures remained arbitrary.[34]

A Typology of Civil-Militia Relations

This section integrates the various considerations that come into play in determining civil-militia relations into a typology. My aim is to provide the analyst and the practitioner with a tool for evaluating the expected degree of difficulty of current and future humanitarian crises. I also suggest certain strategies that will help to secure militia compliance with IHL concerning the treatment of civilians.

Militia-Specific Considerations

In spite of their many differences, the various groups described here exist as part of a continuum of nonstate forces that resort to violence in the pursuit of their objectives. More specifically, these groups can be thought of as varying along two axes. The first plots the nature of militia objectives. The more general the objectives (in the sense that they seek to improve society at large), the more likely it will be that the international community will find a way to engage combatants on the issue of civilian protection. The narrower a militia's objectives, the less receptive it is likely to be to pleas to respect and protect the civilian population.

The second axis plots the degree of organizational complexity of a militia. Structure implies a certain degree of responsibility by clarifying command and control. It also allows the group to establish rules of conduct toward civilian populations and to develop enforcement mechanisms to this effect. However, structure and the development of institutions and procedures do not automatically imply compliance with the norms of conduct at the heart of this discussion. Therefore, structure is at best an enabling condition. It is neither necessary nor sufficient to secure that civil-militia relations are in harmony with the letter or spirit of IHL.

These characteristics are illustrated in Figure 3.1. In terms of humanitarian access negotiations, militias can usefully be divided into four ideal types. The militias that seek the improvement of general societal conditions and possess clear lines of command and control are expected to be the *least challenging* interlocutor because they have both an interest in and the capacity to engage the issue of civilian protection. By contrast, militias with very narrow objectives and with a loose structure are expected to be the *most challenging* interlocutor because they lack the motivation and the capacity to improve civilians' conditions. Militias falling in the remaining two quadrants are considered *moderately challenging*.

Figure 3.1   Militia-Specific Considerations for Difficulty of Negotiations

	Loose Structure	*Clear Structure*
Narrow Objectives	Most challenging	Moderately challenging
Broader Objectives	Moderately challenging	Least challenging

Non-Militia-Specific Considerations

Having provided a rough typology of militias, it is now possible to integrate other considerations. These are included in the biaxial diagram in Figure 3.2.

Figure 3.2   Civil-Militia Relations—A Typology

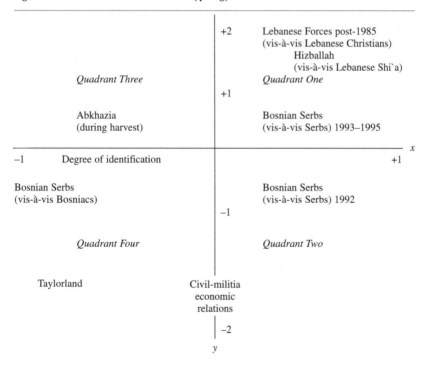

The horizontal (*x*) axis represents the degree of identification between civilians and the militia. As indicated earlier, the higher the perceived identification between a militia and the civilian population that it controls (in-group), the lower the likelihood that the militia will hurt this population. In the diagram, in-groups are assigned the arbitrary value of +1, and out-groups are assigned the arbitrary value of –1. Of course, these two labels represent ideal types and there is potential for variation on this axis. In-groups are not always treated well by combatants who identify with them; similarly, out-groups may be treated well by militias.

The Abkhaz conflict provides an example of militias treating out-groups well. In Abkhazia, more specifically along the Gali River, combatants are said to negotiate security bargains across the demarcation line. These bargains benefit parties on both sides financially. Under the terms of the bargains, internally displaced people are allowed to return to their farms periodically for the harvest season. These policies result in the manipulation of refugees into cycles of migration. Nevertheless, during the harvest season—albeit for financial considerations rather than out of loftier motives—militias treat out-groups better than is otherwise the norm.[35]

The vertical (*y*) axis represents civil-militia economic relations. The higher a militia's symbiotic dependence on the civilian population, the less likely it is that the militia will harm the civilians. From the discussion of civil-militia economic relations, the various types of relations may be collapsed into four broad categories:

1. *Independent militia sources of revenue:* The militia depends largely on external trade connections for survival and for income generation. Examples include Taylorland—the part of Liberia under NPFL control. (Assigned the value –2.)

2. *Predatory civil-militia relations:* The militia extracts resources from civilians by force. A good illustration is the relationship between the Bosnian Serb militias and the Bosnian Muslim population. (Assigned the value –1.)

3. *Parasitic civil-militia relations:* Civil-militia relations are extremely lopsided with the militia benefiting far more than civilians, but there is at least minimal contribution to the economy by the militia. Examples include relations between the Bosnian Serb militias and the Bosnian Serb civilian population. (Assigned the value +1.)

4. *Symbiotic relations:* The militia contributes largely to the economic well-being of the population; it is involved in the economy in positive ways. Lebanon's Hizballah approximates this type of civil-militia economic relations. (Assigned the value +2.)

In Figure 3.2, quadrant one represents the most propitious civil-militia relations. The militia not only identifies with the civilian population over which it rules but has also become positively involved in the economy of the territories under its control. Quadrant four, by comparison, represents the most difficult set of cases, where the militia not only rules over an out-group but civil-militia economic relations are either nonexistent or predatory.

Discussion and Practical Recommendations

Two broad sets of factors that influence civil-militia relations have been identified in this chapter. The first set includes militia-specific considerations, notably the impact of militia objectives and structure. In this respect, it is hypothesized that inclusive objectives are more likely to generate sensitivity to issues of civilian protection than narrow interests. One would also expect higher degrees of control to enable militia leaders to enforce norms of conduct vis-à-vis civilians and to hold violators accountable. However, a tighter structure does not automatically give rise to concern for civilian protection.

The second set of factors relates to potential ties between the combatants and the population. In general, it is expected that militias will treat in-groups better than out-groups. Economic ties can also influence militia attitude toward civilian protection. The more heavily a militia depends on the population it controls, the more likely it will be to limit the harm done to this population.

This section brings together these factors to discuss the challenges and opportunities that face international organizations acting in this area.

Engaging Militias on Humanitarian Issues

In this chapter, I have established that there is room to engage militias on issues pertaining to the protection of civilians in war. In quadrant one of Figure 3.2 above, militia identification with the civilian population and symbiotic economic relations provide the international community with such an opportunity. A militia that depends in part on the population for support and sustenance may find it in its interest to cooperate with the international community to improve humanitarian access and enforce certain norms of conduct toward civilians. The challenge here depends on the type of militia. If the militia has command and control, it may be in a position to accept responsibility for its commitments to the international community. If the militia has a weak structure, by contrast, the leadership may be unable to speak for individual militiamen or to vouch for their compliance.

Larger, more organized groups often set up networks to regularize relations with the populations of the areas that they control. They may build elaborate infrastructures to provide collective goods to communities. For militias that seek the right to represent a given community at eventual peace negotiations, the establishment of patrimonial relations is one way of securing de facto legitimacy through the creation of client networks. In the early to mid-

1980s, the Lebanese Forces' involvement in legal and illegal economic activities was an indirect source of internal legitimization. Revenue generated from these activities was instrumental in the development of parastatal institutions and with the provision of collective goods to the population of the Christian enclave. The establishment of services such as a subsidized public transport network, garbage collection, a police force, and a legal system reinforced perceptions of the militia as "of and for the people." In practical terms, the militia was building a base of popular support, a policy the success of which was reflected in the population's use of the term *shabab* to refer to militiamen.[36]

Such groups tend to see themselves as either governments-in-waiting or as independent political entities. Either way, they seek legitimacy. Therefore, when they cannot engage their domestic adversaries, they commonly turn to the international community to seek redress for grievances. This conjuncture (militia attempts to gain domestic support and international recognition) provides the international community with an opportunity to engage such groups on issues of treatment of civilians. It also provides civilian populations with leverage on the militias. In the Lebanese example, there was intermittent exasperation with extortion committed by individual militiamen. This exasperation grew as the Lebanese Forces became a complex and coherent organization endowed with the means to put an end to such extortion. In time, the infractions of individual militiamen—in spite of efforts by the leadership to impose sanctions on transgressors—reinforced the stereotype of militiamen as brigands.[37] The growing estrangement of a population tired of the war system dominated the popular evaluation of the militia.[38] Post-1988, this exasperation would outweigh the patrimonial benefits in the decision of many Christians to join the campaign of General Michel `Awn to "restore the rule of law."

Identifying Constraints on the Use of Coercion

When militias are not responsive to the concerns of the international community, the use of coercion is often considered as a policy option. However, this option may be counterproductive in some cases. For example, in quadrant two of the typology, the militia identifies with the population, but civil-militia economic relations are predatory. Situations characterized by this set of relationships are particularly challenging: on the one hand, the population may exhibit strong identification with the militia; on the other, the economic relations between both are such that the militia does not hesitate to take advantage of noncombatants if the need arises.

The strong identification factor may lead outside observers to believe that sanctions imposed on the community as a whole might bring the militia into compliance with the norms of conduct toward civilians on the opposite side of the conflict. This is often not the case. Rather, it may lead to a deterioration of the conditions of noncombatants over whom the militia rules. A thorough understanding of the nature of civil-militia economic ties is important to assess the kind of sanctions to be imposed as well as their potential efficacy.

The imposition of economic sanctions on the Serbs worsened the condition of civilians in Republika Srpska. A few months into the war, an extremely lucrative black-market economy developed.[39] Local commanders organized some of this activity for personal benefit. In Republika Srpska, the black market was "run by [Karadzic's Serb Democratic Party] and delegated to people that it trusts, upon which it takes a percentage of the gains. . . . After Serbia imposed sanctions on the [Republika Srpska], criminality increased."[40] For black-market profiteers, the embargo provided an excellent opportunity for enrichment. They could increase their activities by selling goods not only to Bosnian Muslims and Croats but also to ordinary Serbs that the sanctions affected most directly. General consumption goods became a source of financial gain as core party members traded these goods tax-free in return for contributions to their "bosses" in the state structure. Gas station owners had to pay racketeers on a monthly basis.

Using Economic Arguments to Humanitarian Ends

Of course there are instances when the international community cannot engage militiamen on issues of civilian protection by using the notion of militia legitimacy in the eyes of in-groups. In cluster three of the typology, for example, a militia will not be persuaded by humanitarian arguments that it should care for the civilian population under its control. Indeed, there is no strong bond between the population and its rulers. However, civil-militia economic relations may provide a venue to engage the militia on issues of civilian protection, as even these militias depend at least in part on the population for sustenance and economic resources.

It should, however, be noted that the changing nature of the militia ought to be given utmost attention. Under the impact of international pressure, some groups are likely to move from quadrant three to quadrant four while others may move to quadrant one.

Pulling the Economic Plug on Militias

If asked to identify a worst-case scenario, the analyst would point to quadrant four of the typology. This is by far the worst situation that international observers concerned with the fate of civilian populations can face. Not only does the militia have control over a population with which it does not identify, civil-militia economic relations deprive the population of effective means of leverage on its "rulers." When the militia does not have totally independent sources of revenue, it resorts to looting, revolutionary taxation, and other predatory economic practices.

In such cases, it is extremely doubtful that the international community will be able to affect the nature of civil-militia relations short of imposing measures that cut off the militia's external sources of support. This is where it becomes crucial to understand the international financial networks within which the militia acts, be it in the case of the diamond trade of Sierra Leone or the drug trade of Colombian warlords. One of the most promising ways of putting pressure on such militias may lie in the notions of social responsibility increasingly adopted by multinational enterprises. Only by removing the sources of their revenues will such militias even consider discussing the fate of civilians.

Conclusion

The ultimate objectives of combatants, their internal organizational structure, and their belief-systems all affect civil-militia relations. The degree of identification and the nature of civil-militia economic ties are also variables in this equation. Unless they are scrutinized and understood, policymakers will not be able to make effective recommendations to limit the humanitarian disasters associated with civil wars. We sin by omission when we fail to grasp the dynamics that shape civil-militia relations. When external mediators do not understand the complex calculus at work within militias, these groups may be dismissed too easily as fanatics who refuse to settle a dispute. By doing so, however, the international community itself may prevent the timely resolution of such conflicts. And when it comes to the fate of noncombatant populations, the most important priority is to stop the killing.

Notes

The author would like to thank Bruce Jones, Simon Chesterman, and Chandra Lekha Sriram for comments on an earlier draft of this chapter. Thanks are also due to participants in the IPA-Carnegie conference "Civilians in War: 100 Years After the Hague Convention."

1. See Paul Lewis, "Downside of Doing Good: Disaster Relief Can Harm," *New York Times,* Feb. 27, 1999. Accusations that Dutch UNPROFOR soldiers actually helped the Bosnian Serbs commit the massacres of Srebrenica are an example in point. See Joe Lauria, "UN, Annan Accept Blame in Serb Massacre; Blunt Report Details Faults in '95 policy," *Boston Globe,* Nov. 16, 1999.

2. The chapter does not delve into the wider challenges for humanitarian assistance and protection because these challenges have been widely discussed elsewhere, especially in relation to the issue of refugees, internally displaced persons, and safe areas: see, for example, Howard Adelman, Astri Suhrke, and Bruce Jones, *The International Response to Conflict and Genocide: Lessons from the Rwanda Experience— Study 2, Early Warning and Conflict Management* (Steering Committee of the Joint

Evaluation of Emergency Assistance to Rwanda, 1996); Howard Adelman and John Sorenson (eds.), *African Refugees: Development Aid and Repatriation* (Boulder, CO: Westview Press, 1994).

3. Comi M. Toulabor, "Sur un continent en quête de stabilité: La 'Bataille finale' du général Eyadéma au Togo," *Le Monde diplomatique*, March 1993, pp. 18–19.

4. For a comprehensive review, see Walter Laqueur, *Guerrilla: A Historical and Critical Study* (London: Weidenfeld and Nicolson, 1977).

5. Early in the Red Army's history, guerrilla operations were "on the whole subordinate to regular army activities." Mao denounced the use of such tactics, arguing that the army should not be dispersed but that it should instead "establish and consolidate revolutionary bases." The Long March proceeded largely along regular military lines, but the Red Army reverted to guerrilla tactics after the massive defeat that it incurred at Kuang Chang in April 1934. In the first Vietnam war, Vietnamese Communists set up a regular army early on. But in the beginning the war was "mainly guerrilla in character." The guerrillas built a counterstate, one in which they "levied taxes, collected rice, recruited soldiers and disseminated their propaganda." It was not until 1950 that major units of the Communist regular army entered the battle. Laqueur, *Guerrilla*, pp. 246–266.

6. William Reno, *Warlord Politics and African States* (Boulder, CO: Lynne Rienner, 1999), p. 3.

7. Informal interviews with former militiamen (both leaders and soldiers) conducted in Lebanon (twenty-five interviews) between 1992 and 1997, and in Bosnia (ten interviews) in summer 1998 as part of the author's doctoral dissertation research.

8. For example, following the April 1996 Israeli "Grapes of Wrath" operation in South Lebanon, Hizballah stated that it "repaired 5,000 Lebanese homes, rebuilt many roads, and paid compensation to 2,300 farmers." According to outside observers, the figures are not exaggerated and compare favorably with government aid to the victims. See "Lebanon, Hizbullah in Politics," *The Economist*, Sept. 7, 1996.

9. Ibid.

10. *An-Nahar* (Beirut), Sept. 11, 1979.

11. See, e.g., Douglas Johnson, "The Sudan People's Liberation Army and the Problem of Factionalism," in Christopher Clapham (ed.), *African Guerrillas* (Oxford: James Currey, 1998).

12. R. T. Naylor, "The Insurgent Economy: Black Market Operations of Guerrilla Organizations," *Crime, Law and Social Change* 20 (1993), p. 21.

13. See Daniel Compagnon, "Somali Armed Movements: The Interplay of Political Entrepreneurship and Clan-Based Factions," in Clapham, *African Guerrillas*, p. 86. See also John Prendergast, *Frontline Diplomacy: Humanitarian Aid and Conflict in Africa* (Boulder, CO: Lynne Rienner, 1996).

14. Naylor, "The Insurgent Economy," p. 16.

15. Louis Snyder, *Global Mini-Nationalisms: Autonomy or Independence* (Westport: Greenwood Press, 1982), pp. 58–59.

16. Laura Silber and Alan Little, *Yugoslavia: Death of a Nation* (New York: Penguin, 1997), p. 246.

17. Georges Corm, "The War System: Militia Hegemony and the Reestablishment of the State," in Deirdre Collings (ed.), *Peace for Lebanon? From War to Reconstruction* (Boulder, CO: Lynne Rienner, 1994), p. 217.

18. Lawrence Weschler, "High Noon at Twin Peaks," *New Yorker,* Aug. 18, 1997, pp. 29–30.

19. Timothy P. Wickham-Crowley, *Exploring Revolution: Essays on Latin American Insurgency and Revolutionary Theory* (Armonk, NY: M. E. Sharpe, 1991), p. 39.

20. Norman Gall, "The Continental Revolution," *New Leader* 48 (1965), p. 5, cited in Wickham-Crowley, *Exploring Revolution,* p. 39.

21. *An-Nahar* (Beirut), July 3, 1982.

22. Elizabeth Picard, "La Matrice libanaise," in François Jean and Jean Claude Ruffin (eds.), *Les Économies de guerre* (Paris: Pluriel, 1996).

23. Taylorland is reportedly France's third-largest African supplier of logs: Marchés Tropicaux, cited in *Economist Intelligence Unit* 3 (1992), p. 33.

24. Reno, *Warlord Politics,* pp. 79–111.

25. Ibid., p. 76, and sources therein.

26. For more detail, see Christopher Clapham, "Introduction," in *African Guerrillas,* pp. 12–14.

27. Militias engaged in civil wars typically seek to champion the cause of their community. The groups' objectives can range from renegotiation of the current political system to secession. Attempts to secure renegotiation suggest that a militia wants guarantees that other groups in the polity will respect its community's political and other rights. Attempts to seek secession or independence indicate a belief that such rights can only be secured through the establishment of an independent nation-state.

28. Martha Finnemore, "Norms, Culture, and World Politics," *International Organization* 50, 2 (Spring 1996), p. 332.

29. I. William Zartman, *Ripe for Resolution: Conflict and Intervention in Africa* (New York: Oxford University Press, 1989), p. 256.

30. Mohammad Selim, "The Survival of a Non-State Actor: The Foreign Policy of the Palestine Liberation Organization," in Bahgat Korany and Ali Hillal Dessouki (eds.), *The Foreign Policy of Arab States: The Challenge of Change,* 2d ed. (Boulder, CO: Westview Press, 1991).

31. Susan Woodward, *Balkan Tragedy: Chaos and Dissolution After the Cold War* (Washington, DC: Brookings Institution, 1995), p. 242.

32. See ibid., pp. 236–246.

33. The case of Biafra may be considered as a counterexample. According to historians of the conflict, during the Biafran civil war the Nigerian government paid particular attention to the fate of civilians precisely because the government's ultimate objective was to reintegrate Biafra in the larger Nigerian polity. See John De St. Jorre, *The Brothers' War: Biafra and Nigeria* (London: Hodder and Stoughton, 1972).

34. Johnson, "The Sudan People's Liberation Army," pp. 68–69.

35. Oral comments, conference on "The Uses and Abuses of Refugees by Warring Groups," Stanford University, Nov. 1999 (commentator's identity withheld by request). For more details on the manipulation of refugees in Abkhazia, see United Nations, *Report of the Secretary-General Concerning the Situation in Abkhazia, Georgia,* July 20, 1999, especially pp. 5–6, at www.un.org/Docs/sc/reports/1999/s1999805.htm, accessed on May 5, 2000. For more background information see Catherine Dale, "The Dynamics and Challenges of Ethnic Cleansing: The Georgia-Abkhazia Case," *REFWORLD-WRITENET Country Papers,* Aug. 1997, www.unhcr.ch/refworld/country/writenet/wrigeo.htm, accessed on Mar. 15, 2000.

36. The term *shabab* literally means "the young ones." It is used socially to refer to adolescents within one's familial and close social networks.

37. A strongman known for committing such extortion, Commander Abu Jawdeh later became a high-profile military official. His military prowess and the fact that his units managed to secure `Ayn al-Rummaneh, one of the most dangerous areas along the demarcation line, could not offset the resentment of the local population at his fre-

quent excesses. They subsequently migrated en masse to the ranks of supporters of General Michel `Awn in 1989. Interview data, Beirut, Aug. 1993. (Identity of the interviewees withheld at their request.)

38. By 1988, a study conducted by Theodor Hanf of the Arnold Bergstraesser Institut in Freiburg, Germany, revealed that all militias had lost as much as 50 percent of their 1984 support: Ghassan Tuéni, "Peut-on refaire le Liban?" *Politique étrangère* 2 (Summer 1990), pp. 344–345.

39. The examples are drawn from Tim Judah, *The Serbs: History, Myth and the Destruction of Yugoslavia* (New Haven, CT: Yale University Press, 1998), pp. 247–251.

40. Author interview, Branko Peric, editor-in-chief, Alternativna Informativna Mreza [Alternative Information Network], Banja Luka, Sept. 5, 1998.

4

Colombia: Persuading Belligerents to Comply with International Norms

Pierre Gassmann

Reducir lo sucio a solamente lo irregular en el caso de los insurgentes y de los paramilitares, someterse estrictamente a las leyes en el caso del gobierno.

[Restrict the dirty to only the irregular with insurgents and self-defense groups; in the case of the government, submit it strictly to the law.][1]

Since the struggle for its independence in 1830, Colombia has suffered from periodic eruptions of political violence. This has been largely for two reasons. The first concerns the distribution of power between the central state structure and the regions and larger cities, between the Conservative Party, claiming the heritage of the centralist "liberator" Simón Bolívar, and the Liberal Party, beholden to the ideas of Bolívar's companion—later federalist political adversary and successor—Francisco de Paula Santander. The second reason is that Colombians, often forgetful of the political content of their strong traditional allegiances to these political parties, are accustomed to violent disputes over the control of the country's vast natural resources, including arable land, and over the revenue from recurring bonanzas of gold, coal, emeralds, coffee, oil, and, lately, illicit drugs. It is characteristic of Colombia that until very recently, these conflicts played out without any major regional impact, and that warring parties did not depend on outside military or financial support.

Colombians are also extremely wary of attempts to promote a more federalist structure that would give regions a greater autonomy, and of meddling by foreign powers in their internal affairs. Their history is marked by the successive peeling-off of territories that were once part of "Gran Colombia"— Venezuela, Ecuador, Bolivia, and finally Panama in 1903. The latest factional fighting dates back to *La Violencia*, the civil war that erupted after the assassination of the Liberal Party's political leader, Eliezer Gaitan, in 1948. That war cost over 300,000 lives in the first half of the 1950s, mostly rural poor killed by government-sponsored militias. In the early 1960s, a coalition government was formed to replace Colombia's only military dictatorship; its inability to satisfy the land claims of the oppressed peasantry gave rise to new, particularly liberal militia groups, which allied themselves with the Communist Party and founded, in 1964, the Revolutionary Armed Forces of Colombia (FARC). A splinter group of FARC, driven by liberation theology and closer to Castroist ideas of revolutionary momentum, later founded the National Liberation Army (ELN). FARC's base is largely rural, its historical roots being the coffee-growing center of the country. Its first strongholds lie on the western slopes of the Andean Cordillera and the beginning of the Amazonian river basin.[2] The ELN is more connected to part of the intellectual elite of the country and has stronger links to the urban population and trade unions.

During the 1970s, several other groups appeared on the political scene—most notoriously the M19, a predominantly urban guerrilla force with strong links to student movements. Some of the smaller opposition groups, including dissident groups from FARC, made deals with successive administrations and attempted to participate in the democratic political process, including in elections to the Constitutional Assembly in the early 1990s. While a few of their leaders have now successfully established their "civilian" credentials, thousands of militants, mostly members of FARC spin-off Union Patriotica (UP), were assassinated by paramilitary forces in the late 1980s. These events have left a deep distrust among ELN and FARC militants with respect to governmental offers of reconciliation and rehabilitation in exchange for unilateral disarmament. The insurgents also point to the historical connections between the government's armed forces and paramilitary groups—connections that successive Colombian governments have not denied, but whose institutional nature they continue to contest. Indeed, a former Colombian high commissioner of peace has noted that "there is no doubt that the Colombian state had a great deal of responsibility in the creation and development of the paramilitaries, and today has yet to produce sufficient efforts to disband or attack them."[3]

While the most spectacular acts of violence of the early 1990s can be attributed to narco-terrorists fighting extradition, guerrilla strength has grown enormously in the past decade, as has, since 1995, the "new" self-defense militia, or Autodefensas Unidas de Colombia (AUC).

I will in this chapter consider the activities of the International Committee of the Red Cross (ICRC) in Colombia and the response of the various parties to the conflicts that have troubled it over the past decades. I will also provide some necessary background for the reader to understand the underlying difficulties in holding belligerents to international norms.

ICRC Activities in Colombia

One of the crucial questions humanitarian agencies and human rights groups must address is the nature of the violence to which they are responding. One ICRC representative has summarized the problem as follows:

> Amongst armed groups, the distinction between politically-motivated action and organized crime is fading away. All too often, the political objectives are unclear, if not subsidiary to the crimes perpetrated while allegedly waging one's struggle. The predatory dimension of armed groups is directly related to the waning of political and economic support enjoyed during the Cold War.[4]

The applicability of international humanitarian law (IHL) in many ways depends on the context. The case of Colombia is particularly complex, as each of the above-mentioned categories of violence apply, and, moreover, are interlinked. Colombian *violentologues* endlessly debate whether the common-law violence is induced by the war itself or just a law-and-order problem, whether the Colombian guerrillas are still politically motivated or have all but forsaken politics for economic motives, and whether the *autodefensas* have a political foundation.

To indicate the scale of the violence in Colombia, a comparison with the United States may be helpful. Colombia's territory is about one-eighth of the surface of the continental United States, and its population is about one-eighth that of the United States. If the Colombian data were transposed to the United States, 240,000 Americans would have been assassinated annually during the past five years; U.S. jails would hold over twenty thousand political detainees; every year, more than fifteen thousand Americans and some four hundred foreigners would be taken hostage for ransom; and more than eight million Americans would have been forced to leave their homes in the past five to six years because of political violence. Looking at the military picture, one would find over 160,000 guerrillas in the United States, scattered across some eight hundred relatively autonomous "fronts" from two major groups, over more than three quarters of the national territory; there would also be a loose alliance of local "self-defense" militia, counting close to 100,000 members present in varying strength in roughly a third of the country. According to estimates, the legitimate armed forces and national police would count annually over five thousand dead and wounded in combat; four thousand others would be held in captivity by the major guerrilla group. Seen in this light, there is no doubt that Colombia is at war with itself. The Heritage Foundation is certainly wrong, then, when it demands that the government "manage the insurgency as a law enforcement problem."[5] FARC commander Manuel Marulanda is equally wrong when he says that "crimes against humanity and the ferocity of the war against the people cannot be humanized. The war cannot be humanized, it has to be ended."[6] While that war lasts, and especially when peace talks are taking place, the perpetrators of the armed violence must abide by the minimum standards of human rights and IHL. This is what the ICRC is attempting to achieve in Colombia, while trying, at the same time, to satisfy the most urgent needs of the victims of the war.

Before delving into the application of human rights and IHL, it is necessary first to consider the ICRC's efforts to address some of the immediate needs of the population. In this section I consider the protection of persons detained in relation to the armed conflict, alleviating the plight of hostages, and the protection of civilians in conflict areas.

Beginning with People in Jail

Complex emergencies almost always begin with internal tensions, combined with outbursts of political violence, the detention of large numbers of political opponents, accusations of inhumane treatment in detention centers, and other signs of brewing political unrest, sometimes evolving into a full-fledged civil war. Colombia is consistent with this general trend; as indicated earlier, it has a long history of political violence.

In Colombia, the ICRC did not intervene in any way during *La Violencia* in the 1950s, nor did it respond to the calls of the nascent FARC, which was under pressure in Marquetália in 1964. This is something FARC still holds against the ICRC:

> Confronting the imminence of the aggression by the government, those 48 men [in Marquetália] addressed themselves to the Congress, the Governors, to the National and International Red Cross, to the Church, to the United Nations, to the French intellectuals and other democratic organizations, to prevent the beginning of a new armed confrontation in Colombia, with its foreseeable consequences. Unfortunately, nobody heard us, with the exception of the Church.[7]

It was only during the violent repression of political opponents during the Turbay Ayala administration in the early 1970s, and in parallel with its growing involvement with the communist insurgencies in Central America, that the ICRC sought to gain access to the political detainees in Colombian jails in a systematic way. Beginning in 1969, Geneva-based missions toured Colombian prisons once a year. The ICRC opened an office in Colombia in 1980; the following year it concluded a headquarters agreement, giving it license to visit administrative detainees and carry out its humanitarian mandate. Its activities remained intermittent. The main thrust of its work was, like that of other human rights activists worldwide, to seek compliance by the Colombian state with its commitments under international human rights treaties and to obtain the Colombian government's ratification of the 1977 Protocols Additional to the Geneva Conventions.

Only in the late 1980s did the ICRC open offices in Colombian cities other than the capital, primarily to get more systematic access to political detainees being held in different jails throughout the country and to train Colombian army units in IHL. This, in turn, brought the ICRC into contact with other aspects of a gradually spreading insurgency and government repression, combined with more extensive paramilitary action. On a number of occasions, ICRC delegates were called to facilitate fledgling negotiations and to be witnesses to and go-betweens in hostage releases, as in the case of the occupation of the embassy of the Dominican Republic in 1980. In the early 1990s, the ICRC at times became embroiled in the efforts of the Colombian state to deal with drug traffickers and the waves of political abductions and subsequent negotiations for surrender. It was at that time that the ICRC began to consider seriously the possibility of forming working relationships with these armed groups that had only tenuous political motives and whose methods of warfare were clearly outside any of the prevailing rules of IHL. Until that time, the delegation had been told to distance itself clearly from paramilitary groups and armed actors that were primarily involved with the drug traffic.

By interviewing guerrilla leaders in jail—many of whom sooner or later found themselves returning to the mountains or sitting at a negotiating table during the manifold partial surrender agreements reached during the Betancour and Barco administrations—the ICRC gained precious knowledge about the parties involved in the conflict, their motives, their history, and their structures. It also gained the trust of many of these leaders as it strove to ameliorate the conditions of detention and to help their families. At the same time, the ICRC could also convey to many members of the insurgency the purpose and methods of its work. On the government side, the ICRC's confidential and factual approach helped it alleviate the fears of Colombian officials who did not want any foreign institution to interfere with its heavy-handed justice.

As the ICRC's presence in the country expanded, it gained access not only to prisons run by the Ministry of the Interior but also to detention centers maintained by the armed forces. In September 1996, the ICRC and the Ministry of Defense signed an extensive agreement on improved modalities of ICRC access to military facilities. The agreement stated explicitly that "the objective of those visits is determined by strictly humanitarian motives" and that "these visits do not confer any special juridical and political status to detainees, and do not put them into a special legal situation."[8] In theory, the ICRC now had unlimited immediate access to persons captured in relation to the armed conflict and could therefore attempt to prevent disappearances and ill-treatment immediately after arrest.

Today the ICRC routinely visits more than 160 prisons in the country and each year registers an average of fifteen hundred inmates accused of political crimes. The average stay of a political detainee in prison is approximately eighteen months. Even though few have been captured in combat, it is not uncommon for a guerrilla fighter to remember a delegate met somewhere in the mountains or the jungle, or, when met out in the field, to recognize him or her from his or her visits to a prison. Those who were jailed as sympathizers and who somehow benefited from the ICRC's work in prisons serve to strengthen the recognition and trust of the ICRC among their own immediate friends and family, many of whom maintain links to combatants.

Since 1995, authorities and inmates alike have often called on the ICRC to facilitate the settlement of prison riots and to be present as guarantors in transfers of important inmates. In Colombia there is an ongoing public debate concerning the issue of political detention and the decaying prison system. Overcrowding, corruption, and failure to respect minimal judicial guarantees are recurring themes. Numerous national and international human rights non-governmental organizations and activists vocally denounce abuses. In the three years that I spent in Colombia, 1996–1999, the director of the National Penitentiary Institute (INPEC) changed seven times; this trend appears to be continuing under the Pastrana administration. In fact, political detainees receive most of the human rights activists' attention but are not, materially, the worst off. The conditions of common-law prisoners, particularly those with no resources and the mentally ill, are much, much worse. There is little interest in the fate of these thirty thousand or so people, however. Human rights institutions, including the Colombia Office of the High Commissioner for Human Rights, should tackle that problem as a priority.

The routine presence of ICRC staff in military barracks has improved working relations with the armed forces (an important asset when it comes to the training of military staff in IHL) and helps ensure the respect and safety of ICRC field missions. Most important, it has permitted delegates to find more attentive interlocutors for their inquiries and representations on behalf of civilians affected by the war.

The ICRC's consistent interest in people detained by the government has also gradually brought home the need to respect international standards of treatment for persons deprived of their liberty, both to the insurgents and, from the late 1990s, to the *autodefensas*. Detainees who wish to do so are registered by the ICRC. Political detainees usually do—they consider themselves to be prisoners of war and thus entitled to visits and assistance by the ICRC. This is also clear from the negotiations on conditions for the release of the over five hundred members of the armed forces FARC currently holds in captivity. As Manuel Marulanda observed, "The proposal by FARC to create a prisoner exchange law is fundamentally humanitarian. And it is based specifically on

Article 44 of the Second Protocol Additional to the Geneva Conventions of 1977 [Additional Protocol II]."[9]

As political prisoners are held in various prisons around Colombia, they are often detained in the same jails as the *autodefensas*, even though they usually occupy separate buildings within the prison compounds. Some of the *autodefensas* also wish to be registered by the ICRC. While the ICRC considers the *autodefensas* to be an actor in the internal conflict, it neither qualifies nor legitimizes their motives and their political status. This is clearly expressed in the 1996 agreement on access to military facilities.[10] The insurgents see this from a different angle. They believe that only they are waging a just war; they identify the *autodefensas* entirely with the government: "These gentlemen [the leaders of the AUC] are legitimate sons of the state and defend the very same state. Thus they cannot receive a political treatment, as some political leaders pretend."[11] This issue will be addressed in more detail below.

The Hostage Quandary

Another problem that the ICRC has faced in Colombia is the question of its involvement with the detention of hostages taken for ransom by the insurgents and, since 1996, by the *autodefensas* for the purpose of exerting political pressure.

As a rule, the ICRC has always adopted the view that capturing civilians for the purpose of extortion of any kind is a grave breach of the absolute prohibition of the taking of hostages included in Article 3 common to the Geneva Conventions and in Article 4 of Additional Protocol II. The ICRC has consistently drawn the attention of parties to a conflict to the International Convention Against Taking of Hostages and its definition of hostage-taking.

The ELN and FARC strenuously deny that the civilians they detain are hostages. The ELN considers it "permissible to recover war taxes, and to detain persons who refuse to pay them as a form of pressure in order to obtain payment. These detentions cannot be considered 'hostage-taking,' because we never use these persons as shields during hostilities."[12] FARC has voiced similar arguments, although it generally rejects the accusation of hostage-taking outright. Practice, however, contradicted the commitment FARC made under the La Uribe Accord with the Betancour administration in 1984.[13] As of April 26, 2000, FARC appeared to have resolved its public relations dilemma and now openly claims the right to take hostages.[14]

The guerrilla groups, in particular the ELN, have a habit of calling for the presence of the Catholic Church, journalists, and the ICRC as a condition for the release of hostages, and then using these events to make political statements. In such circumstances, families may have paid the requested ransom prior to the release. This has led to accusations that by dealing with hostage-takers and giving them a false "humanitarian image," the ICRC is essentially abetting a crime.

Nevertheless, facing increasing demands for help by the families of the victims, and in view of the ever-growing number of cases reported to the ICRC (close to sixteen hundred were attributed to insurgent groups in 1999), the ICRC decided to systematize its approach. In the 1996 Memorandum of Understanding signed with the Colombian government, the following was agreed:

> Article 2(3): In order for the ICRC to be able to deploy its humanitarian activities, it shall have free access to all the civilian population. To the same end, the ICRC shall be, if required, allowed to have contact with the actors of the internal violence.
> Article 3(1): The ICRC shall be allowed to carry out its traditional activities related to restoring family links and to searching persons reported missing, those deprived of their liberty, those held prisoners or kidnapped.[15]

The ICRC's quest to help families get in touch with their relatives, to facilitate safe contacts with kidnappers, and to facilitate the safe return of hostages was supported by the Presidential Office for the Defense of Personal Liberty, the office handling this issue on behalf of the Colombian government. The ICRC committed itself to notifying this office (dubbed "the Anti-Hostage-Taking Tzar") of its activities without being compelled to go into details concerning the dates and locations of meetings with the guerrillas and *autodefensas*. It also avoided dealings with common-law hostage-takers, always trying to establish first which group actually held an abducted person.

The results of these efforts have been mixed. Although the ICRC was able to reassure families as to the whereabouts of their relatives and help with their safe return in several hundred cases, it obtained access to long-term hostages and hostages reported to be in ill health only a few dozen times. Visiting these hostages remains controversial, for many insurgents attempt to use such visits as proof of their "legitimate prisoner status."

Whereas the material treatment the ELN and FARC provide to their hostages certainly improved as a result of ICRC insistence on this point, the practice of hostage-taking itself has expanded. In fact, rather than being restricted to selective targets—such as the wealthy, or supporters of the *autodefensas*—kidnapping took a turn for the worse in 1998–1999. At this time, both FARC and ELN engaged in so-called miraculous fishing expeditions—stopping cars randomly at roadsides, taking both owner and vehicle (particularly if the latter was four-wheel-drive), and releasing them against ransom; the ELN also hijacked a passenger aircraft and abducted hundreds of people attending mass in a Cali church. The ICRC contributed to securing the release of dozens of persons in the initial stages of these attacks.

Although the ICRC has a strict practice of not becoming involved with the actual negotiations for ransom and payment, some private security firms, as well as certain individual negotiators expecting material gain from their activity as intermediaries, have attempted to hinder the purely humanitarian approach of the institution. At the same time, some local guerrilla commanders, notably from FARC, have been irked by the fact that ICRC has had too much knowledge of individual cases. They equally resented the ICRC's forwarding of such information to their national general secretariat, whose commanders were keen on "humanizing" the practice, or on keeping it at least selective, and who occasionally remonstrate with them for their excesses.

Working in Conflict Areas

The ICRC's raison d'être is to alleviate the suffering of people affected by war—providing emergency relief and protecting civilians and combatants *hors de combat* (wounded and sick combatants, prisoners) from the excesses of war by intervening with the powers that be to request that they abide by IHL. It is impossible to achieve this in Colombia without getting out into the field where most of the victims remain, where villagers are caught in the middle of warfare, and where one can find the interlocutors that count.

Any international agency that wants to work in conflict areas in Colombia first requires the host state's consent. For any national agency, the hard part is to avoid polarization by the various parties and accusations of partiality. The major problem faced by humanitarian agencies in Colombia is that negotiating access with the government, with the general staff of the armed forces or the national secretariat of FARC, or with the Central Command of the ELN or AUC leader Carlos Castaño alone will not do. For the security of its staff—and for the sake of the continuity of its work—any agency also needs to ensure that it is accepted or at least tolerated by all parties concerned, in particular the leaders of local military, guerrilla, and *autodefensa* units in the area where it wishes to work.

The ICRC, which today operates out of seventeen offices throughout Colombia, required more than a decade to gain a measure of trust with all belligerents, sufficient to enable its staff to work in nearly all conflict areas. In that time, it has woven a network of working relations with more than 150 different guerrilla fronts, with their regional and national command structures, with ever-expanding *autodefensa* units, and with the ever-changing commanders of regional and local military units. In order to maintain these relationships and to strengthen the impact of its arguments for the respect of IHL, the ICRC has continued its policy of discreet and confidential persuasion, putting its complaints exclusively to the alleged perpetrators and restricting its public condemnation of breaches of IHL to statements of principle.[16] It also counts on the complementary pressure of those human rights groups and inter-

national agencies that attempt, with strong public condemnations of particular violations of human rights or breaches of IHL, to shame the belligerents
into changing their ways.

Other organizations periodically get their moment in the limelight, such
as when they are invited by the military high command, the guerrilla leaders,
or the *autodefensas* to highly publicized meetings—typically in the hope that
they will condemn the other parties. These public condemnations often back-
fire, however, as they contribute to the polarization of the issues; at times they
take the place of continued and unhindered access to the victims by others.

Attitudes of the Parties to the Conflict Toward International Humanitarian Law and ICRC Approaches

The Government

The Colombian government ratified the 1949 Geneva Conventions only in
1961. For many years, as political violence remained scattered and of low
intensity, the issue of the applicability of Article 3 common to the Geneva
Conventions to the Colombian context was not on the agenda.

Colombia participated actively in the diplomatic conference leading to
the adoption of the 1977 Additional Protocols. Political violence at that time
was on the increase, and it feared that these protocols could provide a platform
for international political recognition of the insurgent movements within its
territory. Colombia's diplomats attempted to introduce into Additional Protocol II, which concerned noninternational armed conflict, subjective criteria for
its application. The text they supported would have stated that "the determination of the conditions [of the applicability of Additional Protocol II] shall
be a matter for the State where the conflict occurs."[17] This position was not
supported, and the text as adopted provides for objective conditions for its
application.[18] From this point on, the issue of the ratification of the protocols
became a feature in Colombian political debate, as government and insurgents
seized on these treaties as arguments for the qualification of the status of the
latter.

At the Caracas peace talks in 1991, the ELN demanded that Additional
Protocol II be ratified. In a surprising sign of the changes to come, the government replied that it would be willing to submit it for the consideration of
the Congress "if and when the guerrilla demonstrates with its actions that it
will not continue to systematically violate Human Rights and the provisions
of Additional Protocols I and II."[19] In contrast to the virtually continuous dec-
larations of a state of siege by earlier governments, as a gesture to armed
opposition groups the 1991 Political Constitution states that "Human Rights

and fundamental liberties may not be suspended. In all cases the rules of IHL will be respected."[20] In 1993, President Gaviria's minister of defense, Rafael Pardo Rueda, introduced new rules of engagement for the armed forces, demanding strict respect for IHL.

President Ernesto Samper finally introduced legislation to ratify Additional Protocol II to Congress immediately after his election in 1994; it had been one of his electoral promises to do so, in order to pave the way for peace talks with the insurgents. Congress passed the law in December 1994. A review of the law by the Constitutional Court in 1995 affirmed the applicability of the protocol to the Colombian context: the court clearly stated that IHL, as international law, superseded Colombian national law, and it commented positively on the nonpolitical character of agreements between the government and the insurgents under Article 3 common to the Geneva Conventions.[21] The court also heard arguments on the key issue of the distinction between civilians and combatants, ultimately supporting the position that "the persons who contribute ideologically and politically to the cause of the organizations risen up in arms may not be considered objectives of military attacks, because in a strict sense they are not combatants."[22]

In 1997, a large group of human rights activists, NGOs, and pacifists, supported by the government, introduced notions of IHL in the "Citizens Mandate," which coincided with elections to regional and municipal authorities. More than ten million Colombians confirmed that minimum standards of IHL had to be respected at all times by all parties to the armed conflict: "No more atrocities; respect IHL. Do not involve persons under 18 years of age in the war—do not kill—do not kidnap people—do not forcefully displace people—do not attack people nor force them to flee from their homes—do not include the civilian population in the armed conflict."[23]

The Samper administration has attempted to use IHL as the basis for concluding agreements with the warring parties in order to "humanize" the war. It achieved some success when it reached a deal with FARC to release unilaterally seventy soldiers in FARC captivity[24] and when it encouraged a group of civil-society representatives—including government officials acting as private citizens—to reach an accord with the ELN in 1998.[25] On May 8, 1998, President Samper also signed a decree giving extended protection to the Red Cross emblem and to relief societies operating in conflict areas.[26]

President Pastrana came into office in 1998 with a promise to demilitarize some forty thousand square kilometers of territory in southwest Colombia. Although the state did not relinquish either its sovereignty over the territory or its prerogatives to assure law and order, it effectively left FARC in charge of some 120,000 civilians. The ICRC had suggested to the parties that they come to an agreement that would provide both the population and elected officials with assurances as to the rules applicable within the territory, in particular with regard to justice and other relations between civilians and the de facto powers of FARC. The closest parallel in IHL to this unique situation is in Section III of the Fourth Geneva Convention on the protection of civilians, concerning occupied territories. These provisions regulate issues such as population transfers, enlistment, justice, relief supplies to the population, health, and the exercise of religious freedom. Regrettably, neither FARC nor the government has acted on these suggestions, and recurring problems concerning allegations of forced recruitment, extrajudicial executions, and limitations of religious freedom continue to mar the experiment of the "peace laboratory."

Members of Congress did solicit the ICRC's help when considering FARC's proposal to pass a law permitting the exchange of political detainees (FARC presently holds over five hundred soldiers and policemen captive). The ICRC suggested that the parties conclude, if that was their political decision, an agreement under Article 3 common to the Geneva Conventions. The issue is still pending.

Recently, in an extraordinary joint experiment, government and FARC negotiators toured Europe, including a visit to the ICRC headquarters, to discuss the different issues pertaining to IHL. They later stated in a joint communiqué that

> we have advanced significantly with the discussion of a subject that preoccupies both Colombians and the International Community, namely the respect of IHL and Human Rights. From the discussions with the President of the ICRC we conclude that it is necessary to make a distinction between the two bodies of law. Furthermore, we have reached a consensus on another aspect: that the defense of Human Rights is the duty exclusively of States, while IHL is a norm that must be respected universally, by all.[27]

In addition, when it reactivated the National Human Rights Commission, the Pastrana government launched a new plan for the Respect of International Humanitarian Law. The plan included signing humanitarian accords, creating protected areas for civilians and internally displaced persons, a prohibition on recruiting minors into the armed forces, preventing sexual exploitation of and violence against women linked to the armed conflict, and the elimination of antipersonnel mines.[28]

The fact that IHL and its underlying humanitarian principles are at the core of negotiations between warring parties is a positive development, although the process of translating debate into reality remains slow. Even if "one can legitimately question the practical relevance of these legal developments in situations where governments have lost their capacity to bring nonstate actors to trial, or have relinquished this authority as part of a peace process,"[29] it is encouraging to note that belligerents remain convinced that a "clinical war" has better chances of achieving a negotiated ending than a protracted "dirty" one.

Colombia is unique in the sense that IHL has become a household word of public debate. In no other country of the world embroiled in internal armed conflict does one find such a high degree of knowledge and awareness of the rules of IHL, both of which are essential prerequisites to preventing excesses of armed violence. In one way, the ICRC's efforts at promoting IHL, training the armed forces, and advising the Colombian government on issues related to this body of laws have paid off: the ICRC can rightly claim that the behavior of the armed forces has improved over time as a consequence of these efforts. However, these positive developments are tempered by the fact that both government and guerrillas, and now the *autodefensas*, are regularly tempted to use IHL selectively to further their own political aims.

National Liberation Army (ELN)

The ELN was the group most enthusiastic to see Colombia ratify the protocols. This is clearly due to the numerous connections that the ELN intelligentsia maintains with the academic world, and its contacts, in the 1980s, with the Salvadoran and Nicaraguan insurgencies, both of which had made public commitments to abide by IHL. In bids to achieve political status and to seek, in particular, special treatment for its detained commanders, the ELN has always requested that the government conclude agreements on the implementation of IHL.

> In times of war, the ELN will work to reduce the human sacrifices and sufferings which are not necessary to defeat the enemy; because our combatants limit their action in compliance with their mission; and thus respecting the code of ethics of the combatant, that is the rules of behaviour recommended by the International Committee of the Red Cross.[30]

The ELN's position of making the applicability of IHL dependent on such agreements remains unchanged today:

> The war is tough. It's been going on for a long time. We don't want it to go on longer than that. But while it lasts, and that is the tragedy we are going through, we have proposed already four years ago to sign, with immediate effect, a "convention for life," which would humanize the conflict, which would protect the civilian population from the horrors of the war.[31]

In the Mainz agreement of 1998, civil-society representatives and ELN introduced another, rather strange, financial condition by agreeing as follows:

> The ELN commits itself to suspending the detention or deprivation of liberty of persons for financial motives, provided that the problem of the avail-

> ability of sufficient resources for the ELN by other means is resolved, and provided that . . . this will not result in a strategic weakening of the ELN.[32]

The agreement goes on to suggest that rather than combatants identifying themselves as such, civilians and their property should be identified specifically so as not to be subject to guerrilla attacks:

> With the objective of removing them from the attacks of the armed actors we will, together with the leadership of civil society and the coordination of the office of the Attorney-General of the nation and the National Ombudsman, proceed with the identification and demarcation of all objects protected by International Humanitarian Law, such as:
>
> • schools;
> • pipelines and aqueducts;
> • ambulances and hospitals, health centers and fire brigades;
> • educational, sports and religious infrastructure;
> • campaigns for public health;
> • electrical infrastructure, etc.[33]

Finally, the ELN has shown great interest in the International Fact-Finding Commission called for by Article 90 of Additional Protocol I, though neither the Samper nor the Pastrana administration has taken all the necessary steps to reach agreement on how the commission could be deployed.[34]

The ICRC's presentations to ELN's Central Command and its front commanders on the application of key provisions of IHL have been met with open minds and resulted in a number of improvements in the way the ELN has dealt with civilians in particular cases. Nevertheless, the ICRC has not surmounted the obstacle of ELN's demand for formal agreements with the government to put its avowed good intentions into practice, nor has it overcome the ELN's determination to use IHL only selectively. The ELN is undoubtedly also unhappy about the fact that its professed faith in IHL has not yielded full political recognition in Colombia and on the international level, but has instead resulted in a burden of compliance its combatants cannot sustain.

Revolutionary Armed Forces of Colombia (FARC)

FARC commanders are generally reluctant to engage in discussions on compliance with international humanitarian law. They look back with suspicion at accords reached in other contexts, notably in Central America, where they feel that IHL and human rights have been used by the international community to lure opposition forces into political agreements that have not kept their promises for the peasantry and the urban poor. They also insist that they will not commit themselves to legal obligations they have not entered into themselves:

"It is supposed that for one to abide by the norms set forth in a pact, one should have participated in its drafting, in its discussion and should be in agreement with its conclusions."[35]

FARC asserts that its own rules of "revolutionary humanism" encompass the principles underlying IHL. It points to its norms of behavior toward civilians:

> To the Civilian Population: FARC-EP does not use the technical terms of International Humanitarian Law, but in some documents there are norms which seek to protect the civilian population from the effects of conflict, establishing criteria which coincide with basic principles of Humanitarian Law, such as the distinction between combatants and non-combatants, and the immunity of the civilian population.[36]

In recent efforts to achieve acceptance by the international community, FARC has also referred to IHL:

> For FARC-EP, the subject of International Humanitarian Law is important, as well as the Humanization of the war, and repeatedly our Comandantes have explained publicly that the war as an expression of death and destruction and humanism as expression of life and social justice are opposed and mutually exclusive. . . . [W]e have presented to different Governments solutions for the problems and social factors which have generated this confrontation, with a view to ending the war.[37]

IHL also found its way into the agreement between the Pastrana administration and FARC on the agenda for preliminary talks about formal negotiations, on May 6, 1999. Agenda item 9 lists, under "Agreements on international humanitarian law," "no child involvement in conflict; protection of the civilian population; land-mines; [and] respect for international agreements."[38]

In any event, efforts to convince FARC to adopt IHL rules in combat seem to have had some resonance, as it prides itself on this internal rule: "commanders and combatants shall study and put into practice rules of international humanitarian law applicable to the conditions of our revolutionary war."[39]

In discussions with the ICRC, FARC has repeatedly said that it would agree to examine a reformulation of IHL, which would make it applicable to the situation in Colombia. In particular, FARC considers that no mobile guerrilla force can satisfy the demands for minimum judicial guarantees as contained in Article 6 of Additional Protocol II. As indicated earlier, it also refuses (as does the ELN) to acknowledge that FARC's practice of "retaining civilians" for the purpose of "collecting taxes" is hostage-taking, a practice prohibited by both Article 3 common to the Geneva Conventions and Additional Protocol II.

The Autodefensas Unidas de Colombia (AUC)

Terrorists, paramilitary arm of the armed forces, or autonomous actor in the armed conflict? A key question for the ICRC in Colombia has been the issue of approaching the paramilitaries, or *autodefensas,* in an attempt to persuade them to abide by the minimum standards of IHL.

During the 1970s and the 1980s, the legitimacy of contacts between the humanitarian agencies operating at the time and armed groups opposing colonial regimes or waging ideologically motivated insurgencies against governments was critically appraised along the ideological lines drawn by superpower antagonism. In most contexts today, the question of whether it is politically correct for the now more numerous humanitarian agencies to deal with armed groups of all kinds is more likely to be determined by the perceived legitimacy of their political, religious, ethnic, economical, or cultural causes—and therefore more fragmented along new fault lines.

Many intrastate armed conflicts are fought by a much wider array of armed groups than the ideological confrontations of the recent past. While Article 2 of Additional Protocol II refers only to armed groups opposing the government and dissident armed forces, the 1998 Rome Statute of the International Criminal Court foresees group and individual accountability in "protracted armed conflict between governmental authorities and organized groups *or between such groups*."[40]

The issue of the actual methods of warfare of these armed groups is today at the forefront of international debate, counterbalancing positions exclusively determined by the national interest of states and "just" causes supported by "international civil society." At its most extreme, the latter view holds that no armed opposition to a democratically elected regime, however tenuous its claim to this title, should be considered through the prism of IHL. Such armed opposition groups are generally dismissed as terrorists and therefore not legitimate subjects of IHL. (It is interesting to note that whereas FARC and ELN figure prominently on the U.S. State Department's list of terrorist organizations, the AUC is not included therein. This may be due to the fact that the drafters of this list consider the AUC as an institutional arm of the Colombian Armed Forces.)

Recent debate in the UN Security Council on the protection of civilians in armed conflict suggests that there is increasing consensus that international law may apply to such armed groups.[41] Broadly speaking, as pointed out by Martin Scheinin,

the move from the notion of the Law of Nations to International Law entails a paradigm shift as to the addressees of the norms. Where the former deals with rights and obligations of the traditional subjects of international law, i.e.

the states, the latter represents a development toward a more complex system of right-holders and duty bearers.[42]

Returning to the specific question of whether the AUC should be considered a party to the internal conflict in Colombia, the recent draft report of the International Council on Human Rights Policy (ICHRP) suggests that armed groups should be defined as groups that are "armed and use force to achieve their objectives and are not under state control."[43] It then rejects the idea that the Colombian *autodefensas* should be considered within that category:

> Examples might be the paramilitary forces in Colombia, the *Autodefensas Unidas de Colombia*, which find their origin in self-defense groups set up and authorized by the State, and that worked closely with the military. Even though they are now illegal, and the Government regularly denounces their activities, the evidence of their continued collusion with state military forces leads to the conclusion that they are still best dealt with as de facto state forces.

The report does, however, consider that, for example, Loyalist forces in Northern Ireland qualify, although, just as the *autodefensas* in Colombia, they "generally do not attack state forces."[44]

The key test is the degree to which a paramilitary group is within or beyond the control of state forces. Most human rights organizations consider that it makes sense to continue to hold the state responsible for any abuses it commits.[45]

State responsibility for abuses committed by armed nonstate actors. States that are accused of human rights violations are wary of bearing exclusive responsibility for such abuses when their national security is challenged by activities of armed groups: "States must take effective measures to protect human rights, even when the immediate threat comes from non-State actors. If States fail to comply with this duty, they are themselves guilty of violating human rights."[46] The following finding of the Inter-American Commission on Human Rights concerning Colombia is significant in this respect:

> The Inter-American Commission on Human Rights reiterates that it fully understands that there are many actors contributing to the situation of violence in Colombia and that the State is not internationally responsible for all of the harm caused to its citizens by non-State agents. The Commission also fully acknowledges that the State has the right and duty to guarantee its security and that of its citizens. The State is justified in taking actions against armed dissident groups, drug traffickers and others who commit crimes or threaten to destabilize or overthrow the constitutional order.[47]

The Commission goes on to note, however,

that the State will incur responsibility for the illegal acts of private actors when it has permitted such acts to take place without taking adequate measures to prevent them or subsequently to punish the perpetrators. The State also incurs responsibility when these acts by private parties are committed with the support, tolerance or acquiescence of State agents.[48]

In 1994 the Samper administration, under pressure from the UN Commission on Human Rights to accept a special rapporteur, offered to have the UN High Commissioner for Human Rights (UNHCHR) open an office in Colombia. In discussions on the agreement between the Colombian government and the UNHCHR, the government insisted that the office report not only on government human rights violations but also, in the context of the internal armed conflict, on breaches of IHL by all parties to the conflict, including the *autodefensas* as an entity separate from the government.

The final agreement did not entirely satisfy this request. It states only that the office should be "receiving complaints on human rights violations and other abuses, including breaches of humanitarian law applicable in armed conflicts," and that it should report to the UN Human Rights Commission "on the human rights situation in Colombia, bearing in mind the climate of violence and internal armed conflict."[49] The office has since reported consistently on alleged breaches of IHL committed by insurgents, government, and *autodefensas* alike.[50]

In light of the commission's findings, it is interesting to examine the responsibility of the Colombian state with regard to abuses FARC or other groups may commit in the area unilaterally demilitarized by the Pastrana administration.

The ICRC's approach to the AUC. The above assertion that "it makes sense to continue to hold the state responsible for any abuses the *autodefensas* commit" is convenient as a political credo for the insurgents.[51] It may also be useful for human rights organizations that are not working in the areas where the *autodefensas* are active, usually for reasons of security.

The ICRC soon found, however, that drawing the attention of the armed forces to alleged abuses by the *autodefensas* did not change the behavior of the latter—the armed forces either were irked by the suggestion of collusion, were falsely denied responsibility, or had actually lost control over the situation they had contributed to creating. The ICRC therefore decided to approach the *autodefensas* directly. This in turn gave rise to accusations that ICRC was giving undue recognition to these groups:

> The interaction of humanitarian agencies with organized armed groups is essentially a political act in itself, conferring an element of recognition and legitimacy on the group or individual. . . . [T]he image of a humanitarian

agency engaging with a particular faction can appear political despite the humanitarian agencies' claims of neutrality and impartiality.[52]

Even the fact that the ICRC had signed an agreement with the Colombian government that mentioned the *autodefensas* as actors in the armed conflict has been severely criticized by FARC and the ELN:

> For the purpose of this agreement, the term *actors of the internal violence* applies to all armed organized groups, independently of their denomination, and to all private armed groups, such as the commonly called self-defense [*autodefensas*] groups and to paramilitary groups.[53]

However, such perceptions by belligerents should not give rise to doubts about the intrinsic neutrality of humanitarian work, as suggested in a recent study:

> Neutrality, under these circumstances, either by humanitarians wishing to be even-handed and above the fray or by local population groups determined on non-involvement, has little meaning. It follows that in the world they now inhabit, humanitarians must acknowledge and analyze the explicitly political nature of their work.[54]

This is the classical conundrum of post–cold war intrastate armed conflicts: Is neutrality toward the new actors of armed conflict—those funded through drug trafficking, those committing terrorist acts, those using illegitimate means of warfare—still possible? Should there be a standard based exclusively on the political motives of different armed groups? Should all armed actors, with the exception of the armed forces of democratically elected governments, now be considered terrorists? And what if the latter themselves use illegitimate means of warfare?

If the criteria used to justify paying attention to armed groups were not exclusively ideological or political but essentially based on the degree to which armed groups abide by national law (or, more specifically, by IHL), where would we draw the line? Which is more illegitimate: financing the war through protection money earned from cocaine growers, laboratory operators, and transporters at the low-income end of drug trafficking, as FARC admits it is doing, or the funding of the *autodefensas* by landowners and drug lords? When it comes to kidnapping, which is worse: the "miraculous fishing expeditions" of FARC and the ELN, or the kidnapping of parents of the guerrilla leaders and of human rights activists by the *autodefensas*?

It is precisely because of the impossibility, for humanitarian purposes, of answering these questions that the ICRC follows a pragmatic approach. The key issue that determines whether the ICRC will attempt to persuade armed groups to abide by international standards is not their moral qualification, whether that is self-styled or attributed by political pundits. The questions it asks are, rather: Are there large numbers of victims? To whom do ICRC staff have to talk in order to get access to them and to be able to protect them from the worst excesses of hostilities and heavy-handed justice? If command structures can be identified, can these people be persuaded to change their ways? And can victims be assisted without altering the material equilibrium of forces?

The AUC's perception of international humanitarian law. The analysis of the war by the AUC closely resembles the arguments made by FARC when it demanded that IHL be adjusted to fit the type of guerrilla warfare in Colombia:

> The low intensity war model and the irregular nature of such war imply the development of a military confrontation conceived within a context of permanent movement that demands permanent logistic support. This support, in the jungle or the mountains, facilitates protecting the lines of communication, ensuring supplies, . . . infiltrating enemy zones, carrying out political campaigns, recruiting forces, collecting extortion taxes, covering up war actions, fostering forced displacement of persons, gathering information, harboring fugitives, hiding weapons and war equipment etc. All these activities, carried out by non-combatant personnel sheltered in the towns and camouflaged as civilians, are of vital importance to the survival and permanence of an armed party in a region. Taking into consideration the above-mentioned facts, we must necessarily conclude that the civilian population is trapped in the war theater of operations.[55]

According to the AUC, civilians are therefore legitimate targets, and the distinction between combatants participating actively in hostilities and civilians is impossible.

Carlos Castaño, the AUC leader, has often argued that IHL as presently understood is not applicable to the war in Colombia, and that if it was applied it would make the war impossible. His position is that the AUC is willing to abide by the rules, provided that FARC and ELN do likewise.

> We believe that, as a fundamental progress in the humanization of the war, as a gesture of intention of peace and as an expression of respect for International Humanitarian Law, it is necessary to exclude the civilian population from the armed conflict. Accordingly, and in agreement and simultaneously with the guerrilla movement, the Autodefensas Unidas de Colombia would be willing to redefine the strategies and tactics of war for the purpose of reciprocally aiming at not involving the civilian population in activities directly or indirectly related to the armed conflict.[56]

For the ICRC, the respect of the AUC was of vital importance in order to be able to operate in areas where it had a significant presence. The ICRC's policy of not condemning publicly the violations of IHL by either side was both helpful and suspect in this regard. It was difficult to convince the AUC that failing to condemn FARC and the ELN's practices is not the same as taking a position against the AUC, just as failing to condemn the AUC's excesses is difficult to explain to the insurgent groups; helping civilians affected by the violence of the AUC was initially considered to be direct assistance to the enemy. Gradually, however, the AUC accepted the ICRC's presence and engaged in debate on complying with IHL—one reason for this might have been that in 1995, the ICRC was among the few organizations that would talk to the AUC at all. Rejecting the AUC as pure criminals would not make them listen to arguments about implementing essential rules of warfare: "strategies to change an armed group's behavior, however dehumanized that group may be, are not likely to succeed if they involve dehumanizing the group even further."[57] The only means to achieve a constructive dialogue is, to paraphrase Carlos Pizarro, the M19 leader, "to build up interlocutors."[58]

In practically every situation, compliance dynamics can be identified that may yield some positive results. In the case of the *autodefensas*, the best possible argument was a political one: if the *autodefensas* pretended to have a political motive, they could be made to reflect on the longer-term impact of the gruesome methods of their antiguerrilla war. "Another factor [for compliance with IHL] could be stated to be the policy reasons, rather than the humanitarian or philosophical purposes behind the rules of warfare. . . . Targeting civilians is not only inhumane, but also wasteful, and far from destroying their will to resist, it usually strengthens it."[59]

The ICRC's engagement with the *autodefensas* has led to endless debate with FARC and the ELN as well as a great deal of criticism from human rights activists. These accusations largely subsided when ICRC delegates were able to visit captive members of the guerrilla commanders' families in 1997 and later obtain their release, and when they facilitated the release of a number of human rights activists captured by the AUC. It is now also accepted that relief activities in favor of civilians in the Uraba area are greatly facilitated by the ICRC's working relations with the AUC. Even FARC military commander and member of the National Secretariat Jorge Briceño grudgingly admitted to me in 1998 that talking to the AUC made sense in order to increase protection of civilians in certain areas.

Besides the relative security of the ICRC's work in the field and some successful démarches for individual cases, it remains difficult to measure the impact of the ICRC's continued representations to the AUC. Castaño's argument that without the ICRC's and the Catholic Church's insistence on human rights and IHL, the AUC's behavior would be much worse, borders on the cynical. The only credible argument he might have is his lack of complete control over all groups claiming to operate under the AUC umbrella.

Conclusion

Many observers believe that Colombia is on the verge of becoming a disintegrated state.[60] The ELN's member of the Central Command, Nicolás Rodriguez "Gabino," says that

> the state as regulatory institution of society does not exist in Colombia, because disputes between dominant classes which are subordinating the state never permitted it to constitute itself. Ultimately, this is because the state has renounced or has lost the functions it was to accomplish. Today, it guarantees neither life, honor nor property, not even for the minority oligarchy of this country.[61]

At the same time, U.S. Assistant Secretary for Human Rights Harold Hongju Koh warns that

> the judicial system, the sick man of Colombia, remains inefficient, severely backlogged, and overburdened, with 90% of all crimes going unpunished. Such a weak institution cannot repair the damage done the country's polity by abuses of the past, nor can it serve as an effective deterrent to similar threats in the future.[62]

Dino Kritsiotis argues that "the absence of any state structures may be considered to facilitate and possibly even create an appropriate climate for systematic violations of humanitarian law. . . . [E]stablished compliance mechanisms are barely operating, if at all."[63]

It is necessary, however, to put the issue of compliance with human rights and IHL in Colombia into perspective. First, the violence in Colombia today is not worse than during the years of *La Violencia*—in some ways it is less indiscriminate than during the repression in the 1970s and the terrorist bombings of the late 1980s and early 1990s. Second, today's staggering numbers of war victims cannot simply be attributed to more indiscriminate and criminal conduct by the actors of the conflict: they are due mainly to the quantitative increase in warfare, now much more widely spread over the national territory. Third, the fact that human rights and IHL are now widely discussed is itself significant, as this is a promising step in the direction of a negotiated settlement of the political crisis. Almost everyone in Colombia agrees that military victory in this war is impossible. The warring parties know that compliance with international norms has a direct relationship to the achievement of an eventual peace settlement; a "cleaner" war is more likely to produce an earlier and less protracted peace agreement between the parties, certainly one that is less fraught with the prospect of persecutions.

As long as political arguments remain a key motivation of the belligerents, these groups should be taken on their word, and compliance with international standards should be the measure of their political credibility. All their interlocutors should keep this in mind, from representatives of governments that consider themselves "friends of Colombia" to representatives of international corporations wishing to exploit Colombian natural resources, and from the Colombian government itself to intergovernmental organizations involved in mediation between the parties. These interlocutors should insist on some minimal standards, in line with the demands of Colombian civil society. Perhaps then the hope expressed by a civilian character in a recent political cartoon, referring to the current peace dialogues between FARC and the Pastrana administration, will come true:

Pues ahora que los malos y los buenos se están poniendo de acuerdo, a ver si nos dejan en paz a los demás.
[Well, now that the goodies and the baddies are agreeing, let's see if they leave the rest of us in peace.][64]

Notes

This chapter was written by the author in a personal capacity and does not necessarily reflect the opinion of the ICRC.

1. Tomás R. Campos, *Lectura política de los secuestros* (San Salvador: Estudios Centroamericanos, 1985), p. 695.

2. Some of these historical locations, such as El Pato and Guayabero, are within the territory unilaterally demilitarized as *Laboratorio de paz* [laboratory of peace] by the Pastrana administration at the end of 1998, in response to a FARC condition for reinitiating the peace dialogue. (FARC and the government use the term *laboratory of peace* to emphasize the exceptional situation of de facto control of the guerrilla with the blessing of the government.)

3. Daniel García-Peña Jaramillo, "Humanitarian Protection in Non-International Conflicts: A Case Study of Colombia," paper presented for the research project on Humanitarian Protection in Non-International Armed Conflicts at the International Institute of Humanitarian Law, San Remo, Dec. 2–4, 1999, p. 7. García-Peña is a former high commissioner of peace of the Samper administration.

4. Jacques de Maio, "Holding Armed Groups to International Standards," ICRC contribution to the research project of the International Council on Human Rights Policy, Geneva, 1999, pp. 2–3.

5. John P. Sweeney, *Tread Cautiously in Colombia's Civil War*, Backgrounder 1264 (Washington, DC: Heritage Foundation, 1999), p. 16.

6. FARC, "Derechos humanos y DIH," in *Revista Resistencia* 23 (March 2000), www.farc-ep.org/Revista/Resistencia23/html/dih.html.

7. Manuel Marulanda, "Queremos una paz, sin hambre y sin represión," speech at the peace dialogues in San Vicente del Caguán, Jan. 7, 1999, read by Comandante Joaquim Gómez, available at www.ciponline.org/colombia/tirofijo1esp.htm, p. 5.

8. Memorandum of Understanding Between the ICRC and the Republic of Colombia, Bogotá, Feb. 16, 1996, art. 3, para. 2 [MOU]; Annex to the MOU, Bogotá, Sept. 16, 1996.

9. FARC, "Derechos humanos y DIH."

10. MOU, art. 3, para. 2; Annex to the MOU, Bogotá, Sept. 16, 1996: "The objective of those visits is determined by strictly humanitarian motives. These visits do not confer any special juridical or political status, and do not put them into a special legal situation."

11. Marulanda, "Queremos una paz," p. 4.

12. Nicolas Rodríguez Bautista, "Qué es humanizar el conflicto colombiano?" May 1, 1996, available at www.voces.org/ddhh/queeshu.htm, p. 11.

13. 1984 La Uribe Accord, in García-Peña, "Humanitarian Protection," p. 9: "FARC once again condemns and does not authorize kidnapping, extortion and terrorism in all its forms and will contribute to ending its practice, such as assaults on liberty and human dignity."

14. In a communiqué of Apr. 26, 2000, FARC announced that the Central General Staff had introduced a "Law No. 002 on Taxation," stating: "Art. 1. FARC-EP will claim a peace-tax from all natural and juridical persons whose capital is superior to one million US Dollars. Art. 2. From this day, those concerned by this law must present themselves in order to comply with this legislation. A second request will increase the amount of the tax. Art. 3. Those who do not comply with this demand will be retained. Their release will depend on the payment of the sum that will be determined." Available at www.ciponline.org/colombia/000ley002.htm.

15. MOU, arts. 2(3), 3(1).

16. In addition to the hostage cases and complaints registered from persons in detention, the ICRC annually registers over 1,500 individual complaints from victims of breaches of IHL committed by the various actors of the armed conflict. These complaints may concern extrajudicial executions, nonrestitution of bodies, and threats against life and property. In many instances, ICRC delegates transmitting such complaints can help to establish authorship of the violations, demand and sometimes obtain reparation, clarify the seriousness of threats and at times obtain the retraction thereof, identify location of graves, and negotiate the restitution of corpses. The ICRC also regularly submits confidential reports on such complaints and reminders of prevailing provisions of IHL to the government, the insurgents, and the *autodefensas*.

17. Statement of Ambassador Hector Charry Sampér, head of the Colombian delegation to the CDDH, 1977, as quoted in Frits Kalshoven, "Protocol II, the Diplomatic Conference on Reaffirmation and Development of International Humanitarian Law Applicable in Armed Conflicts (CDDH) and Colombia," in Karel Wellens (ed.), *International Law, Theory and Practice, Essays in Honor of Erik Suy* (The Hague: Martinus Nijhoff, 1998), p. 601.

18. "This Protocol . . . shall apply to all armed conflicts . . . which take place in the territory of a High Contracting Party between its armed forces and dissident armed forces or other organized armed groups which, under responsible command, exercise such control over a part of its territory as to enable them to carry out sustained and concerted military operations and to implement this Protocol": Additional Protocol II, art. 1(1).

19. García-Peña, "Humanitarian Protection," p. 4.

20. Colombian Political Constitution, art. 214(2), Bogotá, 1991.

21. Article 3 common to the Geneva Conventions provides that parties to a conflict "should further endeavor to bring into force, by means of special agreements, all or part of the other provisions of the present Convention."

22. Statement of Guillermo Rueda Montaña, quoted in Kalshoven, "Protocol II," p. 612.

23. Mandato Ciudadano para la Paz, la Vida y la Libertad, quoted in "La Paz sobre la Mesa," ICRC–Comisión Nacional de Conciliación, *Cambio* 16 (June 1998); English translation available at www.ciponline.org/colombia/pot-civsoc.htm.

24. See José Noé Ríos Muñoz, *Liberación en el Caguán* (Bogotá: Planeta, 1998).

25. Acuerdo de Puertas del Cielo, Mainz, July 15, 1998, in *Correo del Magdalena*, II Epoca, No. 85, July 12–18, 1998; available at www.voces.org/info/resu85.htm.

26. Decreto No. 860, May 8, 1998.

27. Press release of the Joint Delegation of the Colombian Government and FARC-EP in Europe, Mar. 2, 2000.

28. Instituto de Investigación sobre Seguridad y Crimen Organizado, "Agenda Colombia: Informe de conyuntura," Sept. 7, 1999, p. 1, available at www.ba.ucsa.edu.ar/isco/doc/agencol3.htm.

29. Claude Bruderlein, *The Role of Non-State Actors in Building Human Security: The Case of Armed Groups in Intra-State Wars* (Geneva, Mar. 5, 2000), p. 7.

30. Manuel Pérez Martínez, Nicolas Rodríguez Bautista, Antonio García, Central Command of the Ejercito de Liberación Nacional (ELN), *Derechos humanos, nuestra ética en la doctrina militar* (Montañas de Colombia, Mimeograph, 1996), p. 1, also available at www.voces.org/ddhh/carta.htm.

31. Pablo Beltrán and Milton Hernández, "Dialogo y paz," ELN press release, July 3, 1998, p. 10. Pablo Beltrán is a member of the Comando Central (COCE) of the ELN; Milton Hernández is an ELN representative in Europe.

32. Acuerdo de Puertas del Cielo, para. 8.

33. Ibid., para. 14.

34. See Beltrán and Hernández, "Dialogo y paz," pp. 11–13.

35. Alfonso Kano (one of the most influential members of the National Secretariat), quoted in Jaramillo, "Humanitarian Protection," p. 8.

36. FARC-EP, Comisión Internacional, "Normas de comportamiento ante las masas," reproduced in a FARC press release on the occasion of the invitation to attend the first public audience of the peace process between FARC and the Colombian government, Apr. 2, 2000.

37. FARC, "Derechos humanos y DIH."

38. Center for International Policy, www.ciponline.org/colombia/agendaing.htm.

39. Autodefensas Unidas de Colombia, "Proposals for the Negotiated Political Settlement of the Internal Armed Conflict," letter dated Apr. 13, 1998, addressed to the ICRC and the Comisión Nacional de Conciliación, published in *Cambio* 16 (June 1998); English translation available at www.ciponline.org/colombia/pot-paramil.htm, p. 4.

40. Rome Statute of the International Criminal Court, UN Doc. A/Conf.183/9 (1998), art. 7(2)(f) (emphasis added).

41. Report of the Secretary-General to the Security Council on the Protection of Civilians in Armed Conflict, UN Doc. S/1999/957 (1999), para. 36.

42. Martin Scheinin, "Fundamental Standards of Humanity," background paper for the International Expert Meeting, Stockholm, Feb. 22–24, 2000, p. 25.

43. David Petrasek et al., *Ends & Means: Human Rights Approaches to Armed Groups*, draft report for consultation (Geneva: International Council on Human Rights Policy, 1999), p. 5.

44. Ibid., p. 7.

45. Ibid.

46. Scheinin, "Fundamental Standards of Humanity," p. 28.

47. Inter-American Commission on Human Rights, *Third Report on the Situation of Human Rights in Colombia* (1999), pp. 1–2.

48. Ibid.

49. Agreement on the Establishment of an Office of the United Nations High Commissioner for Human Rights in Colombia, Nov. 29, 1996, UN Doc. E/CN.4/1997/11 (1996), Annex, arts. V.7(f), V.10.

50. It seems probable that states hoping for more "balanced" public reporting, which does not focus exclusively on them but also highlights violations of IHL by armed groups, will support the recommendation of the Secretary General's Millennium Report, in which he calls for the establishment of "a mechanism to monitor compliance by all parties with existing provisions of international humanitarian law": Millennium Report of the Secretary-General, "We, the Peoples": The Role of the United Nations in the 21st Century, UN Doc. A/54/2000 (2000), p. 46.

51. Petrasek et al., *Ends & Means*, p. 7.

52. Robin Hart, Report on the 591st Wilton Park Conference, "Humanitarian Principles: Engaging with Non State Actors," Feb. 7–11, 2000, para. 3.

53. MOU, art. 3(d).

54. Michael Byers, Bruce D. Jones, and Janice Gross Stein, "Mean Times, Humanitarian Action in Complex Political Emergencies—Stark Choices, Cruel Dilemmas," Report of the NGOs in Complex Emergencies Project, Program on Conflict Management and Negotiation, University of Toronto (1999), vol. 1, no. 3, p. 30.

55. Autodefensas Unidas de Colombia, "Proposals for the Negotiated Political Settlement," p. 4.

56. Ibid.

57. Petrasek et al., *Ends & Means*, p. 5.

58. Quoted by José Noé Ríos Muñoz, *Cómo negociar a partir de la importancia del otro* (Bogotá: Planeta, 1996), p. 389.

59. Dino Kritsiotis, "Humanitarian Protection in Non-International Conflicts," paper presented for the research project on Humanitarian Protection in Non-International Armed Conflicts at the International Institute of Humanitarian Law, San Remo, Dec. 2–4, 1999, p. 20.

60. Ibid., p. 7: "Disintegrated states involve overwhelmed governments that are almost, if not completely unable to discharge basic governmental functions. The state is judged unable to perform six crucial functions of statehood: to exercise control over territory; have sovereign oversight and supervision of the nation's resources; exercise the effective and rational collection of revenue; maintain an adequate national infrastructure, such as roads and telephone systems; and have the capacity to govern and maintain law and order." See also Luis Jorge Garay S., *Construcción de una nueva Sociedad* (Bogotá: Tercer Mundo Editores, 1999), pp. 1–6; Luis Jorge Garay S., *Globalización y crisis, hegemonía o corresposabilidad* (Bogotá: T. M. Editores, 1999), pp. 143–200.

61. Bautista, "Que es humanizar," p. 4.

62. Harold Hongju Koh, "Colombia: Progress and Pitfalls on the Road to Human Rights," remarks at the U.S. and Colombia Coordinating Office Conference, Washington, DC, Oct. 15, 1999.

63. Kritsiotis, "Humanitarian Protection," p. 23.

64. From a political cartoon by Caballero, *Semana*, Mar. 27, 2000, p. 138.

5

Gaining Compliance Without Force: Human Rights Field Operations

William G. O'Neill

The United Nations and its member states have always found it difficult to secure compliance with human rights and international humanitarian law (IHL), a problem exacerbated by the extent and severity of modern conflicts. I argue in this chapter that the traditional UN compliance mechanisms have serious limitations and that new responses are needed.

Human rights norms have proliferated over the past fifty years. General treaties cover the gamut of civil and political rights, and economic, social, and cultural rights. Specialized treaties ban torture, racial discrimination, and slavery; others elaborate the rights of particular groups, such as women, children, and refugees. Standards on police conduct, the use of force, treatment of prisoners, the independence of the judiciary, and juvenile justice have issued from UN headquarters in six languages. The UN has excelled at creating such standards, and most states have incorporated most of these obligations into their domestic law. It is not a question of aspiration or "good works"—for most states, human rights are the law of the land. Enforcing those rights and holding people accountable for violating rights has been more difficult.

Regional organizations such as the Organization of American States (OAS), the Council of Europe, and the Organization of African Unity (OAU) have created human rights standards for their regions. These three entities have regional human rights treaties that largely mirror the UN-sponsored human rights treaties. Most states in each of these regions have ratified their respective treaties. The regional human rights bodies in Africa and the Americas are weak; usually the most they can do is issue public criticisms of violations. Europe is the exception here: the European Court of Human Rights has the power to hear cases and issue binding decisions that are generally obeyed. Asia and the Middle East do not even have regional human rights

93

treaties or oversight bodies, so people in these regions can rely only on the UN for redress. Some governments in these regions resist strenuously the very notion of "human rights," seeing it as an infringement of their sovereignty.

The International Committee of the Red Cross (ICRC) is "an impartial, neutral and independent organization whose exclusively humanitarian mission is to protect the lives and dignity of the victims of war and internal violence and to provide them with assistance. . . . It also endeavors to prevent suffering by promoting and strengthening humanitarian law and universal humanitarian principles."[1] It is sometimes described as the "guardian" of IHL.

The four Geneva Conventions and the two Additional Protocols spell out in great detail the obligations of combatants toward each other and toward civilians caught in the conflict zone. The six treaties contain over five hundred articles in total, covering everything from defining a prisoner of war to specifying those cultural heritage sites that should be spared during conflict. ICRC experts have written extensive commentaries on IHL that clarify and expand on these general principles. ICRC staff have devoted tens of thousands of hours and Swiss francs to creating training materials and disseminating information on IHL to military and irregular forces alike. The ratification record for IHL is even better than that for human rights law; virtually every state has ratified the four conventions with slightly fewer having ratified the protocols.

The ICRC has no power or means to enforce the laws of armed conflict. At best, the ICRC can complain to the party at fault, though even this is often done in private. There are no reporting requirements under the Geneva Conventions or Additional Protocols, and each state is responsible for ensuring its own compliance.[2] The ICRC works hard through its private interventions with states parties to improve this compliance, and its prison visits and missing persons tracing systems have saved many lives.

The imbalance between setting standards and enforcing those standards is enormous in both human rights and humanitarian law. The blame does not rest solely with the UN and its Secretariat. The member states of the UN have intentionally kept oversight and compliance mechanisms weak by failing to provide sufficient money and personnel to the High Commissioner for Human Rights; many states use the shield of "sovereignty" to deflect investigations or criticisms of their human rights performance.

A glance at any major international daily newspaper shows that states and insurgent groups violate human rights and IHL in every part of the world every day of the week. Children's hands are chopped off in Sierra Leone. The regime in Burma uses forced labor to lay an oil pipeline. Combatants rape thousands of women and young girls in Liberia. Serbian authorities shut down television and radio stations. Detainees languish for months without being charged or tried in Rwanda and Haiti. Insurgents and paramilitary groups kidnap civilians in Colombia. A rocket is fired at a UNHCR bus carrying forty-nine elderly Serbs and children while escorted by French troops in Kosovo. The list could go depressingly on and on.

In this chapter I will review, first, the traditional mechanisms available to the UN for protecting human rights: the Commission on Human Rights, special rapporteurs and working groups, the various treaty bodies, and the High Commissioner for Human Rights. Second, the emergence of the human rights field operation as a mechanism for monitoring and protecting human rights and compliance with the law of armed conflict will be considered. In the third section I provide a case study of the International Civilian Mission in Haiti (MICIVIH), and in the final section I consider various attempts to monitor the effectiveness of this approach to enforcing international human rights and the law of armed conflict.[3]

Seeking Compliance the Old-Fashioned Way

The Commission on Human Rights

Before the UN had even defined "human rights," it created the Commission on Human Rights in 1946. Currently comprised of fifty-three members, the Commission is highly politicized. In its early days, the Commission did not consider that it should even entertain allegations of rights abuses and certainly did not seek to have the state involved change its behavior. State sovereignty trumped any meaningful action to condemn, punish, or enforce human rights standards in the Commission's first twenty-five years. The Commission gradually grew more assertive, although its overwhelming focus on the situations in Israel and South Africa, grave as they were, exposed it to criticisms of bias and double standards. Pinochet's coup in Chile in 1973, followed by the 1976 "Dirty War" in Argentina, energized the Commission to create new procedures to receive and assess complaints of human rights violations and demand action from offending states. Blocs formed along predictable political lines during the cold war; similar blocs form now, usually based on a North-South divide or with regions trying to "protect" one of their own from a negative resolution. While the Commission no longer shies away from condemning states for abuses, its resolutions rarely lead to concrete improvements in the human rights situations.

William Shawcross's assessment of the Security Council's handling of the Srebrenica "safe area" in Bosnia in 1995 applies equally to the Commission: "For many members of the Security Council, adoption of the resolution was enough. Implementation was a detail with which they seemed less concerned."[4] The Commission's efforts regarding the war in Chechnya during the 2000 session is only the latest example of its largely symbolic role.

Special Rapporteurs and Working Groups

Other human rights mechanisms evolved alongside and within the Commission. In the late 1970s, the Commission started naming special rapporteurs on both individual countries and specific issues. Often after heated debates and backroom deals, the Commission would appoint an individual—usually a lawyer, judge, or academic with an international reputation—to be the special rapporteur. The Commission has named country rapporteurs for Iraq, Rwanda, Afghanistan, Cuba, Burundi, El Salvador, Guatemala, Haiti, Sudan, the former Yugoslavia, Colombia, and others. Thematic rapporteurs' mandates cover the whole world and investigate allegations within their mandates; these rapporteurs investigate extrajudicial, summary, or arbitrary executions; torture; violence against women; religious freedom; and the independence of the judiciary, among other topics.

States generally try to resist having a special rapporteur appointed, since this is the Commission's most serious sanction. The special rapporteurs receive information from a variety of sources and ask the government for its response or clarification. The rapporteur then submits an annual report to the Commission, which may be transmitted to the General Assembly. These reports, both the country-specific and thematic, include recommendations and may demand compliance by the offending state with its human rights treaty obligations. Recently, some thematic rapporteurs have conducted joint visits; for example, the rapporteurs on extrajudicial, summary or arbitrary executions, and torture visited Colombia and Indonesia together.

Another compliance tool is the working group. The Commission has created numerous working groups, each composed of five people who serve in their individual capacities; these groups work on such issues as contemporary forms of slavery, "disappearances," arbitrary detention, and the right to development. They seek and receive information from a variety of sources, confront states with allegations, and issue annual reports.

Though they constitute an advance in the effort to secure compliance, the working groups and special rapporteurs have serious limitations. First, they cannot visit a state unless invited. Second, their reports are often ignored not only by the state in question but by nearly everyone else. For example, the special rapporteur on summary or arbitrary executions visited Rwanda in early 1993 and wrote in his April 1993 report that Rwanda would experience massive killings unless action was taken to curb the militias, stop hate speech inciting genocide, and end the practice of specifying ethnicity on identity cards. His warnings were not heeded, and Rwanda's genocide began twelve months later.[5] Third, the special rapporteurs and working group members serve as volunteers, so they work only part-time. Because of limited resources in the Office of the High Commissioner for Human Rights, support staff is limited and each rapporteur and working group faces a crushing burden of communications needing responses; the all-important follow-up on cases is nearly impossible.

Human Rights Treaty Bodies

The remaining compliance mechanism in the UN system is the treaty body. Many human rights treaties create their own compliance and oversight bodies. For example, the Human Rights Committee, which is made up of eighteen experts serving in their individual capacities, receives and reviews reports submitted periodically by all states that have ratified the International Covenant on Civil and Political Rights (ICCPR). The Human Rights Committee meets three times a year; during these sessions committee members question state representatives on the human rights situation in their countries and on matters raised in the state's report. Nongovernmental organizations (NGOs) may also submit reports to the Human Rights Committee—these reports may differ greatly from the generally positive self-assessment in the state reports. In some cases, the committee has made states change their practices. The committee also publishes its findings and issues "Commentaries" on the ICCPR. These commentaries form an important part of the emerging jurisprudence on human rights. The Human Rights Committee also hears complaints of human rights violations from individuals in states that have ratified the First Optional Protocol to the ICCPR. This protocol allows individuals, once they have exhausted all domestic possibilities for redress, to petition the committee directly. This is a potentially powerful compliance tool.

The other major human rights treaties have similar oversight and compliance procedures, characterized by reporting, periodic appearances before an independent committee of experts, findings made by experts, and occasional condemnations. A few treaties have mechanisms for considering individual complaints.

The major weakness of treaty bodies is their lack of enforcement power. Compliance is further weakened by the very nature of periodic reports, many of which are produced late and are vague or downright misleading. Experts serve as part-time volunteers and have limited support from the High Commissioner's office, again largely because of severe resource constraints. Moreover, although some states with largely positive human rights records take the reporting obligation and the Human Rights Committee's comments seriously, many states with poor human rights records are defensive and sometimes submit reports that are sketchy if they are submitted at all. The treaty bodies seem to have a limited impact on those states with the most serious human rights problems. They have no jurisdiction over states that have not ratified the applicable treaty; states that have failed to ratify these treaties include some with abysmal human rights records.

The High Commissioner for Human Rights

In April 1994, in the midst of the genocide in Rwanda, the first UN High Commissioner for Human Rights took office. Human rights NGOs had fought a long battle to create this post; some member states opposed the idea, as did some in the UN bureaucracy, including the then Secretary-General, Boutros Boutros-Ghali.

The High Commissioner is the senior human rights official in the UN. Mary Robinson, the current High Commissioner, is charged with ensuring that human rights abuses are condemned, that future violations are prevented, and that human rights concerns permeate the entire UN system. It is an enormous mandate, perhaps an unrealistic one given the limited resources allocated to her office. The High Commissioner receives less than 1 percent of the annual UN budget, and staff are overwhelmed in the main Geneva office. The limited funding and the office's relative isolation from the power and decisionmaking center in New York restrict the High Commissioner's potential effectiveness in enhancing compliance with human rights standards.

A New Tool to Improve Compliance: The Human Rights Field Operation

The end of the cold war and the disintegration of the Soviet Union have made the world increasingly safe for violent, local conflicts. As superpower intervention and the chance for escalation to a larger, potentially nuclear war have diminished, existing conflicts have intensified and new ones emerged. At the same time, the outside sponsors of many conflicts have lost interest because they are no longer of strategic importance. Several such conflicts accordingly became ripe for long-overdue resolution.

Some key officials in the United Nations in the early 1990s sensed an opportunity to use human rights and IHL as tools to resolve long-standing conflicts. This idea and the subsequent initiatives came from New York, in particular the Department of Political Affairs (DPA), rather than from the Center for Human Rights, as it was then called, in Geneva. The DPA proposed to deploy specialists in human rights and IHL to the states in question, if possible alongside traditional UN peacekeepers. The UN mission to Namibia in the late 1980s was an early prototype of this model; it included a contingent of international police to monitor and report on compliance by local forces and to train a Namibian police force.

The first full-blown human rights field presence came a few years later, in El Salvador. As part of the efforts to end a conflict that had extended over two decades, UN negotiators proposed sending a team of civilians to El Salvador to monitor compliance with human rights and IHL by both the state security forces and the FMLN guerrillas. The two sides agreed, primarily because each did not trust the other and believed that independent monitors would verify the other side's violations. The UN exploited this opening, and the 1991 San Jose Accords sent to El Salvador the first major UN human rights field operation, the United Nations Observer Mission in El Salvador, known by its Spanish acronym, ONUSAL.

ONUSAL constituted a remarkable departure for both the UN and a member state. Traditionally, the notion of state sovereignty has frustrated UN efforts to garner compliance with human rights standards. Many member states have relied on Article 2(7) of the UN Charter to deflect any criticism of a state's treatment of its residents, asserting that this is "essentially within the domestic jurisdiction" of the state. ONUSAL was a major breach in the wall of state sovereignty. Deployed even before the parties had agreed to a cease-fire, the 42-member team had a far-reaching mandate, highly intrusive and unprecedented for a UN mission. ONUSAL could move freely and had the right to set up offices anywhere in El Salvador. Its members could visit all places of detention, unannounced if they so chose. They could speak to any-one they wished in the course of their monitoring; the government and the FMLN promised not to harm anyone who had met with them, and ONUSAL's offices and correspondence were immune from search. The mission was also mandated to report periodically to the Secretary-General on the parties' obser-vance of human rights and IHL.

The ongoing presence of a team of international observers—roaming around the country, asking difficult questions, visiting prisons, writing reports, and establishing contacts with leading NGOs—constituted a major advance in the UN's efforts to seek greater observance of human rights and IHL. ONUSAL was a qualitative leap from the somewhat hidebound Geneva-based mechanisms. It was proactive, on the ground, and its findings could not be easily ignored or dismissed. Unlike other initiatives, ONUSAL also had staying power: its presence in El Salvador did not end until May 1995, when it was reduced in size and the UN responsibility for the mission passed from the Security Council to the General Assembly. This longevity ensured that fol-low-up occurred and key cases or issues were neither ignored nor forgotten.

Once the ONUSAL precedent was established, other human rights field missions soon followed. These missions were sometimes part of broader peacekeeping operations with military and police components; in a few cases a human rights mission was deployed alone. The host state usually consented to the presence of the human rights field office, often under some pressure from the peace negotiators; in a few cases, Haiti and Kosovo, the state's con-sent was lacking and the mission entered under a Chapter VII mandate from the Security Council.

The UN Transitional Authority in Cambodia (UNTAC) followed the El Salvador mission. Created as a result of the Paris peace negotiations in 1991,

UNTAC had sweeping powers amounting to what some experts saw as a new form of UN trusteeship. Although the human rights component of the Cambodian mission was relatively small, it monitored the human rights situation throughout the country and helped start projects with a longer-term impact, such as judicial reform and helping to create and then reinforce Cambodian NGOs. UNTAC even had its own prison, prosecutors, and judges, and it participated in drafting new laws for Cambodia.

The OAS/UN International Civilian Mission in Haiti (MICIVIH) began its work in 1993. Guatemala was next, with the UN Verification Mission (MINUGUA) starting in 1994. These were both large operations that also grew out of negotiations led by DPA personnel from New York. These missions had no input from the Center for Human Rights in Geneva or its successor, the Office of the High Commissioner for Human Rights. There was also minimal contact between the field missions and the various special rapporteurs, working groups, and treaty bodies.

The UN Geneva office finally entered the fray in mid-1994 after the beginning of the genocide in Rwanda that April. The first High Commissioner, José Ayala-Lasso, visited Rwanda and promised to send several hundred human rights observers. This represented a radical shift for the Geneva office, which had no experience in recruiting for, training, or mounting a large field operation. This deficiency became clear as the mission started slowly and its staff, while well meaning, were poorly organized and equipped, had received no training, committed some fundamental errors, and sometimes alienated the very people they had come to protect.

The rest of the 1990s saw a dramatic increase in UN-sponsored human rights field missions. The picture grew more complicated as the High Commissioner, despite inexperience and budget limits requiring these missions to be funded by voluntary contributions from member states, established field operations in Bosnia and Herzegovina, Colombia, Cambodia, Burundi, Croatia, Indonesia, and the Federal Republic of Yugoslavia. The Department of Peacekeeping Operations (DPKO) in New York also became a player. The DPKO incorporated a human rights office in several of its operations, including Sierra Leone, the Central African Republic, Angola, and Kosovo.

Meanwhile, the DPA continues to be involved. It deployed a team of about a dozen "civil affairs officers" in Afghanistan in 1999 whose work includes following human rights issues. The mission in East Timor has an Office of Human Rights Affairs that monitors, investigates, and reports on human rights violations; there are human rights officers in every province. Strengthening the capacity of Timorese NGOs is a mission priority.

Regional organizations have also mounted human rights field operations, especially the Organization for Security and Cooperation in Europe (OSCE). The OSCE has large human rights missions in Bosnia (forty-two field officers) and Kosovo (seventy-one officers). It has smaller operations in numerous states of the former Soviet Union and has a joint human rights office with UN/DPKO in Abkhazia/Georgia. The European Union (EU) was a joint sponsor of the mission in Rwanda until 1997, and the OAS cosponsored the mission in Haiti until June 1999.

This explosion of human rights field operations in just ten years is a welcome advance. Putting people on the ground for extended periods to investigate and follow up allegations, report publicly, and intervene with local officials to request corrective action may secure an improvement in human rights more quickly and decisively than by holding periodic meetings in Geneva and New York, or issuing reports and resolutions that few people ever read. This ongoing presence permits human rights officers to participate in projects that can embed human rights in national institutions, and to work closely with the all-important local NGO community. Human rights field operations offer the chance to go beyond the Geneva mechanisms to offer meaningful, realistic, and practical programs addressing the actual abuses.[6]

Before discussing how to assess the impact of these field missions on the observance of human rights, it is useful to examine in more detail the exact workings of a field mission. The human rights operation in Haiti in its early phases (1993–1996) serves as a good model for the larger missions. Its terms of reference, staffing, structure, division of labor, and principal activities closely resemble those of other missions and provide a clear window on the work of a field operation.

Anatomy of a Human Rights Field Operation: The Haiti Experience

Background and Terms of Reference

The International Civilian Mission in Haiti (MICIVIH) began operations in February 1993.[7] Arising out of the efforts to broker an agreement between the military and the deposed President John-Bertrand Aristide, MICIVIH was the first mission sponsored by the UN and a regional group, the OAS. The mission's Terms of Reference were to "obtain information on the human rights situation in Haiti and to make any appropriate recommendations to promote and protect human rights . . . to pay special attention to respect for the right to life, personal safety and security, freedom of expression and association."[8]

Two omissions from the Terms of Reference quickly became evident. First, there was no mention of economic, social, and cultural rights. In a country as poor as Haiti, this choice seriously affected the daily work of the mission's field officers. While they sought information on specific cases of violations of civil and political rights, the person providing the information and sitting across from them was hungry, needed medicine for her child, or did not have enough money even to return home. It was an intolerable dilemma for many observers, who often used their own funds to assist Haitians. This omission of economic, social, and cultural rights has been repeated in most mission mandates. Second, the Terms of Reference did not mention the importance of working with Haitian groups, especially local human rights and civic organizations. Some Haitian human rights advocates believed that MICIVIH had come to replace them. There were serious misunderstandings and lack of trust between MICIVIH and what should have been its most natural and crucial local partners. Despite these shortcomings, however, the Terms of Reference created a powerful basis for the work of MICIVIH's field officers.

Staffing. At its height, MICIVIH had 204 internationals from forty-five states. These people came from a variety of backgrounds, including lawyers, judges, doctors, nurses, engineers, teachers, anthropologists, and journalists. Most had experience in either human rights or some type of fieldwork under fairly arduous conditions. Most were between the ages of twenty-eight and forty-five.

On arrival, all observers had three weeks of training, including lessons on Créole, Haitian history and culture, human rights norms, Haitian law, and Haitian media. Skills essential to performing their tasks were also taught, such as interviewing techniques, report writing, conducting prison visits, monitoring demonstrations, and presenting "negative" findings to hostile officials. Transportation, security, radio communications, and health questions were also covered. This training model was later adapted for use in other missions.

Structure. MICIVIH established a headquarters in the Haitian capital, Port-au-Prince, and regional offices throughout the country. An executive director and his deputy led the mission. The headquarters was divided into various departments, including investigation and research, legal, human rights education, public information, and training.

The Investigation and Research Department received daily reports on the human rights situation from the regional offices. It analyzed these reports and highlighted any trends or serious cases for the mission leadership and for UN and OAS headquarters. The department's analysis and reporting, building on the core facts conveyed by the field officers, formed the basis of the mission's public reporting. Staff also assisted in investigating complex cases.

The Legal Department staff analyzed all public reports to ensure that their conclusions about human rights violations were consistent with international law. The unit also worked with Haitian lawyers and judges to enhance their understanding of human rights law. Finally, the unit provided daily legal advice to headquarters and regional staff on human rights legal questions.

The Human Rights Education Department created materials to promote human rights for schools, the media, and community organizations. It organized workshops and radio programs and created banners, posters, and other teaching tools. Staff worked with teachers, journalists, and community leaders. With support from the UN Development Program (UNDP), the department published a Créole version of the Universal Declaration of Human Rights, with illustrations by Haitian artists to convey the meaning of the articles for Haitians unable to read.

The Public Information Department dealt with the international and local press. It issued press releases and ensured that the mission's public reports reached key journalists. It conducted workshops for the local press on responsible reporting. The Training Department was responsible for all in-house training of new human rights field officers.

The regional offices' structure mirrored headquarters. Led by a regional coordinator, each office was responsible for a specific geographic area, usually corresponding to one of Haiti's *départements,* or provinces. Headquarters tried to ensure that each regional office had people with the expertise to cover each of the mission's main activities. Each office usually had some staffers especially skilled in interviewing, investigating, and reporting; other officers might be lawyers, who could monitor and analyze the workings of the local justice system. Still others would take the lead in human rights education and promotional work. Some further specialization soon developed among staff, in areas such as conducting prison visits or organizing training for community groups.

MICIVIH's structure and division of labor, with some variations, was typical of most major human rights field operations.

Activities. Armed with broad Terms of Reference, MICIVIH's field observers roamed all over Haiti seeking information on the human rights situation. This was, during 1993–1994, a complicated job, since the military ruled Haiti and barely tolerated the mission's presence. For the first time in Haitian history, international observers were watching and reporting on the Haitian military's treatment of the population; judges and lawyers were assessed on whether they were upholding Haitian law while police behavior was being observed and scrutinized.

MICIVIH's goal was to improve compliance with human rights standards. To achieve this goal, mission observers sought information from reliable sources on the current human rights situation. Every day, Haitians would visit the regional offices and tell their stories; some were victims of abuse or were witnesses or relatives of victims. After taking down the essentials, field officers would seek corroboration of the information. Once they had obtained sufficient confirmation of the veracity of a case, the field officers would raise it with local military officials or the judiciary. The most serious cases were referred to headquarters for action to be taken at a higher level. These cases usually were included in the regular reporting to UN and OAS headquarters in New York and Washington.

Observers visited Haitian prisons and detention centers. When possible, they did so without prior notice. Sometimes Haitian military authorities, in violation of the Terms of Reference, refused entry. Once inside, MICIVIH personnel would check the prison register, though in many cases the prison kept no register, so that no one—not even the head of the prison—knew who was in the facility or the number of prisoners. Observers would supply the prison with a notebook and pens and then show the officer how to maintain this new register and what kind of information was to be included. On follow-up visits, the field officers would check the register to see whether it was accurate. The observers interviewed prisoners and assessed the conditions of detention. Haitian prisons were miserable places, with no running water, toilets, or showers; relatives had to bring food since the prison provided none. Medical care was nonexistent. Observers alerted other UN and humanitarian agencies who tried to fill these gaps. MICIVIH field officers often found that the detainees had been in prison for months, in some cases years, without being charged, let alone tried. Many had been beaten. MICIVIH raised these cases with the authorities, requesting that they respect national and international law.

In response to the findings made during these prison visits and from observing the virtual collapse of the Haitian judicial system, MICIVIH created two initiatives. The first was to assign the doctors in the mission the task of creating an emergency medical unit, in collaboration with Haitian medical professionals, to treat torture victims and prisoners. This unit successfully treated dozens of Haitians and also documented cases of torture and mistreatment for possible future use in trials against their abusers. This task was dangerous. The military and police knew that their abuses were now being uncovered and recorded; the Haitian doctors and nurses took great risks in doing this work, but they saved lives and probably deterred further torture and mistreatment. In just four months in 1993, the unit treated eighty-five victims of human rights violations, including knife, machete, and gunshot wounds; beatings; and one case of torture by electric shocks.[9]

The second project was the creation of a Haitian Legal Aid network. With financing from two donor countries, the MICIVIH Legal Department identified Haitian lawyers willing to take cases referred to them by the mission. MICIVIH paid these lawyers a fee, and they represented torture victims and others detained illegally. Again, this was a potentially life-threatening job. Yet some brave Haitian lawyers went to court and argued, for the first time in Haitian history, that the military was acting illegally. These lawyers secured the release of numerous people. They also made Haitian judges apply the law and thus improved the functioning of the judicial system. MICIVIH field officers observed these court hearings; this also exerted pressure on the judiciary to do its job and in turn protected the judges from subsequent criticism or worse by the military, who were unhappy with this sudden concern for applying the law. Judges could tell the military that they had to enforce the law because the international human rights mission would report right away if they did not. According to one Haitian judge,

At least [the military and the *macoutes*[10]] were a little afraid that the members of the international community were observing them. Whenever they arrested someone or tortured him, members of the mission turned up to demand that the victim be released or to give him medical attention. That is to say, the presence of the mission has caused a certain decrease in cases of human rights violations.[11]

This strategy of constant presence, follow-up, and intervention is the hallmark of a human rights field operation. International human rights NGOs, the UN's own special rapporteurs, and others usually visit a country for several days or a few weeks at most each year; though valuable and important, these limited visits cannot have the same impact as an ongoing presence spread out over an entire country. By showing up every day in court, by continually meeting with local government authorities, by returning to the same prisons each week, by offering ongoing training to local human rights advocates, MICIVIH secured improved compliance with human rights law.[12] A MICIVIH report noted that

the Mission has seen an increasing willingness by judges to apply the law on arrest and detention, and a marked increase in granting provisional liberty to detainees. Prisoners have been processed through the system faster and some now even receive a hearing within 48 hours after arrest, as is required by the Constitution but was exceedingly rare before the presence of the Mission.[13]

MICIVIH was active in areas beyond monitoring, investigating, and reporting. Field officers conducted training sessions on human rights for local community leaders, journalists, and human rights NGOs. They distributed human rights materials, helped launch a national human rights awareness campaign, and created short announcements in Créole for radio broadcasts. The observers developed good working relations with priests, nuns, journalists, community organizers, and schoolteachers and frequently held meetings with them to discuss how MICIVIH could help them and how best to promote human rights in Haiti. Observers sometimes walked for hours over Haiti's mountainous trails to meet people whom the Haitian authorities—except for the military and the police—had ignored for decades.

Reactions to MICIVIH: The Limitations of a Human Rights Field Presence

MICIVIH's positive impact created negative reactions from the military, which in turn affected the human rights situation. This is common in human rights field operations and makes assessing their overall effectiveness complex. For example, the Haitian military modified its behavior in 1993 so that it could continue to intimidate the population. Instead of illegal arrests and detention, soldiers beat people without arresting them. When MICIVIH discovered and denounced this practice, the military assigned the task of beating and intimidating to a newly created corps of paramilitary known as *attachés*. This created "plausible deniability" for the military, which claimed that it was not responsible for these violations.

As the political impasse grew in mid-1993, the Haitian army became increasingly uncooperative and bold. Despite clear guarantees in the Terms of Reference, soldiers denied observers access to prisons and threatened those Haitians who gave information to MICIVIH or who merely attended MICIVIH general human rights meetings. After an initial flurry of peaceful public demonstrations, the military banned all public meetings and did not hesitate to beat those who flouted its illegal regulations, sometimes directly in front of observers.

The failure to reach a political settlement undermined MICIVIH's effectiveness during the latter part of 1993 and throughout 1994, until the U.S.-led military intervention in September. A team of human rights experts sent by the UN Secretary-General to Haiti before MICIVIH's establishment foresaw this scenario. They noted:

> We predict the rapid emergence of serious problems for the Mission if many months elapse before a legitimate government enjoying public confidence returns to power. If the Mission is indeed initially successful in raising the confidence of the population, it will lead rapidly to increasingly assertive attempts to exercise freedom of expression. . . . On the other hand, we have found little indication that the military and *de facto* authorities are prepared to tolerate such activity in practice. . . . For all these reasons we believe that the very success of the Mission could rapidly bring difficulties that would imperil its further success, and perhaps the security of its personnel. We find it hard to envisage the Mission performing successfully the role of protecting human rights, including freedom of expression and association, for more than a few months, without clear progress towards a political solution of the crisis satisfactory to the majority of the population.[14]

The experts' prediction of "serious problems for the mission" if a political settlement was not reached was soon borne out. MICIVIH was evacuated from Haiti on October 15–16, 1993, after a total breakdown in the political negotiations and amid rising violence. A core group of mission members returned in early 1994, only to be expelled by the authorities in July. This expulsion helped set the stage for the U.S.-led military intervention in September 1994.

The link between a political resolution of the crisis and the ongoing effectiveness of a human rights field operation is not only true for Haiti but is a general principle of peacekeeping. This is underscored by the experience of human rights missions in Burundi, Kosovo (during the period of the Kosovo Verification Mission from November 1998 to March 1999), and Colombia. The absence of an underlying solution to the conflict limits the effectiveness of the human rights field operation. In these cases, the observers can only monitor and report on the violations, making sure at least that the outside world knows the extent of violations and the likely perpetrators. The opportunities to prevent violations, ensure that those responsible are punished, and promote human rights principles are limited in these situations.

MICIVIH's Final Chapter: Another Chance to Improve the Observance of Human Rights

Following the 1994 military intervention, MICIVIH resumed its monitoring and reporting but could now devote more resources to training and human rights promotion. President Aristide abolished the Haitian army, a new police force was being recruited, and there were judges and prosecutors to train. The government was now predisposed to cooperate rather than contest or resist.

The possibility of obtaining improved compliance increased correspondingly. Working with community organizations and professional associations (lawyers, journalists, physicians) was much less dangerous; from 1995 until its mandate concluded in early 2000, MICIVIH sponsored countless symposia, workshops, training sessions, radio shows, and other forums for spreading human rights awareness. Observers taught at the various law faculties, helped train teachers and created human rights curricula for schools, advised and loaned staff to the new Ombudsman, and taught Haitian human rights monitors how to investigate and document human rights abuses.

Though the other human rights missions might not have followed the same phases of development as MICIVIH, they have all had to struggle with periods of conflict, lack of political support, and opposition from the host state's government, military, and police—sometimes compounded by opposition to human rights work by armed insurgents.

Field missions generally also strive to combine monitoring and reporting with efforts to improve local capacity, both governmental and nongovernmental, to guarantee human rights. Some missions initially saw monitoring and institution building as two separate, and even irreconcilable, tasks. However, observers in missions from Sierra Leone to Cambodia and from Bosnia to Guatemala have recognized that the two tasks are inextricably linked. As a group of experts convened by the Aspen Institute concluded,

> There is an intimate and supportive relationship between the dual monitoring function and institution building functions of human rights missions. Human rights monitoring can identify problems with the armed forces, the

police, the judicial system, the prisons and other areas of concern, while technical cooperation for institution building helps to ensure that those concerns are addressed by the appropriate institutions.[15]

The challenge faced by every mission is to identify whether its programs, including both monitoring and institution building, are leading to greater compliance with human rights standards. To do this, missions must identify benchmarks to gauge the impact of their work.

Performance Measures for
Human Rights Field Missions

Many people who work in human rights missions are frustrated because they cannot see whether they are having a positive impact on the human rights situation. Their primary "clients"—the local population, including NGOs and some government agencies—sometimes express similar frustrations at a human rights operation's apparent inability to learn from its experience.

Two assumptions underlie the deployment of human rights missions: that their very presence will deter human rights violations, and that their proactive engagement in human rights education and promotion will lead to greater respect for human rights during their stay and after they leave. Yet few have attempted to test these assumptions rigorously. The UN, OAS, EU, and OSCE, which have all fielded human rights missions, have not systematically assessed the performance of their missions. While some "lessons learned" exercises have occurred, their findings have not been widely shared; more important, there is little evidence that organizations have actually made changes—at best, some lessons have been "identified" but not applied. The UN does not have a central repository or even a unit responsible for assessing the performance of the human rights field missions and ensuring that lessons or "good practices" are identified and shared with new missions. The Aspen Institute has published two studies examining human rights field operations,[16] and the Lawyers Committee for Human Rights has published assessments of the missions in El Salvador and Haiti,[17] but the UN has not incorporated the recommendations made in these reports into standard operating procedures.

Lessons from Other Spheres

"You can't improve what you can't measure." This axiom from business management and health care is equally true for human rights field operations. As one such study has shown, "measurement and improvement are intertwined; it is impossible to make improvements without measurement."[18] Similarly, human rights field operations need to identify certain key measures of their work to gauge performance.

Many human rights experts shy away from trying to measure the impact of their work, believing that mere presence is good enough and that human rights values will take hold somehow. After nearly ten years' experience of human rights field operations, however, it is simply not good enough to say that "we know our work is doing some good here." Some resist the idea of measuring because it creates greater accountability and may reveal shortcomings in performance. Others note that in complex emergencies it is sometimes difficult to establish a causal chain between a human rights field activity and a specific result or change. Yet there needs to be a more hard-nosed approach to evaluating human rights field missions if we are serious about making them more effective.

What should those measures be? Again, some lessons from the health care and business communities are instructive. First, missions should focus on a few critical measures. "What you measure is what you get," so the measures should reflect the key objectives of the mission.[19] These should be simple; combine qualitative and quantitative information; measure small, representative samples; and balance process or "output" (such as getting public reports out on time) with outcome (determining whether the reports help raise awareness of human rights issues and lead to improved behavior by the military or a change in policy by the international community toward the host state). In addition, measurement should become part of the team's daily work.[20]

This last point is important: interviews with many human rights field officers have shown that morale frequently suffers due to a failure to see the point of all their efforts. As shown above, human rights field missions often face daunting challenges, many of which may be outside the control of individuals on the ground. These range from the severe resource limitations that affect virtually every mission, to the failure of a particular peace process, as in Haiti in 1993, as well as in Burundi, Kosovo, Angola, and Colombia. Performance measures, if properly chosen, can be both "motivating and obligating": they can show where progress occurs, which can get lost in the complexities and rush of a field operation; they can also help hold field officers accountable to implementing the mission's overall strategy and mandate.[21] They can reinforce teamwork, crucial to any field operation, sharpen focus, and boost morale.

But how can one be sure that a change, as indicated by such performance measures, results from the mission's work, producing either an improvement or deterioration? For example, police often measure reported crime rates to assess their performance. Yet many crimes go unreported, and the police are only one part of the "judicial chain." Incompetent prosecutors, weak judges, poor parole procedures, and prison overcrowding all contribute to increased crime and are outside the police force's control.[22] Similarly, failure of political will can lead to weak messages from the international community to government officials responsible for human rights violations, resulting in a worsening human rights climate outside the control of the field mission.

One way to minimize distortion is to mix output/quantity measures with outcome/quality measures. Output measures can be particularly attractive because they are relatively easy and inexpensive to measure; management also controls the activities leading to outputs, so manipulation is always possible.[23] Measuring quality may be more time-consuming and involve outsiders who are not subject to management's control. But a few well-chosen quality measures are essential to determining both the extent to which the activity of a mission is responsible for change and whether the mission is achieving its stated objectives.

One important measure to assess the impact of a human rights field mission should be the opinion of the local population, the mission's primary "clients." Their perception of the mission is crucial. Surveys and other "feedback" mechanisms are important evaluation tools and fall into the outcome/quality basket. Yet a problem arises for certain field operations: in states with extremely polarized groups, how does one get a truly representative opinion?

Another problem with performance measures is that much of what a human rights mission tries to do will not have many visible results for a long time. "Building a human rights culture" and "creating respect for the rule of law" in places like Cambodia, Rwanda, Guatemala, and Kosovo, where it is arguable that such attitudes never existed, are not short-term goals. One needs to be modest here and avoid uncritically transplanting concepts that work well in business or health care but may be less useful in human rights fieldwork. In an important study of the U.S. Agency for International Development's (USAID) democratization efforts in Romania, Thomas Carothers notes:

> USAID and other US assistance providers should be wary of trying to impose on democracy assistance programs pressure for short-term, quantifiable results. Such an optic not only misses important elements of what is being achieved by the assistance but also tends to distort and limit the evolutionary development of the assistance programs. Faced with expectations of rapid, measurable results, persons involved in assistance at the working level will end up designing and implementing programs just to produce those sorts of results—no matter how artificial or mechanistic—instead of doing what is actually necessary to foster long-term, sustainable democratisation.[24]

With this warning, it is useful to review several attempts by human rights missions to identify performance measures and to attempt to highlight how missions might better assess their efforts to improve compliance with international law.

Examples of Human Rights Performance Measures

Several human rights missions have tried to develop performance measures or indicators. These have tended, first, to assess any progress in the observance of human rights and, second, to determine what impact their work was having on the human rights situation. I will consider assessment measures in five missions: Haiti, Rwanda, Bosnia and Herzegovina, Angola, and Sierra Leone.

Haiti. The OAS/UN mission in Haiti (MICIVIH) tracked the number of illegal arrests and cases of mistreatment of prisoners throughout the country in the summer of 1993. The mission focused on Haitian military officers who made the most arrests and informed them of the legal requirements for a valid arrest. Observers increased prison visits and relayed all complaints of mistreatment to the military officer in charge. For several months following these efforts, MICIVIH noted a decline, backed up by statistics, in the number of illegal arrests and of complaints of mistreatment while in detention. This decline ended in fall 1993, when the international political climate changed drastically and the Haitian military resumed its brutal behavior.

This example shows something quite important. The Haitian military could not claim (if, indeed, it had ever been able to) that it was unaware of national and international legal standards governing arrest and proper treatment of detainees. After fall 1993, soldiers consciously decided to flout these standards, based on their assessment of the consequences for illegal behavior—being perceived as "illegitimate" by the international community. At this point it would have been futile for MICIVIH to propose training for the Haitian military: lack of knowledge was not the problem. If the political backing had been there, the mission could have proposed strengthening the military's disciplinary mechanism to punish soldiers; based on their observation of the military courts, however, field officers determined that the military would not punish its own. It became clear to MICIVIH leaders that only stronger action, including clear warnings that the military risked an intensifying economic boycott and even military intervention, would change the undesirable behavior. MICIVIH's work thus helped to reveal the true intentions of Haiti's military; in such situations, it is better to know sooner rather than later that compliance without force is not going to work.

In situations where the authorities are intransigent, a field operation's most important tools are its reporting and its ability to provide limited help and protection to key local actors. Haiti's military in 1994 were triumphant; they had chased away the world's lone superpower in October 1993, when the USS *Harlan County* refused to land with its four hundred U.S. and Canadian soldiers after demonstrators opposing its arrival protested at Port-au-Prince's main dock. MICIVIH continued to document human rights violations, helping to keep Haiti in the news and on policymakers' screens; it was reported that President Bill Clinton even brought up some of the more violent incidents documented by the mission (such as the practice of disfiguring the dead victim's face so that he or she could not be identified) in White House strategy sessions.

MICIVIH's steady denunciations of the abuses of the Haitian military and its paramilitaries finally drove the authorities to expel the mission on July 13, 1994. Its expulsion helped set the stage for Security Council resolution 940 (1994), adopted on July 31, which called on the international community to use "all necessary means" to establish a secure and stable environment in Haiti.[25] This was the first Security Council resolution to authorize enforcement action under Chapter VII in a situation where there was no conflict as such, but purely internal, state-sponsored terror.[26] MICIVIH's reporting and the Haitian government's harsh reaction helped convince a reluctant international community that only force would resolve Haiti's long-standing human rights nightmare.[27]

When the authorities are more flexible, reporting can be used to help change minds. In 1995, when Haiti's constitutional government had resumed power, MICIVIH developed a working relationship with several ministries, especially the Ministry of Justice. Haiti's justice system was in a shambles, and MICIVIH helped find basic supplies (paper, pens, law books, desks, filing cabinets, and so on) and organized training sessions for judicial officials.[28] MICIVIH also ran a number of radio advertisements condemning lynchings and other forms of street justice. It then hired a local consulting firm to conduct a survey among the population to see if these advertisements had affected people's attitudes toward taking justice into their own hands.[29] MICIVIH also tracked the number of lynchings before and after the ad campaign to see if there had been a decline. Finally, the mission held a number of training sessions on conflict resolution for the new Haitian police and community leaders. MICIVIH then periodically surveyed both groups to see whether the training had helped improve community-police relations and lowered incidents of police abuse.

Rwanda. The UN Human Rights Field Operation in Rwanda (HRFOR) adopted a fairly hard-nosed approach to its work starting in 1995. In mid-1997, after numerous internal meetings, HRFOR adopted "program-based planning and assessment."[30] Each unit and regional office was required to craft a quarterly work plan. These plans described the objective of every initiative, the "client" or target group, the time frame, the amount of resources (personnel, equipment, and money) required, constraints, and, most important, means to verify the impact or success of the project. The teams identified three or four projects for each quarter. The teams then met with the head of the mission and other concerned senior managers, who signed off on the plans following discussion.

For example, one regional office identified overcrowding in the local prison as a serious human rights problem. Most of the prisoners had no case files, or dossiers, in violation of Rwandan law. The office decided to make this a priority issue, with the goal of reducing the number of prisoners without dossiers in detention. Their goal was a 20-percent reduction in the next three months, with priority given to those who had been in detention for up to three years without charge. The team responsible for the prison went to the prison's governor, explained Rwandan and international law, and offered to provide training for police investigators responsible for creating the dossiers. They also offered to help the prison administration set up a review panel, with the aim of granting provisional release to those who had been in detention the longest, unless credible evidence emerged that they were implicated in a serious crime or human rights violation. HRFOR officers even provided transport to police investigators and prosecutors so that they could interview witnesses and victims in far-flung villages to gather evidence; the mission also provided paper, pens, and files. At the end of the first three months, the team noted a 10-percent decrease in the number of persons held in detention without a dossier. The goal for ensuing quarters was a further reduction in the prison population among those with no case files.

The Rwanda mission used questionnaires and surveys to determine what a target group—local human rights groups, for example—knew about human rights and also what they wanted to learn. HRFOR then designed training programs based on this information. As a quantity measure, the mission tabulated how many people had received basic human rights training. As a quality measure, the mission tested the individuals' knowledge before and after the training. Finally, depending on the group, the mission tried to track the training's impact. HRFOR gave dozens of training seminars to hundreds of judges, prosecutors, and military officers. Mission monitors then compared the number of illegal arrests before and after the training; they also analyzed the lengths of time in pretrial detention. After learning that women did not receive credit for small business activities as easily as did men, the mission conducted workshops in several parts of Rwanda for women; it then tracked the number of loans women received after the workshops, noting a substantial increase.

Disappearances became a major problem in Rwanda in 1997. HRFOR trained local human rights monitors to investigate disappearance cases, then assessed the groups' ability to follow such cases and gradually yielded the lead role from mission members to local groups. The number of cases declined in late 1997, but it is not clear to what extent this decline resulted solely from HRFOR's efforts.

When designing radio programs and plays with human rights themes, HRFOR collaborated with Rwandan journalists, playwrights, and actors. After the shows and plays, HRFOR conducted audience surveys to gauge both the size of the audience and the impact of the broadcast and play. After seminars on international law for prison guards and officials, HRFOR used its ongoing prison visits to assess whether the seminars had led to improved treatment and conditions for detainees. It also used these visits as a form of ongoing, on-the-job training. Following seminars for judges and police inspectors, field officers checked to see whether these officials had visited prisons in their areas more frequently than before (as they are required to do by law).

Wielding reports, both internal and public, as a wedge, field officers sought to increase the frequency with which they met with officials to discuss human rights concerns. The number and quality of these substantive meetings became an important performance measure for HRFOR. Following these meetings, depending on the issue, HRFOR would offer assistance. For example, after a study showing that prison guards had adopted a shoot-to-kill policy for prisoners trying to escape, the mission leadership sat down with senior military officers and the chief military prosecutor. HRFOR pointed out that international norms prohibit the use of deadly force except when lives are immediately in danger. References were made to the Geneva Conventions and Protocols and to the UN Basic Principles on the Use of Force and Firearms. After some heated debate, the Rwandan military agreed to change its policy, and the number of such shootings dropped dramatically. HRFOR agreed to provide training for prison guards and the military on human rights and IHL relating to detainees. HRFOR distributed hundreds of copies in English and French of the relevant international standards to the military and to human rights groups.

Another example concerned the indiscriminate use of force by Rwanda's army in its fight against Hutu extremists and militias. Violence intensified in 1997, resulting in several large massacres in the northwest; many women and children were killed, allegedly caught in the "cross-fire" between the militias and the Rwandese Patriotic Army (RPA). When mission officers visited the sites of some massacres and interviewed survivors, however, there was no indication of "cross-fire" or a battle. All evidence indicated that the shooting was from one direction: the RPA's. Despite several meetings with senior officers, no progress occurred on the issue. HRFOR felt compelled to document the most severe cases and to issue a public report in the face of such resistance and denial. Following the public report, senior RPA officers agreed that some "excesses" might have been committed. The chief military prosecutor launched investigations, and several officers were arrested. The prosecutor also asked HRFOR for assistance in training his staff in investigating violations of the Geneva Conventions and in training senior RPA officers in the provisions of the Conventions and Protocols.

HRFOR made several important, measurable improvements in the human rights situation in Rwanda. Nevertheless, in the absence of strong political backing and meaningful progress toward resolving the root causes of the conflict, such gains may be only temporary. In July 1998, following a dispute with the Rwandan authorities about the mission's ability to continue to monitor and report on violations, HRFOR withdrew from Rwanda.

Bosnia and Herzegovina. The OSCE's Human Rights Department (OSCE/HRD) in Bosnia and Herzegovina has deployed over forty field officers throughout the country; since the 1995 Dayton Accords, it has focused on both civil and political, and economic and social rights. Because the Office of the High Representative (OHR), the senior civilian official in Bosnia and Herzegovina, has the power to remove government officials for malfeasance or noncooperation, the OSCE/HRD has an unusually strong capacity to enforce compliance with international norms.

Property rights are crucial to the human rights situation in Bosnia, and an important indicator of the state of human rights is whether an ethnic group can return to an area in which it is a minority. The OSCE/HRD has established several programs to encourage and monitor "minority returns." First, it launched an intensive campaign to inform pre-war occupants of their right to return to their homes, and how to file a claim to repossess their property. By April 2000, 190,000 such claims had been filed.[31] Second, the OSCE/HRD and other groups helped establish Double Occupancy or Property Commissions, charged with identifying cases where pre-war occupants should receive authorization to repossess their property.

Next, it drafted police guidelines for evictions. It distributed these guidelines to the police, including the International Police Task Force (IPTF), and discussed the human rights components of an eviction from property. Before these guidelines were developed, police presence at evictions had been rare, resulting in violence, recriminations, and failure to enforce judicial orders. Police now regularly attend evictions and ensure that they are carried out lawfully.[32] The OSCE/HRD now can assess its impact in the property rights area by measuring the effectiveness of the claims procedure, police presence and willingness to enforce eviction orders, and the number of people able to return to their pre-war homes, thus providing an important measure to assess its work. Moreover, each of the forty-two international human rights officers in the HRD and all its units at headquarters have adopted quarterly work plans to identify priorities, goals, and performance measures, especially those related to property issues.

The OSCE/HRD has also drafted guidelines for local prosecutors in cases involving officials who block minority returns. This initiative began in the spring of 2000; the plan is to monitor whether prosecutors use the guidelines and to follow the number of cases prosecutors launch against obstructive officials. The OHR can then remove any official who persistently refuses to apply the law. In November 1999 alone, the OHR removed twenty-two officials, mostly for property-related matters and largely on information documented by the OSCE/HRD. These removals had a salutary effect on the human rights situation.

Seemingly mundane, administrative matters can be very important in Bosnia and Herzegovina, and the OSCE/HRD, along with UNHCHR, has recognized this and acted. OSCE human rights field officers and UNHCHR protection officers noticed that people without identification cards could not receive essential municipal services. So the OSCE/HRD and other international agencies are in the process of drafting a new Bosnia and Herzegovina identification card that will allow access to services without specifying the bearer's ethnic identity.

Because of the wide-ranging power of the OHR, a type of modern "trusteeship," and the presence of thousands of NATO peacekeeping forces, the OSCE/HRD has unique opportunities to affect the human rights situation in Bosnia in concrete and measurable ways.

Angola. The Human Rights Department of the UN Mission in Angola (MONUA) found itself alone in March 1999 after the military, political, administrative, and international civilian police (CIVPOL) components left Angola. Before these units departed, however, the Human Rights Department interviewed 173 members of MONUA and solicited their views on the human rights work of MONUA, whether the mission had identified the key human rights issues, their assessment of the department itself, and the working relations between it and the various MONUA components.[33] This last point is crucial and often overlooked: success in human rights often depends on all the components of a peacekeeping operation working together.

The department has also commissioned an Angolan company to conduct a survey of knowledge and awareness of human rights issues in several Luanda neighborhoods in which it has run human rights promotion projects. The initial survey will provide baseline data for subsequent efforts to gauge whether its human rights promotion and training initiatives are increasing the population's understanding of human rights and their ability to exercise those rights.

Long-term pretrial detention is common in Angola, in violation of both international and national law. People are detained for months, sometimes years, without being charged or tried. The department recently installed a computer database in the Prosecutor-General's office in Luanda to track arrests and detentions; local prosecutors have received training on how to provide raw data to the system. Similar databases are planned for prosecutors in Benguela and Lubango. The department realizes that the problems stem not only from the absence of a case-tracking system but also because different parts of the judiciary do not communicate with each other. All want to be part of the computer database, however, so the technology may act as a catalyst for better institutional cooperation and efficiency, which may in turn reduce illegal pretrial detention. At the very least, the computer system will create base-line data to measure whether there are improvements in this crucial area.

Finally, the Angola mission has employed Angolan nationals as human rights counselors (60) and human rights promoters (300) in Benguela province. A few other missions, including Rwanda, Haiti, Yugoslavia, Kosovo, and Bosnia and Herzegovina, have also engaged locals in core human rights work. This is one of the best ways to ensure a human rights mission's work takes root and does not collapse once the foreigners inevitably leave. In Angola, the counselors have been trained to receive and resolve cases of human rights abuse while the promoters work on human rights education. The department is identifying criteria to judge the effectiveness of the promoters' work. Once established, these criteria will help shape a new training program for the promoters, who up to now unfortunately have received minimal training due to resource constraints.

Sierra Leone. The United Nations Observer Mission in Sierra Leone (UNOMSIL) had a human rights unit of five people that began work in May 1998. A major component of its work was monitoring, investigating, and reporting on the human rights situation. The unit contributed its human rights analysis to the weekly reports that UNOMSIL sent to UN headquarters, which helped the Security Council understand the human rights elements of the conflict and craft a framework for action that included a human rights perspective.[34] Human rights issues also soon predominated in Security Council discussions of how to understand and react to the Sierra Leone crisis. The unit also reported on human rights abuses committed by the West African peacekeeping forces (ECOMOG) in early 1999, which led to a huge public outcry and immediate improvement in ECOMOG's behavior.

UNOMSIL also worked closely with the numerous humanitarian agencies present in Sierra Leone. Forging a close partnership, humanitarian agencies soon started providing the human rights unit with information on violations of human rights and IHL from all parts of the country.[35] This exchange and consultation helped to enhance human rights–based programming by the agencies. A humanitarian Code of Conduct was also created and led to more uniform interactions between the humanitarian community and both rebel troops (RUF) and ECOMOG. For example, all agencies agreed to a common policy when confronted by demands for money or goods at RUF checkpoints.

Similar to other missions, UNOMSIL invested considerable time and effort to provide human rights skills training to local human rights groups. One clear measure of the effectiveness of this training was when UNOMSIL had to evacuate from Sierra Leone in January 1999 due to a rebel offensive. Local NGOs produced high-quality reports on their own while UNOMSIL was absent. The unit also promoted the status of human rights NGOs within civil society, which had the measurable effect of moving them from the periphery to the center of the debate on the peace accords. One concrete example of this "empowerment" of human rights NGOs was the statutory role given to them in the Truth and Reconciliation Commission.

The human rights unit, working first in UNOMSIL and then later in the follow-on mission called UNAMSIL, promoted human rights awareness in the various UN military components. A decrease in human rights and IHL violations was noted; also, the unit played a key role in convincing UN military observers to break up a child prostitution ring in the eastern town of Kenema.

The unit also had an impact on the way the amnesty issue was treated. The Lomé negotiations, which attempted to end the conflict, included a sweeping amnesty for the RUF despite its well-documented atrocities against civilians. Members of the unit went to Lomé and helped craft the human rights language and formulations of the agreement. The unit conveyed its concerns about the amnesty provisions to DPKO in New York and the Office of the High Commissioner for Human Rights in Geneva and helped convince the UN to distance itself from the amnesty. This was a major step for the UN in its fight against impunity. The collapse of the Lomé Agreement, the resumption of fighting, and the RUF's abduction of UN peacekeepers in May 2000 have borne out the unit's warnings.

Conclusion

The role of human rights in the UN system, in regional bodies, and in peacekeeping expanded dramatically in the last ten years of the twentieth century. Though the static, Geneva-based mechanisms still have a role to play, the focus has shifted to where violations occur and to strengthening those local organizations that will sustain the necessary oversight, investigation, and reporting. The challenge is to identify how to improve the performance of the human rights teams now being deployed by the UN and regional bodies to various trouble spots.

The above examples from five human rights field missions show that performance measures help sharpen an operation's focus, identify ongoing problems, and gauge the effectiveness of its activities. In some cases, the measures have identified the need to add, drop, or change a project. In others, the mission has discovered that the roots of the human rights problems lie in areas outside its control or even influence. Contrary to what some think about such measures—that they will show that the missions are not effective, thus undermining support for them—the opposite is usually true. What most often happens is that by identifying benchmarks and seeking to hold human rights officers accountable for results, missions show the positive impact of their work and presence through demonstrable measures, thereby gaining further support and raising mission morale.

Human rights field missions are here to stay; they may even increase. The UN is currently undertaking a major review of peacekeeping. Given the nature of current conflicts, which are largely caused by massive human rights violations and are internal, not international, the importance of including a well-resourced and dynamic human rights component in any peacekeeping operation should be evident. Since many states fear contributing troops to peacekeeping operations because they may take casualties, it is ironically falling increasingly to civilians, who are untrained and unarmed for conflict, to put themselves in harm's way to tell the world exactly what is happening. Ensuring that they are trained, equipped, and managed to do the best possible job is paramount. The performance-measuring tools described in this chapter can provide a way to judge the quality and impact of a human rights field operation while also providing policymakers with essential information.

As we have seen, even with a solid peacekeeping mission that includes an effective human rights unit, stronger enforcement measures may be needed and can come from only the principal political actors or through the use of military force. Even in these cases, however, at least the human rights missions can flush out the true reasons for ongoing violations, help identify those responsible, and eliminate excuses or alleged justifications for abuses. It is then up to the UN Security Council to determine the appropriate reaction.

Notes

1. "About the ICRC," available at www.icrc.org/eng/icrc.

2. Article 90 in Additional Protocol I creates an International Fact-Finding Commission consisting of "fifteen members of high moral standing and acknowledged impartiality." They serve in their individual capacities and inquire into allegations of "grave breaches" or other serious violations of the Geneva Conventions and Additional Protocol I. This resembles somewhat the treaty body overseeing compliance with international human rights law described below.

3. The other major innovation during this period was the creation of the International Criminal Tribunals for the Former Yugoslavia and Rwanda. These tribunals, and the effort to create a permanent International Criminal Court, are discussed in Chapter 7.

4. William Shawcross, *Deliver Us from Evil: Peacekeepers, Warlords and a World of Endless Conflict* (New York: Simon & Schuster, 2000), quoted in Brian Urquhart, "In the Name of Humanity," *New York Review of Books*, Apr. 27, 2000, p. 20.

5. UN Doc. E/CN.4/1993/7/Add.1 (1993).

6. Kenneth L. Cain, "The Rape of Dinah: Human Rights, Civil War in Liberia, and Evil Triumphant," *Human Rights Quarterly* 21 (1999), p. 297. The author strongly criticizes several international human rights groups for advocating "abstract, ideal standards . . . and articulat[ing] aspirational human rights goals that had no hope of actually being implemented in the real world." He called this "human rights cheerleading."

7. For an excellent analysis, see Lawyers Committee for Human Rights, *Haiti: Learning the Hard Way—The UN/OAS Human Rights Monitoring Operation in Haiti, 1993–1994* (New York: Lawyers Committee for Human Rights, 1995).

8. OAS/UN International Civilian Mission in Haiti, Terms of Reference, paras. 1 and 2 (on file with the author).

9. William G. O'Neill, "Human Rights Monitoring vs. Political Expediency: The Experience of the OAS/UN Mission in Haiti," *Harvard Human Rights Law Journal* 8 (1995), p. 115.

10. A Haitian paramilitary force created by longtime dictator Francois Duvalier in the late 1950s.

11. Lawyers Committee for Human Rights, *Haiti: Learning the Hard Way*, p. 57.

12. These tactics are common to all human rights field missions, and their use in other countries will be described below.

13. See Note by the Secretary-General, The Situation of Democracy and Human Rights in Haiti, Report of the International Civilian Mission in Haiti, UN Doc. A/48/532 (1993), pp. 28–29.

14. See Report Submitted to the Secretary-General by the Team of Human Rights Experts on the International Civilian Mission to Monitor Human Rights in Haiti, UN Doc. A/47/908 (1993), pp. 15–16.

15. Aspen Institute, *Honoring Human Rights: From Peace to Justice* (Washington, DC: Aspen Institute, 1998), p. 29.

16. Aspen Institute, *Honoring Human Rights: From Peace to Justice*; Aspen Institute, *Honoring Human Rights and Keeping the Peace: Lessons from El Salvador, Cambodia, and Haiti* (Washington, DC: Aspen Institute, 1995).

17. Lawyers Committee for Human Rights, *Improvising History: A Critical Evaluation of the United Nations Observer Mission in El Salvador* (New York: Lawyers Committee for Human Rights, 1995); Lawyers Committee for Human Rights, *Haiti: Learning the Hard Way*.

18. Eugene Nelson, Mark Splaine, Paul Batalden, and Stephen Plume, "Building Measurement and Data Collection into Medical Practice," *Annals of Internal Medicine* 128 (1998), pp. 460–466.

19. Robert S. Kaplan and David P. Norton, "The Balanced Scorecard: Measures That Drive Performance," *Harvard Business Review* 92105 (1992), pp. 72–79.

20. Nelson et al., "Building Measurement," p. 460.

21. This phrase is used by Robert S. Kaplan and David P. Norton in "Using the Balanced Scorecard as a Strategic Management System," *Harvard Business Review* 96107 (1996), p. 80.

22. Mark H. Moore, "Police Accountability and the Measurement of Police Enforcement," Harvard University, John F. Kennedy School of Government, Nov. 1991 (on file with the author).

23. Ibid., p. 3.

24. Thomas Carothers, *Assessing Democracy Assistance: The Case of Romania* (Washington, DC: Carnegie Endowment, 1996) pp. 129–130.

25. SC Res. 940 (1994), para. 4.

26. The vote was 13–0, with China and Brazil abstaining precisely because they saw no threat to international peace and security. Ironically, the Hutu-led government of Rwanda was on the Security Council at the same time that it was committing genocide at home.

27. In a different context, the OSCE's human rights report on Kosovo after the NATO bombing campaign helped change policy and the debate swirling around Kosovo. The report demonstrated clearly that attacks on Serbs, Roma, and other minorities

were not isolated acts of revenge but were organized, systematic, and the policy of hard-line Kosovo Albanian groups: OSCE, *Kosovo/Kosova: As Seen as Told* (Vienna: OSCE, 1999).

28. See "An Assessment of the Justice System in Haiti," internal MICIVIH report, March 1994 (on file with the author); and *Paper Laws, Steel Bayonets: The Breakdown of the Rule of Law in Haiti* (New York: Lawyers Committee for Human Rights, 1990).

29. Interview with Colin Granderson, former executive director of MICIVIH, New York, Apr. 7, 2000.

30. The author was chief of mission of HRFOR when these work plans were introduced.

31. OSCE Human Rights Department, "Examples of Impact of Human Rights Officers in the Field," Apr. 2000 (on file with the author).

32. Ibid.

33. Letter from Nicholas Howen, former director of the Human Rights Division of the UN Mission in Angola, Apr. 4, 2000 (on file with the author).

34. This information and much that follows are drawn from correspondence with Michael O'Flaherty, former head of the Human Rights Unit, UNOMSIL, May 5, 2000 (on file with the author).

35. The role of humanitarian agencies and their possible collaboration with human rights missions is growing in importance. This issue is explored in William G. O'Neill, "A Humanitarian Practitioner's Guide to International Human Rights Law," Thomas Watson Institute for International Studies, Occasional Paper No. 34 (1999).

6

Children of War: Understanding War and War Cleansing in Mozambique and Angola

Alcinda Honwana

This chapter considers the impact of political violence on children. In it I examine indigenous understandings of childhood, war and "war cleansing," and the ways in which protection of children in times of armed conflict can be undertaken at the local level. The ethnographic settings for this study are Mozambique and Angola, drawing on field research in Mozambique from 1993 to 1999, and in Angola during 1997–1998.[1] Both countries are former Portuguese colonies that became independent in 1975 after long wars of national liberation. In both countries, the postcolonial governments, led by the nationalist movements of the Front for the Liberation of Mozambique (FRELIMO) and the Popular Movement for the Liberation of Angola (MPLA), adopted a Marxist orientation and socialist models of development. This met with resistance from the rebel movements of the Mozambique National Resistance (RENAMO) and the National Union for the Total Independence of Angola (UNITA) respectively, which waged war against the incumbent governments. In the process of these wars, which lasted more than fifteen years in Mozambique and continue in Angola, thousands of children were drawn into armed conflict. These children of war constitute the subject of this chapter.

In this study I convey the experiences of children directly and indirectly involved in the armed conflicts: child soldiers, child victims of land mines, and abused young girls. I discuss the limitations of international conventions in ensuring children's protection against war and violence. And I argue for a bottom-up rather than a top-down approach—in other words, an approach that entails greater community participation in protecting children from conflict, and in enforcing their humanitarian rights. I also examine the issue of "universalization" of childhood. In this regard, the study emphasizes the diverse ways in which the notion of childhood is socially constructed in different contexts. In Mozambique and Angola, war is often conceptualized in opposition to society, as a "space" in which people are rewarded for breaking norms and social codes. Those who are exposed to war are not easily accepted back into society, as they are considered to be in a state of pollution caused by the anger of the spirits of the dead killed in the war. War pollution is often considered to be a threat to society, so a process of cleansing mediates the transition from the "space" of war into normal society, both for civilians and the military. Analyzing these cleansing or purification rituals shows that strong family and community involvement is vital for the processes of healing, reconciliation, and social reintegration of war-affected children. The effectiveness of these rituals lies in the shared understandings of war, war pollution, and cleansing. Drawing on these notions of war cleansing, I suggest that efforts to prevent children's involvement in war would benefit from a better understanding of local worldviews and meaning systems. This implies a strategy that marries local and global views on the protection of children in armed conflicts.

The Context of Political Violence in Mozambique and Angola

In Mozambique, the war between the government and the rebel forces started in 1977 with the creation of RENAMO by the Rhodesian Central Intelligence Organization (CIO). The Rhodesian government created and sponsored the rebel movement in retaliation against FRELIMO's full implementation of UN sanctions and, more important, its support of the Zimbabwe National Liberation Army's (ZANLA) armed struggle for the independence of Zimbabwe. Immediately after Mozambique's independence, a number of Portuguese settlers and former members of the colonial army left Mozambique for Rhodesia. This provided the Rhodesian security services with a recruiting pool for founding members of RENAMO. At its inception RENAMO (initially known as MNR) was totally dependent on Rhodesia and served a twofold purpose. First, it assisted the Rhodesian forces in operations against ZANLA inside Mozambique, mainly through intelligence gathering. Second, it implemented the agenda of those resentful Portuguese settlers who wanted to unseat the "communist" government of FRELIMO.[2]

From 1977 to 1980 RENAMO's role was expanded to include the sabotage of FRELIMO's economic and social policies and the disruption of normal life in rural areas. In addition, RENAMO was deployed against ZANLA infiltration routes into Zimbabwe. It must be noted that RENAMO's actions were far less damaging than the direct attacks of the Rhodesian army and air force on economic and military targets in the provinces of Tete, Manica, and Gaza. In response, Mozambican government forces took the war back to

Rhodesia by infiltrating a well-trained guerrilla force to operate alongside the Zimbabwean nationalists. In addition, they launched offensive operations against RENAMO bases, which culminated in the capture of the rebel stronghold of Gorongosa in late 1979.

With the independence of Zimbabwe in 1980 following the Lancaster House agreements, RENAMO lost its Rhodesian support and was taken over by South African Security Forces and some groups in the western countries. RENAMO grew rapidly in size and in military effectiveness. By mid-1983, the rebels had regained control over the strategic mountains of Gorongosa in central Mozambique and were operating in eight of the country's ten provinces. RENAMO's attacks against development and aid projects, roads, bridges, railways, schools, hospitals, farms, and entire villages were characterized by acts of extreme cruelty. Systematic torture and massacres of civilians became tragically frequent and "ordinary" events in rural areas, particularly in the southern part of the country. RENAMO's strategy was to disrupt the rural infrastructure, isolate the government in garrison towns, and render the country ungovernable, thus forcing FRELIMO into compliance with South Africa's security concerns by eliminating the ANC presence in Mozambique. At this stage, RENAMO was primarily the military conduit of the South African regional strategy of destabilization in Mozambique.[3]

In spite of its massive cruelty against the civilian population, RENAMO succeeded in attracting the sympathy of the peasantry, especially in the central and northern regions of the country. Many peasants felt disempowered by the government's antagonism to the rural cultural heritage and "traditional" authorities, and by its policies of forced "villagization."[4] The war in Mozambique peaked in 1987 when RENAMO made significant gains in the northern and central areas of the country and undertook actions in the south. The Homoine massacre in July 1987, in which more than four hundred people died, was one of RENAMO's most notorious attacks in the south. In this period there were widespread attacks and atrocities throughout the country, most of which were attributed to RENAMO. However, there are reports that government soldiers also committed some abuses, acting outside of the orders of their commanders.[5] With its economy devastated and development projects paralyzed, the country became increasingly dependent on foreign aid. As a result, the government decided to undertake far-reaching economic reforms, abandoning its former Marxist policies in favor of political and economic liberalization. In 1990 a new Constitution was adopted, enshrining the principles of multiparty democracy. Furthermore, with its resources dissipated by years of war, the government was incapable of imposing a military solution to the conflict. RENAMO was also unable to sustain its war effort as South African support decreased following a process of internal reforms to end apartheid. With this military impasse, the possibilities of a political solution gained strength.[6] Following several months of negotiations, the government and

RENAMO in October 1992 signed a General Peace Agreement in Rome. The first democratic elections took place in October 1994. FRELIMO won these and formed a new government. Five years later in the elections of 1999, FRE-LIMO renewed its mandate, though by a very narrow margin.

The Mozambican conflict was one of the most brutal wars of its time. The social costs were enormous. Its consequences for the civilian populations were catastrophic. Hundreds of thousands of Mozambicans died as a result of the war, about five million people were internally displaced by 1989, and more than one million became refugees in neighboring countries. Besides the many thousands of children who died as a direct consequence of the war, it is estimated that more than 250,000 children were either orphaned or separated from their families. School enrollments were reduced by an estimated 500,000, and medical facilities servicing approximately five million people were destroyed.[7]

In Angola, UNITA was one of the anticolonial movements that had fought against colonial rule since the early 1960s, alongside the MPLA and the UPA-FNLA (Popular Union of Angola–National Front for the Liberation of Angola). After the 1974 coup in Portugal, which marked the end of the Por-tuguese colonial wars, the three Angolan nationalist movements engaged in a bitter internecine war to gain exclusive access to power. The MPLA emerged victorious, the UPA-FNLA faded in importance, and UNITA reconstituted itself with mainly U.S. and South African support and continued its war against the MPLA government.[8] UNITA portrays itself as anti-Marxist and pro-Western. In the height of the cold war, the Angolan conflict directly involved South African and Cuban troops giving support to UNITA and the MPLA respectively. By 1987 there were major battles in the south of the country, culminating in the siege of Cuito Cuanavale by South African and UNITA forces. Although fighting over Cuito Cuanavale ended in a stalemate, the outcome was a psychological defeat for the South African Defense Force (SADF), which came to realize that it could not win militarily in Angola. This prompted a significant rethinking of South African military strategy.[9] Cuito Cuanavale also marked the beginning of new diplomatic attempts to end the conflict. The following eighteen months saw simultaneously the most sus-tained efforts to achieve a peaceful settlement, accompanied by some of the fiercest fighting of the entire war.

The first chance for peace came in May 1991 with the signature of a cease-fire agreement between the government and UNITA. This cease-fire held until the elections in September 1992, the first democratic elections in the country's history. In these elections, deemed free and fair by the international community, the MPLA won a majority of the votes. UNITA refused to accept the election results, claiming electoral fraud, and Savimbi ordered his troops to return to war, restarting full-scale conflict in October 1992.[10] This brutal and intense war lasted until 1994, taking a heavy toll on the civilian population—especially children. In November 1994 a new peace agreement was signed in Lusaka between the government and UNITA. The Lusaka Protocol was aimed at restoring peace in the territory and promoting national reconciliation through a cease-fire, followed by complete disarmament and cantonment of troops. In April 1997 a government of National Reconciliation and Unity, which brought UNITA members as well as some from other political parties into the cabinet, was established. Peace didn't last long. In October 1998, following disagreements with the government, UNITA went back to war.

Even before the renewed war at the end of 1992, the UN estimated that more than $30 billion had been lost during the Angolan conflict. It is estimated that in the 1992–1994 war more than 100,000 people died from war-related causes, the number of land mine victims rose to seventy thousand, and about 1.2 million people were displaced by September 1994.[11] According to the 1997 UN Development Program Report on Human Development in Angola, about 280,000 people were living in neighboring countries as refugees, and approximately 1.2 million Angolans were internally displaced. The urban population rose by 50 percent in 1995, compared to 15 percent growth in 1970. It is estimated that around one million children have been directly affected by the war, with more than 500,000 children dead. About half of the displaced population were children under 15 years of age. UNICEF statistics for 1993 have nearly 840,000 children living in difficult circumstances.[12] Thousands of children are unaccompanied, orphaned, or separated from their families, and many were dragged into armies and militia. In 1997 it was estimated that about 8,500 underage soldiers would be demobilized by March 1997.[13] About ten thousand were registered in the 1996–1997 demobilization process.

Indirectly, the war has affected many more children. Malnutrition has increased due to low food production and displacement. The deterioration of health-care services during the war resulted in higher infant and child mortality rates. Many children were prevented from attending school due mainly to displacement and destruction of schools. The situation of children in the aftermath of the armed conflict in the country is therefore devastating. In addition to problems of death and physical trauma, dire poverty, hunger, and ongoing social and emotional problems caused by this prolonged exposure to political violence make their situation much worse.

Children of War: Living in the Front Lines

It is estimated that more than ten thousand children in Angola and between eight thousand and ten thousand in Mozambique participated in the conflicts as soldiers, mostly recruited by UNITA and RENAMO respectively. There are also accounts of the use of children in the government forces in the two countries, although to a lesser extent. Children were used to carry weapons and other equipment, in the front lines, in reconnaissance missions, in planting land mines, and in espionage. This systematic preference for children as soldiers was often based on the assumptions that children are easier to control and manipulate, that they are easily programmed to feel little fear or revulsion for their actions, and that they are easily programmed to think of war and only war. Children were also believed to possess excessive energy that could be used to the rebel forces' advantage; once trained, they would carry out attacks with greater enthusiasm and brutality than adults.[14] It has been argued that the use of children as soldiers was also a result of shortage of adult reserves, exhausted by war, poverty, and disease.

Despite conscription laws and regulations, in times of war such rules were broken, and many children were abducted and kidnapped, especially by rebel forces. During the war in Mozambique, RENAMO forces regularly kidnapped children from their homes, gave them basic military training, and then sent them to the battlefield:

> I was kidnapped by RENAMO soldiers. One night, they came to my house and, while my brothers and I were sleeping, they tied us up and took us with them. The soldiers who abducted us burnt down many houses and shops in the village and after that they took us all to the base . . . we walked to the base. . . . Later I was sent for (military) training . . . they taught me how to disassemble and reassemble guns. I trained for four months.[15]

The same technique is used in Angola, where children are forcibly recruited by UNITA as soldiers. Not all children are forcibly conscripted, though. In fact, many enlist of their own volition. Many children join the government or rebel forces for protection, to secure food and shelter, because they are attracted by the possibility to loot, or for the sense of power they derive from holding a gun.[16]

Studies in northern Mozambique show that many young people became attracted to RENAMO due to the socioeconomic crisis in the countryside.[17] Many youths migrated to towns and returned to the rural areas unable to find work. These returned youths found life in the rural areas utterly unattractive, dominated as it was by gerontocratic authority, coupled with the lack of food, education, and employment opportunities. RENAMO offered these discontented youths a sense of purpose and power by putting a gun in their hands. A similar situation applies in Angola. Many of the children interviewed pointed out that insecurity, vulnerability, boredom, and lack of food were some of the reasons that led them to volunteer. Particularly important was the sense of security and power that the possession of a gun seemed to provide. "When you have a gun you can defend yourself," said one former underage soldier from Malanje in Angola. Sometimes, the inducement to take up arms may also come from the impulse to avenge the deaths of relatives, or by the sheer fun and adventure of wearing military gear and carrying an AK-47:

> I started military service in 1994, I volunteered to join the government army because we were suffering a lot in my village. . . . I wanted to defend my province and help my family with the products that I could get from the military ambushes.[18]

A sense of patriotism and/or ethnic grievance can also be a factor in children's volunteering for service. In a war situation rules and norms are completely disregarded, to the extent that traditional chiefs and parents send their very children to join the military. In Angola, for example, traditional chiefs from Bie, Huambo, and Malanje provided UNITA with underage recruits. Many did so out of their ethnic allegiance to UNITA, while others might have been forced to do it. In many cases, parents had to give their young boys to the *soba*, who would then send them to UNITA.[19]

> UNITA asked the *sobas* to give a certain number of boys. Parents were responsible for encouraging the boys to stay with UNITA, and to return them if they escaped. If the boys escaped and were not returned to the *soba*, the families would suffer.[20]

In these circumstances, parents are unable to protect their own offspring either from becoming killers or from being killed. In the context of such profound social crisis, parents can view their children joining either armed force—government or rebel—as a form of protecting the children and themselves. The guns give these children the ability to defend themselves and their relatives, as well as access to whatever food, clothing, and shelter the armed forces may provide.[21]

Playing a direct role in the war as a soldier seems to be the most terrible experience for a child in a context of political violence. Equally, living in military camps, being sexually abused by soldiers, being a victim of antipersonnel land mines, or witnessing the killing of family members is no less traumatic. Large numbers of children were abducted and forced to live in military camps. They were used as domestic workers, cooks, water and firewood searchers and carriers, and sexual partners to soldiers. The hardships endured by children who did not carry and fire guns, especially young girls, is often referred to only in the margins. Wars are generally portrayed as an essentially "male affair," executed and endured by men. Very little is usually said about the role female soldiers play, as combatants, cooks, and domestic workers, and the sexual abuse they often suffer. Here is the testimony of a seventeen-year-old girl from Manhica, Mozambique, about her life in a RENAMO military camp:

> I was kidnapped with three friends of mine when we were in the bush looking for firewood. A group of RENAMO soldiers stopped us and forced us to go with them to the military base. We had to carry the products they had looted. . . . We walked for three days until we reached the base. I lived in the base for three years. During the day we had to cook, clean the base and look for firewood and water. During the night soldiers came to take us to sleep with them . . . a soldier per night. . . . The lucky ones were those who were chosen by an "officer" who had a hut for them to live in, and who protected them as his wives.[22]

Many other children were affected by war in their towns and villages when these were attacked. This often meant losing relatives and friends and being deprived of the bare necessities of life. Many were victims of antipersonnel land mines. Land-mine victims carry a permanent reminder of the war with them every day of their lives, for this is a reality that is inscribed in their bodies and from which they cannot escape or hide. This is the story of a nine-year-old girl from Kuito in Angola:

> I stepped onto a landmine when my mother and I went out looking for food. . . . When I stepped onto it, I didn't hear any noise or feel anything. I just saw myself lying on the floor, and a lot of blood coming out of my leg. . . . I started to shout and cry, my mother shouted and cried too. . . . My uncle took me to the hospital. At the hospital, I didn't see anything; I just remember waking up to see that my leg had been amputated. I started crying again.[23]

The inability to produce food in times of war and the massive displacement increased malnutrition and infant mortality rates, which were aggravated by the deterioration of health-care services. School attendance also decreased during the war, due to social instability and forced movement to find safer places.

This is the predicament of most children in zones of ongoing conflict, not only in Africa but also in Europe, Asia, and South America. In fact, the tales of war of Mozambican and Angolan children presented in this chapter are not so different from the ones experienced by children in several conflict zones around the world. From Croatia to Afghanistan, from Sierra Leone to Cambodia, from Nicaragua to Palestine, and from Sri Lanka to the Democratic Republic of Congo, the similarities in recruitment strategies are striking.[24] How can the recruitment of underage soldiers be prevented? How can millions of innocent children be protected from the devastating effects of war? Are the instruments of international humanitarian law helpful in this regard? If so, how can they be enforced? I address some of these questions in the following section.

International Law and Protection of Children Against Political Violence

Several international agreements have been put in place to protect the rights of children and prevent them from participating in political conflicts. The 1977 First Protocol Additional to the Geneva Conventions (Additional Protocol I) provides that states parties shall take "all feasible measures in order that children who have not attained the age of fifteen years do not take a direct part in hostilities and, in particular, they shall refrain from recruiting them into their armed forces."[25] This age limit is repeated in the 1989 Convention on the Rights of the Child, article 38(2) of which provides that states parties shall take "all feasible measures to *ensure* that persons who have attained the age of fifteen years do not take a direct part in hostilities."[26]

The adoption of the age of fifteen was controversial. For other purposes in the Convention, a child is defined as a person below the age of eighteen, unless the law applicable to the child provides otherwise.[27] The African Charter on the Rights and Welfare of the Child promulgated in 1990 by the Organization of African Unity defines a child simply as a person younger than eighteen years of age.[28] Article 22(2) of the African Charter does not stipulate a different age for nonparticipation in armed conflict, merely stating that states parties shall take "*all necessary measures to ensure* that no child shall take a direct part in hostilities and refrain in particular from recruiting any child."[29]

The age limit for recruitment has been the subject of intense debate. Many humanitarian organizations and pressure groups consider that fifteen years of age is too young for military enrollment. The UN constituted a working group to examine the issue, and debates on the need to increase the age limit to eighteen years went on for over six years. An Optional Protocol to the Convention on the Rights of the Child on the Involvement of Children in Armed Conflicts, raising the minimum age to eighteen years, was proposed at the sixth session of the working group in January 2000. The protocol would apply to both national armed forces and nonstate armed groups and would require nations to rehabilitate former child soldiers. However, while compulsory recruitment cannot take place below the age of eighteen, voluntary recruitment can happen at sixteen years of age. It was mainly the United States, the United Kingdom, and Australia that watered down the protocol by insisting on—and charging the panel to agree to—a minimum age of sixteen for voluntary, noncombatant recruits. These countries insisted on a lower age for voluntary enlistment in order to make special provision for allowing enrollment of sixteen-year-olds into educational institutions operated by the military.[30]

Some humanitarian organizations have expressed disappointment with the failure of the international community to reach a "straight-eighteen position." They believe that by failing to raise the age of voluntary recruitment of children to eighteen, governments continue to base their positions primarily on narrow military interests rather than on the best interests of children. The new protocol also creates a double standard by prohibiting all recruitment of children under eighteen but allowing the recruitment of *volunteers* under eighteen. This also raises an important issue in respect of the connection between "voluntary" and "forced" recruitment. Governments and armed groups can find space for underage recruitment by considering it voluntary. Although in some cases young people do indeed volunteer to join military institutions, not all "volunteers" are truly voluntary. Indirect coercive mechanisms can be used to persuade young people to join the military. Intimidation, social pressure, physical protection, the possibility of taking revenge, access to food and shelter, security, and adventure are some of them. Therefore, the dividing line between voluntary and forced recruitment can sometimes be imprecise and ambiguous. Moreover, the distinction between recruitment for combatant and noncombatant roles—as expressed in the proposed amendment protocol—can be blurred. In some cases that distinction can be used as an expedient to justify the presence of children on military bases in deceptive "noncombatant" roles.

Changes in age limit are important, but they may not have the desired impact in terms of enforcing international humanitarian law concerning child recruitment. The question of children's involvement in war easily arouses strong emotions. Images of children carrying guns and wearing military uniforms create demands that their use in armed conflicts be put to an end. Whatever the reasons behind the moral engagement caused by contemporary images of children as soldiers, it represents an important motivation for changing the situation. The crucial issue now is how to change it. The raising of the minimum age of recruitment into military activities to eighteen years constitutes a crucial measure, but it is not enough. On the one hand, it formally strengthens international laws protecting children from armed conflict. On the other hand, however, it is of little practical importance to the thousands of children in many remote areas of the globe where these laws are not known, understood, or implemented. The challenge, therefore, is how to make international conventions understood and recognized at the local level. Beyond strengthening international laws, it is vital to consider local understandings and norms about notions of childhood, child protection, and armed conflict. A marriage between international and national, or even local, mechanisms of child protection seems critical. It is this symbiosis between global and local strategies that can enable the creation of an environment conducive to the effective protection of children against armed conflict in places where such protection is most needed.

Local Versus Global:
The Universalization of Childhood

The dominant framework that informs the understanding of childhood today maintains that children are vulnerable, dependent, and innocent human beings who need to be protected by adults. Child development happens through the process of socialization and follows a predetermined path composed of several stages that children go through on their way to a state of adulthood.[31] Thus, the notion of childhood stands in opposition to adulthood, and children are seen as "people in the process of becoming, rather than being."[32] This conception of childhood and child development is generally taken to be a natural and universal phase of human existence, shaped more by biological and psychological factors than social ones.[33] This view is also predominant in international law regarding the rights of children. The need to establish global standards of childhood in order to protect them led to a "universalization" of what constitutes childhood. In international law, children often appear as presocial and passive recipients of experience who need to be protected up to the age of fifteen or eighteen. They need protection, nurturing, and enlightenment, as they are vulnerable, immature, and incapable of assuming responsibilities. Thus, they should be excluded from work and other responsibilities, and confined to the protection of home and school. This is a predominant concept of childhood among middle-class people, especially in Europe and North America, who have "universalized" children in such a way that children who do not follow this path are considered to be at risk. By traditionally embodying the image of the dependent child and the potential victim, international law has failed to look at childhood as a social and historical construction.

Various authors have stated the importance of understanding childhood as a social construction. As James and Prout pointed out, looking at childhood as a social construct means "the institution of childhood provides an interpretative frame for understanding the early years of human life. In these terms it is biological immaturity rather than childhood which is a universal and natural feature of human groups."[34] But notions of childhood cannot be understood in universal terms. They vary across societies, as they are attached to culture, class, gender, and other variables. Also, notions of childhood are historical constructs that change over time. Hendrik refers to the shifting notions of childhood in nineteenth- and twentieth-century Britain, from an idea of childhood fragmented by geography (urban/rural) and class to one that was much more uniform and coherent.[35]

However, in many other contexts the situation of children differs from the one outlined above. Being a child in Mozambique and Angola, for example, seems to have less to do with age than with social roles and responsibilities. Children are often identified through roles—they are even called according to what they do or are supposed to do as they grow.[36] As expressed by an elderly Angolan,

> In the past there wasn't this thing of saying that this person is 18 or 10 years of age and, therefore, must do this and that. The elders in the family identified the passing of time through the seasons: the time to plant the maize; the time of the harvest etc. . . . and in this way children just grew freely, and parents would know what tasks to assign them depending on the way they were developing. . . . Some children grow faster than others both mentally and physically.[37]

Moreover, unlike the middle-class children whose parents can afford to provide for them up to eighteen years of age, many children in different parts of the world are exposed to work at an early age. They participate actively in productive activities, household chores, and care of younger children. In these societies children learn by participating in, rather than being protected from, social and economic processes. Mozambican and Angolan children are often portrayed as strong, as survivors, and as actively growing, often in difficult conditions.[38] In many African societies, children are often synonymous of wealth because of the contribution they can make to the productive work of the family. Children are also valued as a source of security for the future. Therefore, and as various authors have emphasized, children need to be studied as an analytical category in themselves. One should not focus on children simply as proto-adults or future beings but rather, and essentially, as beings-in-the-present, and as social actors with an active presence of their own.[39]

In some societies, the boundaries between adulthood and childhood become very ambiguous, as children actively create and re-create their roles according to the situations presented to them. In fact, in both Angola and Mozambique, extreme social crises, such as war, favored a displacement of roles between adults and children. As mentioned above, many children were and are active soldiers, assuming roles that in "normal" circumstances would be fulfilled by adults. The shifting of roles in such a dramatic way, in which children become killers and commit the most horrific atrocities, is intrinsically linked to the breakdown of society's structures and morality in the context of a crisis such as war. What kind of social, political, and economic conditions makes possible the eruption of these violent conflicts? What makes possible this massive participation of children in armed conflicts? How can they be protected from war? What effect may this phenomenon have on their generation? And what will their future be like?

These are some pertinent questions to be asked in this context. International humanitarian law is far from being able to enforce human rights in times of war. Even when the age limit for recruitment was fifteen, many children as young as eight continued to be recruited systematically into military activities. The increase in the age of recruitment offers no guarantees for improving the current situation. As mentioned above, in Mozambique and Angola children have been recruited well under the age of fifteen. The issue goes beyond raising age limits. It has to do with dissemination of information about the conventions, with knowledge about rights, with understanding those rights, and with translating the rights and norms into local worldviews and meaning systems in order to make them recognizable and locally sanctioned.

Importantly, the wars in Mozambique and Angola fall outside the "traditional" notion of warfare. These postcolonial conflicts do not exhibit the features of the wars contemplated in the traditional rules of international humanitarian law: they represent a new type of guerrilla war.[40] Children are particularly vulnerable to military recruitment in these conflicts; sometimes they are referred to as "easy prey."[41] These wars constitute a total crisis in people's lives. They destroy not only people's material possessions but also their moral fiber and sense of dignity. This may partially explain why parents have to give their own children to the military, and why traditional leaders have to become recruiters of young soldiers. This raises also the issue of the distinction between civilians and soldiers, because in such context many civilians are forcibly called into performing military tasks. Many are given arms and forced to fight without proper training. In such chaotic conditions, it becomes extremely difficult to enforce international humanitarian laws, especially if these come only from above and are not understood at the local level.

Families and communities play a crucial role in the postwar healing and social reintegration of war-affected children, suggesting a possible role prior to and during conflict. Parents and traditional leaders are often coerced into participating in recruitment, unable to protect even their own children. In times of war, protection may in fact mean enlisting the child into one side or the other, to ensure that the child will at least have access to food, shelter, and a gun to protect him- or herself and eventually the relatives and the village. Nevertheless, in some situations protection may be possible if people are aware of their rights and can understand them within the framework of their own values and norms. A more effective protection strategy may therefore be found by merging global worldviews with local ones and by involving local agents—such as families and community members—in this process. Trying to deal with child protection in these catastrophic conditions by solely expecting governments to act is not enough. Similarly, heavy reliance on international agencies and organizations that come to impose rights and norms established outside that local context, without looking at local understandings and without framing them within local ideologies, may also be ineffective.

With this project in mind, I use the next section to explore some local understandings of the wars in Mozambique and Angola as well as some indigenous mechanisms for the social reintegration of war-affected children.

War: The "Space" of Abnormality

In Mozambique and Angola war is often conceptualized in opposition to society, and as a normless "space." People are trained to kill and harm others and are rewarded for breaking norms and social codes. Therefore, those who are exposed to war are not easily reaccepted into society, as they are considered "polluted" by war. "War pollution" is believed to arise from contact with death and bloodshed. Individuals who have been exposed to war, who killed or saw people being killed, are believed to be polluted by the wrongdoings of the war, and contaminated by the spirits of the dead. These persons are perceived as potential contaminators of the social body. Contamination comes from the anger of the spirits of dead killed during the war. In southern Mozambique these spirits are called *Mipfhukwa*, the spirits of those who did not have an adequate burial to place them in their proper positions in the world of the ancestors. They are believed to be unsettled and bitter spirits who can cause harm to their killers or to passersby. In Angola, too, burial rituals for the dead are considered to be of utmost importance to ensure peace and well-being. The role of the spirits of the dead is central to the life of many people, especially in rural settings in Mozambique and Angola.[42]

Individuals who fought in wars or lived in military camps are seen as the vehicles through which the spirits of the war dead can enter and afflict entire communities. Such spirits are believed to contaminate not only the individual killer but also family relatives, neighbors, and even passersby. After the war, when soldiers and refugees return home, cleansing or purification rituals are seen as a fundamental condition for individual and collective healing and protection against pollution. They are also important means of conflict resolution, reconciliation, and social reintegration of war-affected people into society. I will next discuss how families and communities heal the social wounds of war in the postwar period through ritual performance. It must be noted that not everybody performs cleansing or purification rituals or rituals to appease the spirits of the dead. Such practices are more common in rural areas than in urban settings. The availability of health-care alternatives as well as religious and political affiliations also determines the ways in which people make decisions concerning treatment of war trauma and other related afflictions.

The Aftermath of War: Healing Social Wounds

Cleansing Rituals for War-Affected People

Rituals for former child soldiers are similar to those performed on war-affected individuals in general. These rituals deal with what happened to people during the war period. For combatants (in this case child soldiers), an acknowledgment of the atrocities committed and a subsequent break from that past are articulated through ritual performance. Traditional healing for war-affected children in Angola and Mozambique seems to consist principally of purification or cleansing rituals, attended by family members and the broader community. During these rituals the child is purged and purified of the "contamination" of war and death as well as of sin, guilt, and avenging spirits of those killed by the child soldier. These ceremonies are replete with ritual and symbolism, the details of which are distinctive to the particular ethnolinguistic group but whose general themes are common to all groups.

Case one: Samuel, a former child soldier. Samuel was only nine years old when he was abducted by RENAMO forces during an attack on his village. He was ordered to carry a bag of maize meal and walk for four days to the military camp. Later he was submitted to a month of military training and forced to serve as a soldier for more than two years. After the cease-fire Samuel was reunited with some of his relatives. On the day of his arrival his relatives took him to the *ndumba* (the house of the spirits). There he was presented to the ancestral spirits of the family. The boy's grandfather addressed the spirits, informing them that his grandchild had returned, and thanked them for their protection, as his grandson had returned alive. A few days later a traditional healer was invited by the family to help them perform a cleansing ritual for Samuel. The practitioner took the boy to the bush, where a small hut covered with dry grass had been built. The boy, dressed in the dirty clothes he brought from the rebel camp, entered the hut and undressed himself. Then the hut was set on fire, and an adult relative helped the boy out. The hut, the clothes, and everything else that the boy brought from the camp had to be burnt. This symbolized the rupture with that past. A chicken was sacrificed for the spirits of the dead, and the blood was spread around the ritual place. The chicken was then cooked and offered to the spirits as a sacrificial meal. The boy had to inhale the smoke of some herbal remedies and bathe himself in water treated with medicine. In this way his body was cleansed both internally and externally. Finally, the spirit medium made some incisions in the boy's body and filled them with a paste made from herbal remedies, a practice called *ku thlavela*. The purpose of this procedure is to give strength to the boy. During this public ritual, relatives and neighbors were present and assisted the practitioner by performing specific roles, or just by observing, singing, and clapping.

Case two: Healing Pitango. When Pitango, of Cambandua in Angola, returned home, his family organized a ritual for him. The ritual happened the day Pitango arrived, before he was allowed to socialize with relatives and friends. His body was washed with cassava meal, and chicken blood was placed on his forehead (the chicken was killed during the proceedings). Then his mother took some palm oil and rubbed it on Pitango's hands and feet. During these proceedings the ancestral spirits of the family were often called in to protect the young man who was back from war and had to start a new life. This was done through addresses made by elderly relatives. The elderly in his family, who spoke to Pitango upon his arrival, explained that the performance of this ritual was needed so that the spirits of those killed in the war would not harm him. This was necessary for him to start a new life. Pitango said that because he did not kill anybody during the war he did not need to go through a ritual performed by a *kimbanda* (traditional healer).

Case three: Nzinga's cleansing. Nzinga is a fifty-five-year-old traditional healer in Malanje, Angola. When her nineteen-year-old nephew Pedro returned after more than seven years of fighting with UNITA, she performed a ritual for him. When asked about it, she said,

> I could not let him stay without the cleansing treatment. He needed it because there he might have done bad things like kill, beat and rob people. . . . Without the treatment the spirits of the dead would harm him. I do not know what happened there, he said he did not do anything . . . young people sometimes lie . . . I decided to go for full treatment because otherwise he could become crazy or even die.[43]

Traditional healers generally perform the "full treatment" to which Nzinga refers. It lasted four days and took place in her house. It required a chicken, a *luando* (mat), and some wine or beer. She put her nephew Pedro in a place of seclusion called *mwanza* (place of ritual treatment), and there she placed the mat for him to sleep on. She put some powdered medicine (*ditondo* and *dikezo*) under the mat and in his food and drink. Pedro had to stay inside the *mwanza* for three days. At dawn on the fourth day he was taken to the river to be washed. After this he was not allowed to look back. He had to break with the past, and asking him not to look back at the river symbolized that break with the dirty war (the dirt of the war was washed from his body and left to flow downstream). Back home, Nzinga opened an egg, put some sugar and powdered medicine inside, and threw it away, saying, "You malevolent spirits here is what you want . . . leave us now." The ritual chicken and drinks that Pedro ate and drank throughout the duration of his treatment were likewise prepared with herbal medicines. During the ritual, family members were present and contributed food and drink, which they shared during the proceedings.

Each of these rituals addresses the idea of pollution that the children bring to their homes and villages. They have to be cleansed in order to be able to socialize freely with relatives and friends. In Samuel's case, the cleansing ceremony happened a few days after his arrival and was performed by a specialist. In Pitango's case, he was "washed" the day of his arrival. Pedro's aunt decided to give him the "full treatment" because she was not sure about what he had done during the war. Another important element that these cases reveal is the idea of symbolically breaking with the past—the washing of the body in the river stream so that the dirt of the war would go away; the burning of the hut and the clothes brought from the war. It is interesting to see in all three cases the use of chickens in the rituals (the blood for cleansing, the meat for the sacrificial meal shared with the ancestors) and of herbal remedies to cleanse the body internally (inhaling and drinking) and externally (bathing and rubbing). In these cases the Cartesian dichotomy that separates body and mind cannot be applied, for individuals are seen as a whole body/mind composite, as part and parcel of a collective body—their wrongdoings can affect their families as well. This explains the direct involvement of the family (both the living and the dead) in the cleansing and healing processes. The ancestors are believed to have a powerful role in protecting their relatives against evil and misfortune. That is why Samuel's relatives took him to the hut of the ancestors and thanked them for the fact that he was alive and safely returned home. Pitango's family also addressed the ancestors, and Nzinga put Pedro in the place of the ancestors for the duration of his ritual treatment.

These healing and protective rituals do not involve verbal exteriorization of the experience. Healing is achieved through nonverbal symbolic procedures, which are understood by those participating in them. That is why clothes and other objects symbolizing the past have to be burned or washed away to impress on the individual and the group a complete break from that experience and the beginning of a new life. Recounting and remembering the traumatic experience would be like opening a door for the harmful spirits to penetrate the communities. Viewed from this perspective, the well-meaning attempts of psychotherapists to help local people deal with war trauma may in fact cause more harm than help.

The performance of these rituals and the politics that precede them transcend the particular individuals concerned and involve the collective body. Family and friends are involved, and the ancestral spirits are also implicated in mediating for a good outcome. The cases presented above show how the living have to acknowledge the dead—both ancestors and the war dead—in order to carry on with their lives. The rituals are aimed at seeking forgiveness, appeasing the souls of the dead, and preventing any future afflictions (retaliations) from the spirits of the dead, closing in this way the links with that "bad" past.

There is no doubt that these rituals are instrumental in building family cohesion and solidarity and in dealing with the psychological and emotional side of these children's problems. The fact is, however, that the children return to a countryside that remains as poor as it was when they left, with no job opportunities and no vocational schools. In Mozambique, the end of hostilities gave rise to some degree of confidence, and the economy is slowly showing signs of improvement. In Angola, however, the war did not stop. Fighting continues, children continue to be recruited into the military. Community mechanisms of healing, social rebuilding, and conflict resolution are important, but on their own they cannot be a solution to the problem. These community interventions have to be complemented by job creation and skills training programs, as well as a general alleviation of poverty, in order to give these children and youths some perspective of a better future.

Conclusion

The examination of local healing strategies demonstrates that biomedicine and psychotherapy are only two of many ways of understanding and healing distress and trauma. Considering that the majority of the Mozambican and Angolan population affected by war is rural, a combination of several healing approaches seems to be necessary in order to take into account their worldviews and systems of meaning. I have suggested that local understandings of war trauma, of healing, and of community cohesion and stability need to be taken into account when dealing with postconflict healing, reconciliation, and social reintegration. Traditional healers, religious leaders, the family, and elderly members of the community are already creating their spaces in these processes of healing the social wounds of war. They are not waiting for the government to bring them psychologists and other medical practitioners to solve their problems. They are using the means available to them to restore peace and stability in their communities.

I also have suggested that community participation should be engaged in protection of children against recruitment into armed violence. More and more often, governments, international organizations, and other pressure groups are now called upon to protect children during war. Although the role played by these institutions is vital, better results might be achieved by increasing the participation of local agents in child protection. Moreover, it is fundamental to disseminate information and knowledge about humanitarian law at the local level, and to make it compatible with local understandings. International conventions have to be understood within the context of local worldviews and meaning systems. This is what will allow them to be recognized, accepted, and enforced at the local level, where protection of children from armed conflicts is greatly needed.

Notes

1. The author's work in Angola was possible thanks to a Christian Children's Fund (CCF) consultancy in 1997/1998. The Angolan data presented in this article were collected by the author and by members of the CCF team in Angola.

2. E. Hall, "The Mozambican National Resistance Movement (Renamo) and the Reestablishment of Peace in Mozambique," paper delivered at a workshop on Security and Cooperation in Post-Apartheid Southern Africa, Maputo, Sept. 1991. J. Honwana, "The United Nations and Mozambique: A Sustainable Peace?" *Lumiar Papers* No. 7 (Lisbon: Instituto de Estudos Estrategicos e Internacionais, 1995).

3. R. Gersony, "Summary of Refugee Accounts of Principally Conflict Related Experiences in Mozambique" (Washington, DC: Bureau for Refugee Programs, State Department, 1988); A. Vines, *Renamo: Terrorism in Mozambique* (London: Centre for Southern African Studies, University of York and Indiana University Press, 1991).

4. C. Geffray, *La Cause des armes au Mozambique: Anthropologie d'une guerre civile* (Paris: Credu-Karthala, 1990).

5. United Nations, *The United Nations and Mozambique, 1992–1995* (Blue Book Series) (New York: UN Department of Public Information, 1995).

6. Ibid.

7. Ibid.

8. Vines, *Renamo*; W. Minter, *Apartheid's Contras: An Inquiry into the Roots of War in Angola and Mozambique* (London: Zed Books, 1994).

9. Human Rights Watch, *Easy Prey: Children and War in Liberia* (London: Human Rights Watch Children's Project, 1994).

10. Minter, *Apartheid's Contras*; UN Development Program, *Relatorio do Desenvolvimento Humano, Angola* (1997).

11. Minter, *Apartheid's Contras*.

12. Ibid.

13. UNDP, *Angola*.

14. O. Furley, "Child Soldiers in Africa," in O. Furley (ed.), *Conflict in Africa* (London: Tauris, 1995).

15. Author interview, identity withheld, Ilha Josina, Mozambique, Apr. 1999.

16. Furley, "Child Soldiers."

17. See Geffray, *La Cause des armes*.

18. Author interview, identity withheld, Huambo, Angola, Feb. 1998.

19. A. Honwana, *"Okusiakala Ondalo Okalye* (Let's Light a New Fire): Local Knowledge in the Post-War Healing and Reintegration of War-Affected Children in Angola," research report for Christian Children's Fund, Luanda, Angola, 1999.

20. Author interview, "Ben," Malanje, Angola, Feb. 1998. Ben served as a UNITA soldier and was demobilized in 1997.

21. A. Honwana, "Negotiating Post-War Identities: Child Soldiers in Mozambique and Angola," *CODESRIA Bulletin* 1/2 (1999); Paul Richards, *Fighting for the Rain Forest: War, Youth and Resources in Sierra Leone* (Oxford: James Currey, 1996); Furley, "Child Soldiers."

22. Author interview, identity withheld, Ilha Josina, Mozambique, May 1999.

23. Interview conducted by the CCF team in Angola, identity withheld, Kuito, 1997.

24. C. Dodge and M. Raundalen, *Reaching Children in War: Sudan, Uganda and Mozambique* (Uppsala: Sigma Forlag, 1991); R. Brett and M. McCallin, *Children, the Invisible Soldiers* (Växjö, Sweden: Rädda Barnen [Swedish Save the Children], 1996); I. Abdullah, "Violence, Youth Culture and War: A Critical Reading of Paul Richards,"

Lionenet: A Discussion of Sierra Leonean Issues, Mar. 19, 1996; J. Boyden and S. Gibbs, *Children and War: Understanding Psychological Distress in Cambodia* (Geneva: UN, 1997).

25. Additional Protocol I, art. 77(2).

26. Convention on the Rights of the Child, UN Doc. A/44/49 (1989), art. 38(2) (emphasis added).

27. Convention on the Rights of the Child, art. 1.

28. African Charter on the Rights and Welfare of the Child, OAU Doc. CAB/LEG/24.9/49 (1990), art. 2.

29. See further Ilene Cohn and Guy S. Goodwin-Gill, *Child Soldiers: The Role of Children in Armed Conflict* (Oxford: Clarendon Press, 1994).

30. Radda Barnen, "Children of War," *Newsletter on Child Soldiers* 1 (March 2000).

31. S. Gibbs, "Post-War Reconstruction in Mozambique, Reframing Children's Experiences of War and Healing," *Disasters* 18, 3 (1994), pp. 268–300.

32. A. James, *Childhood Identities: Self and Social Relationships in the Experience of Childhood* (Edinburgh: Edinburgh University Press, 1993).

33. M. Freeman, *The Rights and Wrongs of Children* (London: Francis Printer Publishers, 1993).

34. A. James and A. Prout (eds.), *Constructing and Reconstructing Childhood: Contemporary Issues in the Sociological Study of Childhood* (London: Falmer Press, 1990).

35. Ibid.

36. Honwana, "Negotiating Post-War Identities."

37. Interview conducted in 1997 by members of the CCF team with 75-year-old Antonio Sonama, Uige.

38. Gibbs, "Post-War Reconstruction"; Honwana, *"Okusiakala Ondalo Okalye."*

39. J. Boyden, "Childhood and the Policy Makers: A Comparative Perspective on the Globalization of Childhood," in James and Prout, *Constructing and Reconstructing Childhood*; A. Dawes, "Helping, Coping and 'Cultural Healing,'" *Recovery: Research and Co-operation on Violence, Education and Rehabilitation of Young People* 1, 5 (1996); James, *Childhood Identities*; P. Reynolds, *Traditional Healers and Childhood in Zimbabwe* (Athens: Ohio University Press, 1996); Boyden and Gibbs, *Children and War*.

40. John Ellis describes guerrilla wars as not simply a military phenomenon but also a political activity that involves popular participation. It is a "struggle of the weak against superior members and technology." Normally, in such wars the political program of the leadership has to mesh with the basic aspirations of the people in order to channel their ability to fight. The people are persuaded to fight, rather than being coerced by repressive structures. This was the case of many liberation wars, including the one Angolans fought against Portuguese colonialism. Although these postcolonial wars still maintain some of the features of guerrilla warfare, in many respects their relationship with the people is often one of repression and complete disrespect. They abduct people and force them to fight and support their struggle. This seems to be dramatically different from the traditional guerrilla warfare discussed by Ellis; see John Ellis, *A Short History of Guerrilla Warfare* (London: Allan, 1975).

41. Human Rights Watch, *Easy Prey*.

42. See A. Honwana, "Healing for Peace: Traditional Healers and Post-War Reconstruction in Southern Mozambique," in R. Porter and J. Hinnels (eds.), *Religion, Health and Suffering* (London: Kegan Paul, 1997); Honwana, *"Okusiakala Ondalo Okalye."*

43. Author interview, "Nzinga," Malanje, Angola, Feb. 1998.

PART 3

Enforcing Compliance

7

No Justice Without Peace? International Criminal Law and the Decision to Prosecute

Simon Chesterman

In a recent book on crimes against humanity, Geoffrey Robertson quotes a joke that did the rounds of foreign correspondents in Sarajevo during 1994: "When someone kills a man, he is put in prison. When someone kills 20 people, he is declared mentally insane. But when someone kills 20,000 people, he is invited to Geneva for peace negotiations."[1] The black humor captures a dilemma central to the project of international criminal law: to what extent should the larger goal of peace take precedence over the prosecution of individual justice?

Following the establishment of ad hoc tribunals for the former Yugoslavia and Rwanda in 1993 and 1994, and the adoption in 1998 of the Rome Statute of the International Criminal Court (ICC), much has been written on the history and future of international criminal law.[2] In this chapter I focus on the specific questions of whether individual criminal responsibility should be pursued as part of the resolution to a conflict and the extent to which the international community can and should be involved in any such proceedings.

I begin with the legacy of the Nuremberg trials. Whether or not these proceedings are regarded as tainted by "victor's justice," they provided an unrealistic template for the development of international criminal law. In particular, the trials took place following unconditional surrender to an occupying power—as a result, amnesty for the Nazis was never seriously contemplated. Of primary interest here is the decision to pursue legal rather than military means at all; this was in large part due to the view that the desire for retribution had to be tempered by the need to deter similar atrocities in future.

I then turn to the modern experience of international criminal tribunals, focusing on the two ad hoc tribunals for the former Yugoslavia and Rwanda. The work of these tribunals—each created by the United Nations Security

Council as a measure to restore "international peace and security"—also discloses distinct and not always compatible policy objectives. Their qualified successes appear to be responsible for moves toward the creation of a permanent International Criminal Court; at the same time, it is noteworthy that the prospect of additional ad hoc international tribunals has since been abandoned in Cambodia and East Timor.

Finally, I consider the role of domestic courts. Even assuming that the International Criminal Court comes into existence, domestic proceedings are likely to remain the most important forum for the enforcement of international criminal law. In this respect, the *Pinochet* case is rightly recognized as a landmark decision in confirming that former heads of state do not enjoy immunity from prosecution.[3] That case was followed by the indictment in Senegal of the former Chadian dictator Hissene Habre. At the other extreme, the Lomé Peace Agreement that gave temporary pause to Sierra Leone's civil war in July 1999 included a blanket amnesty for crimes committed in the course of the conflict. The discussion here will concentrate on the political context of such cases, focusing in particular on alternatives to the two extremes of criminal prosecutions and unconditional amnesties.

The Legacy of Nuremburg

The Nuremberg trials of the major Nazi war criminals are generally seen as a pivotal moment in international criminal law. In his opening arguments before the tribunal, U.S. Chief of Counsel Justice Robert H. Jackson presented the trials as an historic victory for the rule of law:

> That four great nations, flushed with victory and stung with injury, stay the hand of vengeance and voluntarily submit their captive enemies to the judgment of the law is one of the most significant tributes that Power has ever paid to Reason.[4]

Even in the closing moments of the war, however, it was far from clear that the Allies would pursue legal avenues to punish the Nazi leadership. British Prime Minister Winston Churchill, for example, had favored the summary execution of fifty or so leading members of the Nazi apparatus. Joseph Stalin approved: in a "semi-jocular" recommendation he suggested that fifty thousand German general staff officers be shot.[5]

This exchange is commonly dismissed as an aberration, but it was a serious proposition at the time. Such an approach enjoyed the virtues of simplicity and candor. It would spare the Allies the tedious process of organizing the mechanisms and material necessary to present a watertight case, precluding legal rationalizations and dilatory tactics that the guilty might employ to delay their judgment. And, crucially, the victors would not be required to "disguise a punishment exacted by one sovereign upon another by appeal to the neutral instrument of the law."[6]

That this course was avoided was due largely to American involvement. Henry Stimson, the U.S. secretary for war, believed that a duly constituted international tribunal would have a greater effect on posterity; the Germans would not be able to claim (as they had of the Treaty of Versailles) that admissions of war guilt had been exacted under duress.[7] President Franklin Roosevelt wavered, but his successor, Harry S. Truman, had utter contempt for the British solution of summary executions. In the event, the final decision to cede "Power . . . to Reason" was formalized on a particularly inauspicious date. In one of history's more brutal ironies, the treaty that established the Nuremberg trials—power's celebrated tribute to reason—was signed by the Allies on the same day that the United States dropped its second atomic bomb on Japan.

These debates highlight competing objectives in the Allies' decision to prosecute the Nazi leadership for war crimes: retribution and deterrence. The retributive element was clear from the earliest preparations for war crimes trials. In October 1941, Churchill articulated his horror at the "Nazi butcheries," stating that "retribution for these crimes must henceforward take its place among the major purposes of the war."[8] By 1942, the United States and the Soviet Union had publicly affirmed their commitment to punishing the "barbaric crimes of the invaders."[9] The Moscow Declaration of November 1, 1943, captured the Allies' ambivalence as to the relative worth of a juridical or purely military resolution, however: "most assuredly the three Allied Powers will pursue them to the uttermost ends of the earth and will deliver them to their accusers in order that justice may be done."[10]

The second desired outcome of the Nuremberg trials was that they should serve a deterrent function. This stemmed in part from the view that World War II might have been prevented if the initiators of World War I had been justly punished.[11] Similarly, the Tokyo trials and other war crimes tribunals allocating individual responsibility were justified on the basis of their capacity to reach individual actors and, presumably, to deter other individuals from performing such acts in future.[12] The applicability of international law to individuals came to constitute the first of the "Nuremberg Principles" adopted by the United Nations General Assembly in 1950.[13] Over the course of the trials, this was variously justified by reference to the precedent established by piracy as an international crime,[14] to international duties that "transcend the national obligations of obedience imposed by the individual state,"[15] and to the results that would flow from allowing individuals to hide behind the veil of sovereignty:

> The principle of personal liability is a necessary as well as logical one if International Law is to render real help to the maintenance of peace. An International Law which operates only on states can be enforced only by war because the most practicable method of coercing a state is warfare. . . . Only sanctions which reach individuals can peacefully and effectively be enforced.[16]

The Nuremberg trials thus marked a significant development in the law, but the political and historical circumstances that made them possible came to be seen as unique to World War II.[17] The trials presaged legal instruments codifying the crime of genocide in 1948[18] and the laws of war in 1949,[19] but attempts to create a comprehensive regime of individual criminality soon foundered. The International Law Commission adopted a draft Code of Offenses against the Peace and Security of Mankind in 1954[20] but then suspended work until 1983. With the notable exception of episodic national prosecutions of Nazi war crimes, the field of international criminal law remained essentially dormant for half a century.[21]

The failure to realize the promise of Nuremberg was commonly attributed to the geopolitics of the cold war. Attempts to codify the law—let alone create institutions to enforce it—were hamstrung by political differences and widespread suspicion of the utility of international law in resolving issues of power. These concerns found voice in the reification of sovereignty as the brittle shell around individual polities: impermeable, but occasionally shattered by violence.[22] A second factor was that few wars concluded with the clarity of World War II. Postwar Germany was (initially, at least) regarded as a clean slate upon which the Allies could inscribe a new legal and political culture. There was, therefore, no serious consideration of amnesties being granted to the Nazi leadership as part of a peace deal; as indicated earlier, the dilemma was whether to dignify their punishment with the trappings of legal procedure. Similarly, the ad hoc legal institutions that were created in Germany were limited in their jurisdiction and could not be used against the victorious Allies that were enforcing the law. As Marvin Frankel has observed, the trial of war criminals of a defeated nation is "simplicity itself as compared to the subtle and dangerous issues that can divide a country when it undertakes to punish its own violators."[23]

In any event, Allied enthusiasm for prosecutions quickly waned. Many senior officers were considered too valuable to prosecute; others either escaped or were not pursued. As Adam Roberts notes, "in the end, an implicit principle of Nuremberg and Tokyo was to hold highly publicized trials of a few leaders primarily responsible for a process of criminality in which hundreds of thousands had in fact been culpable in one way or another."[24] In terms of retribution, the Nuremberg trials were thus highly selective; in terms of deterrence their effect appears to have been negligible.

International Criminal Tribunals

The political impediments to international criminal prosecution after Nuremberg and Tokyo were overcome in 1993 when the Security Council adopted resolution 827 establishing the International Criminal Tribunal for the former Yugoslavia (ICTY). As in the case of the Nuremberg and Tokyo trials, this was a quasijudicial body, established by one group of states to try the nationals of others. Its creation was made possible by the conjunction of three factors: the unprecedented unanimity of the Security Council in the heady days of what U.S. President George Bush had termed the "new world order"; the savagery of such a conflict in Europe that conjured images of Nazi concentration camps; and frustration, particularly on the part of the United States, at the failure of other methods to stem the flow of blood.[25]

The ICTY was established by the Security Council under its powers to take measures to restore international peace and security. The preamble to the resolution first deciding that such a tribunal should be created stated that the Council was

> *Determined* to put an end to [widespread violations of international humanitarian law] and to take effective measures to bring to justice the persons who are responsible for them, [and]
> *Convinced* that in the particular circumstances of the former Yugoslavia the establishment of an international tribunal would enable this aim to be achieved and would contribute to the restoration and maintenance of peace.[26]

This decision to commence prosecutions while the conflict continued was a substantial departure from the Nuremberg mold. Some commentators interpreted this as attempting to achieve through law what the international community was not prepared to achieve through force: "The Yugoslavia Tribunal seeks to make history; but the true lesson of Nuremberg is that *the power of law to reduce history to its terms can only be accomplished where history— victory and surrender—has been made elsewhere*."[27] Others saw it as having far more modest goals: Richard Holbrooke, architect of the 1995 Dayton Accords, notes that the tribunal was initially viewed as "little more than a public relations device."[28]

The ineffectual response to the war in the former Yugoslavia was repeated in relation to Rwanda. Its hand-wringing inaction during the genocide in April–July 1994 shamed the international community into creating a parallel tribunal with almost undignified haste. The tribunal's statute was substantially modeled on that of the ICTY,[29] and it shared the same prosecutor—based over four thousand miles away at the seat of the ICTY in The Hague. The tribunal itself was based outside Rwanda in neighboring Tanzania, a decision that led Rwanda (occupying one of the rotating Security Council seats at the time) to vote against the Security Council resolution establishing it. Whereas the Yugoslav Tribunal had ongoing jurisdiction over events in the former Yugoslavia, its Rwandan counterpart was limited to events that took place in 1994. A more important difference was political. The establishment of the ICTY was justified as a necessary step toward prosecuting those responsible for atrocities in the former Yugoslavia; given the military and political climate, it is unlikely that many such prosecutions would have taken place in Yugoslavia itself. The Rwandan Tribunal, by contrast, was established to try the perpetrators of the Tutsi genocide in Rwanda during 1994; the target population of these atrocities later held power in Rwanda, and the country commenced its own trials. Indeed, it is tempting to conclude that the only similarity between the two situations was the international community's sense of helplessness at its failure to prevent slaughter.[30]

These political subtexts to the work of the two ad hoc tribunals have been reflected in their jurisprudence. There appears to be a tension, for example, between what might be called the legal and historical views of the tribunals' work. On the one hand is the minimalist view that the tribunals are legal bodies established simply to adjudicate the cases presented to them. On the other, deriving from the ad hoc nature of the tribunals, is the view that they were established, in essence, to tell the story of what happened in the former Yugoslavia since 1991 and in Rwanda in 1994; this may at times require a more expansive view of their mandates. These different views are illustrated in the inconsistent positions adopted on the issue of *concours d'infractions*. Usually translated into English as "cumulative charges," *concours d'infractions* is a civil law concept that has no real parallel in common-law systems. A more appropriate (if less economical) translation is "multiple offenses in relation to the same set of facts." If, for example, a person is proven to have murdered a member of a particular ethnic group, and the act was committed with intent to destroy the ethnic group as such (the requirement for proving genocide), *and* that it was committed as part of a widespread or systematic attack directed against a civilian population (the requirements for proving crimes against humanity), should the person be convicted of one or both offenses? The Trial Chambers of the Rwandan Tribunal have reached different conclusions on this question. Trial Chamber I, in *Akayesu*, held that the different crimes protect different interests and that it may be necessary to record a conviction for more than one offense in order to reflect accurately an accused's conduct.[31] In *Kayishema and Ruzindana*, Trial Chamber II came to the opposite conclusion: where the same evidence is relied upon for the two offenses, multiple convictions would amount to convicting the accused twice for the same offense. This would be "highly prejudicial and untenable in law."[32] The two positions reflect distinct and to some extent incompatible conceptions of the role of the tribunal.

A second set of policy differences more directly concerns the political background to the ad hoc tribunals: their relationship to reestablishing peace and security in the region. The ongoing mandate of the Yugoslav Tribunal and the continuing conflicts that are its subject matter have politicized the exercise of prosecutorial discretion in predictable ways. This was clearest in relation to the failure to indict either of the presidents of the Federal Republic of Yugoslavia and Croatia in the period 1993–1995, apparently in order to secure Milosevic and Tudjman's cooperation in the eventual peace settlement. (The Dayton Accords were remarkable for the lack of any amnesty-for-peace clause, but indicted war criminals were excluded from participation.[33]) Similarly, political considerations appeared to lie behind the decision to indict President Milosevic in the middle of the North Atlantic Treaty Organization's (NATO) legally questionable air campaign in 1999, and the reluctance to investigate alleged violations of the laws of war by NATO forces.[34] A related problem was the difficulty of enforcing the prosecutor's indictments when issued, most prominently in the failure to apprehend either Radovan Karadzic or Ratko Mladic.

These political undercurrents were revisited in the drafting of the Rome Statute of the International Criminal Court. The provisions governing the jurisdiction of the Court gave rise to some of the most difficult negotiations. One crucial question concerned the Court's relationship to the Security Council. The International Law Commission's 1994 draft had prohibited the commencement of a prosecution if it arose from a "situation" that was being dealt with by the Council under Chapter VII of the Charter, unless the Council decided otherwise.[35] This gave each of the permanent five members of the Council an effective veto over prosecutions. The statute as adopted reflects the "Singapore compromise" whereby the Council's negative veto was replaced by a positive arrangement, providing that the Council may defer investigation or prosecution for a period of twelve months by adopting a Chapter VII resolution.[36] This loss of the veto power was cited by the United States as one of the reasons for its decision to vote against the statute. In subsequent discussions it has appeared as though the basic reason for U.S. opposition to the Court is the absence of a cast-iron guarantee that no U.S. national will ever appear before it.[37] This is a remarkable demand to make of any court, but it also ignores the complementarity provisions built into the Rome Statute. Under the statute, cases that have been investigated or prosecuted by a state with jurisdiction over them (as each state has over its own nationals) are inadmissible, unless it can be shown that the proceedings were undertaken "for the purpose of shielding the person concerned," or that delays or lack of impartiality are inconsistent with an intent to bring the person concerned to justice.[38] Continuing fears of "show trials" of U.S. citizens are premised on the unlikely possibility that a court will find that a bona fide U.S. investigation into impugned conduct would fall foul of these provisions.

The creation of an International Criminal Court may avoid some of the political complications seen in relation to the two ad hoc tribunals, but it is a mistake to place too much value on the internationalization of the criminal process. The Rwandan Tribunal was created in a form not approved by the people it was intended to help; similar tribunals were abandoned in Cambodia and East Timor when it became clear that they would not receive local support. After requesting assistance in 1997 to investigate and prosecute crimes committed under Pol Pot between 1975 and 1979, Cambodia later rejected the prospect of an ad hoc tribunal in the mold of the ICTY. In August 1999, the UN released plans for a joint Cambodian-international tribunal. The tribunal was to have applied Cambodian law, but with a foreign prosecutor and a majority of foreign judges. Prime Minister Hun Sen rejected the plan, insisting on coprosecutors, one foreign and one Cambodian—effectively giving Cambodia a veto over prosecutions. This was unacceptable to UN negotiators; at the same time, China stated that it would veto any Security Council resolution that would impose a tribunal against Cambodia's wishes. In the absence of agreement it seems probable that Cambodia will conduct select trials on its own or not at all.[39]

In East Timor, the International Commission of Inquiry on East Timor issued a report on January 31, 2000, calling for an international tribunal to conduct prosecutions arising from atrocities committed after the plebiscite in September 1999. On the same day, an Indonesian inquiry also recommended prosecutions of senior Indonesian military officials but stated that they should be tried by Indonesia. Indonesian President Abdurrahman Wahid was reported to have said that he wanted to preempt an international tribunal by conducting a credible investigation and trial within Indonesia. In response, the Secretary-General stated that the Security Council would "keep an eye on the process" but did not plan to establish a tribunal.[40]

Speaking in the Security Council, U.S. Permanent Representative Richard Holbrooke expressed strong support for the Secretary-General's call to encourage Indonesia to conduct a more thorough investigation and to take action on its own:

> We support Attorney-General Marzuki and the other brave members of the Indonesian Government and the [National Commission of Inquiry (KPP-HAM)] . . . in their efforts for full accountability on an internal basis. The Indonesian Commission did impressive work, but if they cannot deal with their problem internally they must recognize that international pressure on them will mount, and the pressure for the recommendations as called for by the International Commission of Inquiry on East Timor for an international tribunal will also increase.
>
> I hope that people in Indonesia understand that the world is listening. The best way to avoid what they do not wish—which is an international tribunal—is to have a credible internal effort. That is strongly our view. There-

fore, we applaud the international report, and we await the Indonesians' full response to it.[41]

These developments suggest one way in which the International Criminal Court might profitably be used: as a tool for pressuring governments to conduct investigations and trials that are "credible." A strong argument can be made that such internal processes, where possible, will almost always be preferable to externalized solutions. A lingering concern, however, is that the choice between the alternatives continues to be defined by reference to the Nuremberg paradigm of criminal trials. As the experiences of many countries show, this is an unrealistic template for evaluating domestic proceedings.

Domestic Proceedings

The question of how an emerging regime should deal with the abuses of its predecessor has become a leitmotif in the literature on emerging democracies.[42] Here the focus will be on the role that the international community can and should play in "transitional justice." A central problem in this respect is that commentators with an international perspective often view such internal transitions through the lens of international criminal law: either the wrongdoers are held accountable, or they enjoy impunity.

In fact the situation is more complex. First, a useful distinction may be made between *acknowledgment*—whether to remember or forget the abuses— and *accountability*—whether to impose sanctions on the individuals who were responsible for the abuses.[43] This helps to distinguish among four types of responses to past abuses. At either extreme of the spectrum are criminal prosecutions and unconditional amnesty. Criminal prosecution was the official policy toward collaborators in all Western European states occupied by Germany during World War II, a history that continues to inform current attitudes to war crimes. This may be contrasted with the general position of post-Communist Eastern and Central Europe, and the postauthoritarian regimes of Latin America, which have tended to favor amnesties. Between the extremes lie policies such as lustration and conditional amnesties, typically in the form of a truth commission.

The word *lustration* derives from the Latin term for the purificatory sacrifice that followed a quinquennial census. In the present context, it denotes the disqualification of a former elite, of the secret police and their informers, or of civil servants from holding political office under the new regime. Such disqualification of political and civil rights may accompany a criminal conviction, as it did in postwar Belgium, France, and the Netherlands. In situations such as post-Communist Eastern and Central Europe, it has sometimes provided a way to sidestep prosecutions.[44]

    Conditional amnesties linked to truth commissions serve a different agen-
da, putting a high priority on investigating the abuses of the former regime.
The goal of such a commission is not to prosecute or punish but to disclose
the facts of what took place. Truth commissions have been established with
varying success across Latin America,[45] but the linkage between truth and
amnesty is epitomized by the Truth and Reconciliation Commission (TRC) in
South Africa. The goals that it embodies are expressed in the 1993 Interim
Constitution: "there is a need for understanding but not for vengeance, a need
for reparation but not retaliation, a need for *ubuntu* but not for victimization."[46] Under the TRC, a person may apply for amnesty for any act, omission,
or offense that took place between March 1, 1960, and May 11, 1994. To be
granted amnesty, the person must satisfy the Committee on Amnesty that the
act was associated with a political objective committed in the course of the
conflicts of the past, and that full disclosure of all relevant facts has been
made.[47]

    Various peace agreements concluded in the 1990s have incorporated pro-
visions demanding individual accountability. The Cambodia settlement
accords adopted in 1991 included a requirement that Cambodia recognize its
obligations under relevant human rights instruments, which would include
obligations under the Genocide Convention to prosecute those responsible for
genocide.[48] The 1992 El Salvador peace agreements provided for the creation
of a truth commission, along with a watered-down pledge to end impunity, but
were followed by a broad amnesty law.[49] The 1995 Dayton Accords included
a pledge by the parties to the conflict in Bosnia and Herzegovina to cooperate
with the ICTY, as well as the exclusion of indicted fugitives from positions of
authority in the new state.[50] The Guatemala peace accords committed the government to criminalize disappearances and extrajudicial executions, though
this was accompanied by an amnesty for past crimes.[51] Significantly, though
each of these agreements obliged parties to establish particular regimes of
accountability, none contained an explicit obligation to punish any offenses.[52]

    A far more common feature of such peace agreements is provision for
amnesty. Amnesty laws of varying breadth covering governmental atrocities
have been passed or honored throughout Latin America in the past decade in
Chile,[53] Brazil,[54] Uruguay,[55] Argentina,[56] Nicaragua,[57] Honduras,[58] El Salvador,[59] Haiti,[60] Peru,[61] and Guatemala.[62] A similar practice now appears to
be accompanying transitions to democracy in Africa, reflected in Côte
d'Ivoire,[63] South Africa,[64] Algeria,[65] and Sierra Leone.[66]

    The international reaction to such amnesties has been, at best, ambiguous.
With a few notable exceptions, the UN and its member states have been reluctant to condemn amnesties. Following the amnesty in Guatemala in 1996, for
example, the General Assembly adopted a weak resolution in which it recognized "the commitment of the Government and civil society of Guatemala to
advance in the fight against impunity and towards the consolidation of the rule

of law."[67] In 1994, the United States actively encouraged the democratically elected government that it had helped to return to power in Haiti to grant amnesty to the prior junta.[68]

Exceptions to this trend include the U.S. criticism of Peru in 1997 and the UN Secretary-General's criticism of El Salvador in 1997.[69] More robust criticism has come from the UN Human Rights Committee established under the International Covenant on Civil and Political Rights. It first condemned amnesties by reference to their effect on respect for the prohibition of torture but later extended its concern to blanket amnesties generally.[70] In its observations on the 1995 amnesty in Peru, it stated that

> amnesty prevents appropriate investigation and punishment of perpetrators of past human rights violations, undermines efforts to establish respect for human rights, contributes to an atmosphere of impunity among perpetrators of human rights violations, and constitutes a very serious impediment to efforts undertaken to consolidate democracy and promote respect for human rights.[71]

In Sierra Leone, the international community was heavily involved in the peace process but backed away from criticizing an amnesty that granted impunity to participants in a conflict notorious for its viciousness. The Lomé Peace Agreement, signed on July 7, 1999, was brokered by the United Nations, the Organization of African Unity (OAU), and the Economic Community of West African States (ECOWAS). It nevertheless provided for the pardon of Corporal Foday Sankoh and a complete amnesty for any crimes committed by members of the fighting forces during the conflict from March 1991 up until the date of the signing of the agreement.[72] At the last minute, the UN Secretary-General's Special Representative, Francis Okelo, appended a handwritten disclaimer to the agreement, stating that the UN would not recognize the amnesty provisions as applying to genocide, crimes against humanity, war crimes, and other serious violations of international humanitarian law. Secretary-General Kofi Annan acknowledged that the sweeping amnesty in the peace agreement was difficult to reconcile with ending impunity:

> As in other peace accords, many compromises were necessary in the Lomé Peace Agreement. As a result, some of the terms under which this peace has been obtained, in particular the provisions on amnesty, are difficult to reconcile with the goal of ending the culture of impunity, which inspired the creation of the United Nations Tribunals for Rwanda and the Former Yugoslavia, and the future International Criminal Court. Hence the instruction to my Special Representative to enter a reservation when he signed the peace agreement, explicitly stating that, for the United Nations, the amnesty cannot cover international crimes of genocide, crimes against humanity, war crimes and other serious violations of international humanitarian law. At the same time, the Government and people of Sierra Leone should be allowed this opportunity to realize their best and only hope of ending their long and brutal conflict.[73]

The Lomé Peace Agreement encapsulates the central policy dispute over prosecutions as opposed to amnesties, and their relative potential to end cycles of state violence and consolidate democratic transitions.[74] The terms of this debate are usually limited to the question of criminal accountability for past abuses—there is general agreement that ongoing or future violations should not be the subject of amnesties. Opinions fall broadly into two camps. On the one hand, officials and organs in states undergoing transitions frequently claim that criminal accountability undermines the transition to democracy and must therefore be limited in whole or in part. On the other hand, human rights NGOs, victims groups, certain international bodies, and most commentators argue that criminal punishment is the most effective insurance against future repression.[75]

The first view has been voiced by heads of state, legislatures, and courts, though different rationales have been advanced in support of it.[76] In a minority of cases it has been justified in terms of simple realpolitik: a regime promulgates a self-amnesty or refuses to surrender power unless it is granted such an amnesty. More commonly it is linked to the question of reconciliation and the argument that criminal prosecutions may be an obstacle to this goal. This may be due to fears about the power of the former regime and the prospect of instability if trials are carried out (for example, Chile, Argentina, and Uruguay) or due to a political decision that persons who committed abuses should nevertheless remain part of the polity (for example, South Africa and Mozambique). A related concern may be the practical impossibility of prosecuting large numbers of people.

The view that accountability supports democracy also has its variants. The UN Human Rights Committee has declared that impunity is "a very serious impediment to efforts undertaken to consolidate democracy."[77] Human rights NGOs often stress a link between accountability, reconciliation, peace, and democracy.[78] Others have argued the more conservative point that trials serve to advance liberal government or the rule of law.[79] The specific concern that trials may also foster instability is frequently ignored, however, with the result that the debate often resolves to a simple opposition of idealists and realists.

It seems clear that claims for a causal relationship between accountability and democracy—either positive or negative—are overstated. Carlos Nino, a human rights adviser to post-junta Argentinean President Alfonsín, notes that trials can be destabilizing but concludes that the link ultimately

> depends on what makes democracy self-sustainable. If one believes that self-interested motivations are enough, then the balance works heavily against retroactive justice. On the other hand, if one believes that impartial value judgments contribute to the consolidation of democracy, there is a compelling political case for retroactive justice.[80]

It is also arguable that a distinction must be drawn between internal and international conflicts. The second Additional Protocol to the Geneva Conventions, which concerns the law applicable to noninternational armed conflicts, calls on states after the conclusion of civil wars to "grant the broadest possible amnesty to persons who have participated in the armed conflict."[81] It has been argued that this was not intended to include amnesties for those having violated international humanitarian law, but in practice such amnesties have tended to be blanket ones.[82] This provision may be contrasted with the Geneva Conventions themselves, which require that states parties undertake to enact legislation necessary to provide effective penal sanctions for persons committing grave breaches, such as willful killing, torture, and inhuman treatment.[83] In a case examining the constitutional legitimacy of the Truth and Reconciliation Commission, the South African Constitutional Court explained the distinction as follows:

> It is one thing to allow the officers of a hostile power which has invaded a foreign state to remain unpunished for gross violations of human rights perpetrated against others during the course of such conflict. It is another thing to compel such punishment in circumstances where such violations have substantially occurred in consequence of conflict between different formations within the same state in respect of the permissible political direction which that state should take with regard to the structures of the state and the parameters of its political policies and where it becomes necessary after the cessation of such conflict for the society traumatised by such a conflict to reconstruct itself. The erstwhile adversaries of such a conflict inhabit the same sovereign territory. They have to live with each other and work with each other and the state concerned is best equipped to determine what measures may be most conducive for the facilitation of such reconciliation and reconstruction.[84]

These qualifications on the appropriateness of legal and political approaches to dealing with a postconflict situation do not provide answers to simple questions, such as whether the international community should push for international tribunals as part of a peace deal. As the case of East Timor shows, it may come down to a more subtle question of pressuring a state to make its legal investigations credible. At the same time, it is clear that criminal prosecutions are not regarded as an unqualified good—there seems to be no political will to force South Africa to prosecute those given amnesties by its TRC, for example.

Nor does the Rome Statute provide solutions. In the course of the drafting negotiations, the question of how the Court should deal with amnesties or pardons was dropped when it appeared unlikely that a compromise could be reached.[85] This presents two points of uncertainty in the Rome Statute. In the case of amnesties, the statute appears to require that a case is or has been the subject of a *criminal* investigation in order to be inadmissible before the

Court.[86] A blanket amnesty would clearly not fall within this provision. Nor, however, would a truth commission of the nature of South Africa's TRC, where immunity from prosecution is drawn from the simple telling of truth to a nonjudicial body. Unless the Security Council intervened,[87] the decision of whether or not it is appropriate to commence a prosecution before the Court after such proceedings would fall to the discretion of the prosecutor.[88] This discretion is considerable: the Rome Statute permits the prosecutor to decline to initiate an investigation or to continue with a prosecution where there are "substantial reasons to believe that an investigation would not serve the interests of justice."[89] The reconciliation process in South Africa would seem to fall within this provision; the amnesty granted in the Lomé Peace Agreement may not. The position is still less clear concerning pardons that follow a criminal prosecution. If it could be established that those proceedings were undertaken for the purpose of shielding the person from criminal responsibility, or if the proceedings were not otherwise conducted independently or impartially, the Court would not be precluded from hearing the case. This might be difficult, however, particularly if the prosecution and the pardon are undertaken by different political organs.[90]

Conclusion

> Justice may be essential, then, but it is best to be modest about what trials can achieve. The great virtue of legal proceedings is that rules of evidence establish otherwise contestable facts. In this sense, war crimes trials make it more difficult for societies to take refuge in denial. But if trials assist the process of uncovering the truth, it is doubtful whether they assist the process of reconciliation. The purgative function of justice tends to operate on the victims' side only. While victims may feel justice has been done, the community from which the perpetrators come may feel that they have been made scapegoats. All one can say is that leaving war crimes unpunished is worse: the cycle of impunity remains unbroken, societies remain free to indulge their fantasies of denial.[91]

Martha Minow, author of *Between Vengeance and Forgiveness*, begins her work with a warning against hopes for conceptual neatness in any consideration of this subject. In the first place, the context of any society facing up to past horrors will be different: In what circumstances did the regime change take place? Did the abuses affect a large or small proportion of the population? How was it motivated? To what extent does the population believe in a spiritual reckoning for temporal events? Second, it is an illusion to think that any particular response can be adequate to deal with the consequences of atrocities committed against oneself or one's loved ones.[92]

I have argued that there are, at least, more than two responses. The Nuremberg trials made international criminal law possible, but the standard that they set—a completely legal (if one-sided) reckoning with past atrocities—was itself impossible. In the event, they remained an icon, resurrected when the horrors of war and human inhumanity returned to Europe. The trials continue to inform debate on the International Criminal Court, both in the belief that criminal prosecutions are the most appropriate way to deal with a bloody past and (in the case of the United States, at least) that law is something for Great Powers to make but not to follow.

The Nuremberg trials also inform consideration of peace agreements within states and the Faustian pacts whereby power is exchanged for impunity. The International Criminal Court will provide an instrument and useful institutional knowledge to assist states in dealing with postconflict situations, but the tension between ethical imperatives and political constraints that underlies all such proceedings will remain. As the work of the South African TRC and other less high-profile reconciliation processes has shown, the failure to prosecute all alleged wrongdoers need not be the same as granting a blanket amnesty. At the same time, it is important to remember that the process of reconciliation must ultimately take place within the state whose history is in the dock.

Notes

The author would like to thank Michael Byers, Sven Koopmans, and Patricia Shuming Tan for their helpful comments on an earlier draft of this chapter.

1. Geoffrey Robertson, *Crimes Against Humanity: The Struggle for Global Justice* (London: Allen Lane, 1999), p. 190.

2. See generally M. Cherif Bassiouni, *The Statute of the International Criminal Court: A Documentary History* (Ardsley, NY: Transnational, 1998); Herman A. M. von Hebel, Johan G. Lammers, and Jolien Schukking (eds.), *Reflections on the International Criminal Court: Essays in Honor of Adriaan Bos* (The Hague: T.M.C. Asser Press, 1999); and Roy S.K. Lee (ed.), *The International Criminal Court: The Making of the Rome Statute* (The Hague: Kluwer, 1999). See also Simon Chesterman, "Never Again . . . and Again: Law, Order and the Gender of War Crimes in Bosnia and Beyond," *Yale Journal of International Law* 22 (1997), p. 299, and sources there cited.

3. *R. v. Bow Street Metro. Stipendiary Magistrate, ex parte Pinochet Ugarte [No. 3]* [1999] 2 WLR 827.

4. *Trial of the Major War Criminals Before the International Military Tribunal* (1949), vol. 2, p. 99.

5. Telford Taylor, *The Anatomy of the Nuremberg Trials: A Personal Memoir* (New York: Knopf, 1992), pp. 29–30.

6. Lawrence Douglas, "Film as Witness: Screening Nazi Concentration Camps Before the Nuremberg Tribunal," *Yale Law Journal* 105 (1995), pp. 457–458. In the case of the Israeli prosecution of Adolf Eichmann, the difficulties in extraditing him

from Argentina led to "frequent" mention of the alternative of "kill[ing] him there and then, in the streets of Buenos Aires": Hannah Arendt, *Eichmann in Jerusalem: A Report on the Banality of Evil* (London: Faber and Faber, 1963), p. 265.

7. Robertson, *Crimes Against Humanity*, p. 199.

8. Quoted in United Nations War Crimes Commission, *History of the United Nations War Crime Commission and the Development of the Laws of War* (London: HMSO, 1948), p. 88. The declaration, issued on October 25, 1941, was part of a joint declaration with the United States—then neutral in the war.

9. President Roosevelt, Declaration of Aug. 21, 1942, quoted in UN War Crimes Commission, *History*, p. 93. See also the note of the Soviet Union, Oct. 14, 1942, quoted in ibid., p. 94.

10. Moscow Declaration, Nov. 1, 1943, reprinted in *The Times* (London), Nov. 3, 1943.

11. See Chesterman, "Never Again," pp. 304–305.

12. See, e.g., Egon Schwelb, "Crimes Against Humanity," *British Yearbook of International Law* 23 (1947), pp. 198–199.

13. UN General Assembly, Principles of International Law Recognized in the Charter of the Nuremberg Tribunal and in the Judgment of the Tribunal, 5 UN GAOR Supp. (No. 12) 11, UN Doc. A/1316 (1950), reprinted in *American Journal of International Law (Official Documents Supplement)* 44 (1950), p. 126.

14. The analogy with piracy is questionable at the least; the prosecution of pirates falls within international criminal law as their crimes do not fall within the jurisdiction of any one state: see, e.g., A. Carnegie, "Jurisdiction over Violations of the Laws and Customs of War," *British Yearbook of International Law* 39 (1963), p. 421.

15. *Trial of the Major War Criminals*, vol. 22, p. 466.

16. Robert H. Jackson, *The Nürenberg Case* (New York: Knopf, 1947), p. 88.

17. Indeed, early criticisms of the Yugoslav Tribunal argued that a juridical resolution to a conflict is possible only when "an army sits atop its vanquished enemy": Kenneth Anderson, "Nuremberg Sensibility: Telford Taylor's Memoir of the Nuremberg Trials," *Harvard Human Rights Journal* 7 (1994), p. 292.

18. Convention on the Prevention and Punishment of the Crime of Genocide, Dec. 9, 1948, 78 UNTS 277.

19. See the four Geneva Conventions of Aug. 12, 1949.

20. *Yearbook of the International Law Commission* (1954-II), p. 140.

21. See Timothy L.H. McCormack and Gerry Simpson (eds.), *The Law of War Crimes: National and International Approaches* (The Hague: Kluwer, 1997).

22. Ironically, the main sticking point in debates on the criminal code was the precise definition of the term *aggression*: see Bassiouni, *The Statute of the ICC*, pp. 12–14. The term remains undefined in the Rome Statute: Rome Statute of the International Criminal Court, UN Doc. A/Conf.183/9 (1998), art. 5(2).

23. Marvin E. Frankel, *Out of the Shadows of Night: The Struggle for International Human Rights* (New York: Delacorte Press, 1989), quoted in *Azanian Peoples Organization (AZAPO) v. President of the Republic of South Africa* (1996) 4 SA 671, para. 31 [*AZAPO*].

24. Adam Roberts, "The Laws of War: Problems of Implementation," *Duke Journal of Comparative and International Law* 6 (1995), pp. 26–27; David Wippman, "Atrocities, Deterrence, and the Limits of International Justice," *Fordham International Law Journal* 23 (1999), pp. 480–481.

25. See, e.g., James Crawford, "The ILC Adopts a Statute for an International Criminal Court," *American Journal of International Law* 89 (1995), p. 404.

26. SC Res. 808 (1993).

27. Anderson, "Nuremberg Sensibility," p. 294.

28. Richard Holbrooke, *To End a War* (New York: Random House, 1998), pp. 189–190.

29. See Simon Chesterman, "An Altogether Different Order: Defining the Elements of Crimes Against Humanity," *Duke Journal of Comparative and International Law* 10 (2000), p. 307.

30. It might be argued that the Rwandan Tribunal enables the trial of persons who would not otherwise be extradited to Rwanda. In the case of alleged *génocidaires*, however, such trials can take place in national courts exercising universal jurisdiction under the Genocide Convention. By April 2000, Rwanda itself had conducted 2,500 trials, with over three hundred people sentenced to death. Some 120,000 suspects still await trial.

31. *Prosecutor v. Jean-Paul Akayesu*, Case No. ICTR-96-4-T, Judgment (Int'l. Crim. Trib. Rwanda, Trial Chamber I, Sep. 2, 1998), para. 469.

32. *Prosecutor v. Clément Kayishema and Obed Ruzindana,* Case No. ICTR-95-1-T, Judgment (Int'l. Crim. Trib. Rwanda, Trial Chamber II, May 21, 1999), para. 649. See further Chesterman, "An Altogether Different Order," p. 341 n. 165.

33. See Holbrooke, *To End a War*, p. 333; Jurek Martin, "U.S. Fears Wider War in Balkans If Bosnia Talks Fail," *Financial Times* (London), Nov. 2, 1995.

34. Roger Cohen, "Warrants Served for Serbs' Leader and 4 Assistants," *New York Times*, May 28, 1999; Elizabeth Becker, "Rights Group Says NATO Killed 500 Civilians in Kosovo War," *New York Times*, Feb. 7, 2000.

35. Report of the International Law Commission on the Work of Its Forty-Sixth Session, Draft Statute for an International Criminal Court, UN Doc. A/49/10 (1994).

36. See Lionel Yee, "The International Criminal Court and the Security Council: Articles 13(b) and 16," in Lee, *The ICC*.

37. See, e.g., UN Doc. A/C.6/53/SR.9 (1998), extracted in Lee, *The ICC*, pp. 634–635.

38. Rome Statute, art. 17.

39. See Elizabeth Becker, "Cambodia Spurns UN Plan for Khmer Rouge Tribunal," *New York Times*, Mar. 13, 1999; Philip Shenon, "UN Plans Joint War Crimes Tribunal for Khmer Rouge," *New York Times*, Aug. 12, 1999; Seth Mydans, "Terms of Khmer Rouge Trials Still Elude UN and Cambodia," *New York Times*, Mar. 23, 2000; and "Justice for the Khmer Rouge" (editorial), *New York Times*, Apr. 3, 2000.

40. See Seth Mydans, "Jakarta's Military Chiefs Accused of Crimes," *New York Times*, Feb. 1, 2000; Seth Mydans, "Governing Tortuously: Indonesia's President Outflanks the General," *New York Times*, Feb. 15, 2000.

41. Statement of U.S. Permanent Representative Richard Holbrooke in the Security Council, Feb. 3, 2000, available at www.un.int/usa/00hol0203.htm.

42. See generally Neil J. Kritz (ed.), *Transitional Justice: How Emerging Democracies Reckon with Former Regimes* (Washington, DC: United States Institute of Peace Press, 1995).

43. Luc Huyse, "Justice After Transition: On the Choices Successor Elites Make in Dealing with the Past," *Law and Social Inquiry* 20 (1995), p. 52.

44. Ibid.

45. See Priscilla B. Hayner, "Fifteen Truth Commissions—1974–1993: A Comparative Study," *Human Rights Quarterly* 16 (1994), p. 597.

46. Constitution of the Republic of South Africa Act 200 of 1993 (South Africa), Epilogue. *Ubuntu* may be translated as the essence of being human, linked to an inclusive sense of community: see Desmond Tutu, "The World Can Learn from South Africa's Restitution," *Independent* (London), Oct. 31, 1999.

47. Promotion of National Unity and Reconciliation Act 34 of 1995 (South Africa), s. 20.

48. Agreement on a Comprehensive Political Settlement of the Cambodia Conflict, Oct. 23, 1991, art 15(2), 31 ILM 174, p. 186 (1992).

49. Mexico Agreements, Commission on the Truth, in Steven R. Ratner, "New Democracies, Old Atrocities: An Inquiry in International Law," *Georgetown Law Journal* 87 (1999), p. 717. But see Law on General Amnesty for the Consolidation of Peace, Decree No. 485, Mar. 20, 1993 (El Salvador), reprinted in *Transitional Justice*, vol. 3, p. 546. See further Thomas Buergenthal, "The United Nations Truth Commission for El Salvador," *Vanderbilt Journal of Transnational Law* 27 (1994), p. 497.

50. General Framework Agreement for Peace in Bosnia and Herzegovina, Dec. 14, 1995, Bosnia and Herzegovina–Croatia–Federal Republic of Yugoslavia, art. 9, 35 ILM 75, p. 90 (1996); ibid., Annex 4 (Constitution), art. 9(1), 35 ILM 75, p. 125 (1996).

51. Comprehensive Agreement on Human Rights, Dec. 29, 1996, art. 3, 36 ILM 258, p. 276 (1997). But see Ley de Reconciliación Nacional, Decreto No. 145–196, Dec. 18, 1996 (Guatemala), in Ratner, "New Democracies, Old Atrocities," p. 723.

52. Ratner, "New Democracies, Old Atrocities," p. 717.

53. Decreto Ley No. 2.191, Apr. 18, 1978 (Chile), in Ratner, "New Democracies, Old Atrocities," p. 722.

54. Lei No. 6.683, Aug. 28, 1979, art. 1 (Brazil), in Ratner, "New Democracies, Old Atrocities," p. 722.

55. Law 15,848 of Dec. 22, 1986 (Uruguay), reprinted in Kritz, *Transitional Justice*, vol. 3, p. 598. See Inter-American Commission on Human Rights, *Annual Report, 1992–93* (1993), p. 154 (concluding that the law is incompatible with the American Convention on Human Rights).

56. Law No. 23.492, Dec. 23, 1986 (Argentina), reprinted in Kritz, *Transitional Justice*, vol. 3, p. 505. See Aryeh Neier, "What Should Be Done About the Guilty?" *New York Review of Books*, Feb. 1, 1990, p. 32.

57. Law No. 81 on General Amnesty and National Reconciliation, May 9, 1990 (Nicaragua), reprinted in Kritz, *Transitional Justice*, vol. 3, p. 591.

58. Decreto Numero 87–91, July 23, 1991 (Honduras).

59. See above note 49.

60. Loi Relative à l'Amnistie, Oct. 10, 1994 (Haiti), in Michael P. Scharf, "Swapping Amnesties for Peace: Was There a Duty to Prosecute International Crimes in Haiti?" *Texas International Law Journal* 31 (1996), p. 1.

61. Ley No. 26479, June 14, 1995, available at www.congreso.gob.pe/ccd/leyes/cronos/1995/ley26479.htm (Peru).

62. Ley de Reconciliación Nacional, Decreto No. 145–196, Dec. 18, 1996 (Guatemala), in Ratner, "New Democracies, Old Atrocities," p. 723.

63. "Amnesty Law for Ivory Coast," *Independent* (London), July 30, 1992 (law passed July 29, 1992).

64. See above notes 46–47.

65. After his inauguration on Apr. 27, 1999, President Bouteflika unveiled a draft Civil Harmony law, which developed the terms of a 1995 clemency decree—it was adopted by Parliament in July 1999 and endorsed in national referendum on Sept. 16, 1999: "Bouteflika Urges Algeria to Pass Amnesty for Insurgents Today," *New York Times*, Sept. 16, 1999.

66. See below notes 72–73.

67. GA Res. 51/197 (1997), para. 8.

68. Scharf, "Swapping Amnesties for Peace," pp. 6–8.

69. Ratner, "New Democracies, Old Atrocities," p. 724 n. 79.

70. Human Rights Committee, General Comment 20(44), art. 7, para. 15, in *Report of the Human Rights Committee*, UN GAOR, 47th Sess., Supp. No. 40, Annex 6, UN Doc. A/47/49 (1992): "Amnesties are generally incompatible with the duty of States to investigate such acts."

71. Human Rights Committee, Preliminary Observations on Peru, UN Doc. CCPR/C/79/Add.67 (1996), para. 9.

72. Peace Agreement Between the Government of Sierra Leone and the Revolutionary United Front of Sierra Leone, Lomé, Togo, July 7, 1999, UN Doc. S/1999/777 (1999).

73. Seventh Report of the Secretary-General on the United Nations Observer Mission in Sierra Leone, July 30, 1999, UN Doc. S/1999/836 (1999), para. 54.

74. Diane F. Orentlicher, "Settling Accounts: The Duty to Prosecute Human Rights Violations of a Prior Regime," *Yale Law Journal* 100 (1991), pp. 2541–2542.

75. Ratner, "New Democracies, Old Atrocities," p. 734.

76. See ibid.

77. Human Rights Committee, *Preliminary Observations on Peru*, para. 9. Cf. *Hugo Rodriguez v. Uruguay*, Comm. No. 322/1988, UN Doc. CCPR/C/51/D/322/1988 (1994), para. 12.4.

78. See, e.g., Human Rights Watch, *Justice in the Balance: Recommendations for an Independent and Effective International Criminal Court* (New York: Human Rights Watch, 1998).

79. Ratner, "New Democracies, Old Atrocities," p. 735.

80. Carlos Santiago Nino, *Radical Evil on Trial* (New Haven, CT: Yale University Press, 1996), p. 134.

81. Additional Protocol II, art. 4.

82. Naomi Roht-Arriaza, "Combating Impunity: Some Thoughts on the Way Forward," *Law and Contemporary Problems* 59 (1996), p. 97.

83. First Geneva Convention, art. 49; Second Geneva Convention, art. 50; Third Geneva Convention, art. 129; Fourth Geneva Convention, art. 146.

84. *AZAPO*, para. 31.

85. John T. Holmes, "The Principle of Complementarity," in Lee, *The ICC*, p. 60; Scharf, "Swapping Amnesties for Peace," pp. 521–522.

86. Rome Statute, art. 17, refers to "investigation," which might in isolation be interpreted as including the work of a truth commission. Nevertheless, the standard for determining that an investigation is not genuine is that the proceedings are "inconsistent with an intent to bring the person concerned to justice," suggesting a criminal proceeding.

87. Rome Statute, art. 16.

88. See Holmes, "Complementarity," p. 77.

89. Rome Statute, art. 53(1)(c), (2)(c). This applies also to situations where a state party has filed a complaint. The decision is subject to review by the Pre-Trial Chamber: Rome Statute, art. 53(3).

90. Rome Statute, art. 20(3). See Holmes, "Complementarity," pp. 76–77.

91. Michael Ignatieff, *The Warrior's Honor: Ethnic War and the Modern Conscience* (London: Vintage, 1999), p. 184.

92. Martha Minow, *Between Vengeance and Forgiveness: Facing History After Genocide and Mass Violence* (Boston: Beacon Press, 1998), pp. 4–5.

8

Sexual Violence in Times of Conflict: The Jurisprudence of the International Criminal Tribunal for Rwanda

Navanethem Pillay

In this chapter I consider the legal response to sexual violence in times of conflict. In particular, I focus on the definitions of rape and sexual violence in international law. The judgment of the International Criminal Tribunal for Rwanda in *Akayesu* was a landmark in this area for two reasons: it was the first time that an individual had been found guilty of rape as an act of genocide, and it marked a departure from "mechanical" definitions of the crime of rape toward one more in line with the experiences of victims. I will first outline the legal framework within which acts of sexual violence must be considered, before examining the jurisprudence of the ad hoc tribunals for Rwanda and the former Yugoslavia.

The Legal Framework

Rape has long existed as a lacuna in the legal framework of human rights and international humanitarian law.

International human rights instruments seek to enshrine a common standard of rights and freedoms for all people, reflecting recognition of the fundamental, inalienable, inherent, and equal dignity of all human beings. The preamble to the Universal Declaration of Human Rights (UDHR) states that such recognition is the foundation of freedom, justice, and peace in the world. Article 3 of the UDHR proclaims the right to life, liberty, and security of person. Article 5, repeated in Article 7 of the International Covenant on Civil and Political Rights (ICCPR), affirms the right not to be subjected to torture or to cruel, inhuman, or degrading treatment or punishment. While the UDHR is a proclamation of the General Assembly of the United Nations, the ICCPR has been ratified by 144 states.[1] Article 7 of the ICCPR may not, according to Article 4 of the same document, be derogated from, even in times of public emergency.

In addition to these standards and others that apply at all times, the four Geneva Conventions of 1949 govern the behavior of their contracting parties in times of international armed conflict. Article 3 common to the Geneva Conventions provides that "persons taking no active part in the hostilities . . . shall in all circumstances be treated humanely, without any adverse distinction founded on race, color, religion or faith, sex, birth or wealth, or any other similar criteria." It goes on to state that with respect to these people, "violence to life and person, in particular murder of all kinds, mutilation, cruel treatment and torture" and "outrages upon personal dignity, in particular humiliating and degrading treatment," are prohibited. Article 76 of the 1977 First Protocol Additional to the Geneva Conventions (Additional Protocol I) specifically provides that "women shall be the object of special respect and shall be protected in particular against rape, forced prostitution and any other form of indecent assault."

The International Criminal Tribunal for Rwanda (ICTR) was established by UN Security Council resolution 955 (1994) for the prosecution of persons responsible for genocide and other serious violations of international humanitarian law in Rwanda.[2] The ICTR was created by the Security Council under Chapter VII of the Charter of the United Nations. During deliberations on the appropriate response to events in Rwanda in 1994, the Security Council took into consideration the report of the Commission of Experts, which had documented systematic, widespread, and flagrant violations of international humanitarian law in Rwanda, with massive loss of life, rape, and acts of sexual violence.[3]

The Security Council is not a legislative body; it lacks the competence to enact substantive law that could form the subject matter jurisdiction of a tribunal like the ICTR. The ICTR Statute therefore incorporates provisions from various existing legal instruments. It confers on the ICTR the power to prosecute persons for the crimes of genocide, as set forth in the Genocide Convention;[4] crimes against humanity, as defined in the Nuremberg Charter;[5] and violations of Article 3 common to the Geneva Conventions[6] and Additional Protocol II.[7] It is noteworthy that Rwanda became a party to the Geneva Conventions after independence in 1962 and acceded to the Genocide Convention in 1975 and to Additional Protocol II in 1984.

The statute also confers on the ICTR the authority to hold persons individually criminally responsible for crimes that they "planned, instigated, ordered, committed or otherwise aided and abetted in planning, preparation or execution" as well as for crimes committed by their subordinates. These crimes are enumerated in Articles 2 to 4 of the statute.

Article 2 confers on the ICTR the power to prosecute any person who commits, conspires, directly and publicly incites, attempts, or is complicit in committing genocide. Genocide is defined as any of the enumerated acts committed with intent to destroy, in whole or in part, a national, ethnic, racial, or religious group, as such. These enumerated acts are:

a. Killing members of the group;
b. Causing serious bodily or mental harm to members of the group;
c. Deliberately inflicting on the group conditions of life calculated to bring about its physical destruction in whole or in part;
d. Imposing measures intended to prevent births within the group; and
e. Forcibly transferring children of the group to another group.

This definition of genocide, while dealing with discrimination on "national, ethnical, racial or religious" grounds, does not specifically cover gender, nor does it explicitly enumerate categories for rape or other forms of sexual violence.

Pursuant to Article 3 of the statute, the ICTR has the power to prosecute persons responsible for crimes against humanity, specifically:

a. Murder;
b. Extermination;
c. Enslavement;
d. Deportation;
e. Imprisonment;
f. Torture;
g. Rape;
h. Persecutions on political, racial, and religious grounds; and
i. Other inhumane acts;

where any such acts are perpetrated as part of a widespread or systematic attack against any civilian population on national, political, ethnic, racial, or religious grounds. Here, rape is specifically included as a prohibited act, and it may therefore constitute a crime against humanity in itself. Other forms of sexual violence are not explicitly prohibited. This is regarded as a weakness of the ICTR Statute (reflected also in the Statute of the Yugoslav Tribunal). It is noted that the provisions of the Rome Statute of the International Criminal Court address this shortfall. Article 7(g) of the Rome Statute expressly stipulates that "rape, sexual slavery, enforced prostitution, forced pregnancy, enforced sterilization, or any other form of sexual violence of comparable gravity" may constitute crimes against humanity.

Serious violations of common Article 3 and Additional Protocol II are incorporated in Article 4 of the ICTR Statute. These violations include but are not limited to:

a. Violence to life, health, and physical or mental well-being of persons, in particular murder as well as cruel treatment such as torture, mutilation, or any form of corporal punishment;
b. Collective punishments;
c. Taking of hostages;
d. Acts of terrorism;
e. Outrages upon personal dignity, in particular humiliating and degrading treatment, rape, enforced prostitution, and any form of indecent assault;
f. Pillage;
g. The passing of sentences and the carrying out of executions without previous judgment pronounced by a regularly constituted court, affording all the judicial guarantees which are recognized as indispensable by civilized peoples; and
h. Threats to commit any of the foregoing acts.

Article 4(e) of the ICTR Statute certainly provides a broad category of conduct that may constitute sexual violence. For successful prosecution, however, not only must the elements of the sexual conduct be proved—the general elements of common Article 3 and of Additional Protocol II must also be proved.

In *Akayesu*, the Trial Chamber held that where an accused is indicted for one or more of the violations enumerated under Article 4 of the ICTR Statute, the prosecutor has the burden of proving, among other elements, that there existed an armed conflict, not of an international character, and that the violation was committed in support of, or in furtherance of, that conflict. The Trial Chamber stated:

> Akayesu would incur individual criminal responsibility for his acts if it were proved that by virtue of his authority, he is either responsible for the outbreak of, or is otherwise directly engaged in the conduct of hostilities. Hence, the Prosecutor will have to demonstrate to the Chamber and prove that Akayesu was either a member of the armed forces under the military command of either of the belligerent parties, or that he was legitimately mandated and expected, as a public official or agent or person otherwise holding public authority or *de facto* representing the government, to support or fulfil the war efforts.[8]

The prosecutor has noted an appeal on the Trial Chamber's application of common Article 3 and Additional Protocol II, and the decision of the Appeals Court is pending.

The Jurisprudence of the ICTR

In *Akayesu* the original indictment against the accused, dated February 13, 1996, did not include sexual crimes. On June 17, 1997, the Trial Chamber granted leave to amend this indictment to include three additional counts of sexual violence, following a motion by the prosecutor, pursuant to Rule 50 of the ICTR's Rules of Procedure and Evidence. In support of this motion, the prosecutor submitted that in the testimony presented at trial and in their investigations,

> there had been hints that there were acts of sexual violence occurring in the Taba commune. It came up . . . in the testimony of Witness J or Witness H. . . . It also came up in prior investigations, but the prior investigations were not enough . . . to link the accused to the acts of sexual violence.[9]

The prosecutor outlined the difficulties in conducting investigations in matters of sexual violence, in part because a large part of Rwanda

> was categorized as what is known as phase 4. . . . Phase 4 means that our investigators cannot travel into the field without armed escort [and] . . . attempting to conduct investigations when there are such sensitive issues as witness protection . . . [accompanied by] armed escorts is not practical. The investigators stick out like a sore thumb and it draws attention to the witnesses.[10]

The prosecutor submitted that the shame and stigma that are associated with acts of sexual violence served as an obstacle in getting victims to testify to their ordeals, thus contributing to the difficulties in investigating matters of this nature.[11] The prosecutor also submitted that members of staff at the prosecutor's office were not as sensitive as they ought to have been in conducting investigations pertaining to matters of sexual violence.[12]

The prosecutor also submitted that, due to an improvement in the security situation and creative investigation on the part of their investigators, it had become possible to conduct investigations closer to Taba commune, although they were still unable to get into the commune itself. Following these investigations, five witnesses were interviewed and their statements reduced to writing. These witnesses spoke of "horrific [and] . . . shocking acts . . . that can be attributable to the accused, acts that were done with his knowledge and his approval."[13]

The amended indictment set out the following allegations in support of the three additional counts:

> 10A. In this indictment, acts of sexual violence include forcible sexual penetration of the vagina, anus or oral cavity by a penis and/or of the vagina or anus by some other object, and sexual abuse, such as forced nudity. . . .
>
> 12A. Between April 7 and the end of June, 1994, hundreds of civilians (hereinafter "displaced civilians") sought refuge at the bureau communal. The majority of these displaced civilians were Tutsi. While seeking refuge at the bureau communal, female displaced civilians were regularly taken by

armed local militia and/or communal police and subjected to sexual violence, and/or beaten on or near the bureau communal premises. Displaced
civilians were also murdered frequently on or near the bureau communal
premises. Many women were forced to endure multiple acts of sexual violence which were at times committed by more than one assailant. These acts
of sexual violence were generally accompanied by explicit threats of death
or bodily harm. The female displaced civilians lived in constant fear and
their physical and psychological health deteriorated as a result of the sexual
violence and beatings and killings.

12B. Jean Paul AKAYESU knew that the acts of sexual violence, beatings
and murders were being committed and was at times present during their
commission. Jean Paul AKAYESU facilitated the commission of the sexual
violence, beatings and murders by allowing the sexual violence and beatings
and murders to occur on or near the bureau communal premises. By virtue
of his presence during the commission of the sexual violence, beatings and
murders and by failing to prevent the sexual violence, beatings and murders,
Jean Paul AKAYESU encouraged these activities.[14]

In determining whether the acts of rape and sexual violence constituted
genocide in *Akayesu*, the Trial Chamber had first to decide whether genocide
had occurred in Rwanda. The special intent to commit genocide lies in the
intention to destroy in whole or in part a national, ethnic, racial, or religious
group as such. Neither the Genocide Convention nor the ICTR Statute defines
these categories. After having consulted the *travaux préparatoires* of the
Genocide Convention, the Trial Chamber concluded that the drafters perceived the crime of genocide as targeting only stable and permanent groups,
whose membership is determined by birth, and excluded mobile groups such
as political or economic entities, where entry is voluntary.[15]

The Trial Chamber examined the criteria for defining each of the groups
and found that there was no clear distinction between Tutsi and Hutu in
Rwanda. They belonged to the same national and religious group and shared
a common language and culture. Any hereditary physical features that distin-
guished Hutu and Tutsi as different racial groups had been obliterated with the
passage of time. The Trial Chamber relied on evidence of witnesses who identified themselves and other victims as Tutsi, Hutu, or Twa—the ethnic classi-
fications on official Rwandan identity cards—and on the subjective perceptions of the Rwandan people, rather than adhering to an objective formalistic
definition of ethnicity. Consequently, the Trial Chamber established as precedent the concept that a court may regard any stable or permanent group,
whose membership is largely determined by birth, as an "ethnic" group for the
purposes of the Genocide Convention. In so doing, the Trial Chamber expanded the interest group that will be afforded protection under the Genocide Convention.

In its deliberations on the element of genocidal intent in *Akayesu*, the
Trial Chamber did not confine itself to evidence of the accused's acts alone

but reasoned that "it is possible to deduce the genocidal intent in a particular act charged from the general context of the perpetration of other culpable acts systematically directed against that same group, whether these acts were committed by the same offender or by others."[16] The Trial Chamber inferred genocidal intent from the evidence of the large scale of the atrocities committed, their general nature, and the deliberate and systematic targeting of people because of their membership in a particular group, to the exclusion of members of other groups.

In determining whether the acts of rape and sexual violence to which witnesses testified constituted crimes against humanity and genocide, the Trial Chamber noted that "there is no commonly accepted definition of the term [rape] in international law. For historical reasons, the crime of rape has been viewed as prohibiting involuntary *coitus per vaginam*"; other sexual acts not involving this form of coitus have not been treated as rape. The Trial Chamber considered that the prosecutor's definition of rape was in explicit physical terms and required graphic descriptions of sexual acts, an approach referred to by the Trial Chamber as a "mechanical" or "body part" definition of rape.

A survey of the definitions in national legal systems reveals that there is some adherence to this narrow conception of the crime and that even in countries where the legal definition of rape has been broadened, the crime is not defined in the explicit physical terms used by the prosecutor in the *Akayesu* indictment. In France, rape is defined as:

> *Tout acte de pénétration sexuelle, de quelque nature qu'il soit, commis sur la personne d'autrui par violence, contrainte, menace ou surprise est un viol.*
>
> [Any act of sexual penetration, of whatever nature, committed on the person of another by violence, constraint, threat or surprise constitutes rape.][17]

In England, rape is defined as follows:

> (1) It is an offence for a man to rape a woman or another man.
> (2) A man commits rape if:
>   (a) he has sexual intercourse with a person (whether vaginal or anal) who at the time of intercourse does not consent to it; or
>   (b) at the time he knows that the person does not consent to the intercourse or is reckless as to whether that person consents to it.[18]

The German Penal Code section 177 states that:

> (1) A person who commits or acts in a manner that enables a third person to commit sexual abuses on a person:
>   1. with use of force;
>   2. under threat with immediate danger for life or limb;

3. by the use of a location where the victim will not be able to receive any protection against the actions of the accused;

will be sentenced to not less than two years of imprisonment.

In South Africa, rape "consists in the intentional unlawful sexual intercourse with a woman without her consent."[19] This crime is committed only by penetration of the vagina by the penis. Any other form of sexual congress between the parties cannot constitute rape.

In recounting their experiences, however, women tend to portray the entire act of violence as a violation of their bodies. In the course of direct examination during the *Akayesu* trial, the prosecutor asked a witness, "When you say they raped you, I need to ask you whether or not there was penetration by this man's penis or by some other object into your vagina." The witness's response was, "It is indeed the penis. But they were doing it in an atrocious manner, especially after having killed our brothers and our father, and these people were mocking us, they were taunting us." The witness perceived her experience in terms of violence, fear, and pain, and not merely as a penetration of her vagina by a penis.

In evaluating testimony, the Trial Chamber in *Akayesu* took into consideration cultural and language constraints experienced by witnesses in testifying to intimate private details. The Trial Chamber stated:

> The terms *gusambanya*, *kurungora*, *kuryamana* and *gufata ku ngufu* were used interchangeably by witnesses and translated by the interpreters as "rape". The Chamber has consulted its official trial interpreters to gain a precise understanding of these words and how they have been interpreted. The word *gusambanya* means "to bring (a person) to commit adultery or fornication". The word *kurungora* means "to have sexual intercourse with a woman". This term is used regardless of whether the woman is married or not, and regardless of whether she gives consent or not. The word *kuryamana* means "to share a bed" or "to have sexual intercourse", depending on the context. It seems similar to the colloquial usage in English and in French of the term "to sleep with". The term *gufata ku ngufu* means "to take (anything) by force" and also "to rape".
>
> The context in which these terms are used is critical to an understanding of their meaning and their translation. The dictionary entry for *kurungora*, the most generic term for sexual intercourse, includes as an example of usage of this word, the sentence "*Mukantwali yahuye n'abasore batatu baramwambura baramurongora*," for which the dictionary translation into French is "*Mukantwali a rencontré trois jeunes gens qui l'ont dévalisée et violée*" (in English "Mukantwali met three young men who robbed her of her belongings and *raped* her").[20]

In *Akayesu*, the Trial Chamber articulated a conceptual definition of rape. In its view, rape constituted a form of aggression similar to torture, and it looked to the Convention Against Torture and Other Cruel, Inhumane and

Degrading Treatment or Punishment as a guide to formulating a definition of rape. This Convention does not catalogue specific acts in its definition of torture, focusing rather on the conceptual framework of state-sanctioned violence. The Trial Chamber reasoned that rape, like torture, is used for such purposes as "intimidation, degradation, humiliation, discrimination, punishment, control or destruction of a person."[21] Like torture, rape is a violation of personal dignity; rape constitutes torture when inflicted by or at the instigation of or with the consent or acquiescence of a public official or other person acting in an official capacity.

The Trial Chamber also noted that though rape has been defined in certain national jurisdictions as nonconsensual intercourse, variations may include acts that involve the insertion of objects and/or the use of bodily orifices not considered to be intrinsically sexual in nature.[22]

Taking all these elements into account, the Trial Chamber defined rape as "a physical invasion of a sexual nature, committed on a person under circumstances which are coercive."[23] It considered sexual violence, which includes rape, "to be any act of a sexual nature which is committed on a person under circumstances which are coercive."[24] The Trial Chamber reasoned that sexual violence is not limited to the physical invasion of the human body but may also include acts not involving penetration or even physical contact. An example of this type of sexual violence is the incident described by Witness KK in which Akayesu ordered the Interahamwe to undress a student and force her to do gymnastics naked before a crowd in the public courtyard of the bureau communal.

According to the Trial Chamber, coercive circumstances included not only physical force but threats and intimidation. It made a factual determination that the acts of rape and sexual violence caused serious bodily or mental harm to members of a group as defined in Article 2(2) of the ICTR Statute, concluding that sexual violence was an integral part of the genocide committed in Rwanda in general. In arriving at this conclusion, the Trial Chamber stated that that rape and sexual violence

> constitute genocide in the same way as any other act as long as they were committed with the specific intent to destroy, in whole or in part, a particular group, targeted as such. Indeed, rape and sexual violence . . . are even . . . one of the worst ways of inflicting harm on the victim as he or she suffers both bodily and mental harm. . . . Sexual violence was an integral part of the process of destruction, specifically targeting Tutsi women and specifically contributing to their destruction and to the destruction of the Tutsi group as a whole. . . . Sexual violence was a step in the process of destruction of the Tutsi group—destruction of the spirit, of the will to live, and of life itself.[25]

The Trial Chamber in *Akayesu* attributed individual criminal responsibility to the accused for acts of rape and sexual violence, pursuant to Article 6 of the ICTR Statute. Although the accused did not personally perpetrate any acts of rape or sexual violence, the Trial Chamber held that he had aided and abetted in the commission of these acts by allowing them to take place at or near the premises of the bureau communal. The Trial Chamber also held that the accused verbally ordered and encouraged the commission of these acts of rape and sexual violence. These orders and encouragement served as a clear signal of official tolerance for criminal conduct of this nature, by virtue of the accused's position of authority in the commune of Taba.

Akayesu was also convicted of crimes against humanity (rape and other inhumane acts). In so finding, the Trial Chamber held that acts of sexual violence were committed as part of a widespread and systematic attack directed against a civilian population on discriminatory grounds—namely discrimination on grounds of ethnicity.[26]

In the International Criminal Tribunal for the former Yugoslavia (ICTY), Trial Chamber II, in *Delalic*, adopted the conceptual definition of rape and sexual violence articulated in *Akayesu*.[27] In *Furundzija,* another ICTY case, the Trial Chamber held that

> the forced penetration of the mouth by the male sexual organ constitutes a most humiliating and degrading attack upon human dignity. The essence of the whole corpus of international humanitarian law as well as human rights law lies in the protection of the human dignity of every person, what ever his or her gender. The general principle of respect for human dignity is the basic underpinning and indeed the very *raison d'être* of international humanitarian law and human rights law, indeed in modern times it has become of such paramount importance as to permeate the whole body of international law. This principle is indeed to shield human beings from outrages upon their personal dignity, whether such outrages are carried out by unlawfully attacking the body or by humiliating and debasing the honor, the self-respect of the mental well being of a person. It is consonant with this principle that such an extremely serious sexual outrage as forced oral penetration should be classified as rape.[28]

In *Musema*, Trial Chamber I of the ICTR reiterated the definition of rape and sexual violence set forth in *Akayesu*. The Chamber also recognized that the essence of rape is not the particular details relating to the body parts that have been violated and the objects used in the perpetration of such violation; rather it is the aggression that is expressed in a sexual manner, under conditions of coercion.[29] The Trial Chamber held that the definition of rape and sexual violence set forth in *Akayesu* is clear and establishes a framework for judicial consideration of individual incidents of sexual violence and allows for a determination, on a case-by-case basis, as to whether such incidents constitute rape. This definition of rape, according to the Trial Chamber, encompasses all the conduct regulated in the definition of rape set forth in *Furundzija*.[30]

The Trial Chambers in *Musema* and *Furundzija* noted that there is a trend in national legislation to broaden the definition of rape. In *Musema*, the Trial Chamber held that, in light of the dynamic ongoing evolution of the understanding of rape and the incorporation of this understanding into principles of international law, a conceptual definition of rape, as set forth in *Akayesu*, is preferable to a mechanical definition. This conceptual definition will better accommodate evolving norms of criminal justice.

The ICTR's *Akayesu* and *Musema* judgments are subject to appeal by both the prosecution and defense. The deliberations and judgments of the ICTR's Appeals Chamber, as well as the deliberations and judgments of the Trial Chambers in pending and future cases, will no doubt contribute to our understanding of the norms and application of international humanitarian law. The rule of international law has the untapped potential to deter violations of human rights and to bring to justice the perpetrators of such violations. To do so, international humanitarian law must provide clear, certain, and progressive direction.

Notes

1. Office of the High Commissioner for Human Rights, Status of Ratifications of the Principal International Human Rights Treaties, May 15, 2000.

2. The full name of the ICTR is the International Criminal Tribunal for the Prosecution of Persons Responsible for Genocide and Other Serious Violations of International Humanitarian Law.

3. Letter dated Oct. 1, 1994, from the Secretary-General, addressed to the President of the Security Council, UN Doc. S/1994/1125 (1994).

4. Convention on the Prevention and Punishment of Crimes of Genocide, Dec. 9, 1948, 78 UNTS 277.

5. Charter of the International Military Tribunal, Annex to the Agreement for the Prosecution and Punishment of Major War Criminals of the European Axis, Aug. 8, 1945, 82 UNTS 279.

6. Geneva Convention for the Amelioration of the Condition of the Wounded and the Sick in Armed Forces in the Field, Aug. 12, 1949, 75 UNTS 31 (First Geneva Convention); Geneva Convention for the Amelioration of the Condition of Wounded, Sick and Shipwrecked Members of Armed Forces at Sea, Aug. 12, 1949, 75 UNTS 85 (Second Geneva Convention); Geneva Convention Relative to the Treatment of Prisoners of War, Aug. 12, 1949, 75 UNTS 135 (Third Geneva Convention); Geneva Convention Relative to the Protection of Civilian Persons in Time of War, Aug. 12, 1949, 75 UNTS 287 (Fourth Geneva Convention).

7. Protocol Additional to the Geneva Conventions of 12 August 1949, and Relating to the Protection of Victims of Non-International Armed Conflicts, June 8, 1977 (Additional Protocol II).

8. See *Prosecutor v. Jean-Paul Akayesu*, Case No. ICTR-96-4-T, Judgment (Int'l. Crim. Trib. Rwanda, Trial Chamber I, Sept. 2, 1998), para. 640.

9. *Akayesu*, transcript of June 17, 1997, pp. 6–7.

10. Ibid., pp. 9–10.

11. Ibid., p. 7.

12. Ibid.

13. Ibid., pp. 10–11.

14. *Akayesu*, para. 6.

15. Ibid., paras. 299–305.

16. Ibid., para. 523.

17. Le Nouveau Code Pénal (France), arts. 222–223.

18. Sexual Offences Act 1956 (Eng.), s. 1, as amended by the Criminal Justice and Public Order Act 1994 (Eng.), s. 142.

19. Jonathan M. Burchell and John Milton, *Principles of Criminal Law*, 2d ed. (South Africa: Juta & Co., 1997), p. 487.

20. *Akayesu*, paras. 152–153 (footnote omitted).

21. Ibid., para. 597.

22. Ibid., para. 596.

23. Ibid., para. 598.

24. Ibid.

25. Ibid., paras. 731–732.

26. Ibid., paras. 685–695.

27. *Prosecutor v. Zejnil Delalic, Zdravko Mucic, Hazim Delic, Esad Landzo*, Case No. IT-96-21-T, Judgment (Int'l. Crim. Trib. former Yugo., Trial Chamber II *quater*, Nov. 16, 1998), paras. 478–479.

28. *Prosecutor v. Anto Furundzija*, Case No. IT-95-17/1-T, Judgment (Int'l. Crim. Trib. former Yugo., Trial Chamber II, Dec. 10, 1998), para. 183.

29. *Prosecutor v. Alfred Musema,* Case No. ICTR-96-13-T, Judgment (Int'l. Crim. Trib. Rwanda, Trial Chamber I, Jan. 27, 2000), para. 226.

30. Ibid., para. 227.

9

Humanitarian Issues and Agencies as Triggers for International Military Action

Adam Roberts

In crises and conflicts since the end of the cold war, considerations specifically identified as "humanitarian" have been repeatedly designated by states and international bodies as grounds for threatening, and embarking on, international military action. Such considerations have been given greater prominence in international decisionmaking than in previous eras. Since 1990, in one episode after another in which international bodies have sought to stop terrible excesses in crisis-torn regions, three main types of humanitarian issues have been cited, for example in UN Security Council resolutions, as grounds for international concern:

- Murder and deliberate infliction of suffering on civilians, prisoners, and others;
- Refusal of parties to a conflict to allow or assist humanitarian relief activities; and
- Violence and threats of violence against humanitarian workers.

In a few cases these types of humanitarian issues have been raised not in the context of an armed conflict but as a result of tyrannical government or a state of uncontrolled violence. However, in most cases these issues have arisen during armed conflicts (whether international or internal, or with elements of both). Thus they necessarily relate directly to the law of war. Security Council resolutions have in fact repeatedly condemned such actions by parties to conflicts as violations of international humanitarian law. In many cases the Security Council, or certain of its leading members, has then gone on to authorize or initiate the use of force in order to end a pattern of violations. In short, the law of war is acquiring a role as a trigger for military action.

The terms *law (or laws) of war* and *international humanitarian law* are used more or less interchangeably in this chapter. They and the various near synonyms also used currently (such as "international law of armed conflict") all refer to what is substantially the same body of law. The term *law of war* is sometimes seen as old-fashioned, but it has the merit of being succinct; and it also encompasses aspects that are not exclusively humanitarian in purpose, such as the law relating to neutrality. At the same time, the term *international humanitarian law* has come to be widely used in diplomatic circles and among nongovernmental organizations; it can be particularly useful in referring to those parts of the law of war that deal with substantially humanitarian matters, such as protection of vulnerable populations and of aid activities.

Military action based on these three types of humanitarian issues is one important response to the questions of how to prevent violations of international humanitarian law and how to protect civilians and other victims of war. Much discussion of the protection of civilians in war has failed to take account of this developing practice of military action. One reason may be that the whole subject is controversial. Any exploration of military action as a response to violations of the law of war challenges the long-standing and important principle that the law relating to resort to war (*jus ad bellum*) is a separate and distinct subject from the law relating to conduct in war (*jus in bello*). Likewise, any suggestion that humanitarian workers and organizations may play some part in triggering military action challenges their deep (and in some cases legally based) commitment to impartiality and neutrality.

Military action is a broad term. As used here, it encompasses the use of military force, or the explicit threat of such use, with the aim of ending persistent violations of international humanitarian norms. The particular purposes of such action can include altering the policies of certain factions or governments; weakening or defeating certain armed forces and the infrastructure that supports them; arresting suspected violators of the law of war; providing humanitarian relief; and providing physical protection for vulnerable people, activities, and institutions. Its forms can include the use of air, naval, and land forces, whether in direct combat operations, in protection, in intervention in a state, or in making threats against a particular state or group. The legal framework for such action includes three main types: (1) UN command and control, as with enforcement operations that are approved by the Security Council and remain directly under UN control; (2) action following a UN authorization under which powers are delegated to national or alliance command and control; and (3) action without explicit UN backing, for example under the auspices of a regional alliance or organization. In some cases, as noted below, military action has the additional legal basis of having the full consent of the government of the state where the action takes place.

The broad subject of military action as considered here overlaps with, but is not quite the same as, humanitarian intervention. *Humanitarian interven-*

tion in its classical sense means military intervention in a state, without the approval of its authorities, and with the purpose of preventing widespread suffering or death among the inhabitants. Shorn of the epithet "humanitarian," the term *intervention* still carries an implication of forcible action against the wishes of the government of the state concerned. Many military actions rooted in considerations of international humanitarian law fit these definitions of intervention, but by no means do all. Some, indeed, may have the explicit consent of the government of the territory in which the action takes place (for example, when such action is taken against insurgents or separatists in a civil war) and therefore do not count as interventions in the classical sense, whether humanitarian or otherwise. Equally, some actions, even if grounded in considerations of international humanitarian law, may have other purposes (for example, concern with international peace and security) that are not strictly speaking humanitarian and are therefore doubtful candidates for inclusion in the category of "humanitarian intervention."

Considerations of international humanitarian law and international human rights law often converge. The same acts may constitute violations of both of these bodies of law and may be cited in a particular instance as justifications for military action or the threat thereof. Sometimes the international humanitarian law element is underplayed, such as when public figures advocate or defend military action or discuss the general issue of humanitarian intervention exclusively on grounds of violations of human rights, when the violations concerned might equally properly be viewed as violations of international humanitarian law. However, considerations of international humanitarian law, which are the main focus of attention here, have come to be emphasized much more since about 1991 than in any previous period, especially in the practice of the UN Security Council.

Military action as a response to violations of human rights and humanitarian norms has a long history, well predating the modern codifications of international law on the subject. In the 1820s, it was largely as a consequence of reported Turkish atrocities that French and British governments decided to give a degree of naval support to the cause of Greek independence from Ottoman rule. The history of European colonialism is replete with cases in which one part of the public justification for intervention was the violation of basic humanitarian norms in one or another part of the non-European world. Similarly, in the period of the cold war (roughly 1945–1989) numerous interventions were justified at least partly in humanitarian terms.

The purpose here is, first, to illustrate the extent to which humanitarian issues have become entwined with the initiation of international military action, especially in the practice of the UN Security Council, in response to a wide variety of situations by no means limited to war. This is followed by an examination of some of the other purposes that may contribute to the initiation of international military action in particular cases, and an examination of the apparent absence of specific authorization of such military action in international law, including the law of war. I then turn to the difficult role of humanitarian organizations in situations where force is threatened or used, and a specific examination of some of the problems that the entwining of humanitarian and military issues has created for the International Committee of the Red Cross (ICRC). This is followed by a brief discussion of the protection of civilians in UN debates, focusing on three key UN documents issued in 1999. Finally, on the basis that "humanitarian" issues will continue to have a bearing on decisions about military force, some possible conclusions for humanitarian organizations, states, and interstate organizations are suggested. Of these, perhaps the most challenging is the question of how peacekeeping forces may need to undergo a complex metamorphosis in order to be effective in carrying out tasks such as protection of civilians in violent situations.

UN Security Council Practice Since 1990

Since early 1991 there have been at least nine crises in which humanitarian issues were referred to prominently in UN Security Council resolutions, after which military action was authorized either by the UN Security Council itself and/or (in the case of northern Iraq and Kosovo) by major Western states, and such action took place. In all but the first of these cases, relevant Security Council resolutions explicitly referred to Chapter VII of the UN Charter, indicating that the Council's powers to take action, including sanctions and enforcement, were being invoked. These nine cases are briefly outlined below, with a few examples of the reference to humanitarian issues in the relevant resolutions. (In almost all cases other issues were also mentioned, including, for example, the maintenance of international peace and security.)

Northern Iraq, 1991

Following a failed uprising within Iraq and a huge exodus of Kurds and others to neighboring countries, a UN Security Council resolution in April 1991 required that "Iraq allow immediate access by international humanitarian organizations to all those in need of assistance in all parts of Iraq."[1] This was not adopted under Chapter VII of the UN Charter, but it did state that Iraqi actions causing refugee flows "threaten international peace and security in the region." The resolution, while less than a formal authorization of intervention, was of considerable help to the United States and its coalition partners when the U.S.-led military operation within northern Iraq began on April 17, 1991. Iraq subsequently consented to the presence of the UN Guards Contingent in Iraq (UNGCI).

Bosnia and Herzegovina, 1992–1995

During this long and atrocious war, from as early as June 1992 onward, several UN Security Council resolutions suggested that if the UN Protection Force (UNPROFOR) and its humanitarian activities were obstructed, further measures not based on the consent of the parties might be taken to ensure delivery of humanitarian assistance.[2]

Also in 1992, the resolution establishing the NATO-enforced "no-fly zone" in Bosnia specified that one of the purposes of the ban on military flights was "for the safety of delivery of humanitarian assistance."[3]

The resolutions on the "safe areas" in Bosnia approved by the Security Council in April–June 1993 all condemned violations of international humanitarian law and referred also to other humanitarian considerations, including the Security Council's duty to prevent the crime of genocide.[4] Certain subsequent uses of force by NATO in Bosnia from 1993 to 1995 were based on these resolutions.

Somalia, 1992–1993

The U.S.-led invasion of December 9, 1992, by the Unified Task Force (UNITAF) was authorized by a UN Security Council resolution passed six days earlier that referred to "the urgent calls from Somalia for the international community to take measures to ensure the delivery of humanitarian assistance in Somalia," expressed alarm at "continuing reports of widespread violations of international humanitarian law occurring in Somalia," and made numerous other references to humanitarian issues.[5]

In 1993, the expanded UN peacekeeping force, UN Operation in Somalia (UNOSOM II), was established on the basis of a resolution that deplored "the acts of violence against persons engaging in humanitarian efforts" and noted with regret "the continuing reports of widespread violations of international humanitarian law."[6] This resolution accorded UNOSOM II specific powers of enforcement, confirming that it was intended to be more than a normal peacekeeping force. It left Somalia in March 1995 following a number of disastrous incidents, mainly in Mogadishu in 1993 and 1994, that raised questions about the command structure and purposes of the international forces in Somalia and about their failures to observe fundamental humanitarian norms.

Rwanda, 1994

The UN response to the genocide in Rwanda in April through July 1994 was marked by weakness and indecision, despite the presence in the country of a small peacekeeping force, the UN Assistance Mission for Rwanda (UNAMIR). When the Security Council did begin to call for forceful action in response to the crisis, it stressed the importance of humanitarian issues as a basis for such action. For example, an early resolution on these lines passed in May 1994 expressed concern over "a humanitarian crisis of enormous proportions" and decided on an expansion of UNAMIR's mandate:

> (a) To contribute to the security and protection of displaced persons, refugees and civilians at risk in Rwanda, including through the establishment and maintenance, where feasible, of secure humanitarian areas;
> (b) To provide security and support for the distribution of relief supplies and humanitarian relief operations.[7]

This mandate was repeated and reaffirmed in a resolution in early June, which referred to "reports indicating that acts of genocide have occurred in Rwanda" and underscored that "the internal displacement of some 1.5 million Rwandans facing starvation and disease and the massive exodus of refugees to neighbouring countries constitute a humanitarian crisis of enormous proportions."[8] Great difficulties arose in obtaining forces to go to Rwanda to carry out the mandate.

On June 22, in a further decision on Rwanda, the Security Council accepted an offer from France and other member states to establish a temporary operation there under French command and control. The Council authorized France to use "all necessary means to achieve the humanitarian objectives" that had been set out in the resolutions cited above.[9] This was the prelude to the controversial French-led Opération Turquoise in western Rwanda in summer 1994.

Haiti, 1994

Following the coup d'état in Haiti in September 1991, the UN Security Council eventually passed a resolution in July 1994 stating inter alia that it was "gravely concerned by the significant further deterioration of the humanitarian situation in Haiti" and authorizing the use of "all necessary means to facilitate the departure from Haiti of the military leadership . . . and to establish and maintain a secure and stable environment."[10] This resolution is remarkable for its unequivocal call for action to topple an existing regime. The U.S.-led invasion followed in September 1994, with the last-minute consent of the military regime to the presence of the Multinational Force in Haiti (MNF). In 1995, the UN Mission in Haiti (UNMIH), a peacekeeping force, took over from the MNF, inheriting the powers, including those under Chapter VII of the UN Charter, that had earlier been accorded to the MNF.[11]

Albania, 1997

In March 1997, during a period of widespread disorder in Albania and a large refugee exodus, the UN Security Council adopted a resolution approving the establishment of an Italian-led multinational protection force (MPF) "to facilitate the safe and prompt delivery of humanitarian assistance, and to help create a secure environment for the missions of international organizations in Albania, including those providing humanitarian assistance."[12] This operation had the consent of the Albanian government. The MPF was deployed in Albania shortly after the resolution was passed, and by the time that the force was withdrawn in June, it had contributed significantly to the restoration of order.

Kosovo, 1998–1999

Following the outbreak of hostilities and atrocities in Kosovo in February 1998 and a worsening of the situation over the summer, the UN Security Council passed a resolution in September 1998 demanding that the parties take certain concrete steps, including a cease-fire and acceptance of an effective international monitoring force in the province. In the course of repeated references to humanitarian issues, this resolution stated that a main purpose was "to avert the impending humanitarian catastrophe." It also demanded that the Federal Republic of Yugoslavia "facilitate, in agreement with the UNHCR and the ICRC, the safe return of refugees and displaced persons to their homes and allow free and unimpeded access for humanitarian organizations and supplies to Kosovo."[13] The subsequent major resolution on Kosovo, endorsing agreements concluded in Belgrade on October 15–16 and adopted just over a week later, made similar references to humanitarian issues as a basis for action.[14]

Regarding Kosovo in 1998–1999, as in the case of northern Iraq in 1991, the Security Council did not explicitly authorize the use of force, but did spell out demands relating inter alia to humanitarian issues: these resolutions were then cited by representatives of NATO member states as evidence that the military action they were taking—even though not endorsed by the Security Council—was in pursuit of goals (including humanitarian ones) that the Council had proclaimed.

Following the war between NATO states and Yugoslavia in March–June 1999, the Security Council passed a further resolution deciding to deploy an international civil and security presence in Kosovo, the latter with substantial NATO participation and with extensive powers. Its assigned tasks included establishing "a secure environment in which refugees and displaced persons can return home in safety, the international civil presence can operate, a transitional administration can be established, and humanitarian aid can be delivered."[15]

East Timor, 1999

After pro-Indonesian elements in East Timor refused to accept the outcome of the referendum of August 30, 1999, which had favored independence for the territory and embarked on large-scale killings and expulsions, the Security Council passed a resolution in mid-September authorizing an Australian-led multinational force to restore peace and security in East Timor and "to facilitate humanitarian assistance operations."[16] The resolution was passed only after Indonesian consent to the multinational force had been obtained: this followed the exertion of considerable pressure on the Indonesian government.

A resolution adopted in the following month made provisions to replace the Australian-led force with the UN Transitional Administration in East Timor (UNTAET), which was authorized "to take all necessary measures to fulfil its mandate." Again, humanitarian considerations and organizations were mentioned.[17]

Sierra Leone, 1999–2000

Faced with the difficult task of ensuring implementation of the Lomé Peace Agreement of July 7, 1999, which was intended to end the long civil war in Sierra Leone, in October 1999 the Security Council adopted a resolution establishing a new UN force there with certain limited enforcement powers. The UN Mission in Sierra Leone (UNAMSIL), which replaced a UN observer mission with fewer powers (UNOMSIL), was authorized "to take the necessary action to ensure the security and freedom of movement of its personnel and, within its capabilities and areas of deployment, to afford protection to civilians under imminent threat of physical violence." The resolution also called on all parties "to ensure safe and unhindered access of humanitarian assistance to those in need in Sierra Leone, to guarantee the safety and security of humanitarian personnel and to respect strictly the relevant provisions of international humanitarian and human rights law."[18]

A subsequent resolution adopted in February 2000 strengthened UNAMSIL's mandate, giving it authority to "take the necessary action" regarding an enlarged range of tasks that included, inter alia, "to facilitate the free flow of people, goods and humanitarian assistance along specified thoroughfares."[19]

Other Purposes in These Military Actions

The fact that humanitarian issues were cited authoritatively in so many UN Security Council resolutions, the great majority of which also referred to Chapter VII and all of which led to military action of some kind, does not mean that states and international bodies had experienced a sudden conversion to humanitarianism. In some crises they adopted a response in the name of humanitarianism because they were unable to formulate, or to agree on, substantive policies dealing with the fundamental issues involved. Nor does the emphasis on humanitarian aspects mean that there were no other purposes, interests, or motives at stake. In each case there were. They included:

Securing return of refugees. While enabling refugees to return home may appear to be a humanitarian cause, it also reflects a strong interest of states faced with a sudden refugee influx or a threat thereof. In many cases states taking a significant role in military action in a crisis, or urging others to do so, were also those that faced major refugee problems. Since 1990, massive refugee flows have often been seen as constituting a threat to international peace and security and hence as justifying involvement and action by the Security Council and by others.

International peace and security. In all the above crises, considerations of international peace and security were mentioned alongside humanitarian issues as a basis for international action. For the UN Security Council, reference to this matter is procedurally important in order to justify the Council concerning itself with a crisis. In general, the crises demonstrate that humanitarian issues are not easily separable from more explicitly political ones, including those relating to peace and security.

Credibility of commitments and/or demonstration of power. If states, or the UN Security Council, have called for certain action to be taken by a party to a conflict, and their calls have been ignored, they may have an interest in taking military action in order to maintain the international credibility of their words and of their military capacity. In addition, some states may embark on military action, including in support of humanitarian causes, partly out of a concern to demonstrate a capacity for exercising power, including in cases where their material interests are not directly involved. Some such motivations may have been involved in the willingness of various countries to support the Sarajevo airlift for three years following the visit by President François Mitterrand of France to Sarajevo on June 28, 1992.

In many cases there may have been other interests at stake, encompassing the protection of fellow nationals, the protection of UN personnel from attack, the security of present or future investments, and the spreading of democracy. Yet the main problem in connection with many of these crises has been the *lack* of solid interests on the part of actual and potential intervening states, and a resulting lack of willingness to take any seriously committing action. In some cases (as in Bosnia) they have acted too late; in other cases (as in Rwanda) most states failed to act at all; in still other cases (as in Somalia) those intervening were not willing to stay for the length of time or to accept the level of casualties that completion of the tasks assigned to the mission might have required.

Lack of Legitimation of Military
Action in the Law of War

There is no treaty that explicitly recognizes a general right of states or international bodies to take military action in response to gross violations of humanitarian norms, including those in the law of war. The nearest to a legal basis for such action is the UN Charter. The wording of Article 2(4) and 2(7), while basically noninterventionist, appears to leave some scope for the Security Council to take enforcement action within a state; and Chapter VII recognizes the Security Council's right to take a wide range of actions, some of which can be military, in cases where there is a threat to international peace and security. Chapter IX, on international economic and social cooperation, contains a pledge by members to "take joint and separate action" to achieve, inter alia, universal observance of human rights, but it has never been suggested that this phrase in Chapter IX legitimizes specifically military action.

Some international agreements concluded since 1945 contain provisions pointing toward a possible right of military action in response to violations. The clearest example (which belongs equally to both the human rights and armed conflict branches of international law) is the 1948 Genocide Convention, Article VIII of which specifies that any contracting state "may call upon the competent organs of the United Nations to take such action under the Charter of the United Nations as they consider appropriate for the prevention and suppression of acts of genocide." Another possible example (which is not in the strict sense a laws-of-war treaty) is the 1994 Convention on the Safety of United Nations and Associated Personnel, Article 7 of which contains a provision that states will cooperate in its implementation, "particularly in any case where the host State is unable itself to take the required measures." Both of these agreements have been cited frequently in the course of UN Security Council resolutions authorizing the use of force.

As to humanitarian interventions (in the classical sense of military interventions on humanitarian grounds) not authorized by the UN Security Council, there is a dearth of any binding legal text that supports such action. Treaties in the fields of human rights and international humanitarian law do require states to observe well-defined standards and to prevent and punish certain violations of those standards. Further, common Article 1 of each of the four Geneva Conventions of 1949 famously calls on states "to ensure respect for the present Convention in all circumstances." This phrase, while open to considerable interpretation, does not go so far as to imply that forcible military action is among the means of implementation.

A number of treaties in the field of the law of war appear to exclude the idea that a state's violations of their terms could provide a basis for military intervention. The 1977 First Protocol Additional to the Geneva Conventions (Additional Protocol I), which relates to international armed conflicts, contains the following caveat in its preamble:

> *Expressing* their conviction that nothing in this Protocol or in the Geneva Conventions of 12 August 1949 can be construed as legitimizing or authorizing any act of aggression or any other use of force inconsistent with the Charter of the United Nations . . .

Additional Protocol II, on noninternational armed conflicts, states in Article 3, entitled "Non-intervention,"

> 1. Nothing in this Protocol shall be invoked for the purpose of affecting the sovereignty of a State or the responsibility of the government, by all legitimate means, to maintain or re-establish law and order in the State or to defend the national unity and territorial integrity of the State.
> 2. Nothing in this Protocol shall be invoked as a justification for intervening, directly or indirectly, for any reason whatever, in the armed conflict or in the internal or external affairs of the High Contracting Party in the territory of which that conflict occurs.

The 1998 Rome Statute of the International Criminal Court (not yet in force) contains a similar provision in its preamble, emphasizing that "nothing in this Statute shall be taken as authorizing any State Party to intervene in an armed conflict or in the internal affairs of any State."

Finally, the 1999 Second Hague Protocol on Cultural Property, in its chapter on noninternational armed conflicts, reaffirms state sovereignty and nonintervention in Article 22(3) and (5), in terms virtually identical to those of Additional Protocol II, quoted above.

The principal purpose of these provisions of agreements on the laws of war seems to be to protect the sovereignty of potential target states, and in particular to exclude the possibility of these treaties being so interpreted as to justify forcible intervention by states in the affairs (internal or external) of another state. However, these provisions by no means exclude all military action in response to violations. For example, they do not rule out action that is by consent of a government involved in a conflict; and they do not appear to deprive the UN Security Council of its powers under the UN Charter.

In the 1990s, the increased interest in how international humanitarian law can be implemented inevitably resulted in a shift away from a rigid insistence on the nonintervention rule in favor of a limited (and far from uniform) acceptance that sometimes international military enforcement action may be needed. However, in those cases where military action takes place without the consent of the government concerned and lacks UN Security Council authorization, international law offers some conflicting principles. In an international crisis the balancing of these principles against one another is a subjective process that cannot always lead to agreed-upon conclusions.

Requests of Humanitarian Organizations for Military Action

In a number of post–cold war crises, international humanitarian workers and organizations have themselves called for outside military intervention in a crisis. For example, in the second half of 1992 a number of agencies called for military action to protect humanitarian aid in Somalia; and in April and May 1994 the UK charity Oxfam described the killings in Rwanda as genocide and called for international action.

In certain cases, even if they do not explicitly call for military action, humanitarian workers and organizations may provide an analysis and description of the crisis in such a way as to assist building a consensus for it. A case in point may be the evidence of the situation in Kosovo presented by a representative of UNHCR to the UN Security Council meeting on September 10, 1998. This contributed something to the subsequent strongly worded Chapter VII resolution on Kosovo.[20]

Even if such workers and organizations are silent, actions taken against them can have the effect of leading to calls for intervention. Today's aid workers may sometimes, involuntarily, have a role similar to Western missionaries in distant lands in the era of European colonialism: violence against them may lead to outside intervention. Such a process may have been reinforced by the 1994 Convention on the Safety of UN and Associated Personnel, especially its Article 7(3), which requires states parties to cooperate in implementation of the Convention, "particularly in any case where the host state is unable to take the required measures."

Special Case of ICRC

Any development that seems to associate international humanitarian workers and organizations, and indeed international humanitarian law, with demands or justifications for military action poses a serious problem for the Red Cross and Red Crescent Movement. For the ICRC in particular, the statutory requirements of impartiality and neutrality are fundamental to its effective performance of the tasks in armed conflicts that are assigned to it in international conventions.

The ICRC's understandable caution about being associated with positions and actions of the United Nations was indicated during the negotiations that led to the conclusion of the 1994 Convention on the Safety of UN and Associated Personnel. The ICRC stated that it did not want its personnel to be protected under this convention. This was partly because ICRC personnel already have international legal protection deriving from the 1949 Geneva Conventions, and partly because the ICRC's role as neutral humanitarian intermediary might be jeopardized if the ICRC were perceived as closely linked with the UN.

The dilemmas that all this poses for the ICRC were well expressed by Jakob Kellenberger, president of the ICRC, in an address at Wilton Park on May 15, 2000. He referred to "the confusion caused by the mixing of humanitarian aims with political and/or military aims in action taken by the international community in armed conflicts." He went on:

> My point is not to criticize military intervention, which can, under extreme circumstances, become the only possibility to prevent a humanitarian situation from worsening or to create the conditions for humanitarian organizations to do their work. But we should be careful with words. Whereas an intervention can well be motivated by humanitarian reasons, "humanitarian intervention" is a problematic expression.[21]

While it is certainly right to be skeptical about the term *humanitarian intervention,* the remarkable trend of the 1990s for humanitarian issues to be cited as a basis for Security Council action is not likely to be reversed. For better or for worse, military and humanitarian issues are now intertwined. The ICRC, to maintain its distinct identity, must necessarily put emphasis on its unique character and on the special roles that it performs: it simply cannot be a typical humanitarian organization, if such a thing exists.

Consideration of the Protection of Civilians in Key UN Documents

Since the early 1990s there have been extensive discussions within the United Nations addressing the role of the military in supporting humanitarian operations. An awareness of the importance of the issue contributed to the fact that the 1994 Convention on the Safety of UN and Associated Personnel, which was negotiated at the UN headquarters in New York, dealt extensively with the legal protection of a wide range of "associated personnel," including those working for intergovernmental bodies, UN specialized agencies, and humanitarian nongovernmental organizations. The discussions at the UN, which became frequent in the second half of the 1990s, gradually moved in the direction of concentrating not just on the legal and physical protection of aid but on the physical protection of civilians at risk; the validity of military action, especially in opposing systematic murder of civilians, was eventually accepted. However, there is little sign that policies that should flow from these conclusions have been understood and acted upon by states, by the UN Security Council, or by the UN Department of Peacekeeping Operations.

One early high-level discussion of the military/humanitarian interface, in which serious differences of opinion were expressed, was the Security Council's daylong session on May 21, 1997, on "Protection for humanitarian assistance to refugees and others in conflict situations," in which senior representatives from many leading international agencies as well as from states took part. This, like many such discussions, was concerned more with the issue of protection of humanitarian operations than with the closely related question of protection of civilians at risk. It exposed a conflict between those in favor of international military support for humanitarian operations and those who are skeptical or even opposed to such support, fearing above all that it would threaten the neutrality and impartiality of humanitarian work.[22]

In 1999, three UN documents addressed directly the question of how the international community should respond when civilians are at risk, whether in armed conflict or at the hands of a brutal regime. These were the Report of the Secretary-General to the Security Council on the Protection of Civilians in Armed Conflict, the Report of the Secretary-General on the Fall of Srebrenica, and the Report of the Independent Inquiry into the Actions of the UN During the 1994 Genocide in Rwanda. With the publication of the reports on Srebrenica and Rwanda, opinion moved in the direction of accepting the importance of military action in certain extreme circumstances.

The three reports all recognize that there can be situations in which "protection" of civilians and prisoners of war in the narrow legal sense may be woefully inadequate: physical protection is needed, and it may have to be provided by foreign armed forces. This is a key lesson from the disasters of the 1990s that must be taken on board by humanitarian agencies, even if they cannot associate themselves directly with such use of force. What follows is in no sense a summary of the reports; rather it is a distillation of their conclusions as to how humanitarian issues should sometimes be a basis for the initiation of military action.

Secretary-General's Report on the Protection of Civilians in Armed Conflict

This report, issued in September 1999, was the follow-up to an open meeting of the UN Security Council on the matter of protection of civilians in armed conflict. It is the most general of the three reports and, perhaps for that reason, the least satisfactory.

One weakness is that it presents a completely negative view of the implementation of the law of war in contemporary conflicts, stating in a typical passage:

> International humanitarian and human rights law set out the rights of civilians and the obligations of combatants during time of conflict. Yet, belligerents throughout the world refuse to respect these statutes, relying instead on terror as a means of control over populations.[23]

There is no recognition that in some conflicts certain basic norms have been observed, at least by some parties; nor is it pointed out that some of those who committed the most egregious violations of humanitarian norms (the Rwandan regime in 1994 and the Serbs at Srebrenica in 1995) subsequently suffered serious military reverses.

The report makes some worthwhile proposals regarding ratification of existing treaties, further development of the law, conflict prevention, and other matters. However, it merely reiterates certain proposals without discussing the tragedies ensuing from their application in practice in the 1990s. Thus it advocates arms embargoes in respect of situations where parties to the conflict target civilians, but it fails to show any awareness of why particular forms of arms embargo came to be seen as deeply unsatisfactory in the former Yugoslavia in 1991–1996 and in Sierra Leone beginning in 1997. Likewise it fails to offer any detailed analysis of the Security Council's actual efforts in the preceding decade to act in various conflicts to secure physical protection of vulnerable populations. On this subject, the report makes an apparently robust statement with a distinctly less-than-robust finale when it recommends that the Security Council

> establish, as a measure of last resort, temporary security zones and safe corridors for the protection of civilians and the delivery of assistance in situations characterized by the threat of genocide, crimes against humanity and war crimes against the civilian population, subject to the clear understanding that such arrangements require the availability, prior to their establishment, of sufficient and credible force to guarantee the safety of civilian populations making use of them, and ensure the demilitarization of these zones and the availability of a safe-exit option.[24]

There is a case for the demilitarization of certain security zones—at least if it can be achieved with the agreement and ongoing consent of parties to a conflict. However, the apparent assumption here that any security zone should be demilitarized is open to two objections. First, it was precisely the zones in Bosnia that were subject to demilitarization agreements (albeit imperfect) that were conquered by Bosnian Serb forces in summer 1995. Second, there is an obvious risk in demilitarizing a zone and then putting all reliance for defense on outside forces, especially if those forces are imbued with the mentality of the "safe-exit option." In short, the report's coverage of the core issue it is supposed to address—the protection of civilians in armed conflict—is not serious.

In the same part of the report the Secretary-General also recommended, in a more robust mode, that the Security Council,

> in the face of massive and ongoing abuses, consider the imposition of appropriate enforcement action. Before acting in such cases, either with a United Nations, regional or multinational arrangement, and in order to reinforce political support for such efforts, enhance confidence in their legitimacy and deter perceptions of selectivity or bias toward one region or another, the Council should consider the following factors:
>
> (a) The scope of the breaches of human rights and international humanitarian law including the numbers of people affected and the nature of the violations;
> (b) The inability of local authorities to uphold legal order, or identification of a pattern of complicity by local authorities;
> (c) The exhaustion of peaceful or consent-based efforts to address the situation;
> (d) The ability of the Security Council to monitor actions that are undertaken;
> (e) The limited and proportionate use of force, with attention to repercussions upon civilian populations and the environment.[25]

The greatest omission in the report is one that is not easily remedied. It fails to discuss the capacity and will of states to act. Proposals such as the one above depend crucially upon major regional or global powers, equipped with intervention forces, being willing to commit their military assets over a substantial period and to accept the possibility of casualties. There is persuasive evidence from the years since 1990 that such willingness is in limited supply. Hence the protection of civilians has sometimes assumed perverse forms: empty promises to protect the "safe areas" in Bosnia, and retaliatory bombing from a safe height as a response to ongoing killings and expulsions in Kosovo.

Secretary-General's Report on the Fall of Srebrenica

The report of the UN Secretary-General on "The Fall of Srebrenica" is an extraordinarily powerful account and analysis of a difficult subject, leaving the reader in little doubt about the complex causes and tragic consequences of the failure of states and the UN to take serious action to protect this "safe area." Its central lesson is put bluntly in the conclusions:

The community of nations decided to respond to the war in Bosnia and Herzegovina with an arms embargo, with humanitarian aid and with the deployment of a peacekeeping force. It must be clearly stated that these measures were poor substitutes for more decisive and forceful action to prevent the unfolding horror.[26]

The report in no way denies the validity of humanitarian considerations as a basis for international involvement, but it does suggest that the resulting policies and deployments need also to involve elements that go well beyond the purely humanitarian. In particular, member states and the UN must on occasion be willing to use armed force, support one side in a conflict and oppose the other, and/or impose a settlement.

Independent Inquiry Report into UN Actions During the Rwanda Genocide

In April–July 1994 between half a million and a million people were killed in massacres in Rwanda in the worst case of genocide since World War II. The report of the independent inquiry examines why the international response was so weak. It focuses on the response to the crisis within the United Nations; it says far less about the equally important subject of the responses of key national governments. The report's narrative confirms that for too long, key UN personnel, especially in New York, failed to heed information about impending or actual massacres and stuck to the concept of impartial peacekeeping when stronger measures were required. A key conclusion of the report consciously echoes the Srebrenica report, issued the previous month, when it states:

While the presence of United Nations peacekeepers in Rwanda may have begun as a traditional peacekeeping operation to monitor the implementation of an existing peace agreement, the onslaught of the genocide should have led decision-makers in the United Nations—from the Secretary-General and the Security Council to Secretariat officials and the leadership of UNAMIR—to realize that the original mandate, and indeed the neutral mediating role of the United Nations, was no longer adequate and required a different, more assertive response, combined with the means necessary to take such action.[27]

Conclusion

Since the end of the cold war there has been a strong trend toward identifying humanitarian considerations as a basis for certain military mandates and actions. This trend has been observed not only in armed conflicts, whether civil or international (for example, Bosnia and Sierra Leone), but also in situations of tyrannical or brutal government (Rwanda and Haiti), uncontrolled violence (Somalia and Albania), and the establishment of international forces to help implement a peace agreement (Kosovo and East Timor). Some of the cases mentioned have had characteristics of several of these types of situations.

It is easy to criticize this trend on several grounds. First, some extremely serious humanitarian crises do not result in military action. Crises that have led to severely limited international military action, or no action at all, include those in Abkhazia in the 1990s, and the war in Chechnya in 1999–2000. There is, inevitably, a selective element in international military responses. Second, military actions taken on largely humanitarian grounds are sometimes too little, too late. They are often characterized by lack of clarity about strategy and aims, reluctance to accept sacrifices, nervousness about siding with one or other of the belligerent parties, and an unwillingness to keep forces in a crisis area for more than a short period. Third, humanitarian issues and organizations get entangled with politico/military matters, potentially undermining their distinctive roles. And fourth, there is no practical prospect of developing a coherent and agreed-upon general international legal doctrine of humanitarian intervention. The legitimacy of military action, as well as the practical aspects thereof, must necessarily be considered, taking into account the unique aspects of each case.

Despite all the problems, there are positive outcomes from the ways in which humanitarian considerations have played some part in the initiation of military actions. Many lives have been saved in many crises, including even the controversial case of Somalia; international military action has helped to end some vicious wars, including in Bosnia; persons indicted for war crimes have been arrested by the NATO-led forces in Bosnia; many refugees, including those from Albania and East Timor, have been enabled to return to their countries; and those who would inflict wanton violence on civilians and prisoners are under notice that they may face serious military consequences.

As to the future, humanitarian issues seem destined to remain intertwined with decisions about the use of force in at least some crises. Whether this development is condemned or celebrated, it must probably be accepted as a fact; and it poses the challenge of how to address some of the problems associated with it, and how to take the matter forward.

For humanitarian organizations it is almost inevitable that there will be a division of labor not just in their activities but also in their moral stance. Some will stress absolute impartiality and neutrality. Others may be more prepared to engage in advocacy—even, occasionally, military advocacy—and also to seek some degree of military protection for their activities. This suggests a key conclusion: while neutrality and impartiality may represent one valid moral position for humanitarian organizations, especially the ICRC, it is not the only moral position that is valid.

For states and intergovernmental bodies, two main challenges need to be faced. The first is that if military force is used in support of at least partly humanitarian goals, or in implementation of international humanitarian law, it is important that it should itself comply with that body of law. Experience suggests that there can be particular pressures in military operations with humanitarian purposes that make observance of the law difficult. The perception of those involved that a military action is disinterested, and in support of high moral purposes, can easily lead to an attitude of superiority over the people they are seeking to save. Whether committed for this or other reasons, the crimes by the forces intervening in Somalia in 1992–1995 are evidence of the seriousness of the problem. The case of the 1999 Kosovo war suggests two further grounds for worry. One is that where a military operation has the purpose of changing the policy of a government, it may involve putting pressure on individuals and installations that are as much connected with the government as they are with the army, and may have some elements of civilian function or character. A second worry exemplified by Kosovo is that conducting low-risk war by bombing from fifteen thousand feet may make it difficult to attack military units or to protect vulnerable civilians. These concerns arising from the Kosovo war suggest that the clear distinction in the laws of war between civilian and military targets is at risk of being eroded. In principle, the application of the laws of war to international forces is not in doubt, and important aspects of this principle have been confirmed by the UN Secretary-General's Bulletin of August 1999.[28] However, ensuring that such application is effective remains a problem.

The second challenge is how to combine humanitarian aims with the effective strategic and political management of armed force. This problem has many dimensions. In particular, there is an urgent need to develop clear concepts and procedures for a process that has recurred in an ad hoc and muddled fashion in the crises of the 1990s: the metamorphosis of a peacekeeping and observer mission into an enforcement operation. For peacekeeping tasks, forces are often spread out widely within a country. For enforcement, forces must be constituted differently: they generally need to be concentrated, and an efficient system of command and control becomes even more important than in peacekeeping. Until there is a clearer idea of how such forces may be deployed and used, humanitarian issues may remain triggers more for failure than for effective intervention to achieve the humanitarian objectives that have been so frequently proclaimed and only rarely achieved.

Notes

1. Security Council [hereafter, SC] Res. 688 (Apr. 5, 1991).
2. See, e.g., SC Res. 758 (June 8, 1992), SC Res. 761 (June 29, 1992), and SC Res. 770 (Aug. 13, 1992), this last being explicitly under Chapter VII.

3. SC Res. 781 (Oct. 9, 1992).

4. SC Res. 819 (Apr. 16, 1993), SC Res. 824 (May 6, 1993), and SC Res. 836 (June 4, 1993), the last two adopted explicitly under Chapter VII.

5. SC Res. 794 (Dec. 3, 1992), adopted under Chapter VII.

6. SC Res. 814 (Mar. 26, 1993), adopted under Chapter VII.

7. SC Res. 918 (May 17, 1994), only part of which was adopted under Chapter VII.

8. SC Res. 925 (June 8, 1994).

9. SC Res. 929 (June 22, 1994), adopted under Chapter VII. The humanitarian objectives to which it referred were those set out previously in SC Res. 925 (1994), and also in SC Res. 918 (1994).

10. SC Res. 940 (July 31, 1994), adopted under Chapter VII.

11. SC Res. 975 (Jan. 30, 1995) provided for UNMIH to take over certain specific powers that had been accorded to the MNF in Haiti by SC Res. 940 (July 31, 1994).

12. SC Res. 1101 (Mar. 28, 1997), adopted under Chapter VII. See also SC Res. 1114 (June 19, 1997), deciding that the operation in Albania was to be limited to a period of forty-five days from June 28, 1997.

13. SC Res. 1199 (Sept. 23, 1998), adopted under Chapter VII.

14. SC Res. 1203 (Oct. 24, 1998), adopted under Chapter VII.

15. SC Res. 1244 (June 10, 1999), adopted under Chapter VII.

16. SC Res. 1264 (Sept. 15, 1999), adopted under Chapter VII.

17. SC Res. 1272 (Oct. 25, 1999), adopted under Chapter VII.

18. SC Res. 1270 (Oct. 22, 1999), adopted under Chapter VII.

19. SC Res. 1289 (Feb. 7, 2000), adopted under Chapter VII.

20. SC Res. 1199 (Sept. 23, 1998), adopted under Chapter VII.

21. Dr. Jakob Kellenberger (president of the ICRC), "Humanitarian Challenges in the Midst of War," address at Wilton Park Conference, May 15–19, 2000, text as distributed at conference, p. 6.

22. "Difficulty of Providing Military Support for Humanitarian Operations While Ensuring Impartiality Focus of Security Council Debate," UN Press Release SC/6371, May 21, 1997.

23. Report of the Secretary-General to the Security Council on the Protection of Civilians in Armed Conflict, UN Doc. S/1999/957 (Sept. 8, 1999), para. 3. There are similarly negative views of implementation in paras. 2, 7, 12, 13, and 21.

24. Ibid., recommendation 39.

25. Ibid., recommendation 40. This report led promptly to the passing of SC Res. 1265 (Sept. 17, 1999) on the protection of civilians in armed conflict.

26. Report of the Secretary-General Pursuant to General Assembly Resolution 53/35: The Fall of Srebrenica, UN Doc. A/54/549 (Nov. 15, 1999), para. 490.

27. Report of the Independent Inquiry into the Actions of the United Nations During the 1994 Genocide in Rwanda, attached to UN Doc. S/1999/1257 (Dec. 16, 1999), pp. 50–51.

28. Secretary-General's Bulletin: Observance by United Nations Forces of International Humanitarian Law, entry into force Aug. 12, 1999, UN Doc. ST/SGB/1999/13 (Aug. 6, 1999).

10

The Enforcement of Humanitarian Norms and the Politics of Ambivalence

Edward C. Luck

Few questions have been posed more sharply or debated more heatedly within the United Nations in recent years than that of economic or military intervention to enforce humanitarian norms. In a series of speeches and reports beginning in mid-1998, Secretary-General Kofi Annan has repeatedly and forcefully reminded member states of the moral, legal, and human consequences of failing to act in the face of mass atrocities in places like Rwanda, Srebrenica, and Sierra Leone. As he warned the General Assembly in September 1999, the tragedy of Kosovo "revealed the core challenge to the Security Council and to the United Nations as a whole in the next century: to forge unity behind the principle that massive and systematic violations of human rights—wherever they may take place—should not be allowed to stand."[1] While the Secretary-General succeeded admirably in focusing intergovernmental attention on the humanitarian challenge, the subsequent debate demonstrated how deeply divided the member states remain on how principles of national sovereignty and humanitarian need should be reconciled.[2] The ambivalence of member states can be seen not only in debates about competing principles but also, more graphically, in their hesitancy to respond even to massive violations of humanitarian norms with effective economic or military enforcement action under Chapter VII of the UN Charter. In this chapter I address some of the reasons why such ambivalence should be expected from individual countries and why the UN's political culture itself emits mixed messages on this score. I then suggest some ways to address these doubts and uncertainties.

The international military responses to repression in Kosovo and East Timor in 1999 encouraged some observers to announce the arrival not only of a new doctrine but also of a new era of humanitarian intervention.[3] Sounding very much like the Secretary-General, Prime Minister Tony Blair of the United Kingdom declared that in Kosovo "we are fighting not for territory but for values. For a new internationalism where the brutal repression of whole ethnic groups will no longer be tolerated. For a world where those responsible for such crimes have nowhere to hide."[4] Calling the Kosovo conflict "a just and necessary war," U.S. President Bill Clinton cautioned that "had we faltered, the result would have been a moral and strategic disaster."[5] Less than four months later, President Clinton declared that in East Timor, "at stake are the lives and way of life of innocent people. At issue is whether the democratically-expressed will of the people can be overturned by violence and intimidation."[6] Although the Security Council remains bitterly divided over the legality and appropriateness of the NATO air campaign against Serbia, it did agree on the deployment of a Chapter VII operation in East Timor once the government of Indonesia gave its consent.[7]

Despite the soaring rhetoric heard in some capitals regarding these two crises, however, why has the international community been so reticent to speak out—let alone act—in dozens of other raging conflicts, some of which have had terrible humanitarian consequences? The "new era" has been undermined by the fact that support by national governments for enforcing humanitarian norms remains selective and, in most cases, halfhearted. Kosovo and East Timor may well prove to be the exception, with Rwanda and Sierra Leone closer to the rule. If those that have the capacity lack the will and those that proclaim the will lack the capacity, the commitment of neither will be tested. Though some states may be less ambivalent than others, few are prepared to make major sacrifices of blood, treasure, or political capital to enforce humanitarian principles in places where they do not have a political, economic, or strategic rationale for becoming involved. Feelings of ambivalence fade, of course, when the risks and costs of intervention are relatively low; when the violator is relatively weak, vulnerable, and unpopular; and when public outrage suggests that a substantial domestic political price would be paid for inaction. But will this not remain a formula for inconsistency and for charges of bias and inequity?

Ambivalence may be prevalent today, but it is arguable that this was always the case. The enthusiasm for taking enforcement measures—as opposed to assistance for the victims and harsh words for the perpetrators—has been even more episodic in the past than it has been in recent years. Though the results have been uneven, there has been more serious governmental and academic study, as well as public interest, in enforcement options over the past decade than at any other point since the Hague Peace Conferences a century ago. During the four decades of the cold war, it would have appeared ludicrous to suggest that NATO's first major combat engagement, albeit from the air, would be triggered by a humanitarian calamity. The virulence of the backlash from developing states and from conservative Western commentators against notions of humanitarian intervention, in fact, attests to how much visibility and political currency these ideas have attained during the 1990s. Enthusiasms aside, however, it is painfully evident that there are a number of challenging practical problems that need to be resolved before credible and effective enforcement mechanisms can be put in place. And the will to overcome such obstacles, at least on the part of those governments with the wherewithal, continues to be markedly insufficient.

To suggest that the persistence of ambivalence is understandable does not mean that it is either acceptable or tolerable. The horrific toll in terms of innocent lives lost, including large numbers of women and children, is repugnant to basic human values.[8] The moral, spiritual, and civic costs have been substantially higher than is generally recognized or acknowledged. The authority and credibility of international law and its institutions have been undermined by the tendency of states to proclaim and codify norms and principles that they are not prepared to defend. This practice has compounded the sense of skepticism, cynicism, and even disillusionment that has pervaded so much of public and official discussion of the prospects for international cooperation and for developing a rules-based international system. More fundamentally, the gap between words and deeds in humanitarian law has fed public disillusionment in and disaffection from national government as well as from intergovernmental institutions. Perhaps the greatest casualty has been the erosion of the credibility and authority of the Security Council itself.

At a time of global media coverage and instantaneous communications, these discrepancies are all the more stark as it becomes more and more difficult to claim that we just "didn't know" what was happening in distant places. Also attentive to the images and accounts of how the world reacts to crises, the perpetrators of the next round of humanitarian abuses can only be encouraged by repeated demonstrations of the unwillingness of the international community to act in the face of obvious violations.[9] In the process, opportunities for deterring future atrocities are being lost. Despite all the talk of prevention, the ambivalence and the divergent perspectives that characterize deliberations in the Security Council may prevent the one body with the legal authority to enforce its decisions from acting with sufficient dispatch and decisiveness to stop major human tragedies from unfolding, as in the case of Rwanda. It is, unfortunately, only *after* the toll of human suffering begins to mount that the rest of the world normally starts to pay attention.

I will address the politics of ambivalence from three broad perspectives. The first is that of the larger political culture of the United Nations, of the values and policy priorities that are widely championed by its Secretariat and intergovernmental bodies on related issues. I will argue that contradictions within the organization's political culture tend to constrain or inhibit the development of effective strategies for enforcement. The second set of impediments relates to structural asymmetries stemming from the very nature of the

UN system, in particular the barriers to coherent collective action in a system where enforcement capacities are held by sovereign and independent-minded member states. The third set of concerns relates to the ambiguous nature of the conflicts themselves and to the costs, risks, and challenges inherent in effective enforcement action under difficult circumstances.

The UN Political Culture

At its core, the political culture of the United Nations is ambivalent about undertaking military or economic enforcement measures. During the cold war years, a divided Security Council could agree on little of either, leaving the provisions of Chapter VII, which the founders had intended to be the organization's centerpiece, largely hypothetical. Chapter VI, which provides for pacific means of dispute settlement, became the primary vehicle for carrying out the UN's responsibilities for the maintenance of international peace and security, with enforcement to be undertaken by others should peaceful means fail. The UN was about peace, not war; about lightly armed, after-the-fact peacekeepers, not combat forces. Economic sanctions were only for outcasts, such as Southern Rhodesia and South Africa. As the UN was transformed from a group of World War II allies to a truly global organization, the idea of undertaking enforcement measures against one of its members (with the exception of a few rogue states) became less and less attractive.

None of the machinery envisioned in Chapter VII, such as a functioning Military Staff Committee and stand-by force agreements under Article 43, has been fully realized.[10] The question of command of UN forces, to be decided "subsequently" according to Article 47(3), was never settled. On the Secretariat side, a strong support staff to assist Security Council consideration of economic and military enforcement options was never developed.[11] In his July 1997 reform plan, Secretary-General Annan candidly noted that "the United Nations does not have, at this point in its history, the institutional capacity to conduct military enforcement measures under Chapter VII. Under present conditions, ad hoc coalitions of willing Member States offer the most effective deterrent to aggression or to the escalation or spread of an ongoing conflict."[12] His report to the Millennium Assembly was even more candid about the organization's incapacity to initiate any substantial peace operation, whether under Chapter VI or VII:

> The structural weaknesses of United Nations peace operations, however, only Member States can fix. Our system for launching operations has sometimes been compared to a volunteer fire department, but that description is too generous. Every time there is a fire, we must first find fire engines and the funds to run them before we can start dousing any flames. The present system relies almost entirely on last minute, ad hoc arrangements that guar-

antee delay, with respect to the provision of civilian personnel even more so than military.[13]

These weaknesses have been endemic, yet the member states have done little to correct them—even over the decade since the end of the cold war, once the excuse for inaction. It appears that states are not eager to see a UN that is either militarily capable or politically assertive. Unlike his predecessor, Boutros Boutros-Ghali, Secretary-General Annan therefore did not suggest in his 1997 or 2000 reports that the UN should acquire even modest enforcement or standing military capabilities.

Many member states are distinctly uncomfortable with the notion of the Security Council having forces at its disposal, whether standing or standby, given its limited membership and broad powers under Chapter VII. These states question the legitimacy of Security Council actions in light of what they claim is its undemocratic, selective, and authoritarian character. Evidently they fear a strong, interventionist UN that they cannot control more than they lament its current weaknesses. Most developing countries, including large ones such as India and China, find the prospect of an interventionist Council that has ready access to military power particularly threatening. Placing great stock in the principles of nonintervention, sovereign equality, and the sanctity of borders, smaller states that have little or no say in Council deliberations are understandably cautious. Seeming to value equity and geographical balance as highly as effectiveness, they tend to champion a major enlargement of the Council (with most of the new seats going to developing countries), further steps toward greater transparency and less emphasis on informal consultations in its work, cutbacks on gratis personnel (provided free by member states) in the UN Secretariat (even in peacekeeping and sanctions monitoring), and deeper cuts in the military capabilities of the major powers. In private, some of them fret about the lack of any power center to counterbalance U.S. dominance in the Council and the organization as a whole, following the demise of the Soviet Union.

Though understandable when seen through the prism of UN politics, these aspects of the prevailing culture tend to work against the UN's potential effectiveness as an enforcer of international humanitarian norms. The larger and more diverse the Council, the longer its decisionmaking process is apt to take and the lower the common denominator of its deliberations is likely to be. The result will be a narrowing, not a broadening, of the geographical and political scope for UN enforcement action. The more UN procedures are shaped to counterbalance U.S. power, moreover, the less probable it will be that the military assets of the one country with global power projection capabilities will be placed at the UN's disposal. Likewise, under those conditions, the United States will be more likely to pursue political, economic, and military options outside of the UN framework, as in Kosovo.[14] Tellingly, with a few modest exceptions aimed largely at peacekeeping contingencies, others are not rushing to develop the kinds of expensive national military capabilities that would be required to conduct enforcement missions overseas without U.S. participation. Most of those countries preaching the importance of joint military action under the authority of the UN have, in fact, so gutted their peacetime military capabilities since the end of the cold war that they have relatively little left to offer against a determined midsized aggressor in another part of the world.

These asymmetries—between rhetoric and capacities, and between the United States and other would-be defenders of international norms—present a considerable quandary. For the foreseeable future, no enforcement regime is likely to work without the U.S. at its center, yet many member states appear to be as worried about U.S. domination of the UN as some prominent members of the U.S. Congress are concerned about UN decisionmaking putting a crimp on U.S. foreign policy options and priorities. Small countries are hardly alone in their concerns about sovereignty.

A related dilemma is that the logic of the effective employment of force does not always coincide with the philosophy of universal political participation. The larger the number of national military units participating in an international enforcement coalition, the more complicated command and control and logistical arrangements become. While there may be political and diplomatic advantages to including twenty or thirty member states in such an operation, from a military perspective it makes most sense if only a few carry out the bulk of the fighting, as in the Desert Storm campaign to expel Iraqi forces from Kuwait in early 1991. The math works the opposite way in the case of economic sanctions, however, and the Secretary-General has pointed out that "the universal character of the United Nations makes it a particularly appropriate body to consider and oversee such measures."[15]

At a more basic level, it is frequently asked at the UN whether military or economic enforcement action is compatible with humanitarian objectives. The ongoing economic sanctions against Iraq and NATO's actions over Kosovo are two cases in point. Although a strong argument can be made that the ends—which included important political and security, as well as humanitarian considerations—justified the means, many delegates at the UN have raised tough questions about proportionality and effectiveness. There has been a rising tide of opposition among UN member states—especially developing ones—to the use of trade sanctions as an enforcement tool. In 1998, for example, the Organization of African Unity (OAU), meeting at the summit level, urged its members to defy the Charter and to violate the Security Council–imposed travel ban on Libya.[16]

It is true that in most cases economic and military enforcement measures do produce additional humanitarian suffering, sometimes on a wide scale, before they have a chance of affecting the plans and calculations of those violating international norms in the first place. As the Secretary-General noted in his report to the Millennium Assembly, "when robust and comprehensive economic sanctions are directed against authoritarian regimes it is usually the people who suffer."[17] In South Africa, antiapartheid activists consistently contended that the pain was worth the gain. But at present, the emphasis in the UN community is on trying to develop targeted sanctions regimes that discriminate more precisely between the "good guys" and the "bad guys"—a laudatory, if elusive, objective.[18] There is a parallel interest in developing a better understanding of how inducements (carrots) might be persuasively coupled with sanctions (sticks), though there may be significant moral dilemmas along this path and the international community could end up rewarding undesirable behavior, as in Sierra Leone, if such steps are not carefully planned and monitored. Also, carrots are unlikely to persuade aggressors and human rights abusers unless the alternative sticks are both credible and punishing. Advocates of low-cost/low-pain options point out, however, that in most cases it will be easier to sustain public support for sanctions that impose less collateral damage on the civilian population in the recipient nation. Yet this tendency to seek painless and guilt-free foreign policy tools also gives one an eerie sense that the international community feels uneasy with the exercise of raw power—something that rarely seems to bother the perpetrators of violence against civilian populations.

It is standard in UN discourse and doctrine to assert that the use of economic or, certainly, military sanctions should be treated as the final resort, to be undertaken only when diplomatic and political tools have failed. As the Secretary-General asserted in his June 1998 Ditchley speech,

> The most effective interventions are not military. It is much better, from every point of view, if action can be taken to resolve or manage a conflict before it reaches the military stage. Sometimes this action may take the form of economic advice and assistance.[19]

He reiterated this in his September 1999 report to the Security Council on the protection of civilians in armed conflict. Among the five factors that he urged the Council to take into account *before* considering the imposition of any sort of enforcement action was "the exhaustion of peaceful or consent-based efforts to address the situation."[20]

Though these are reasonable enough caveats for an organization that contrasts its skills at mediation and good offices with its incapacity for carrying out tough enforcement measures, this trend suggests that the UN's resort to enforcement options will tend to come rather late, if ever, in an unfolding crisis. At what point could it have been said that all possible efforts at peaceful settlement with Slobodan Milosevic or Saddam Hussein had been exhausted? How much havoc should be wreaked on civilian populations before the Council is free to consider the use of enforcement measures? It is possible that such delays will permit the target regime to prepare more thoroughly to resist any sanctions that might eventually be imposed. Aggressors and human rights abusers have always been good at sustaining a seemingly serious diplomatic dialogue on the international level while simultaneously continuing to commit atrocities and to consolidate their ill-gotten gains on the ground. The dominance of Chapter VI in the political culture of the UN has more than once made it vulnerable to the appearance of aiding and abetting such tactics in places like Bosnia and Sierra Leone.

In light of its reluctance to contemplate forceful action in most cases of humanitarian abuse, it is understandable that the UN has instead taken to the doctrine of prevention like a duck to water.[21] To member states, prevention looks a lot cheaper, safer, and tamer than either massive relief missions or high-risk enforcement operations. According to the Secretary-General's 1999 report on the work of the organization,

> More effective prevention strategies would not only save tens of billions of dollars, but hundreds of thousands of lives as well. Funds currently spent on intervention and relief could be devoted to enhancing equitable and sustainable development instead, which would further reduce the risks of war and disaster.[22]

Given statistics like these and the assumption that these "savings" would be shifted to development activities—both questionable projections—it should come as no surprise that the Secretary-General was able to declare in his report to the Millennium Assembly that "there is near-universal agreement that prevention is preferable to cure."[23] Following its debate in late November 1999 on prevention, the Security Council issued a presidential statement that recognized "the importance of building a culture of prevention of armed conflicts" and stressed "the importance of a coordinated international response to economic, social, cultural or humanitarian problems, which are often the root causes of armed conflict."[24] The Secretary-General, in turn, expressed his hope that the debate would "restore prevention to its rightful place as the first responsibility of the Security Council, and of the Organization as a whole."[25]

Perhaps the reliance on prevention is a sound strategy, especially for an organization so allergic to enforcement, and there is no doubt that it is an immensely popular one among both the member states and the Secretariat. But it begs the question of what the UN should do if prevention fails in the future as it has so often in the past.

Prevention is not deterrence. Deterrence can be attained only through a credible threat of effective action to enforce international norms and to deny those who would violate them impunity and the fruits of victory. The work of the existing war crimes tribunals and the progress toward an International

Criminal Court may mark the beginning of the end of the "culture of impunity," but the effectiveness of these new bodies will depend on the willingness and capacity of member states to enforce their judgments. What the UN embrace of prevention seems to be offering, at best, is half a loaf: a "good cop, bad cop" division of labor in which it plays the softie and someone else—usually the United States and a few partners—is left to act as the heavy, the enforcer. This may be an eminently practical formula, given the politics of the day, but it could not be further from the conception behind the UN Charter. The Charter sought to unite the policy tools of Chapters VI and VII within a well-defined framework of international law. A soft prevention-only approach is an invitation to global and regional powers to go outside the mechanisms provided by the Charter in order to enforce their own selective interpretation of international norms when and where they choose.

Global Norms, National Actors

Like the UN Charter, the treaties that make up the substance of international humanitarian law depend largely on national action for their implementation. They, too, lack reliable and effective means for enforcing their provisions or for monitoring or assessing their implementation. They define principles that purport to be universal, indivisible, and timeless yet are to be carried out through ad hoc mechanisms that possess none of these attributes. On the one hand, as the Secretary-General has asserted, in cases of crimes against humanity, "the Security Council has a moral duty to act on behalf of the international community."[26] On the other hand, the enforcement of these moral absolutes is left, paradoxically, to the Council, with its highly political and inherently cautious decisionmaking process that seeks to avoid controversy and to build consensus. National governments, as well, are far more comfortable with the incremental and particular than with the bold and universal.

Humanitarian conventions either lack enforcement provisions or, like multilateral arms control and disarmament agreements, refer disputes back to the UN, and hence to the political dynamics of the Security Council. These, in turn, are under enormous strain from several directions given the increasingly apparent fissures among the five permanent members of the Security Council, the festering crisis in U.S.-UN relations, the chronic disputes noted above over the equity of both the representation and voting arrangements in the Council, the struggles between the Council and the General Assembly over authority and legitimacy, and the organization's limited structural, material, intellectual, and financial capacities for planning, monitoring, and implementing either economic or military enforcement measures in the first place. The Secretary-General is right to assert that "in human rights, the United Nations must have the courage to recognize that just as there are common aims, there are common enemies."[27] But the unity that was to underpin his organization is looking rather frayed these days, especially on questions of intervention. Kosovo brutally illustrated the stark choice between following the rules of the Charter and forcefully upholding international humanitarian norms. Internationalists cannot have it both ways.

The UN's troubles reflect the core dilemma of trying to codify universal moral standards and then to enforce them collectively, objectively, and fairly in the nation-state era, when national governments, not international organizations, have a virtual monopoly on the tools to do the job. States vote in the Security Council whether enforcement is needed, and they then decide in their national capitals whether to provide material support for the effort. Too often, when the enforcement of a collective norm is seen as everyone's responsibility, it turns out to be no one's responsibility in the end. More often than not, no one is held accountable for breakdowns in humanitarian standards or the failure of international organizations to impose effective remedies. As is wholly appropriate at a time when even the UN proclaims the virtues of democratic governance at every opportunity, national leaders remain responsible to the citizens and political forces within their countries—including for the costs and risks of international operations—much more than to international agreements or to a vague concept of international community. Domestic politics, therefore, matter a great deal. In humanitarian affairs, moreover, nonstate actors are often big players, whether as perpetrators of abuses, sources of relief, or mediators of differences. They may not have seats at the UN or be parties to the relevant treaties, but the extent of their cooperation on the ground usually determines whether an intervention succeeds or fails.

Those devoted to transnational humanitarian principles may be tempted to see national interests as narrow and selfish barriers to be overcome. But to deny or denigrate the place of national interest in international decisionmaking would be shortsighted and foolhardy. When the results of international decisionmaking processes and the resources available to carry them out are ultimately determined on a national or even subnational basis, humanitarian needs will not be served unless they are interpreted in capitals as questions of national interest and of domestic political concern. The Secretary-General has recognized this:

> Of course, the traditional pursuit of national interest is a permanent feature of international relations and of the life and work of the Security Council. But as the world has changed in profound ways since the end of the cold war, I believe our conceptions of national interest have failed to follow suit.[28]

Completing this transition and translating global norms into national priorities, of course, has not proven to be a simple or straightforward matter.

Whatever their humanitarian consequences, conflicts have political, economic, and social roots. Their political shadings will encourage some countries to support and others to oppose international intervention. Global interests, too often portrayed as above politics, tend to be seen as abstract, vague, and distracting—someone else's problem—while the costs and responsibilities of putting one's own forces at risk in hostile and uncertain situations—typically those in which enforcement is required—loom all too immediate and real. Unless voters demand that something forceful be done, political leaders are unlikely to perceive that the potential benefits of intervention in such cases outweigh the risks. Otherwise, member state support will normally remain at the level of concerned rhetoric, paper resolutions, and humanitarian band-aids. Though these are not necessarily dilemmas without solutions, their answers would appear to lie in good old-fashioned national political processes, in which the media and NGOs can play a substantial role. Statements of global concern and moral outrage, further norm creation, and appeals to intergovernmental organizations have their place, but it is in support of, not as a replacement for, political action on the national level.

If there is consensus on anything at the UN these days, it is that U.S. reluctance is the biggest barrier to effective UN peace operations and that any political action should begin in Washington. It is widely accepted that when it comes to major international enforcement action, the United States has indeed become "the indispensable nation" (though in East Timor it was a local power, Australia, that got the job done, and in Sierra Leone the May 2000 intervention by the former colonial power, the United Kingdom, may have tipped the balance). The global economic and financial reach of the United States makes it hard to conceive of most forms of trade or financial sanctions, not to mention travel bans or arms embargoes, working effectively without its full cooperation. Though its penchant for imposing sanctions unilaterally has produced results that are at best mixed, its leadership in promoting, monitoring, and implementing multilateral sanctions has often helped to give them real teeth. In terms of military technology and the capacity to protect and maintain forces in distant theaters, the superiority of U.S. capabilities is even more pronounced, and the margin appears to be expanding. Many countries have more peacekeeping experience than the United States, but none has engaged in so many combat operations, particularly in operations so far from home and sustained over such prolonged periods. It is understandable that U.S. defense planners worry about overextension, for even if other states were to provide the bulk of the initial ground troops in a particular enforcement action, U.S. airlift, sealift, logistical support, intelligence, and airpower might well be needed to help overcome stubborn or escalating resistance.

In the Security Council, the United States possesses not only formal veto power but also enormous influence in the informal consultations that determine the issues and texts on which the Council does or does not vote. Enforcement action will not be authorized by the Council without its consent. During the early 1990s, buoyed by the success of Desert Storm, the United States tended to be among the most bullish member states in terms of support for a more proactive and assertive international effort to enforce international norms. Following the October 1993 debacle in Mogadishu and the subsequent Republican revolt in Congress against assertive multilateralism, however, the United States became decidedly bearish on having the UN take on additional enforcement tasks and on giving it further capacities to prepare or undertake such missions.[29] In the early days of the Rwandan genocide, for example, the United States was particularly outspoken about the risks of intervention. The resulting horrors led to some moderation in congressional attitudes, however, and the United States has gone along with Security Council decisions to deploy forces in Sierra Leone, East Timor, and the Democratic Republic of the Congo, as long as U.S. ground forces were not involved and other countries took the lead. At the same time, the United States has been the prime advocate for maintaining sanctions in cases such as Iraq, Serbia, and Libya, where it has deemed its interests to be at stake. Closer to home, the United States (with Canada) led the charge for a Chapter VII resolution to intervene in Haiti, partly on humanitarian grounds.[30] In Kosovo, the United States would have preferred Council authorization for an enforcement action, but it was equally determined to keep military implementation in NATO rather than UN hands.

The U.S. allergy to UN enforcement action has been most painfully evident over the course of the Clinton administration. This has depended in part on the dynamics of Washington politics, including excessive partisanship and a deterioration of congressional-executive relations; it has also been affected by the end of the cold war, marked by declining fears that local conflicts would escalate, the lack of a global strategy, and a heavy focus on domestic issues. Yet the roots of U.S. ambivalence run very deep.[31] In the century since the first Hague Peace Conference, no president has accepted the notion that an international commander should exercise command authority over U.S. forces or, with the exception of a brief flirtation at the end of World War II, that international bodies should have a significant standing force at their disposal. Certainly, the United States has sought the blessing of the UN for military enforcement action from time to time, but with implementation to remain outside of UN channels or oversight. On the other hand, the United States, like the Secretary-General, has recognized the logic of having multilateral economic sanctions carried out through the UN, since they require the cooperation of many countries.

U.S. skepticism about the UN is certainly an obstacle to the development of that organization's full potential for enforcing humanitarian norms, but are U.S. policies and attitudes really so far out of step with those of other countries? Public opinion data, though neither comprehensive nor entirely reliable, suggest that Americans are no less sympathetic than others to the UN or to the plight of civilian victims of conflict.[32] Though the U.S. government might have less confidence in multilateral mechanisms than some other member states, it is not clear that it is uniformly or even generally less willing to act to enforce international norms in such cases. It took the lead both going into and retreating from Somalia, where it had no strategic interests. The United States might have been slow to put forces on the ground in the former Yugoslavia, even as it advocated tougher enforcement measures in the Security Council. Yet it is arguable whether the Europeans or Americans had a stronger (less weak?) track record on enforcement in the Balkans. Should the U.S. position flip-flop once again on the desirability of building a more reliable enforcement regime, would other member states flock to the cause? There is reason for doubt. Some governments may well be engaged in free-riding, letting their constituencies know how much they would like to act if only the recalcitrant United States would let them.

None of the other permanent members appears poised to pick up the torch on enforcement. As noted above, China remains adamant about nonintervention in domestic affairs and opposed to any expansion of UN enforcement capabilities.[33] Whereas most U.S. objections are based on pragmatic considerations—doubts about whether UN efforts will work—Chinese concerns are couched in terms of fundamental principle. Its distaste for enforcement action was only reinforced by the apparently accidental U.S. bombing of the Chinese Embassy in Belgrade in 1999. Beijing, moreover, is understandably sensitive about human rights and humanitarian considerations as a basis for policy given its domestic vulnerabilities in this regard. Focused on urgent domestic economic, social, and political problems, Chinese leaders show relatively little interest in distant events. While reluctant to block the will of the rest of the Council members—except on some issues involving countries that have relations with Taiwan, again showing its local focus—China usually works to water down Council resolutions with enforcement implications. Its guiding word appears to be caution.

Russia has also become decidedly less supportive of humanitarian intervention over the period 1999–2000 in light of widespread condemnation in the West of its brutal tactics in Chechnya. Eager to remain a player despite its receding capacities, Russia had previously sought to assert an activist role for the Security Council, a place where it still benefits from its former status as a world power. In theory, Moscow has long favored giving life to the Military Staff Committee and to the concept of an international military force. In practice, Russia would have liked to see less enforcement and more diplomacy in Iraq and Serbia, places where it has strong national interests. Since the days of the Bretton Woods preparatory meetings, Moscow has also advocated a strict reading of the Charter, particularly concerning the prerogatives of the Security Council and its five permanent members. In seeking to cling to its former status in the international hierarchy while focusing on enormous domestic challenges, including acute security problems, Russia is unlikely to oppose a widely held position in the Council in favor of enforcement measures in places, such as East Timor, where its strategic interests would not be compromised. By the same token, it does not place much of a priority on enforcing humanitarian norms outside of its immediate neighborhood, a task that would in any case have to be left to others.

Among the permanent members of the Security Council, it would probably fall to Britain and France to generate any movement in the direction of a more robust UN enforcement capacity. Acutely aware of the occasional mutterings around the UN community about whether their privileged positions in the Council are not due more to history than to current strategic realities, London and Paris have remained quite active in UN peacekeeping and conflict resolution efforts. At several points when the United States hesitated, they were quick to assert the need for international action to address humanitarian emergencies, as Britain did in response to crises in East Timor and Sierra Leone. France was the only power eventually willing to put its forces on the ground in Rwanda, though many observers saw strategic interests, rather than humanitarian concerns, behind its move and questioned whether it was not on the wrong side from the beginning.[34] Both countries have been cautious about enhancing the UN's enforcement capabilities, and neither can credibly claim that its military has global reach. Though citizens, NGOs, and officials in France and Britain did seem responsive to humanitarian appeals in the succession of crises in the former Yugoslavia, their willingness and ability to respond forcefully, despite the proximity of the crisis, were rather limited given the modest size of their military capabilities. It remains to be seen whether an effective European rapid-response force can be either assembled or employed effectively in such contingencies.

Japan has moved steadily to build its military strength in recent years, but its orientation remains decidedly local and defensive. Despite its prolonged recession, Japan remains an important economic power globally and, especially, regionally, whose active participation in sanctions regimes is often essential. While Japan is less squeamish about UN enforcement matters than it used to be, it is unlikely, in part for historical reasons, either to exercise a leadership position or to participate militarily in such measures. On East Timor, Tokyo adopted a decidedly low-key stance, letting others take the lead not only on the ground but rhetorically as well. Germany has been in a somewhat similar position, though its forces participated alongside those of its allies in the air enforcement campaign in Kosovo and on the ground in the subsequent peacekeeping operation. Denied permanent seats in the Security Council, Germany and Japan might well offer important material as well as financial support to international enforcement efforts, but neither should be expected to take the lead in establishing a new enforcement regime.

This leaves the so-called middle powers: countries whose humanitarian concerns outstrip their physical capacities to compel the parties to conflicts far from their borders to respect international norms in their treatment of civilian populations. These countries have often served as catalysts, in the short term drawing worldwide attention to abuses and in the long term helping to develop international norms and institutions. Countries considered medium powers in global terms may be seen as major powers in a regional context: Nigeria served as the primary enforcer in Liberia and Sierra Leone, as did Australia in East Timor. These cases demonstrate that so-called middle powers can play important roles on the ground—sometimes as part of regional coalitions or under the banner of regional or subregional organizations—if the protagonists in the conflict are not too distant, large, or well connected. Generally, however, middle powers are known for their participation less in enforcement actions than in peacekeeping operations, where their forces have often served as the backbone of UN missions. The disillusioning experiences of the Belgian and Bangladeshi peacekeepers in Kigali and of the Dutch soldiers at Srebrenica, however, underline the risks and costs of putting the troops of smaller countries in harm's way without reliable and robust military support from others.[35]

Ambiguity, Uncertainty, and Risk

There is nothing ambiguous about the scale and depth of civilian suffering during warfare, but the conflicts themselves, especially the ill-defined ones of recent years, are often propelled by circumstances and motivations that are both ambiguous and opaque. Part intrastate and part interstate, from a distance these conflicts may seem to rage without reason, bounds, or principles. For the parties, matters of life and death are at stake. For decisionmakers in distant capitals, however, it may be hard to identify the combatants, much less what they stand for or hope to achieve. Victims abound, but who are the "good guys" and the "bad guys"; which side should be aided, and which opposed? There are few heroes in Sierra Leone, Somalia, Liberia, Angola, Sudan, Afghanistan, or the former Yugoslavia. Relieving suffering and enforcing justice are not the same thing, so is the purpose of a humanitarian intervention simply to stop the fighting or to create the conditions for a durable and just peace?

Ambiguities breed ambivalence, and this subject is replete with both. Perhaps NGOs and relief organizations can make the distinction between the fact and the cause of suffering, but governments, especially powerful ones, usually cannot. Intervention in someone else's war, especially through enforcement measures, means becoming enmeshed—and becoming a factor—in the politics, tactics, and strategies of that conflict. From the perspective of the combatants, enforcement is not a neutral or impartial act, any more than the provision of humanitarian aid is apolitical. Likewise, it is difficult for leaders of democratic states to persuade their parliaments and their constituencies that economic sanctions or military actions are to be taken in some murky, distant, and dangerous conflict in which their country has neither friends nor foes. How are they to employ open-ended, egalitarian humanitarian standards in deciding when to intervene without, in essence, accepting a commitment?

Perversely, it appears that those conflicts with the highest losses to civilian populations are often those that drag on the longest and that produce the most ambiguous and indecisive outcomes. If one side has a decisive military advantage, it can win on the battlefield and then proceed to consolidate its victory in the adversary's unresisting population centers. But when fighting surges back and forth for years over large swaths of territory, as in Afghanistan, Sudan, or Angola; when civil conflict divides cities, towns, and villages, as in the former Yugoslavia; or where guerrilla forces employ terror as a weapon in prolonged strife, as in Sierra Leone and Algeria, then the outcomes tend to be Pyrrhic and inconclusive. In such cases, the international community may end up merely stemming the violence in the short term, rather than resolving the underlying sources of discontent in the long term.[36] In such cases, it is understandable that critics from the major powers question the expenditure of resources and lives for such muddled and indeterminate results.

It is a grisly irony that the very ruthlessness of those committing humanitarian atrocities, including the wave of assaults on aid workers from the UN and voluntary organizations in recent years, may discourage other countries from intervening. One of the more disturbing asymmetries in such operations has been the contrast between the motivations and norms that guide the perpetrators of abuse and those of the forces intervening to protect innocent civilians and to enforce international norms. The perpetrators, driven by hatred, resentment, fear, and avarice, are usually both determined and duplicitous. Deploying children as soldiers and targeting civilians, they do not play by the same set of rules as the international forces, and they usually have a deeper and more personal stake in the outcome of the conflict. Bearing in mind the Mogadishu effect, local forces may be tempted to commit atrocities against the intervening forces in the expectation that the consequent publicity back home will spark calls to "bring the boys home," as happened after the calculated slaughter of the Belgian peacekeepers at the start of the genocide in Rwanda. It is telling, in this regard, that it was after its 1999 democratic elections that Nigeria decided to pull its troops out of atrocity-plagued Sierra Leone. For distant countries motivated by goodwill rather than national interest, the very intensity of the horrors being committed makes intervention in the heat of the violence an unattractive proposition. For military planners, trained to employ worst-case reasoning, the downside risks will be magnified by qualitative factors, even if the overall numbers and relative military capacities look favorable to the intervenors. In the end, a politically relevant calculation in such cases must take into account highly subjective estimates of commitment and will, as well as of military and economic power.

Planning for military enforcement—a term not traditionally employed in professional military doctrine—can be a particularly complex and uncertain enterprise. As indicated earlier, military enforcement action almost always involves taking sides, implicitly if not explicitly. If enforcement is required, then at least one party to the conflict presumably opposes what the international force is trying to achieve. Otherwise, a peacekeeping force could do the job. Military commanders must assume that there will be resistance, perhaps from unexpected quarters, and prepare accordingly. It is hard, however, to know how much is enough. In 1992, media and NGO observers found the by-the-book U.S. marine landing on the beaches of Mogadishu to be comical; less than a year later, following the ill-fated Ranger strike to try to capture Mohammad Aideed, there was much second-guessing in Washington and media circles about why the Clinton administration had not supplied the appropriate armored vehicles and sufficient firepower to get the job done right. The dilemma, in cases such as this, is that to attempt to enforce humanitarian norms can be a lot like going to war, yet without the wholehearted national commitment that would normally go with it. Most of these missions call for something more than a robust peacekeeping force, but less than that demanded by a campaign to repulse an invasion, as in Kuwait and Korea.

These uncertainties pose more than doctrinal confusions, for they stir public and official doubts about what is expected and what risks are entailed. There is always some danger of escalation, as in Freetown, Srebrenica, Kigali, and Mogadishu, when the depth of the international commitment is deliberately tested. Such a challenge would pose less of an obstacle for an all-out operation undertaken by a single country or alliance than for a limited mission carried out by a multilateral organization, whose decisions involve many voices and disparate levels of commitment. Even NATO unity and command procedures have been sorely tested in Bosnia-Herzegovina and Kosovo. Past experience in places like Somalia suggests that when UN operations are put to the test, some states may choose to withdraw their contingents, others to hunker down or to send reinforcements and greater firepower. Such circumstances are bound to raise doubts among inherently cautious military planners in national capitals. In general, missions to enforce international humanitarian norms are likely to require considerable flexibility as midcourse adjustments are needed to meet changing circumstances. Signaling intentions can be very important. The Security Council and other multilateral decisionmaking bodies, however, have not been known for their agility in adapting mandates to changing circumstances in a timely and flexible manner. In the case of

Bosnia-Herzegovina, the Council went to the other extreme, passing such a bewildering array of resolutions under Chapters VI and VII that it was hard to distinguish either its real intentions or the rules of engagement under which the force on the ground was to operate.

Humanitarian emergencies, moreover, come in all shapes and sizes. They need to be addressed and understood on a case-by-case basis, rather than trying to develop and impose a generic model across the board, since in this field one size certainly does not fit all. Those who suggest that a single small force of UN volunteers could respond effectively and credibly to such an array and number of circumstances, terrain, challenges, and specialized tasks throughout the world are decidedly optimistic. Moreover, early warning, reliable intelligence, and strong analytical and assessment capabilities—including an intimate knowledge of local history, customs, and languages—are essential both for permitting (though not, of course, guaranteeing) preventive or early action and for conducting an effective operation under changing conditions. Individual member states might have these capabilities, but, once again, they are not areas of comparative advantage for the UN. The UN's own lessons-learned exercises are replete with references to failure in these areas, often abetted by false expectations and gross miscalculations on the part of influential member states.

Future Prospects

The arguments advanced above strongly suggest that the roots of ambivalence run both deep and wide. Ambivalence is not just an American problem, or only a contemporary phenomenon. Nor is it always counterproductive, for prudence is a virtue when it discourages knee-jerk responses before the local dynamics of a conflict are fully understood or a durable political foundation for a mission can be developed. Enforcement measures are strong medicine that should not be prescribed too often or too quickly. Such measures should be invoked when (1) the violations are particularly abhorrent and dangerous; (2) a sensible plan has been drawn up for addressing them; (3) the international will is sufficiently strong and united to ensure that the required steps will be implemented fully, faithfully, and energetically; and (4) the chances of ultimate success are reasonably good. Nothing breeds ambivalence more quickly than failure, whether it be a failure of understanding or of will.

The persistence of ambivalence in most national capitals cautions against sweeping conclusions and bold promises; those who trumpet the arrival of a new era of humanitarian intervention are premature. There is no doubt that in a media age, with direct strategic threats to the national security of the major powers fading, humanitarian and human rights concerns have assumed a higher place in the public consciousness and on official agendas. While a step in the right direction, however, higher visibility will not make the political and operational dilemmas disappear, or make effective answers any less elusive. The costs and risks inherent in undertaking enforcement measures to deal with these threats to global values and human dignity will still be substantial. But as public attentiveness to these questions grows, so too will the costs of perpetuating the current disjunction between high intentions and weak resolve. Over time, this gap could threaten to undermine confidence not only in international law and organization but also in national leaders who appear more comfortable with words than deeds. The only way to escape this quandary is to strive to build domestic coalitions broad and stable enough to support follow-up action with teeth and staying power.

It would be unfair to suggest that the world has simply stood by as the humanitarian disasters of the 1990s have unfolded. As noted at the start of this chapter, the track record of the past decade, for all of its inadequacies, does not look so bad when compared with previous years. There have been impressive bursts of intellectual creativity, diplomatic energy, and humanitarian norm-building. But in terms of enforcement, it has been a decade of occasional and highly selective experiments, usually invoked only after the worst violations have occurred. There has been an overreliance on hastily concocted and poorly monitored economic sanctions, in the process giving this potentially useful tool a bad name. The use of military options, pursued repeatedly in recent years, has seen a disturbing trend either to have the Security Council delegate authority to whoever is willing to shoulder the costs and bear the risks or to sidestep the UN entirely. This approach has permitted flexibility and has circumvented member-state concerns about UN command structures, but it has had a downside as well. "Ad hockery" does little to reinforce, and may actually undermine, the authority of international law and organization. Since disinterested parties tend to stay home, dependence on those willing to step forward often means letting the most interested parties carry out enforcement tasks. In humanitarian terms, this no doubt beats doing nothing in the face of massive violations, but the practice of effectively excluding more objective voices hardly establishes the most promising model or precedent for meeting future challenges.

Reliance on such stopgap arrangements in the short term, moreover, should not be allowed to stall or divert efforts to develop the political support and the practical plans that are essential to fashioning a reliable multilateral enforcement capacity over the long term. Civil society, working primarily in national capitals, should play a central part in both efforts. For until substantial progress is made in building these twin pillars, the humanitarian enterprise will be caught in a self-defeating cycle. The very weakness of multilateral machinery contributes to doubts about the practicality of multilateral options, feeding the very ambivalence that prevents developing its antidote. In the meantime, each picture and headline reporting another spasm of violence and abuse against civilians should remind us of the terrible human costs of our failure to come to grips with these core dilemmas and contradictions.

Notes

1. Statement by the Secretary-General to the General Assembly, Sept. 20, 1999, UN Doc. SG/SM/7136-GA/9596 (1999).

2. It is striking that when the Secretary-General released his sweeping report to the Millennium Assembly little more than half a year later, it contained only a few brief paragraphs on "the dilemma of intervention," with no specific recommendations or conclusions. He merely noted that "we confront a real dilemma. Few would disagree that both the defense of humanity and the defense of sovereignty are principles that must be supported. Alas, that does not tell us which principle should prevail when they are in conflict": Millennium Report of the Secretary-General, "We, the Peoples": The Role of the United Nations in the 21st Century, UN Doc. A/54/2000 (2000), pp. 47–48.

3. Michael J. Glennon, "The New Interventionism: The Search for a Just International Law," *Foreign Affairs* 78, 3 (May/June 1999), pp. 2–7. For commentaries on Professor Glennon's thesis, see Thomas M. Franck, "Break It, Don't Fake It," and Edward C. Luck, "A Road to Nowhere," *Foreign Affairs* 78, 4 (July/Aug. 1999), pp. 116–119. For a critique of the legal basis for the new doctrine, see Richard B. Bilder, "Kosovo and the 'New Interventionism': Promise or Peril?" *Journal of Transnational Law & Policy* 9 (1999), pp. 153–182.

4. Tony Blair, "A New Generation Draws the Line," *Newsweek*, Apr. 19, 1999.

5. William Jefferson Clinton, "A Just and Necessary War," *New York Times*, May 23, 1999.

6. Statement by the President on East Timor, Sept. 9, 1999, the White House, Office of the Press Secretary.

7. See Security Council resolution 1264 (1999).

8. UN sources estimate that at least three-quarters of the casualties of recent conflicts have been civilians, though the precise numbers are not known: Secretary-General Kofi A. Annan, "Reflections on Intervention," statement made at Ditchley Park, United Kingdom, June 26, 1998, in *The Question of Intervention* (New York: UN Department of Public Information, 1999), pp. 3–16.

9. On the other hand, Tony Blair argued that the NATO success in Kosovo would have a positive effect on Iraq: "Imagine how Saddam will react to this victory; imagine the reactions of other dictators who are tempted to resolve their political problems by terrorizing their own people or attacking their neighbors. They will now know that when we say we will act, we are serious": Tony Blair, "A New Moral Crusade," *Newsweek*, June 14, 1999.

10. One of the benchmarks, or conditions, in the 1999 Helms-Biden Bill (PL106-113, Appendix G, Sec. 921) is that U.S. arrears to the UN will not be repaid if *any* of the 188 member states signs an Article 43 agreement with the UN.

11. For recommendations in this regard, see International Task Force on the Enforcement of UN Security Council Resolutions, Final Report, *Words to Deeds: Strengthening the UN's Enforcement Capabilities* (New York: United Nations Association of the USA, 1997).

12. Report of the Secretary-General, Renewing the United Nations: A Programme for Reform, UN Doc. A/51/950 (1997), p. 36.

13. Millennium Report of the Secretary-General, p. 49.

14. For a discussion of the dynamics of the growing asymmetries between U.S. perceptions of exceptionalism and the prevailing UN emphasis on universalism and "democratization," see Edward C. Luck, *Mixed Messages: American Politics and International Organization, 1919–1999* (Washington, DC: Brookings Institution Press, 1999), pp. 15–40, 280–306.

15. Report of the Secretary-General, Renewing the United Nations, p. 36.

16. For the decision adopted at the Assembly of Heads of State and Government of the Organization of African Unity, held in Ouagadougou, Burkina Faso, June 8–10, 1998, see Gus Constantine, "UN Travel Ban on Libya Collapsing; Egypt's Mubarak Latest African Dignitary to Visit Gadhafi," *Washington Times*, July 10, 1998; and Office of the Spokesman, U.S. Department of State, "Rubin Statement: OAU Resolution on Libya," June 16, 1998.

17. Millennium Report of the Secretary-General, p. 50.

18. Switzerland, a nonmember state, has led the effort to perfect targeted financial sanctions, while Germany has sponsored a series of studies of arms embargoes and travel bans.

19. Annan, "Reflections on Intervention," pp. 8–9.

20. Report of the Secretary-General to the Security Council on the Protection of Civilians in Armed Conflict, UN Doc. S/1999/957 (1999), p. 24.

21. For the most prominent and comprehensive set of recent studies on prevention strategies, see the Final Report of the Carnegie Commission on Preventing Deadly Conflict, *Preventing Deadly Conflict* (New York: Carnegie Corporation of New York, 1997).

22. Report of the Secretary-General on the Work of the Organization, UN Doc. A/54/1 (1999), p. 3.

23. Millennium Report of the Secretary-General, p. 44.

24. Statement by the President of the Security Council, UN Doc. S/PRST/ 1999/34, Nov. 30, 1999.

25. Press Release, "Effective Deterrent Action Is the Key to Conflict Prevention, Secretary-General Tells Security Council," Nov. 29, 1999, UN Doc. SG/SM/7238-SC/6760 (1999).

26. Millennium Report of the Secretary-General, p. 48.

27. "Standing Up for Human Rights," Address by the UN Secretary-General to the United Nations Commission on Human Rights, Geneva, Apr. 7, 1999.

28. Statement by the Secretary-General to the General Assembly, Sept. 20, 1999, UN Doc. SG/SM/7136-GA/9596 (1999).

29. There is some evidence, however, that the Clinton administration's retreat from assertive multilateralism actually began before the Mogadishu incident: see Edward C. Luck, "American Politics and International Organization: Lessons from the 1990s," in Rosemary Foot, Neil MacFarlane, and Michael Mastanduno (eds.), *The U.S. and Multilateral Organizations* (forthcoming). See also Ivo H. Daalder, "Knowing When to Say No: The Development of U.S. Policy for Peacekeeping," in William J. Durch (ed.), *UN Peacekeeping, American Politics and the Uncivil Wars of the 1990s* (New York: St. Martin's Press, 1996); and Michael G. MacKinnon, *The Evolution of U.S. Peacekeeping Under Clinton* (London: Frank Cass, 2000).

30. For the best account of this case, see David Malone, *Decision-Making in the UN Security Council: The Case of Haiti, 1990–1997* (Oxford: Clarendon Press, 1998).

31. These roots are chronicled in Luck, *Mixed Messages*. By spring 2000, there had been a modest thaw in U.S.-UN relations, marked by an exchange of visits between the UN Security Council and the Senate Foreign Relations Committee, led by Senator Jesse Helms. None of the core differences has been resolved, however, and the

honeymoon period could well be short-lived. See Barbara Crossette, "Helms, in Visit to UN, Offers Harsh Message," *New York Times*, Jan. 21, 2000; Barbara Crossette and Eric Schmitt, "UN Ambassadors in Helms Land: Smiles On, Gloves Off," *New York Times*, Mar. 31, 2000; Edward C. Luck, testimony, "Field Hearing on Implementation of United Nations Reform," Senate Foreign Relations Committee, New York, Jan. 21, 2000 (Washington, DC: U.S. Government Printing Office, 2000).

32. See Gallup International Millennium Survey (London: Gallup International Association, 2000); Luck, *Mixed Messages*, pp. 34–40.

33. Statement to the General Assembly by Chinese Ambassador to the UN Qin Huasun, Oct. 6, 1999, UN Doc. GA/9627 (1999).

34. See Philip Gourevitch, *We Wish to Inform You That Tomorrow We Will Be Killed with Our Families: Stories from Rwanda* (New York: Farrar, Straus & Giroux, 1998).

35. See the Report of the Secretary-General pursuant to GA Res. 53/55: The Fall of Srebrenica, UN Doc. A/54/549 (1999); Report of the Independent Inquiry into the Actions of the United Nations During the 1994 Genocide in Rwanda, UN Doc. S/1999/1257 (1999).

36. See, e.g., Richard K. Betts, "The Delusion of Impartial Intervention," *Foreign Affairs* 73, 6 (Nov./Dec. 1994), pp. 20–33; and Edward N. Luttwak, "Give War a Chance," *Foreign Affairs* 78, 4 (July/Aug. 1999), pp. 36–44.

PART 4

Reevaluating Protection

11

The End of Innocence: Humanitarian Protection in the Twenty-First Century

Claude Bruderlein

Recent events in Sierra Leone, Chechnya, East Timor, and Kosovo have shown once again the limited ability of the international community to respond adequately to major humanitarian crises. Despite the renewed commitment of states to abide by the rules of international humanitarian law (IHL), entire populations in Europe, Africa, and Central Asia have been displaced over recent years as a consequence of armed conflicts, or harassed and subjected to extreme forms of violence on political, religious, ethnic, and racial grounds. The international community remains mostly powerless in the face of these human tragedies. On those occasions where the international community has played a role, its actions have been limited, selective, and subject to utilitarian calculations. This has become all the more evident in recent military interventions for the protection of civilians.

The legal and moral basis for military action in these circumstances calls for a certain level of consistency and foresight that has often been missing, causing the legitimacy of international institutions engaged in this exercise to be questioned. This lack of legitimacy results in a poor image for international action that leads to further limiting of financial and military support.

The events of the past few years in particular press us to engage in a substantial review of the international community's approach toward humanitarian crises. In many ways, the traditional assumption of the primary role of states in the protection of civilians in IHL and human rights conventions has hampered our ability to conceive new strategies to enhance the protection of civilians in situations of armed conflict. The increasing role of nonstate actors, including armed groups and large corporations, must be recognized in our protection strategies. International organizations and states have failed to understand this critical development, limiting their capacity to act effectively for the protection of civilians. I argue in this chapter for a critical review of our efforts as a first step toward the expansion of our imagination on new strategic approaches to humanitarian protection. I go on to explore the various strategies developed by humanitarian organizations to address contemporary threats to civilian populations in times of conflict. I first examine the traditional concept of humanitarian protection, its origins and limitations, in light of the changing nature of armed conflicts and the increasing role of nonstate actors. I then proceed to analyze the various strategies adopted in response to the recent report of the UN Secretary-General to the Security Council on the protection of civilians in armed conflict.[1]

The Role of Nonstate Actors

The development of IHL and human rights is deeply rooted in the historical and political environment of the twentieth century and the paradigm of the nation-state. Traditional protection strategies under IHL and human rights conventions have focused primarily on the role of state actors involved in a given conflict. Accordingly, states are the principal agents under such instruments as the Geneva Conventions, charged with ensuring that military operations are restricted to military targets and that populations in need receive adequate relief assistance and protection.

The dynamic of post–cold war conflicts has departed significantly from this paradigm. Protracted and complex emergencies, such as those in Somalia, Zaire/DRC, Angola, Burundi, Sudan, Sierra Leone, and Afghanistan, have challenged the historical foundations of IHL. These new conflicts often surface against the background of collapsed states and involve a number of nonstate actors over which state institutions have little or no control. Such nonstate actors, which range from armed groups and private militias to corporations and nongovernmental organizations (NGOs), may be the only groups able to protect civilians in such circumstances.

The most dramatic and prevalent threats to civilians now arise in internal armed conflict. Of the twenty-five armed conflicts that took place in 1998, twenty-three were internal in character, engaging one or more nonstate actors.[2] A common feature of internal armed conflicts is the widespread violation of IHL and human rights by these nonstate armed groups, in particular by rebel movements and private militias. Threats to civilians also increase with the proliferation of weapons, especially small arms and land mines, and as a result of the organized crime and random violence that occur in these chaotic conditions. The presence of armed groups among civilians plays a particular role in blurring the dividing line between combatants and noncombatants, a crucial distinction in IHL. Corporate interests in natural resources such as diamonds in Angola and Sierra Leone, or illegal trafficking in drugs or timber in Colombia and Myanmar, also play an increasing role in sustaining armed conflicts and thereby contribute to the deterioration of the humanitarian situation. In this context, understanding and promoting the responsibilities of nonstate actors toward civilians have become a crucial element in future protection strategies.[3]

IHL and human rights law offer only limited opportunities to develop new strategies regarding these situations. International law in this area pays little attention to the role of nonstate actors, with the notable but limited exception of the International Committee of the Red Cross (ICRC).[4] The role and responsibility of nonstate actors in the protection of civilians under international law depend largely on the consent and action of states. The current discrepancy between the role of state and nonstate actors in international law illustrates the extent to which political considerations have hampered the development of effective strategies to protect civilians in armed conflict. This exclusion of nonstate actors is unlikely to change under the present circumstances. Nonstate armed groups are repeatedly barred from participating in international conferences on the protection of civilians, and contact with such groups is subject to intense political pressure from many sides. The accountability of private corporations for their conduct in conflict areas remains unclear due to a lack of relevant legal standards and state opposition to the investigation of the role of corporations in war situations.

A recent illustration of the reluctance of states to recognize the role of nonstate armed groups in the implementation of international standards is provided by the Rome Conference of July 1998 on the establishment of the International Criminal Court. While hundreds of NGOs were represented, several in an official capacity, among more than 130 state delegations, no efforts were made to engage armed groups in this process. The statute adopted at the Rome Conference offers very few provisions for engaging armed groups, imposing obligations only on states and individuals. In particular, it confers no legal authority on nonstate actors in the prosecution of war crimes, despite the fact that the leadership of these armed groups may be the only bodies with real control over nonstate combatants. The practical significance of these legal developments may therefore be minimal in situations where governments have lost their capacity to bring nonstate actors to trial or have relinquished their authority to prosecute war criminals as part of a peace process by granting an amnesty—as in Sierra Leone regarding the RUF combatants. The recent developments in Sierra Leone prove that an armed group that has been isolated for many years and has been held unaccountable for its ruthless behavior cannot easily be co-opted into a political process. Yet, from a practical perspective, armed groups remain key actors for protection strategies in four areas: as de facto governments within the territory under their control, as military entities active in combat, as authorities potentially responsible for the protection of humanitarian operations, and as political entities that may eventually be party to a peace settlement.

A related area concerns the role of corporations. Efforts to engage the responsibility of corporations in the protection of civilians are still in their infancy. Recent initiatives by the UN Security Council Sanctions Committee to engage the responsibility of De Beers in the trade of diamonds with UNITA have shown the potential influence of the Council on multinational corporations.[5] Similarly, the California court trial of the oil company Unocal for violations of the Slavery Convention of 1927 in Myanmar shows the potential leverage that can be exerted against corporate actors by national courts.[6] Their economic activities in conflict areas may make corporate actors key elements of new protection strategies—perhaps more important than armed groups, or even states. While armed groups tend to remain obscure and unreliable actors acting outside any legal frameworks, and state representatives benefit from diplomatic immunity, private corporations remain vulnerable to political and legal pressures ranging from consumer boycotts to lawsuits.

Protecting the Innocent

International efforts to enhance humanitarian protection have traditionally focused on stressing the nonmilitary character of civilian persons and infrastructures, which should therefore be spared from attack. Civilian populations and infrastructure are nevertheless increasingly targeted by warring parties—state and nonstate alike—and have acquired, in the view of many combatants, strategic significance in the conduct of hostilities. Civilians are targeted as cover for rebel operations or as the objects of reprisal attacks; they are terrorized and displaced to exert pressure on an opposing force. Civilians are also the victims of chaotic brutality inflicted by uncontrolled combatants taking advantage of the anarchy that follows the collapse of governmental authority. Finally, civilians may become the principal target in the course of ethnic cleansing and genocide.

Some commentators have argued that the focus of humanitarian protection on "civilians" has become inadequate to address the complexity and gravity of the situation of civilians in today's armed conflicts.[7] The scope of IHL protection appears too narrow to answer the concerns of international agencies and NGOs regarding the specific needs of vulnerable groups, such as displaced persons, refugees, women, and children. Moreover, IHL and human rights instruments often seem too technical for easy use in complex situations. Contradictory calls have been made, on the one hand, to develop specific standards to protect vulnerable groups (such as children,[8] women,[9] and displaced persons[10]) and, on the other, to proclaim generic standards or "fundamental principles" to protect all civilians in all circumstances.[11] Questions have been raised concerning whether these new standards and principles would have the same legal authority as the original instruments. A more serious consequence of these debates has been the increasing tendency to see some civilians as more "innocent" than others and, therefore, more deserving of protection. The withdrawal of some international assistance from refugee camps under Interahamwe control in Zaire (1994–1996) and the bombing of civilian infrastructures in the NATO campaign against Serbia represent clear departures from the fundamental assumption in IHL of the general principle of innocence of civilians in situations of armed conflict.

In view of the weakening of traditional humanitarian protection mechanisms, the international community must reexamine its approach to the protection of civilians. The dissemination of basic principles of IHL and human rights law, the development of standards on the protection of women or children—all will be of little help to civilians if these initiatives are not integrated into a far-reaching strategy to induce and enforce compliance of all actors involved in armed conflicts. Ultimately, such a strategy should lay the foundations for stronger and more effective actions under existing enforcement mechanisms at the regional and international levels. In order to build the necessary coalition of states to support such coercive measures against the perpetrators of massive violations of IHL and human rights law, the coherence and consistency of international community action will have to be reconsidered.

Review of Existing Strategies to Enhance Humanitarian Protection

The response of humanitarian organizations to the challenges that these violations pose to traditional protection regimes has varied according to specific mandates and interests. To a large extent, these responses have been mutually reinforcing. However, a common approach has yet to emerge since institutional interests underlying the organizations' objectives are often driven by historical and political considerations. In this section I elaborate the strategies of each of the main humanitarian actors.

Reasserting the Validity of International Humanitarian Law

The first of these strategies, under the leadership of the ICRC, is to stress the role and objectives of IHL and promote further efforts at the national and international levels for the legal enforcement of these rules. IHL is seen as an

essential tool in the determination of the illegal character of the violence perpetrated against civilians in conflict situations and, accordingly, should be at
the center of any strategy to protect civilians.

Proponents of this approach acknowledge that the nature of war has
changed significantly in recent years and that civilians have increasingly
become subject to attack, but they caution against hasty conclusions with
regard to the continuing relevance of the norms of IHL. In their view, violations of those norms do not necessarily signify their obsolescence. On the
contrary, they believe that IHL remains highly relevant in contemporary conflict situations and mobilize considerable efforts to strengthen and expand its
application. The establishment of the International Criminal Court, the adoption of the Ottawa Land-mines Treaty, and the Protocol on the Protection of
Cultural Property are often cited as examples of the dynamism of IHL.[12]

To revitalize discussions on the role of IHL, the ICRC has undertaken two
major qualitative studies of the relevance of IHL in today's armed conflicts.
The first of these studies, requested by the International Conference of the
Red Cross and Red Crescent in 1995, aims to appraise the role of customary
humanitarian law in situations of armed conflict. The second study, undertak-
en on the occasion of the fiftieth anniversary of the Geneva Conventions,
assesses the effectiveness of IHL from the perspective of its agents and beneficiaries, including thousands of interviews throughout the world to assess the
actual impact of IHL on the conduct of hostilities. The results of these studies
were presented at the Twenty-seventh International Conference of the Red
Cross and Red Crescent in November 1999 in Geneva.[13] The reports make
clear that IHL represents an active and evolving field of international law,
which can provide clear guidance for the efforts of the international community in the protection of civilians.

At the same time, it has become difficult to ignore the discrepancies
between the dynamism of IHL in international fora and the poor record of
implementation in the field. To reassert the validity of the law is certainly an
important step toward mobilizing the international community on a more
cogent agenda for the protection of civilians. Such a strategy is essentially
conservative, however. Notably, it fails to address the problem of adapting
IHL mechanisms to the changing environment—in particular the growing role
of nonstate actors, such as armed groups and corporations, and the problems
that follow the collapse of state authority. The efforts of the ICRC to revali-
date IHL through surveys and studies on customary rules offer the prospect of
a renewal in its approach to IHL, from traditional state-centered strategies to
engagement with nonstate actors. Nevertheless, the ICRC's continuing focus
on conventional rules, its insistence on preserving its role under the Geneva
Conventions as the "Guardian of International Humanitarian Law," and its
reluctance to engage in the political and security aspects of humanitarian
operations remain major obstacles to the success of this approach.

Expanding the Scope of Humanitarian Protection

Over recent decades, the involvement of UN agencies and NGOs in humanitarian operations has considerably expanded the number of humanitarian actors in conflict situations. Many of these actors, on the basis of their original mandate or due simply to the availability of funding, have concentrated their activities on particular groups of victims, such as children, women, refugees, displaced persons, and land mine victims. This expansion has changed the perceived scope of humanitarian protection from being driven by IHL to being driven by the needs of specific groups of victims and the circumstances under which this protection should be exercised. Humanitarian protection is now understood to go beyond the narrow role provided for in traditional IHL conventions. Although these conventions remain the primary legal reference in conflict situations, the development of human rights instruments recognizing basic rights of civilians that also apply in situations of armed conflict has encouraged human rights organizations and specialized agencies to engage in the protection of civilians. It has been argued that this expansion of the concept of humanitarian protection has emancipated it from an early parallelism with military necessity.[14]

In this expanded context, humanitarian protection involves both the protection of basic human rights and the provision of durable solutions. Beyond the notion of physical security, humanitarian protection also encompasses a range of activities aimed at ensuring respect for the dignity of individuals and their basic development and signifies a point of convergence among the regimes of IHL, human rights, and refugee law.

The time frame of the concept of humanitarian protection is also being extended. Traditionally, the concept was only applicable during the actual conduct of hostilities (military time frame) whereas it now extends from the emergence of a conflict situation to postconflict and reconstruction periods (humanitarian agencies time frame). The concerns of humanitarian agencies for the protection of particular groups beyond the actual conflict period—such as refugees or internally displaced persons (IDPs) returning to their place of origin, or other vulnerable groups, such as the women and girls of Afghanistan—illustrate the will of the humanitarian community to extend the time frame of its activities from emergency-driven operations to conflict prevention and postconflict peace-building.

Some argue that this expansion reflects the concern of the international community for the situation of civilians as a whole, not simply as victims of armed hostilities. This expansion acknowledges that the overall security situation of civilians may be at the core of the causes of the conflict and not merely a consequence. This connection between the situation of civilians and the political causes of a conflict renders humanitarian strategies that much more difficult and complex. The respective mandates of political, humanitarian, and developmental agencies tend to overlap, and their attention to specific groups of victims may become cumbersome in large crises. These organizations work under pressure to attract donors and develop market-oriented strategies to promote their activities. The simultaneous presence of the OSCE, NATO, the UN, the ICRC, NGOs, and donor agencies in Kosovo with often-competing mandates in political, administrative, and humanitarian terms has hampered considerably the effectiveness of the intervention of the international community in the region.

Diversifying the Agents and Implementation Strategies of Humanitarian Protection

The strategic expansion of the concept of humanitarian protection has resulted in an enlarged understanding of the rights of civilians in times of war. However, protection still relies primarily on the participation of implementing agents such as states, the Security Council, or regional organizations that are willing and able to effect protection. In the case of a failure of the parties to a conflict to respect the rules of IHL, states parties to the IHL instruments have a subsidiary responsibility to "ensure respect" for the rules of humanitarian law.[15]

The actual significance of this subsidiary responsibility and its implications for the protection of civilians remain unclear. For example, the impact on the deliberations of security mechanisms such as the UN Security Council is uncertain. Proponents of a more active humanitarian role for the Security Council are keen to believe a revival of this obligation is implicit in the increasing interest of Security Council members in humanitarian issues. Others are more skeptical about the real impact of the Security Council debates on the protection of civilians that took place in September 1999 and April 2000 with respect to the willingness of member states to allocate the necessary resources to intervene.

Proponents of more assertive and effective protection regimes believe that humanitarian protection requires the elaboration of new political and security strategies to address the immediate needs of the population as well as the root causes of the conflict. Such a protection regime should, in this context, involve political and security actors, such as the Security Council; regional organizations; and specialized departments and agencies, such as the UN Department of Peacekeeping Operations, in the elaboration of the international response to humanitarian crises.[16] Moreover, the actors involved need to be able to propose strategic options to maximize the resources available under the given political and security constraints. Options to enhance the protection of civilians may include creating security zones, establishing humanitarian corridors, and air-dropping relief assistance.[17]

Specific role of the UN Security Council in the protection of civilians. The situation of civilians in times of armed conflict has prompted substantive discussions on protection strategies within the Security Council.[18] A significant observation in the course of these debates has been the linkage made between serious violations of IHL and basic human rights, and the maintenance of international peace and security.[19] Violent assaults on civilians are both a product and a cause of political instability and armed conflicts. In addition, the scope of the human tragedy involved in situations of armed conflict may depend on the action—or inaction—of the UN and other multilateral mechanisms designed to address the causes and consequences of armed conflicts.

In this context, the response to violations of IHL and human rights standards seems to be gaining significance in the eyes of Security Council members, as efforts to protect and assist civilians in times of conflict are seen to play a major role in addressing the potential causes of further conflict. Reciprocally, decisions of the Council on political and security issues are acknowledged to have serious implications for the situation of civilians in times of conflict. Such a link implies the need to elaborate approaches to address the humanitarian dimension of situations of armed conflict and to determine a specific but complementary role for the Council in the protection of civilians. The recent report of the Secretary-General to the Security Council on the protection of civilians in armed conflict presents, in this context, a series of practical recommendations to promote, strengthen, and implement the legal and physical protection of civilians.[20]

The political will of the Council to intervene in an effective and sustainable fashion, however, has yet to materialize. Security Council members, particularly the permanent members, have been reluctant to support Council action on humanitarian issues unless there are clear national interests involved. When they do decide to intervene, they tend to take only minimal risks, remaining particularly concerned with the potential human cost of the intervention and their domestic standing rather than the fate of the attacked civilians. The lack of seriousness of the Council has allowed its members to adopt a populist attitude toward these crises. Humanitarian crises, unlike other security concerns, are considered by Security Council members of little consequence in terms of their core security interests. Decisions in this area are therefore made largely with regard to public opinion rather than strategic considerations for regional peace and security. The level of attention of the Council's members thus depends largely on the visibility of a given crisis in their national press. Even when such crises are documented, the default position of governments remains noninterventionist regardless of the gravity of the situation. During a government's term, the political cost of not intervening will always be less than the military and human cost of intervening in complex and disordered emergencies. In this context, it appears that the *proximity* of the crisis, rather than its gravity, becomes the factor triggering a concerted response.

This minimalist approach may prove to be self-defeating, as it is likely to play into the hands of future aggressors who may tailor their attacks against civilians to the particular reservations of members of the Council. Indeed, there is some evidence that parties to armed conflicts may plan their attacks against civilians with particular attention to (1) the timing of their attacks, for example with regard to domestic agendas of Council members in election years; (2) the profile of their targeted groups, portraying them as "secessionists" or "fundamentalists"; and (3) the most fashionable standards, sparing women and children, for example, but exterminating all men of military age.

In this context, some have raised serious concerns about the mixing of humanitarian and political agendas. The use of force by the Security Council or regional organizations is subject to political agendas that may jeopardize the neutrality of protective humanitarian arrangements.[21] Furthermore, the use of force to protect civilian populations implies the military engagement of international forces against the parties to the conflict. This engagement may put the civilian populations at even greater risk if they become a central issue of the conflict, such as when international demands for the return of displaced populations clash with one or more parties' policy of ethnic cleansing. The role of the Council in addressing such matters remains of critical importance in defining the international community's response to serious violations of IHL and human rights standards. The fulfillment of this role would, however, greatly benefit from the elaboration of guidelines to determine which situations should involve the Council and which measures available under the UN Charter could enhance the protection of civilians in situations of armed conflict.

Specific roles of the Emergency Relief Coordinator and of the representatives of the Secretary-General for internally displaced persons and children and armed conflicts. One of the most significant strategic developments over recent years has been the creation of a series of advocacy and coordination instruments within the UN system to enhance the protection role of the organization. For some years, UN agencies such as the United Nations Children's Fund (UNICEF) and the UN High Commissioner for Refugees (UNHCR) have been active participants in protection actions pertaining to their respective beneficiaries: children and refugees. UN member states, however, have been seeking a more holistic and coordinated approach to international relief and protection efforts. As a result, the Office for the Coordination of Humanitarian Affairs (OCHA), headed by the Emergency Relief Coordinator (ERC), was established by the Secretary-General in January 1998 to strengthen the capacity of the United Nations to respond to humanitarian crises. As part of the reform process of the UN Secretariat, it replaced the Department of Humanitarian Affairs that had been created in 1992 pursuant to General Assembly resolution 46/182.

Under resolution 46/182, the ERC was to "actively facilitat[e], including through negotiation if needed, the access by the operational organizations to emergency areas for the rapid provision of emergency assistance by obtaining the consent of all parties concerned, through modalities such as the establishment of temporary relief corridors where needed, days and zones of tranquility and other forms."[22] In 1997, the Secretary-General confirmed the role of the ERC in the protection activities of the UN system, in particular his or her advocacy role with the UN political organs, notably the Security Council.[23] Sergio Vieira de Mello has held the post since January 1998. His regular briefings of the Security Council and his field assessment missions illustrate the significant role of the ERC in the development of the UN response to humanitarian crises.

In response to the demand for more focused attention on the needs of vulnerable groups, Secretary-General Boutros Boutros-Ghali appointed Francis Deng as his Representative on Internally Displaced Persons in 1992, with a mandate to examine the protection of IDPs. In the absence of an international legal framework spelling out the rights and the freedoms of internally displaced persons specifically, the Representative compiled the Guiding Principles on Internal Displacement, based on existing instruments in IHL and human rights law, which were presented to the Commission on Human Rights in 1998. In 1997, the Secretary-General appointed Olara A. Otunnu as his Special Representative for Children and Armed Conflict. In terms of protection, the primary objective of this office is to raise public and official awareness of international instruments and local norms that provide for the rights, protection, and welfare of children.[24]

These developments have not always been welcomed by other actors such as UNHCR and UNICEF. Even though it is clear that the objectives pursued are compatible with existing mandates, there has been some dissonance in the multiplication of advocacy voices. The programmatic approach of large agencies serving millions of beneficiaries has been disturbed by the more enterprising and expeditious tactics of the representatives of the Secretary-General. Some argue that they have contributed significantly to the renewal of UN approaches to the situation of war victims. Still, the burden of protection schemes elaborated by these ad hoc advocates is likely to fall on the operational agencies. There is, therefore, a need to improve the integration of the advocacy role of these representatives with the operational priorities of other agencies of the UN system.

Development of Field Strategies

Relief NGOs and human rights groups have brought a field-oriented perspective to the debate on humanitarian protection. Compared to the internationalist strategies of the UN, which imposes a universal concept of protection to be implemented by mostly foreign agents, NGOs have been more concerned with nurturing and maintaining domestic mechanisms for the self-protection of people and groups under threat. In the view of many, engagement in protection in no way supplants the critical need for a domestic legal system.[25] In the absence of such a system, protection strategies should involve rather than exclude domestic actors, including tribal and community leaders, NGOs, lawyers, and religious groups.

There are, of course, situations in which it may be difficult to obtain the cooperation of community-based mechanisms—ethnic or communal conflicts, for example. In these circumstances, the intervention of a third-party agent from the international community may become necessary. NGOs have been among the first calling for UN military involvement in all the major crises of the 1990s, in full awareness of the irreversible character of some conflicts and the impending dangers for the civilian population.

There are, however, many examples of situations in which local structures could have been used to enhance indigenous protection mechanisms but were disregarded by international organizations, unnecessarily disempowering the local leaders and perhaps contributing to the erosion of civil society. The use of hate media by the majority Hutu government in Rwanda in 1993–1994, for example, presented an opportunity to collaborate with civil society structures to counter racist propaganda. That opportunity was missed.

From this perspective, some NGOs argue that protection strategies should first be developed at the field level, from the bottom up, with the intervention of foreign agents subjected to a series of domestic requirements. The default response to early abuses against civilians should no longer be the media-driven deployment of foreign observers but a process of consultation and reconciliation among local actors with the support of NGOs. Such engagement may include the presence of international workers in support of these mechanisms. These strategies involve a continuing assessment of the threats against civilians in each conflict and a thorough analysis of the opportunities and constraints of domestic protection mechanisms.[26] Key objectives of this approach are the maintenance of access to targeted civilians and maintenance of a dialogue with all relevant parties at the field level. One clear advantage of this approach is the integration of protection issues into conflict prevention strategies and peace-building efforts. An equally clear shortfall is its limitations in cases of communal and ethnic violence, where reconciliation may no longer be on the agenda of the parties.

Conclusion

In this chapter I have analyzed the traditional assumptions of humanitarian protection and presented some of the strategies currently in debate among humanitarian organizations and actors regarding the future of humanitarian protection. Each of these strategies presents some level of compatibility with the others and could contribute to an overall approach to humanitarian protection.

International humanitarian law should certainly remain the core legal framework of any mechanism of humanitarian protection; it has a high level of acceptability and imposes significant responsibilities on combatants. However, this legal framework of protection strategies can no longer be limited to IHL conventions and should include provisions from refugee and human rights law to address the needs of vulnerable groups. In addition, the increasing number of internal armed conflicts and the incidence of "failed" states have rendered many of the traditional state-centered mechanisms of implementation ineffective. The role of nonstate actors should be carefully reviewed, and efforts should be devoted to promote increased levels of participation of nonstate actors and their accountability to international standards, in particular armed groups and the corporations supporting those groups. The universal competence of national courts to try violations of these actors under IHL should be fully recognized and supported.

The most interesting contribution to the debate has come from the NGO community, which has questioned the sustainability of protection mechanisms established exclusively at the multilateral level. The key elements of humanitarian protection appear to be in the hands of the local actors—namely the parties to the conflict, local governments, and community leaders. Unless the international community is willing and able to intervene militarily to protect civilians in conflict situations such as Sierra Leone, Angola, or Sudan, any effective and sustainable protection strategy is likely to start and end at the local level. Humanitarian protection strategies would gain in effectiveness through integration into overall efforts to prevent conflict and rebuild peace at the local and regional levels.

Ultimately, the effectiveness of future protection mechanisms relies on our ability to adapt the normative basis for protection to the changing reality of conflicts as well as to generate the political will to undertake committed actions. Current international conventions are the product of an age of innocence regarding the role and capability of states in the protection of civilians. This age has been brought to a sharp end by the genocide in Rwanda, the ethnic cleansing in the former Yugoslavia, and other large-scale tragedies of the 1990s. Effective protection strategies can no longer rely solely on the will and capacity of distant and disinterested states to ensure the immediate protection of civilians. On the contrary, every step of these strategies should aim at strengthening the role of local communities, national institutions, and regional organizations committed to the peaceful resolution of each crisis. In this context, the proximity and vitality of local and regional actors are likely to remain factors of central importance for the enabling of effective and relevant protection strategies.

Notes

1. Report of the Secretary-General to the Security Council on the Protection of Civilians in Armed Conflict, UN Doc. S/1999/957 (1999).

2. SIPRI, *Armaments, Disarmament and International Security: SIPRI Yearbook 1999* (Stockholm: Almquist & Wiksell; New York: Humanities Press, 1999).

3. See Chapter 3 by Marie-Joëlle Zahar in this volume.

4. See, e.g., Article 3 common to the four Geneva Conventions.

5. Christopher Munnion, "De Beers Ban on Gem Sales Hits UNITA," *Daily Telegraph* (London), Oct. 8, 1999.

6. William Branigin, "Rights Victims in Burma Want a U.S. Company to Pay; Suit Alleges Army Abuses While Pipeline Was Built," *Washington Post*, Apr. 13, 1999.

7. See, e.g., Thomas G. Weiss, "Principles, Politics, and Humanitarian Action," *Ethics & International Affairs* 13 (1999), p. 11.

8. Commission on Human Rights, Children in Armed Conflict: Interim Report of the Special Representative of the Secretary-General, Mr. Olara A. Otunnu, submitted pursuant to General Assembly Resolution 52/107, UN Doc. E/CN.4/1998/119 (1998).

9. Report of the UN Secretary-General Commission on the Status of Women, 42nd Sess., UN Doc. E/CN.6/1998/1 (1998).

10. Note by the Secretary-General Regarding the Report on Internally Displaced Persons, UN Doc. A/54/409 (1999).

11. See Secretary-General's Report on Protection of Civilians.

12. See Harvard University/OCHA, Report of the Inter-Agency Expert Consultation on Protected Areas (1999), available at www.hsph.harvard.edu/hcpds/report.pdf.

13. See the full report of the survey "People and War" available at www.onwar.org.

14. These instruments include the Convention on the Prevention and Punishment of the Crimes of Genocide (1948); Convention Relating to the Status of Refugees (1951); Convention on the Elimination of All Forms of Discrimination Against Women (1979); Convention Against Torture and Other Cruel, Inhuman or Degrading Treatment or Punishment (1984); Convention on the Rights of the Child (1989); and the Rome Statute of the International Criminal Court (1998).

15. For details on the measures available to states to ensure respect of the Geneva Conventions, see U. Palwankar, "Measures Available to States for Fulfilling Their Obligation to Ensure Respect for International Humanitarian Law," *International Review of the Red Cross* 298 (1994), pp. 9–25. See also L. Condorelli and L. Boisson de Chazournes, "Quelques remarques à propos de l'obligation des Etats de 'respecter et faire respecter' le droit international humanitaire en 'toutes circonstances,' in C. Swinarski (ed.), *Studies and Essays on International Humanitarian Law and Red Cross Principles in Honour of Jean Pictet* (Geneva: ICRC & Martinus Nijhoff Publishers, 1984), pp. 17–36.

16. Cornelio Sommaruga, president of the ICRC, does not reject the use of force to stop humanitarian disasters. In his view, grave breaches of humanitarian law, as witnessed in Rwanda, Somalia, and Bosnia-Herzegovina, represent a threat to international peace and security that may trigger a form of military response. See Cornelio Sommaruga, "Effective Implementation of International Humanitarian Law in Changing Circumstances," *Proceedings of the American Society of International Law* 91 (1997), pp. 519–522.

17. See Inter-Agency Expert Consultation on Protected Areas and related documents.

18. See, e.g., UN Doc. S/PRST/1999/6 (1999).

19. Secretary-General's Report on Protection of Civilians, paras. 28ff.

20. Ibid.

21. Yves Sandoz, "The Establishment of Safety Zones for Persons Displaced Within Their Country of Origin," in Najeeb Al-Nauimi and Richard Meese (eds.), *International Legal Issues Arising Under the United Nations Decade of International Law* (The Hague: Martinus Nijhoff, 1995), pp. 899–927.

22. GA Res. 46/182 (1991), para. 35(d).

23. Report of the Secretary-General, Renewing the United Nations: A Programme for Reform, UN Doc. A/51/950 (1997), paras. 180ff.

24. Mission Statement of the Senior Representative of the Secretary-General on Children and Armed Conflict, available at www.un.org/special-rep/children-armed-conflict.

25. Diane Paul, "Protection in Practice: Field-Level Strategies for Protecting Civilians from Deliberate Harm," in Humanitarian Practice Network (formerly RRN), *Overseas Development Institute (ODI)* 30 (July 1999).

26. Ibid., p. 7.

From Chaos to Coherence?
Toward a Regime for
Protecting Civilians in War

Bruce D. Jones and Charles K. Cater

The centenary of the first Hague International Peace Conference, convened in the wake of the Franco-Prussian war, reminds us of the enduring challenge that first prompted Czar Nicholas II's initiative: limiting the carnage that accompanies war. While the nineteenth-century leaders of Europe may have been primarily concerned with the welfare of their standing armies, the passage of a century has distinctly shifted concern toward the particular vulnerability of civilians and efforts to protect them from the effects of war. In this chapter we analyze both the progress and the failures of the "international community" in this regard—while also pointing the way toward developing a more effective approach for coping with this difficult problem.

The timing of the symposium that inspired this volume on September 23–24, 1999, was fortuitous.[1] In the same week, the protection of civilians took center stage at the United Nations. The UN High Commissioner for Human Rights addressed the Security Council for the first time in its history, helping to introduce a report on the protection of civilians in armed conflict;[2] at the UN's general debate, member states alternately attacked or supported the Secretary-General's defense of humanitarian intervention,[3] a debate that has continued in the pages of leading journals; and, most significantly, the Security Council authorized a peace-enforcement mission to halt ethnic cleansing and deter mass killings in East Timor.[4]

Meanwhile at the symposium, academics, international policymakers, and field practitioners from the legal, security, and humanitarian fields presented a range of views on protecting civilians. Discussion covered the issues of evolving norms and laws, international organizations and their strategies, the interests and behavior of belligerents, and case reviews of the local contexts in which violence against civilians occurs. Underlying the ensuing debate was a determination to focus less on developing new laws or norms than on increasing the prospects for the implementation and enforcement of those norms that already exist but are so persistently violated.

Meaningful protection of civilians in and from war requires greater coherence between distinct types and levels of international response than currently exists. This must begin with a more nuanced understanding of the local contexts in which war and protection efforts take place. From this foundation, more productive efforts need to be made by international actors to develop complementary protection strategies. These, in turn, can be more effectively implemented by the international and regional organizations that design them. Finally, the normative framework that both informs and is informed by such practice warrants ongoing attention.

We address each of these issues in the order listed above: local context, organizational strategies, systemic constraints, and normative developments. Our focus then shifts to a discussion of developing a more effective international response, including better utilization of strategic coordination. In conclusion, we offer suggestions in three areas for future work toward a regime for the protection of civilians: research, organizational development, and domestic political advocacy.

Dealing with the Local Level: Belligerents in War

It is at the local level that protection strategies ultimately succeed or fail, in the highly specific context of a given conflict. There is little doubt that an essential precondition to effective protection of civilians is a nuanced understanding of specific local contexts. While specific contexts can refer to the history of a conflict, or elements of the culture of a people in question, what is arguably most important and certainly most frequently given short shrift is the particular question of understanding those belligerents whose actions expose civilians to violence in the first place. Enhanced understanding requires seeing belligerents in context and examining their varying behavior, objectives, and instruments of war in order to shed light on how belligerents deal with civilians and to draw out the implications for international protection efforts.

Unconventional belligerents—meaning rebel groups, militias, and other nonstate actors—have been significantly understudied for reasons ranging from a bias toward legitimate state actors to the practical and security constraints on close analysis of militia groups. Nonetheless, this is an important area for further inquiry, particularly if the international community wishes to influence the behavior of militias in order to protect civilians and resolve conflicts. Among the first tasks is to draw a number of analytic distinctions that establish a rough typology of the highly diverse types of militias. Such a typology has been developed by Marie-Joëlle Zahar, who has identified three primary dimensions.[5]

The first concerns how militias decide whom they consider to fall within their "in-group" (allies) and their "out-group" (enemies) as well as the implications this determination has for their behavior toward these two groups. Militias are well known for their human rights violations against civilians considered to be in the out-group (such as Bosnian Serb militias and their treatment of Muslim civilians in Bosnia). However, the fact that militias also act quite differently toward civilians in their respective in-groups is often ignored. For example, Hizballah, a group accused of terrorist tactics against Israeli citizens in its drive to push Israel from Lebanon, also sees itself as a provider of social services for the poorest members of Lebanese society.

The second dimension concerns how militias function economically, which Zahar categorizes as either predatory, parasitic, symbiotic, or independent. In a *symbiotic* relationship, militias will attempt to foster economic activities for civil society and then subsequently take a share of the revenue. This is close to what is often termed a "patron-client" relationship. In contrast, a *predatory* relationship involves the direct extraction of wealth from civil society without anything offered in return by the militia. This is similar to what could be called a "protection racket" or extortion. A *parasitic* relationship can be understood as a hybrid between these two extremes. For example, the leaders of Republika Srpska conferred some benefits upon their in-group, but they also extracted significant personal wealth through coercive methods. Finally, an *independent* source of revenue refers to essentially external sources of funds—particularly those derived from natural resource extraction industries. Prominent examples include commerce by Charles Taylor's National Patriotic Front of Liberia (NPFL), Foday Sankoh's Revolutionary United Front (RUF) in Sierra Leone, and Jonas Savimbi's National Union for the Total Independence of Angola (UNITA).

Third, the objectives and structure of a militia must be taken into account. The relative importance of various goals for a particular group is perhaps the most crucial dimension of their relations to civilians. If a militia is seeking legitimacy and/or greater inclusion in the existing political system, then its tactics will be much different than if it is seeking secession (when it may be less likely to respect human rights). For example, some rebel groups in eastern Democratic Republic of the Congo (DRC) have collaborated with international humanitarian organizations to enhance the welfare of populations under their territorial control; this had the dual purpose of enhancing their standing with those populations and with the international diplomatic community. Both purposes served to further their political objective of sustained political rule in eastern DRC.[6] On the other hand, Bosnian Serb militias used ethnic cleansing as a tactic to clear territory of even minimal minority opposition, as part of a wider strategy of consolidating Serb rule in Bosnia. In this latter case, the demands of the Bosnian war also necessitated a more formal military structure for the Vojska Republika Srpska (Serb Republic Army). As Zahar notes, this had the unintended consequence of making the leadership, Radovan Karadzic and Ratko Mladic, more susceptible to international pressure and prosecution.

It is important that behavior be understood in this sophisticated manner. Too frequently, attacks on civilians or other atrocities are portrayed simply as acts of insanity, barbarity, or hatred, without analyzing their strategic purpose. Anticipating the objectives of belligerents is central to the prospects for successful negotiations. It is also important to realize that objectives often change throughout the course of a conflict, greatly influencing the behavior of militias. Thus, with respect to negotiating with belligerents and militia groups, timing emerges as a crucial factor.

Economic objectives are also a significant and understudied element of this equation, as is the varying interest of belligerents in political and diplomatic recognition. The two sets of interests suggest different strategies for engagement on issues of protection and conflict resolution, as well as the importance of strategic flexibility in order to adapt to changing economic and political interests of militias. Economic objectives may rise through the course of a war as militias and others find alternative economic space created by the war. This poses significant challenges, because the ending of wars will entail for belligerents a loss of economic opportunity; however, the evolution of the interests and behavior of belligerents also provides important negotiating opportunities, if it is well understood.

Understanding the different elements of belligerents' interests and behavior at an individual level also helps generate a more pragmatic approach to dealing with them.[7] From the perspective of a combatant, humanitarian considerations are necessarily secondary or tertiary: in the heat of battle, there is little time to reflect upon the Geneva Conventions. This is in part because choices are brutally simple—life or death. Recognizing the horror of such a dilemma helps to humanize belligerents. For instance, in a context where grown men are fighting child soldiers, the choice may be either to fight back or to sacrifice one's own life in order not to draw arms against children. Some belligerents will make such sacrifices. All too frequently, of course, the willingness of belligerents to make use of child soldiers is emblematic of a general tendency to trade civilian life for political and economic gain. In Angola and Mozambique, for example, UNITA and RENAMO respectively used child soldiers as a deliberate strategy of war; government forces also used child soldiers, albeit to a lesser extent. These children were often forced to raid their own villages and were therefore effectively alienated from their own society. Aside from those children who were direct participants, most other children were either victims of war or were forced to carry supplies or do other forms of labor for the armies. Furthermore, belligerents target civilians for labor, manipulate the efforts of humanitarian organizations to achieve power or secure their own survival, and make little distinction in general between civilians and combatants.

In either case, a focus on belligerents highlights the horror, the trauma, and the essential struggle for death and survival that are the reality of war—too often diminished by the abstract words used by policymakers and academics. Moreover, understanding belligerents in their relation to civilian populations, and in particular to their objectives, helps to highlight that there are a number of persistent *patterns* in war, recurrent dynamics that either protect or expose civilians to death and displacement. These patterns are critical, for they serve as an important entry point for international efforts in local contexts.

Understanding the behavior of belligerents is only the first step, however. It is also critical to sufficiently appreciate the needs and motivations of civilians as well, even the most victimized. Take, for instance, the use of general amnesties as a tool for conflict resolution—a tactic opposed by many of those who seek more principled international engagements in civil conflicts. On the one hand, the provision of general amnesty to war perpetrators has been used as a tool for conflict resolution in such settings as Guatemala and Sierra Leone. On the other hand, laws and norms relating to human rights have gained currency and strength, and the international community is increasingly seeking to hold individuals accountable for human rights abuses. The tension between these positions was dramatically evident over Sierra Leone, when the UN High Commissioner for Human Rights publicly declared her opposition to the amnesty negotiated by the Lomé Peace Agreement, signed in 1999. In similar fashion, efforts to ensure that the International Criminal Tribunal for Rwanda (ICTR) is conducted according to universal judicial standards have required the adoption of operating procedures and rules of punishment that appear to have weakened its potential contribution to reconciliation in Rwanda and eroded support from the Rwandan government.

While the pros and cons of amnesties are many and debatable, an oft-overlooked perspective is that of the war-weary civilian, who may prefer an "unjust" end to war to a continuation of hostilities with the possibility of future justice. The disjuncture between what is sought by civilians in war and what the international community may seek to provide is potentially significant. This is but one illustration of the tension between the imperatives of a particular conflict and the aspiration to universal standards, where what is needed to provide protection for civilians on the ground may contradict emerging universal norms. But even this example is not straightforward in its trade-offs, not a simple matter of "peace versus justice"; for as we show in the next section, there is evidence from some cases that human rights strategies can be effective in protecting civilians, not least by providing early warning of impending conflicts.

Strategies for Protection: Evidence from Cases

One step removed from the analysis of belligerents are issues relating to the practical experience of international actors in working with civilians in war. The issues are framed by a number of major challenges, prominently including complications arising from the interactions between the protection strategies of different international organizations, and limited use by those organizations of local resources, both human and cultural, for reasons of both inherent difficulty and inadequate effort on the part of international actors.

The question of interactions—and frequently tensions—between the different strategies used by organizations is well illustrated by the case of Colombia.[8] In Colombia, four main types of international human rights and humanitarian actors play roles related to protecting civilians: Peace Brigades and similar organizations, human rights groups, Médecins Sans Frontières (MSF) and similar organizations, and the ICRC. Each type of organization has its own mandate and mode of operation that frame its interaction with the belligerents (the Colombian government, right-wing militias, and left-wing guerrilla groups). Tensions arise because human rights groups, such as Human Rights Watch, use exposure in order to deter human rights abuses (on the assumption that belligerents are at least somewhat responsive to international public opinion). Organizations such as MSF use their provision of medical services in order to gain access, but they do not hesitate to publicly denounce human rights violations by combatants. The risk of using denunciation as a tactic is that other international actors—namely, humanitarian groups such as the ICRC—may lose access to vulnerable populations because they are conflated with human rights groups who may be seen as partial. The humanitarian organizations typically refrain from publicly denouncing the conditions faced by those in detention. This approach has created a relationship of trust for the ICRC, for example, with all of the combatants and has maintained international humanitarian access in the country. At the same time, in Colombia human rights reporting has provided crucial information to the broader international community, which serves as an indicator of the emergence and escalation of conflict. There are thus a number of tensions between protection strategies in Colombia, most notably a tension between sustained access to civilians *during* conflict and the advocacy and negotiations required to generate sufficient political action to *end* human rights abuses and conflict.

Although adaptation to varying local contexts is responsible for some variation among international strategies, there remains a much deeper and more problematic incoherence in the international system's collective capacity to develop effective protection strategies. In many cases, there is evidence of substantial contradictions between the strategies pursued by different organizations. The risk of seeking greater coherence among international efforts, of course, is a lowering of the common denominator: many have argued, for example, that the effort to develop a common international front for international agencies in Afghanistan forced a compromise of values rather than effecting an appropriate trade-off among humanitarian actors, or between them and their political and development counterparts.

Of course, it is not likely to be the case that any one given strategy is going to be effective in all cases. Rather, different strategies will have varying impacts, depending substantially on the nature of the case and the interests and objectives of the belligerents. However, the evidence suggests that the international community as a whole has done a poor job of identifying the comparative advantages of different organizations, relating those advantages to particular strategies, and identifying mechanisms for ensuring that appropriate organizations, with effective strategies, are deployed to achieve certain tasks at key junctures.

The question of the comparative advantage of different strategies is perhaps best illustrated by reference to the question of neutrality as a strategy. In the discussion above about Colombia, it was clear that neutrality served as an important operational tool for protection *because of the specific context.* But in other situations the limits of neutrality may be evident. Failure to adequately incorporate an understanding of the interests and behavior of belligerents into a program of "neutral" humanitarian assistance and protection strategies can lead to circumstances where one form of protection (for example, food assistance) undermines another (such as when food is diverted by belligerents into military purposes). The case of Sudan is seen as an acute instance of this problem. In other contexts, where belligerents see an important strategic and political gain from launching direct attacks on civilians— one thinks of Burundi, Rwanda, northern Sierra Leone, and East Timor—neutrality loses its vigor as a source of protection. The UN's recent reports on Srebrenica and Rwanda highlight the inadequacy of neutrality as a protection strategy in these cases.[9]

In cases where neutrality runs up against its political limits, humanitarian organizations like the ICRC are often the first to recognize that neutral humanitarian assistance alone will prove inadequate; the onus shifts to those responsible for collective security. Yet in the process of calling on the Security Council or regional organizations, humanitarian organizations themselves, as well as journalists and others, frequently mount their calls in terms and words that muddy the waters for those actors who would seek—for the sake of future action—to retain their neutrality. Again, there is no shortage of different actors with distinct comparative advantages in mobilizing international opinion, negotiating with the Security Council, working with regional actors—but there is little evidence of anything other than ad hoc systems through which these organizations are employed or deployed to perform these various tasks. Put simply, how can the neutrality of traditional humanitarian organizations like the ICRC be protected while also recognizing the limits of neutrality and the need for political and military action to protect civilians in certain kinds of war?

The case of Colombia also illustrates a second theme that arises in terms of strategy: use of local resources. The situation in Colombia is characterized by a seeming paradox where humanitarian and human rights organizations make very limited use of what is in fact a well-developed domestic legal apparatus. More effective use of this system could in theory provide better protection from human rights abuses, in particular. However, in this case, the limited use of these resources by international actors is largely a function of security concerns: the fact that judges and international actors are often taken hostage or assassinated severely constrains the option of using the local court system as a method of protection.

In Somalia, a very different case, the effectiveness of international protection strategies has waxed and waned. Somalia was at war from 1989 to 1992, until the international community intervened militarily; it is estimated that this intervention may have saved the lives of over one million Somalis. Yet, when the third UN peacekeeping force left Somalia in 1995, war broke out again between the two most powerful clans in the country, and regional efforts to mediate the conflict have since been unsuccessful. Since that time, regional efforts have focused on dialogue with warlords, in the perceived absence of viable civic alternatives. The central state of Somalia has collapsed, although in some local cases elders and district councils have successfully maintained a modicum of stability. The only agency currently operating nationwide in the country is the Somali Red Crescent Society, which recently conducted over one thousand surveys among the population as part of the ICRC's People On War campaign.[10] The surveys revealed a widespread sense that Somalia has been abandoned by international humanitarian organizations that operate from Nairobi. In contrast, the Somali Red Crescent Society, which is based in the country and operates in all regions of the country, can conduct humanitarian efforts more credibly. Importantly, the Somali Red Crescent Society draws on traditional Somali codes of conduct during war, which are consonant with the Geneva Conventions but are both more familiar and more authentic in the Somali context. This traditional code is little known and less used by international actors.[11]

The limited use of local culture and rite is often based on a lack of understanding of the way in which war is conceived by local actors. For example, in Angola and Mozambique, according to the local perspective, war has been a "total crisis" that effectively disrupts all previous social norms for behavior. The space of war is conceptualized as an "abnormality" where one is rewarded for letting children kill adults, and vice versa. It is only after war stops and people must once again cope with everyday needs that people "normalize" their situation. At this point, rituals, including those related to burial rites, become extremely important for two reasons: pardon and cleansing. The use

of such rituals has been shown to be an important part of postconflict reconciliation processes, to name only one use.[12]

International humanitarian and human rights agencies, however, rarely
adopt reconciliation and rehabilitation approaches that make effective use of
local rites. The Somalia example is not unique in what it suggests about the
very serious limits on international actors' knowledge of local custom, law,
norms, and culture. These are important but underutilized resources for
enhancing the protection of civilians. This is true in terms of both understanding existing cultural norms that influence the behavior of belligerents
and noting cultural requirements for successful protection strategies. Lack of
attention to local culture, rites, and the role of ritual means that scarce
resources are typically wasted on culturally inappropriate initiatives. This
point echoes the issue raised in the section above, namely the importance of
understanding the perspective of those civilians whose protection is the raison
d'être of engagement.

These problems—the limited use of local resources and the tension
between strategies of different organizations—arise because the approaches
employed are as much a function of the bureaucratic and political realities for
each international organization as they are a response to the specific context
for protection efforts. This dimension of protection strategies must be fully
appreciated. Just as it is necessary to be pragmatic in our understanding of belligerents, so it is crucial to be realistic—though not uncritical—in our understanding of the people and organizations that are involved in humanitarian and
political responses.

Organizations and the International System: Constraints and Challenges

The capacities of international organizations (and their regional and nongovernmental counterparts) are primarily determined by organizational mandates, history, assumptions, personnel, and other such factors. These elements
impose limits on individual organizations and also on the interconnected system of organizations that constitutes the front line of protection. Moreover,
international organizations are part of a wider international system that has its
own premises, logic, modalities, and constraints. The nature of organizations
and the systems in which they are located are an important dimension of the
overall equation of connecting universal protection norms to effective local
actions.

Tackling first the question of the constraints of international organizations, much is revealed by an exploration of the ICRC, the archetypal neutral
humanitarian agency, and guarantor of the Geneva Conventions—one of the
first major efforts to codify the protection of civilians. This organization is

based on the tenets of humanitarian protection that were initially developed at the first of the Geneva Conventions in 1864, and which in turn were based on a set of four key assumptions: (1) that noncombatants have no strategic value (and should thus be spared the effects of hostilities) and that militaries should follow utilitarian considerations, (2) that parties to a conflict should provide access to humanitarian actors, (3) that humanitarian assistance should be neutral, and (4) that an international treaty would serve as an important guarantor of protection mechanisms.

In the evolving international context in which current protection efforts are based, there are reasons to doubt that these assumptions are still valid.[13] Four key distinctions can be made between the validity of the norms in theory and their implementation in practice. First, civilians are targeted during war (e.g., the Spanish Civil War, Burundi), so they must have military value. Second, the distinction between civilians and combatants is often unclear (Sudan, Eastern Zaire). Third, neutrality is very problematic because any assistance provided to warring parties or civilians has both a real and perceived effect upon their capability to maintain the war effort. Fourth, there is some question as to whether a state-centric approach is the most efficient or practical way to provide for humanitarian protection.

The ICRC, however, is an organization with a strong history and its own self-interest, and it may not want to change its mode of operations or its place within the international regime. Moreover, the ICRC is widely noted for its professionalism, a characteristic that emerges out of strict attention to a set of core principles and consistent application of policy parameters that guide the organization as a whole as well as individual delegates. How can a professional organization like the ICRC attune itself to the local situation for each conflict while at the same time maintaining the professionalism that consistency imparts?

This challenge—of being open to learning and adapting to local circumstance while maintaining a consistent, professional capacity grounded in core principles—is replicated across the range of international, regional, and nongovernmental organizations. Moreover, in an era of changing international and legal parameters, many organizations are internally divided on protection questions. The United Nations itself is often seen as conflicted when it comes to humanitarian intervention. First, there is some question regarding its institutional "disinterest" and impartiality—if it is disinterested, then why intervene? Second, there is at times an unrealistic belief in the prospect of sanctions that are both "painless" for civilians and effective as an enforcement measure.[14] Third, there are tensions between the accountability functions (such as the International Criminal Court) and the stability that may be required for a peacekeeping operation. Fourth, there is still division on the question of regional organizations and cooperation with them. Fifth, the United Nations lacks its own capacity for intervention, and member states are reluctant to empower the organization for this purpose; this creates the perception and the reality of inconsistency. Additional problems stem from the institutional limitations of the United Nations to take a long-term approach to conflict prevention. Finally, it is not always clear how to reconcile the potentially competing mandates of creating peace and enforcing humanitarian norms.

It is one thing to understand the constraints facing one organization or government; it is a second question altogether to understand the constraints on getting effective protection from a system of intersecting organizations. Therefore, quite apart from these *internal* issues of mandate, organizational learning, and incentive systems that drive and constrain individual organizations, there are also *external* constraints that arise from the simple fact that all protection organizations exist and operate in a wider international political system. At the level of the international system—and the states that drive it— it is clear that there are major constraints on both the effectiveness of protection efforts and the consistency of their application. These constraints can be understood both in terms of ambivalence toward humanitarian intervention, which should be understood as the rule rather than as the exception, and in terms of the system of incentives and disincentives created by the political and financial context in which organizations function. These issues are addressed in reverse order—starting with analysis at the organizational level and continuing with a discussion of humanitarian intervention in a broader context.

The system of incentives and disincentives within which protection organizations function is one of the least understood dimensions of the question. A substantial organizational challenge of getting appropriate interventions from organizations with a comparative advantage in a given situation lies in the nature of the incentives offered—in terms of funding, professional advancement, prestige, and organizational clout. Protection organizations (and the people that staff them) see an imperative of presence in every major conflict and crisis setting, irrespective of whether the strategies and comparative advantages their organization can bring to bear are in fact relevant to the needs of protection in the given case. (Of course, incentives and disincentives are only one part of what makes an organization act. The people who staff those organizations have their own decisionmaking capacity, and their role is an important but oft-overlooked dimension of the protection equation. The capacity of these individuals to influence selection criteria for intervention and the development of strategy is substantial, usually ignored, and almost wholly unaccountable.)

Second, the international political system constrains protection organizations due to a persistent ambivalence toward humanitarian intervention.[15] There are a number of sources of this ambivalence, among them (1) ambiguity regarding the nature of a particular conflict, (2) a sense that the enforcement of humanitarian norms is an "international" responsibility and thus not the burden of any particular state, (3) frequent competing interests and responsibilities between the United Nations Secretariat and agencies and its member states, and (4) the fact that enforcement mechanisms have real consequences and are therefore usually the result of the strategic calculation of perceived self-interest among member states.

Even where there is not a priori ambivalence, there is need for pragmatism with respect to humanitarian intervention because (1) belligerents are often "thugs" who create a strong disincentive for international action, (2) the risk of escalation is often ignored by the UN Security Council, (3) there are large disparities among the responses of member states that should be understood within the context of their respective domestic political arenas, and (4) each conflict is different and should be addressed on a case-by-case basis.

In order to overcome both ambivalence and pragmatic constraints, the United States is often thought of as indispensable, both in terms of the authorization of humanitarian intervention and the provision of the means for implementation. Practical military considerations—airpower, seapower, logistical support, and intelligence—dictate that U.S. support is almost always necessary for an effective large-scale enforcement action. Given its high profile and massive capabilities, the United States is often criticized for its inconsistency in the enforcement of humanitarian norms. In some ways, however, the United States is not that much different from other states: its international policies are often derivative of domestic political concerns and realities (in recent cases, exerting pressure against international involvement). On the other hand, in some cases, the position of the United States is clearly at odds with the rest of the world (such as the exceptionalism asserted by the Pentagon with respect to the International Criminal Court).

Moreover, a U.S.-backed humanitarian intervention will generally only succeed with the support of other UN member states. Unfortunately, the P-5 states in the Security Council suffer from selective attention to international developments, which limits their scope for intervention. Similarly, the "middle powers" (such as Germany and Japan) lack capacity for enforcement measures, which often renders unconvincing their rhetoric on the need for a more robust international response to crisis situations. As for the developing countries, there is a reluctance to devolve sovereignty, a bias toward noninterference, and a concern for equity—all of which can act contrary to pressures for the international enforcement of humanitarian norms.

Thus, understanding the organizational dimension of protection entails both the way in which individual organizations do or do not learn and adjust their strategies in the face of specific challenges in local contexts, and the complex and evolving way in which those organizations interact with a wider international political system—that both shapes and to a lesser extent is shaped by their activities. If this were not sufficiently complex, there is the added complication that this international system of protection organizations is ultimately grounded in a series of universal norms and principles that are

themselves in flux. It is to this question of transforming international normative frameworks that we now turn.

Universal Norms: A Progress Report

In both their inventiveness and their dysfunction, international organizations
are the primary conduit through which universal norms are developed, refined,
and implemented. Indeed, the flux, competition, innovation, and systemic dysfunction that appear to characterize modern international organizations can be
seen as primarily a function of the current process of transformation that is taking place in the realm of universal norms themselves—particularly where
dealing with various elements of protection.

The recent examples of Kosovo and East Timor demonstrate the apparent
salience of humanitarian intervention as an emerging norm of international
relations, which is even more striking with the historical perspective that systemic efforts toward civilian protection are actually quite new.[16] Civilian protection is largely based on the Fourth Geneva Convention of 1949 and the
1977 Protocols Additional to the Geneva Conventions. Both are limited in
scope. For example, the Fourth Geneva Convention really only deals with
civilians in the context of militarily occupied territories and detention by an
adversarial military force. Nonetheless, an analytic paradigm persists that
places emphasis on breaches of civilian protection and actually overstates the
case regarding the gap between principle and practice. Furthermore, commentary that only portrays civilians as fully innocent bystanders in war situations misrepresents the ugly complexities of war and can lead to dubious conclusions and policy recommendations (for example, that "safe areas" during
the Bosnian war could and should be thoroughly demilitarized). International
law is the product less of ideals than of "hard negotiation" among states,
which unavoidably reflects their self-interests.

Is there a right to humanitarian intervention? According to the classic definition, humanitarian intervention is (1) a military operation, (2) without the
consent of warring parties, and (3) for the purpose of preventing civilian
deaths. Typically, the principle of nonintervention in the affairs of sovereign
nation-states has been conceptualized as being in direct opposition to the practice of humanitarian intervention as defined above. However, one could rein-
terpret humanitarian intervention as not necessarily undermining the overall
integrity of the nonintervention principle. For example, there have been a
number of international interventions, such as the recent operation in East
Timor, where there was an "element of consent" even though formal authorization was lacking for the operation—thus indicating a potential middle
ground between the poles of humanitarian intervention and strict nonintervention.

Obtaining a clear legal doctrine for humanitarian intervention seems unlikely. One reason is the position of China and many of the Non-Aligned Movement countries on this issue (stemming at least in part from the history of colonialism). Second, the issue of consent is actually very complex in practice, as epitomized in the East Timor intervention. Third, more consideration needs to be given to the means of humanitarian intervention—for example, NATO bombing of civilians in Kosovo and Serbia. Fourth, there is a need to recognize that external actors have limited interests and are often reluctant to commit adequate resources. Finally, rather than searching for new legal instruments to further regulate humanitarian intervention, perhaps the international community should concentrate efforts on determining what could be learned from recent Security Council and state practice.[17]

This constitutes one approach to the problem. Another involves historicizing the problem, or more accurately, problematizing the history.[18] In order to understand the laws of war and their application toward civilian protection, these laws should be put into their proper historical context. The framers of the Hague Conventions of 1899 were faced with two crucial juridical puzzles: Can one make a conceptual distinction between "just war" and "justice in war"? And how can one distinguish between combatants and noncombatants? In the former case, a "middle-ground ideology" emerged, which argued that such a determination is possible. According to this line of thought, one can separate issues regarding *how* a war is fought from a discussion of *why* a war is fought. In the latter case, combatants were defined as "those who fight," and noncombatants were termed "those who are passive." In a sense, the perceived need for guidelines that set standards of "neutrality" for the conduct of war effectively created laws of war that are not "neutral" themselves. The Hague Conventions were drafted to "professionalize war" and thus pertain to the conduct of standing armies toward each other. However, practice has shown that war is often between soldiers and civilians (and thus outside the scope of the rules developed at the Hague Conference). To a certain extent, the contemporary inadequacy of international humanitarian law for the protection of civilians in conflict can be traced to earlier failures to resolve the contradictions inherent in legal conceptions of "neutrality" and "combatant." Thus, it may be necessary to think more deeply about our own assumptions regarding these terms and how they relate to protection issues in practice.

A third approach favors exploring new efforts to develop the international law of individual accountability. Ironically, there is some sense that massive human rights violations should be handled at the domestic level, while individual crimes have been dealt with more comfortably at the international level. For example, some Chileans, even those who have opposed Pinochet, view their own past as intrinsically linked with the present and therefore may see a trial abroad of former President Pinochet as a challenge to the nation as a whole. Nonetheless, the case clearly has legal merit as established by the

UK courts, the objections raised by Chileans and their government regarding the issue of sovereignty notwithstanding.[19]

Some recent developments under Chapter VII of the UN Charter—the creation of the International Criminal Tribunal for the former Yugoslavia (ICTY) and the International Criminal Tribunal for Rwanda (ICTR)—paved the way for agreement on the Statute for an International Criminal Court (ICC) via treaty in Rome in July 1998. Despite the fact that a number of suprastate or interstate forms of jurisdiction already exist in international law (including Security Council law, laws on crimes against humanity), the ICC has provoked a number of objections, in part because it is difficult to explain to those who are not international law specialists. Though international lawyers point out that since states consented to the creation of the statutes of the ICC—indeed were instrumental in its creation—the ICC cannot be seen as impinging on national prerogatives, nevertheless the ICC is perceived by many as posing a direct challenge to state sovereignty. Accordingly, some proponents argue for a cautious approach to setting up the ICC so that it will not be marginalized by powerful states (notably the United States). Other advocates argue that the moment is right to push forward with the establishment of the Court—regardless of the objections of certain key state powers.

Despite an apparent "progress narrative," there remains a powerful clash between the "interstate order" model of law and diplomacy and what could be called the "criminal law" model derived from domestic legal systems. Whether the two can be productively reconciled is not yet clear. There are likely to be political pressures for international courts to work preventatively—particularly since political and financial costs for a possible alternative (such as humanitarian intervention) would be much higher. Yet, there are serious potential disadvantages to this approach: (1) the capacity of international courts is limited, (2) prosecuting individuals for violations personalizes conflict, and (3) a backlash may be created, which would lead us back to the emphasis of 1899 on protecting standing armies (although this is somewhat unlikely).

While there is little hope for reaching consensus in the near term regarding such possible solutions, it is also evident that the claims of states to benefit from nonintervention have diminished. Three issues are particularly worth exploring: (1) the question of the "process solution" proposed as a way forward through the current state of doctrinal debate, (2) the question of competition among evolving norms, and (3) the question of how it might be possible to structure interaction within these normative frameworks. Such issues relate closely to the more operational questions of comparative advantages among international and humanitarian organizations. Can the international community find mechanisms or processes whereby the preventive value of accountability laws and norms is maximized while their potential to undermine processes of reconciliation are also minimized?

One suggestion, proposed by international law expert Lori Damrosch, has been to develop a so-called process solution whereby multilateral bodies would be charged with determining the nature and existence of a humanitarian crisis *but not* be asked to expressly authorize a particular response.[20] In theory, such findings would function as a diagnosis of a critical situation, after which states would be permitted *legally* to develop an appropriate response to protect the lives of civilians at risk. Variations on this solution might enable the General Assembly (instead of the Security Council) to make the initial determination, which would then be relayed to the Security Council. The burden of proof would thus be placed on the Security Council by confronting it with findings of fact rather than more contentious issues regarding possible solutions. The advantage of such a system is that a determination of applicability of intervention criteria would be made democratically (and thus presumably more consistently) than is likely if the question were left to a closed body like the Security Council.

Unfortunately, this proposal is also problematic: the General Assembly does not sit permanently, has no independent access to information, and operates through a heavy-handed and slow bureaucracy. Moreover, a high number of members of the Assembly do not endorse humanitarian intervention, because of a concern for the erosion of sovereignty. Of course, this concern is fueled by the suspicion that intervention will operate at the whim of the great powers, rather than on the basis of consistent criteria. Presumably, if the Assembly were able to control the application of the criteria, this concern would diminish. This point notwithstanding, there are a number of other significant obstacles to overcome for such a solution to be effective.

Interestingly, elements of the "process solution" are already to be found in the Convention on the Prevention and Punishment of the Crime of Genocide—the first piece of international legislation to codify the need for military response in the face of gross human rights violations. The Genocide Convention, as it is popularly known, creates a legal opportunity—though not an obligation—for member states to call on the UN to "take such measures under the Charter" as may be necessary to prevent or punish genocide or acts of genocide. The Genocide Convention has been notable not only for the absence of actions taken under its provisions but even more so for the recurrent reluctance of states to refer to the Genocide Convention to justify even bona fide humanitarian actions. Does this mean that a "process solution" could not work?

Not necessarily. There are two substantive differences between the Genocide Convention and the process solution considered here. First, while the black-letter law of the Genocide Convention does not compel international intervention when genocide occurs, there is a widespread perception that such an obligation does exist. This goes a long way toward explaining states' reluctance to make use of the Genocide Convention: namely, fear of creating precedents. Second, and perhaps more important, is the fact that there is nothing in the Genocide Convention to structure the process by which a determination is made that a genocide is in fact occurring. Nothing in the text identifies responsibility for this determination or suggests the means by which such a determination occurs. As a result, an enormously wide range of actors, some credible and competent, others distinctly unprofessional, can raise the flag of genocide and seek action. This generates a "cry wolf" phenomenon that reinforces the unwillingness of states to make use of the Genocide Convention.

Nevertheless, the idea of a "process solution" raises intriguing prospects worthy of further consideration. Research, policy development, and practice are creating new arrangements, pushing the boundaries of existing certainties, and opening up further space for humanitarian engagement because norms, and their implementing organizations, are in a state of flux. This creates complexity but also possibility. Between complexity and possibility—and somewhere between the reach of the International Criminal Court, the ICRC, and the Security Council—lies a combination of effective strategies that can be put together in varying ways to meet the protection needs of civilian populations in a wide range of local conflicts. But, exactly, where?

Developing a Framework for Integrated and Effective Response

How do the different levels explored here—local contexts, strategies, organizations, the international system, and principles—connect, both analytically and in real terms? How does one link universal standards with local challenges and success stories? How can concerned actors ensure that there is consistent, effective protection of civilians while contending with the political constraints and parochial interests of the governments and international organizations ostensibly responsible for ensuring it? What causes one set of norms to be applied in a given case, and another in a second? Are there international mechanisms that manage or coordinate such processes, making best use of the comparative advantage of different bodies of law and the institutions that employ them? Or is protection primarily a function of diffuse organizational and national politics, of shifting interests and competing norms? That symposium participants discerned more evidence of diffusion than coordination raises serious questions about the prospect of consistent, effective implementation of strategies for protection in the wide range of specific contexts in which civilians are exposed to violence.

The first—perhaps the critical—step is to emphasize our starting point: that there are *patterns* in the local success stories. Case studies provide ample evidence of the variation of conflict settings, attributes, and actors. Less attention is typically paid to patterns within that variation, but this symposium made a significant contribution in this regard. These patterns can be mapped, explored, understood, and to a limited extent even predicted. Of particular salience in terms of the protection of civilians are the patterns that emerge in the relationship between belligerents and civilian populations—relations of protection, service delivery, extraction, and abuse. Understanding how these relations vary, principally as a function of the type of war and the objectives of belligerents, provides a critical foundation for strengthening the architecture of international protection efforts.

Improved understanding of these issues can also inform better strategy. To provide effective protection (for example, through humanitarian assistance), strategies must be built on an understanding of how the belligerents and civilian populations relate in a given context. In a situation where militias are important providers of social services and protection to a given population under their control, humanitarian assistance will likely be most effective if it seeks to maximize, rather than displace, that service delivery function. When militias are using civilian populations primarily as a source of extraction, introducing new material goods—that is, food assistance, tools, shelter materials, and other such items—may simply expose civilians to further levels of harassment, attack, and abuse, as militias seek to extract even greater levels of resources from those civilians. At the extreme, when militias either deliberately put civilians between themselves and other belligerents, or directly attack civilians to displace them or generate an environment of fear and uncertainty, in which their rule can flourish, traditional humanitarian assistance is unlikely to do much at all in the way of assistance. Protection of civilians in such circumstances will require either concerted political and economic interventions designed to alter the political economy of warfare from which such militias profit, or direct military intervention to deter abuses. Of course, a greater level of specificity would be required to translate these loose concepts into actual correlations between situations and strategies. For the purposes of this chapter, however, the key is that the range of strategies required does not need to span the full breadth of specific local contexts; it need only match the patterns of variation. In a world in which there were, for example, twenty instances of civil war in which a given organization was trying to protect civilians, the patterns discussed above would likely function in such a way that only a few different types of strategies are needed, not twenty unique ones. Of course, these will be tailored to local contexts; but they will be cut from a more manageable number of patterns.

This is important, because for the organizations involved in providing protection, the complexity of that organizational world is such that matching the wide-ranging, complex, and fractured world of international organizations to each specific context makes for an unwieldy, perhaps impossible, task at the international policy level. Making effective connections between organizations and specific contexts is aided by a degree of conceptual grouping on both sides of the equation—in dealing with the patterns of variation in local contexts but also in understanding the nature and types of organizations engaged in protection efforts and the systems in place for activating or deploying them to intervene in a given context. With reasonably effective systems for matching the capacities and comparative advantages of organizations to particular types of situations, it might be possible to construct the basic framework of a system for provision of adequate, consistent protection. Strong systems of what is referred to as *strategic coordination* would be required to manage a system of matching the comparative advantages of institutions (and the norms they embody) to cases that fit certain patterns.

Of course, there is little evidence of any such systems being in place. There is ample evidence from recent cases—in Bosnia and Kosovo, Sierra Leone and Liberia, East Timor and elsewhere—of the weakness of existing systems for strategic coordination. Each of these cases is characterized by multiple overlapping actors with similar mandates, weak histories of collaboration, competitive fund-raising tools, and separate reporting lines. The situation is particularly difficult in Europe, which is increasingly characterized by a multiplicity of regional organizations able to take on political, economic, and humanitarian functions—including, but not limited to, NATO, the EU, the Council of Europe, and the OSCE. Each of these organizations functions in uneasy relation to one another and to the UN.

The period following NATO's conflict with Serbia is particularly notable for what it revealed about the competition and potential for collaboration among all of these organizations. An extraordinary collection of international and regional organizations seeking to play key protection roles is present in postconflict Kosovo. These include (1) NATO seeking to provide physical protection to civilians, based on Security Council law; (2) the International Criminal Tribunal for Yugoslavia seeking to collect evidence and prosecute war crimes, based on war crimes legislation; (3) UNHCR seeking to provide assistance and legal protection to refugees and internally displaced persons, based on refugee law; (4) the ICRC seeking to provide assistance and legal protection, based on the Geneva Conventions; (5) the OSCE seeking to provide human rights protection to civilians, based on a UN-assigned role in "governance and institution-building," and with particular attention to European human rights conventions; (6) the UN seeking to provide legal protection through its responsibility for justice issues in Kosovo; and (7) the UN High Commissioner for Human Rights seeking to establish a human rights reporting mechanism, based on international human rights law and standards. Yet the challenge of providing effective protection to civilians in Kosovo remains a daunting one. The disjuncture between the array of protection assets deployed in Kosovo and the limits on protection efforts is extraordinary and revealing.

Is civilian protection simply so hard that even with an enormous number of protection assets, assembled by the richest possible collection of regional and international organizations, efforts are bound to fail? Or is it the case that the current complexity and structures of the international systems for protection actually diminish our response capacity? Surely, it is some measure of both.

Effective protection of civilians outside the framework of a functioning and responsible state is extraordinarily difficult. But this argues all the more sharply to ensure that international protection efforts are as focused, disciplined, and well managed as possible. This means, in ideal terms, the creation of systems of incentives that will allow organizations to respond only when they have a comparative advantage to offer, and to do so consistently. It means having methods or systems that regulate or coordinate the conflicting strategies of relevant organizations and helping those organizations find ways more effectively to combine their efforts.

The reality, far too often, is that multiple and in some sense competing norms and a diffuse international political system are driving complex, competing, and frequently ineffective organizations to develop responses based principally on their mandates and expertise rather than on the basis of comparative advantage, serious analysis of the specificity of a given situation, or appropriate response strategies. The result is a far less efficient and effective system for protecting civilians in war than can be imagined or implemented.

In a recent work on peacemaking, I. William Zartman argues that "on the edge of the millennium, the methods of conflict have been more brutal and the methods of conflict resolution more sophisticated than ever before, leaving a tremendous gap between reality and theory that remains to be filled."[21] Surely part of this gap arises from the complexity, diffusion, and normative flux that currently characterizes the international systems for protection. These features inhibit making the kinds of effective connections between norms, organizations, strategies, and local contexts that must be made in order to achieve effective, consistent protection for civilians in war.

Next Steps: Additional Issues and Future Work

If there is to be progress in implementing existing norms and laws for the protection of civilians, the challenge of making effective connections across the four different levels discussed herein emerges as a central one. Taking the agenda forward requires new work in three domains: research, organizational development, and politics.

Research Agendas

A number of specific areas of research would aid the implementation effort. A first field of inquiry addresses the question of the relations between combatants and civilians. These include (1) collecting further data (or presenting existing data in more accessible forms) on the motivation, interests, and incentives of combatants to attack/protect civilians in war as well as mapping the evolution of those interests over the course of protracted conflicts; (2) extending existing analyses to different kinds of contexts, in particular relating to militias that have significant economic agendas for pursuing war strategies (such as UNITA, RUF, and Taleban); (3) mapping the "sublocal" variation in protection—that is, the manner in which, in one given war context, the degree and manner of attacks on civilians, or protection thereof, vary from village to village, county to county; and (4) collecting further data (or presenting existing data in more accessible forms) on traditional modes of social reconciliation and codes for conduct in war.

A second field of inquiry relates to the manner in which the international community gains the consent of local actors to engage on protection issues, short of full-scale military intervention. In this context, the concept of "pressured consent" is useful. A specific proposal would be to research the case of East Timor and the various tools that were used to pressure the Indonesian government into consenting to the deployment of a UN protection force. This would involve tracing the debates within New York, Washington, and other capitals about the decision to apply various forms of pressure, and the evolution of the response in Jakarta. The central question would be to determine which (or which combination) of the various tools led to the change in Indonesia's position. Similar inquiries could be conducted into a representative set of cases in order to establish some guidelines as to "what works" in what circumstances with respect to pressured consent. This could then be extended to consider nonstate armed groups—mapping, for example, the entry points for pressure with respect to militias whose primary objectives are economic and who may prove to be the least responsive to more traditional sources of legal and political pressure.

In addition, several issues that arose only briefly at the symposium should not go unaddressed. These include:

The privatization of security. There is a growing phenomenon where states are functionally unable (let alone politically willing) to provide security for their civilian populations. Private security actors are emerging in this void, but largely in the service of corporate and private interests, not public ones.

The connection between globalization and intractable wars of economic gain.[22] One seminar participant made the point that a diamond contract is infinitely more valuable than a seat on the General Assembly. How can the international community engage corporate and economic actors on a protection agenda? How can it be ensured that private actors are also held accountable?

The role of NGOs, especially regarding North-South links. Local, domestic NGOs are particularly important partners in the protection of civilians.

Links between international and local NGOs are increasing, providing an important channel of resources and a focus of activity. However, there are risks that excessive diversion of resources and political support to NGOs may undermine state formation and democratic processes in weak states.

Prevention and the linkages between security and development.[23] Protection should be the focus of long-term preventive initiatives, not solely emergency responses to conflict situations. Developing effective long-term policy requires research and dialogue to bridge the existing gaps between development and security literatures and practitioners.

In each of these areas, the appropriate methodology is a triangular conversation among case specialists, analytical "framers," and policymakers. This is a methodology for policy-relevant research that is being employed by the International Peace Academy and its research partners (notably, Stanford University's Center for International Security and Cooperation) in a number of different projects, and is proving useful for generating high-quality research that charts the fine line between excessive generalization and over-specification while also being formulated in a way that leads to the development of clear policy options.

Organizational Development

If the organizations involved in developing protection responses are to make use of good research and knowledge about local contexts and the patterns to which they conform, there must also be substantial reform and development of the system of international organizations. This would be in two realms: first, in the realm of strategic coordination, in terms of the systems that exist or do not exist for forging effective linkages between norms, policy, strategy, and specific action; and, second, in the realm of making determinations about where and when protection action—including humanitarian intervention—is needed.

Strengthening the strategic coordination capacities of the international system is a major challenge in a context where there is serious and sustained international debate about the role of the UN vis-à-vis regional and subregional organizations, where the UN itself is embattled and frequently unresponsive, and where much of the energy and innovation lies in the nongovernmental world, which, by nature, is least amenable to strategic coordination. Of course, it remains debatable whether the real problem of strategic coordination lies with inadequate coordination or with poor strategies. There have certainly been a number of situations where lead entities, including the UN, have employed strategies that were well coordinated but ill conceived. Nonetheless, it is surely the case that even with an appropriate strategy, implementation would be dependent on some kind of appropriate coordination capacity. Unfortunately, there is evidence that the collective capacity of international and regional political and humanitarian organizations to collaborate toward implementation of an effective strategy for protection in a given case has been deteriorating, not improving—notwithstanding the multiple efforts toward the creation of policies or frameworks for strategic coordination. Indeed, the proliferation of such efforts is more indicative of the fractured and disparate nature of the international protection "system" than it is of substantive progress. In the UN system, it is only recently that systematic attention to the question of strategic coordination, notably by the Deputy Secretary-General, has begun to bear fruit, and this comes at a time when the demand for increased interaction between the UN and other organizations adds a whole new dimension of complexity.

The question of coordination is most frequently discussed in the humanitarian world. However, recent episodes such as Kosovo reveal that the issues that drive the coordination debate in the humanitarian community—overlapping mandates, resources wasted on duplication, conflicting and competing strategies among ostensibly like-minded institutions—increasingly characterize the political sphere as well. Europe is probably the region where the growth in overlapping, often competing regional and subregional organizations has been most notable, but other regions are not far behind. In this realm, one is repeatedly confronted with the reality that one government may have four or five very different positions on the same protection issue, depending on which organization they are speaking through.

Fundamentally, however, the question of strategic coordination depends on a willingness of both bureaucrats and political actors within organizations, and outside them, to place the protection needs of a given population ahead of the specific interests of their own organization. However, this reflects a problem with the nature of existing organizations: the interests of civilian populations and of protection organizations should be more or less synchronized, but often they are not. Existing financial and organizational structures are such that strategic coordination is so much at odds with the basic parameters of institutional survival and development that substantive initiatives in this realm must overcome serious obstacles. In determining when a situation exists that calls for a concerted international effort to mount a protection response, especially where strong political or military action is needed to protect the basic human rights of civilians, the difficulty of getting consistent criteria for intervention is acute (as noted above in the section on norms). However, progress in this area will likely depend very substantially on prior progress in a third area for further work, namely in the realm of domestic politics.

Politics

Reform of international and regional organizations in a way that will generate more effective strategic coordination and consistency in intervention is highly dependent on the nature of political support for such reforms among member states. But here, dialogue and debate are usually constrained by the "international community"—a collection of generally like-minded individuals and bureaucratic departments that represent and manage "foreign policy" and multilateral agendas. Increasingly, however, the nature of domestic politics in a number of key states is such that this grouping of actors is in fact either unable to represent their government's view or to make credible commitments on the part of their own governments. Rather, a much wider set of actors whose inputs have traditionally been confined to domestic politics is increasingly powerful on international issues, and the process of achieving a coherent policy—let alone action—within a given capital requires a far wider set of negotiations and compromises than most multilateral organizations are typically set up to facilitate. Moreover, existing foreign policy bodies and multilateral agencies have traditionally done a rather poor job of lobbying domestic constituencies in order to develop domestic political support for international policies or action in the humanitarian and protection fields.

This suggests, then, that those concerned with the strengthening of the international capacity to implement international norms and laws to protect civilians in and from wars would be well served to shift some of the emphasis of their intellectual and political work from the international to the domestic arena. The job of building political coalitions among and between domestic constituencies is fundamental if a more consistent, more effective regime for the protection of civilians in and from war is to emerge. Here, the exciting fact is that we live in what must surely be a unique historical moment, when the world's only major power is not only a democracy but a democracy uniquely open to nongovernmental influence. International actors have long decried the ability of a variety of domestic lobbies in Washington to influence foreign policy debates in ways that adversely impact upon their preferred strategies. Until very recently, and still only in small measure, what had not been done was to join the fight; to take the case for consistent, principled international action to the domestic lobbies; to sell the argument in the domestic arena. But the potential to make a case for the rule of law in international affairs and to develop a constituency for principled international action is far greater than the effort that has been given to date. Until a more concerted effort has been made, both in the United States and across a range of other implicated countries, it is unlikely that there will be a major shift in the underlying international systems that condition the pursuit of implementing protection principles.

Conclusion

And so the chapter ends on a paradox—that the search for a more effective and consistent implementation of international norms and laws to protect civilians in war begins with more consistent and effective engagement in domestic politics. Just as the real test of effective protection lies at the local level, so the real political will to make this happen derives from the local level. The complex international system that currently manages and sustains interventions needs to do much less to separate these twin realities and far more to bridge them.

Currently, international protection efforts are too frequently characterized by inconsistency, incoherence, and ineffectiveness. Fledgling international protection efforts are fractured at a variety of levels. Developing a framework for consistent and effective protection requires new energy and political will to solve a range of challenges discussed in this chapter. Enhanced understanding of local dynamics and actors, improved strategies and systems for coordination, strengthened and reformed protection organizations, and a productive mediation between established and emergent laws and norms—these are the building blocks of a more solid international regime for the protection of civilians in war.

Notes

The views expressed in this chapter are those of the authors and are not necessarily those of either the United Nations or the International Peace Academy.

1. This chapter draws from the major themes of an International Peace Academy/Carnegie Corporation of New York symposium, September 23–24, 1999, as well as points developed further within this volume. As a text, it is the responsibility of the authors. As a body of ideas, the authors would like to gratefully acknowledge the contributions of both symposium participants and chapter authors.

2. Report of the Secretary-General to the Security Council on the Protection of Civilians in Armed Conflict, UN Doc. S/1999/957 (1999).

3. UN Doc. A/54/PV.4 (Sept. 20, 1999).

4. SC Res. 1264 (1999).

5. See Marie-Joëlle Zahar, Chapter 3 in this volume.

6. The case is complicated by the differing objectives of the rebels' sometime backers, Rwanda and Uganda, whose objectives have more to do with establishing a security zone along their western borders and with economic interests in eastern DRC.

7. Joao Honwana, "Putting Belligerents in Context: Contemporary Conflict in Africa," panel presentation, International Peace Academy/Carnegie Corporation of New York symposium, September 23–24, 1999. Honwana raised the personal dilemmas faced by combatants.

8. Pierre Gassmann, Chapter 4 in this volume.

9. Report of the Secretary-General Pursuant to General Assembly Resolution 53/35: The Fall of Srebrenica, UN Doc. A/54/549 (1999); Report of the Independent Inquiry into the Actions of the United Nations During the 1994 Genocide in Rwanda, attached to UN Doc. S/1999/1257 (1999).

10. The People On War campaign is an ICRC project aimed at consulting with those civilians who are directly affected by war in order to better target international humanitarian efforts toward local contexts and needs.

11. Abdulkadir Ibrahim Haji Abdi, "Learning from 'People on War' in Somalia," panel presentation, International Peace Academy/Carnegie Corporation of New York symposium, September 23–24, 1999.

12. Alcinda Honwana, Chapter 6 in this volume.

13. Claude Bruderlein, Chapter 11 in this volume.

14. David Cortright and George A. Lopez, *The Sanctions Decade: Assessing UN Strategies in the 1990s* (Boulder, CO: Lynne Rienner Publishers, 2000).

15. Edward C. Luck, Chapter 10 in this volume.

16. Although some have questioned NATO's rationale for intervention in Kosovo as well as the relevance of comparisons with the case of East Timor.

17. Adam Roberts, Chapter 9 in this volume.

18. Karma Nabulsi, Chapter 1 in this volume. Nabulsi also proposed the concept of a "progress narrative."

19. Michael Byers, "Individual Accountability in International Law," panel presentation, International Peace Academy/Carnegie Corporation of New York symposium, September 23–24, 1999. Byers focused on the Pinochet case and its implications for the International Criminal Court.

20. This suggestion was made at the symposium by Anne-Marie Slaughter.

21. I. William Zartman and J. Lewis Rasmussen (eds.), *Peacemaking in International Conflict: Methods and Techniques* (Washington, DC: USIP Press, 1997), p. 3.

22. See, for example, David M. Malone and Mats Berdal (eds.), *Greed and Grievance: Economic Agendas in Civil Wars* (Boulder, CO: Lynne Rienner Publishers, 2000).

23. See, for example, Charles K. Cater and Karin Wermester, *From Reaction to Prevention: Opportunities for the UN System in the New Millennium* (New York: International Peace Academy, International Policy Conference Report, Apr. 13–14, 2000).

Abbreviations and Acronyms

AUC	Autodefensas Unidas de Colombia
CIO	Central Intelligence Organization (Rhodesia)
CIVPOL	international civilian police
DPA	United Nations Department of Political Affairs
DPKO	United Nations Department of Peacekeeping Operations
DRC	Democratic Republic of the Congo
ECOMOG	ECOWAS Monitoring Group
ECOWAS	Economic Community of West African States
ELN	National Liberation Army (Colombia) [*Ejercito de Liberación Nacional*]
EPLF	Eritrean People's Liberation Front
ERC	United Nations Emergency Relief Coordinator
EU	European Union
EZLN	Zapatista National Liberation Army (Mexico)
FAA	Angolan Armed Forces [*Forças Armadas Angolanas*]
FARC	Revolutionary Armed Forces of Colombia [*Fuerzas Armadas Revolucionarias de Colombia*]
FMLN	Farabundo Martí National Liberation Front (El Salvador)
FRELIMO	Front for the Liberation of Mozambique
HRD	Human Rights Department
HRFOR	United Nations Human Rights Field Operation in Rwanda
ICC	International Criminal Court
ICCPR	International Covenant on Civil and Political Rights
ICHRP	International Council on Human Rights Policy
ICRC	International Committee of the Red Cross
ICTR	International Criminal Tribunal for Rwanda
ICTY	International Criminal Tribunal for the former Yugoslavia
IDP	internally displaced person

IHL	international humanitarian law
INPEC	National Penitentiary Institute
IPTF	International Police Task Force (Bosnia-Herzegovina)
IRA	Irish Republican Army
KLA/UCK	Kosovo Liberation Army
MICIVIH	International Civilian Mission in Haiti (Feb. 1993–)
MINUGUA	United Nations Verification Mission in Guatemala (Jan.–May 1997)
MNF	Multinational Force
MONUA	United Nations Mission in Angola (July 1997–Feb. 1999)
MPF	multinational protection force
MPLA	Popular Movement for the Liberation of Angola [*Movimento Popular de Libertação de Angola*]
MSF	Médecins Sans Frontières
NATO	North Atlantic Treaty Organization
NGO	nongovernmental organization
NPFL	National Patriotic Front of Liberia
OAS	Organization of American States
OAU	Organization of African Unity
OCHA	United Nations Office for the Coordination of Humanitarian Affairs
OHR	Office of the High Representative (Bosnia-Herzegovina)
ONUSAL	United Nations Observer Mission in El Salvador (July 1991–Apr. 1995)
OSCE	Organization for Security and Cooperation in Europe
PLAN	People's Liberation Army of Namibia
PLO	Palestinian Liberation Organization
RENAMO	Mozambique National Resistance
RPA	Rwandese Patriotic Army
RUF	Revolutionary United Front (Sierra Leone)
SADC	Southern African Development Community
SADF	South African Defense Force
SAP	South African Police
SPLA	Sudan People's Liberation Army
SWAPO	South West Africa People's Organization
SYL	SWAPO Youth League
TRC	Truth and Reconciliation Commission (South Africa)
UDHR	Universal Declaration of Human Rights
UN	United Nations
UNAMIR	United Nations Assistance Mission for Rwanda (Oct. 1993–Mar. 1996)
UNAMSIL	United Nations Mission in Sierra Leone (Oct. 1999–)
UNDP	United Nations Development Programme
UNGCI	United Nations Guards Contingent in Iraq

UNHCHR	United Nations High Commissioner for Human Rights
UNHCR	United Nations High Commissioner for Refugees
UNICEF	United Nations Children's Fund
UNITA	National Union for the Total Independence of Angola [*União Nacional para la Independençia Total de Angola*]
UNITAF	Unified Task Force
UNMIH	United Nations Mission in Haiti (Sept. 1993–June 1996)
UNOMSIL	United Nations Observer Mission in Sierra Leone (July 1998–Oct. 1999)
UNPROFOR	United Nations Protection Force (Feb. 1992–Mar. 1995)
UNTAC	United Nations Transitional Authority in Cambodia (Mar. 1992–Sept. 1993)
UNTAET	United Nations Transitional Administration in East Timor (Oct. 1999–)
UP	Union Patriotica
UNOSOM	United Nations Operation in Somalia
UPA-FNLA	Popular Union of Angola–National Front for the Liberation of Angola
USAID	United States Agency for International Development
ZANLA	Zimbabwe National Liberation Army

Treaty Abbreviations

First Geneva Convention	Geneva Convention for the Amelioration of the Condition of the Wounded and the Sick in Armed Forces in the Field, Aug. 12, 1949, 75 UNTS 31
Second Geneva Convention	Geneva Convention for the Amelioration of the Condition of Wounded, Sick and Shipwrecked Members of Armed Forces at Sea, Aug. 12, 1949, 75 UNTS 85
Third Geneva Convention	Geneva Convention Relative to the Treatment of Prisoners of War, Aug. 12, 1949, 75 UNTS 135
Fourth Geneva Convention	Geneva Convention Relative to the Protection of Civilian Persons in Time of War, Aug. 12, 1949, 75 UNTS 287 (sometimes referred to as the Civilians Convention)
Additional Protocol I	Protocol Additional to the Geneva Conventions of 12 August 1949, and Relating to the Protection of Victims of International Armed Conflicts, June 8, 1977
Additional Protocol II	Protocol Additional to the Geneva Conventions of 12 August 1949, and Relating to the Protection of Victims of Non-International Armed Conflicts, June 8, 1977

Bibliography

af Jochnick, Chris, and Roger Normand. "The Legitimation of Violence: A Critical History of the Laws of War." *Harvard International Law Journal* 35 (1994), p. 35.

Alao, Abiodun. *The Burden of Collective Goodwill: The International Involvement in the Liberian Civil War.* Aldershot: Ashgate, 1998.

Amnesty International. *Kosovo: After Tragedy, Justice?* London: Amnesty International, 1999.

Annan, Kofi. "Peace-Keeping in Situations of Civil War." *New York University Journal of International Law and Politics* 26 (1994), p. 623.

Aspen Institute. *Honoring Human Rights and Keeping the Peace: Lessons from El Salvador, Cambodia, and Haiti.* Washington, DC: Aspen Institute, 1995.

Bassiouni, M. Cherif. *Crimes Against Humanity in International Criminal Law*, 2d ed. The Hague: Kluwer, 1999.

————. *The Statute of the International Criminal Court: A Documentary History.* Ardsley, NY: Transnational, 1998.

Berdal, Mats R. "The Security Council, Peacekeeping and Internal Conflict After the Cold War." *Duke Journal of Comparative and International Law* 7 (1996), p. 71.

Berdal, Mats, and David M. Malone (eds.). *Greed and Grievance: Economic Agendas in Civil Wars.* Boulder, CO: Lynne Rienner Publishers, 2000.

Best, Geoffrey. *War and Law Since 1945.* Oxford: Clarendon Press, 1994.

Betts, Richard K. "The Delusion of Impartial Intervention." *Foreign Affairs* 73, 6 (Nov./Dec. 1994), p. 20.

Boutros-Ghali, Boutros. *Unvanquished: A U.S.-UN Saga.* New York: Random House, 1999.

Bowden, Mark. *Black Hawk Down: A Story of Modern War.* New York: Atlantic Monthly Press, 1999.

Boyden, J., and S. Gibbs. *Children and War: Understanding Psychological Distress in Cambodia.* Geneva: UN, 1997.

Brett, R., and M. McCallin. *Children, the Invisible Soldiers.* Växjö, Sweden: Rädda Barnen (Swedish Save the Children), 1996.

Brown, Michael (ed.). *Nationalism and Ethnic Conflict: An International Security Reader.* Cambridge, MA: MIT Press, 1997.

Brownlie, Ian. *Basic Documents in International Law*, 4th ed. Oxford: Clarendon Press, 1994.

————. *International Law and the Use of Force by States.* Oxford: Clarendon Press, 1963.

Brownmiller, Susan. *Against Our Will: Men, Women, and Rape.* London: Secker & Warburg, 1975.

Bruderlein, Claude. *The Role of Non-State Actors in Building Human Security: The Case of Armed Groups in Intra-State Wars.* Geneva, Mar. 5, 2000.

Carnegie Commission on Preventing Deadly Conflict. Final report, *Preventing Deadly Conflict.* New York: Carnegie Corporation of New York, 1997.

Cater, Charles K., and Karin Wermester. *From Reaction to Prevention: Opportunities for the UN System in the New Millennium.* New York: International Peace Academy, International Policy Conference Report, Apr. 13–14, 2000.

Cawthra, Gavin. *Brutal Force: The Apartheid War Machine.* London: International Defence and Aid Fund for Southern Africa, 1986.

Chesterman, Simon. "An Altogether Different Order: Defining the Elements of Crimes Against Humanity." *Duke Journal of Comparative and International Law* 10 (2000), p. 307.

————. *Just War or Just Peace? Humanitarian Intervention and International Law.* Oxford: Oxford University Press, 2001.

————. "Never Again . . . and Again: Law, Order and the Gender of War Crimes in Bosnia and Beyond." *Yale Journal of International Law* 22 (1997), p. 299.

Chinkin, Christine M. "Kosovo: A 'Good' or 'Bad' War?" *American Journal of International Law* 93 (1999), p. 841.

Chomsky, Noam. *The New Military Humanism: Lessons from Kosovo.* London: Pluto Press, 1999.

Clapham, Christopher (ed.). *African Guerrillas.* Oxford: James Currey, 1998.

Clark, Walter S., and Jeffrey Herbst (eds.). *Learning from Somalia: The Lessons of Armed Humanitarian Intervention.* Boulder, CO: Westview Press, 1997.

Cliffe, Lionel. *The Transition to Independence in Namibia.* Boulder, CO: Lynne Rienner Publishers, 1994.

Cohne, Ilene, and Guy S. Goodwin-Gill. *Child Soldiers: The Role of Children in Armed Conflict.* Oxford: Clarendon Press, 1994.

Collings, Deirdre (ed.). *Peace for Lebanon? From War to Reconstruction.* Boulder, CO: Lynne Rienner Publishers, 1994.

Copelon, Rhonda. "Surfacing Gender: Re-Engraving Crimes Against Women in Humanitarian Law." *Hastings Women's Law Journal* 5 (1994), p. 243.

Cortright, David, and George A. Lopez. *The Sanctions Decade: Assessing UN Strategies in the 1990s.* Boulder, CO: Lynne Rienner Publishers, 2000.

de Kock, Eugene. *A Long Night's Damage: Working for the Apartheid State.* Saxonwold: Contra, 1998.

Destexhe, Alain. "Humanitarian Neutrality: Myth or Reality," In *Preventive Diplomacy: Stopping Wars Before They Start,* edited by Kevin M. Cahill. New York: Basic Books, 1996.

Dodge, C., and M. Raundalen. *Reaching Children in War: Sudan, Uganda and Mozambique.* Uppsala: Sigma Forlag, 1991.

Draper, G.I.A.D. *The Red Cross Conventions.* London: Stevens, 1958.

Dunant, Henri. *Un souvenir de Solférino.* Geneva: Jules-Guillaume Fick, 1862. Available in French and English at www.icrc.org.

Durch, William J. (ed.). *UN Peacekeeping, American Politics and the Uncivil Wars of the 1990s.* New York: St. Martin's Press, 1996.

Ellis, John. *A Short History of Guerrilla Warfare.* London: Allan, 1975.

Ellis, Stephen. *The Mask of Anarchy: The Destruction of Liberia and the Religious Dimension of an African Civil War.* London: Hurst, 1999.

Evans, Gareth. *Cooperating for Peace: The Global Agenda for the 1990s and Beyond.* St. Leonards, NSW: Allen & Unwin, 1993.

Evans, Glynne. *Responding to Crises in the African Great Lakes.* Adelphi Paper 311. London: International Institute for Strategic Studies, 1997.

Fleck, Dieter (ed.). *The Handbook of Humanitarian Law in Armed Conflict.* Oxford: Oxford University Press, 1995.

Fox, Gregory H. "International Law and Civil Wars." *New York University Journal of International Law and Politics* 26 (1994), p. 633.

Furley, O. (ed.). *Conflict in Africa.* London: Tauris, 1995.

Geffray, C. *La Cause des armes au Mozambique: Anthropologie d'une guerre civile.* Paris: Credu-Karthala, 1990.

Gersony, R. "Summary of Refugee Accounts of Principally Conflict Related Experiences in Mozambique." Washington, DC: Bureau for Refugee Programs, State Department, 1988.

Gibbs, S. "Post-War Reconstruction in Mozambique: Reframing Children's Experiences of War and Healing." *Disasters* 18, 3 (1994), p. 268.

Global Witness. *A Crude Awakening: The Role of the Oil and Banking Industries in Angola's Civil War and the Plunder of State Assets.* London: Global Witness, 1999.

———. *A Rough Trade: The Role of Companies and Governments in the Angolan Conflict.* London: Global Witness, 1998.

Goodwin-Gill, Guy S. *The Refugee in International Law,* 2d ed. Oxford: Clarendon Press, 1996.

Goulding, Marrack. "The Evolution of United Nations Peacekeeping." *International Affairs* 69 (1993), p. 451.

Gourevitch, Philip. *We Wish to Inform You That Tomorrow We Will Be Killed with Our Families.* London: Picador, 1999.

Graber, Doris. *The Development of the Law of Belligerent Occupation 1863–1914: A Historical Survey.* New York: Columbia University Press, 1949.

Green, L. C. *The Contemporary Law of Armed Conflict.* Manchester: Manchester University Press, 1993.

Groth, Siegfried. *Namibia: The Wall of Silence—The Dark Days of the Liberation Struggle.* Wuppertal: Peter Hammer, 1995.

Grotius, Hugo. *De iure belli ac pacis libri tres* [1646]. Classics of International Law. F. W. Kelsey, trans. Oxford: Clarendon Press, 1925.

Hampson, Françoise J. "Using International Human Rights Machinery to Enforce the International Law of Armed Conflict. *Revue de droit pénal militaire et de droit de la guerre* 31 (1992), p. 119.

Harvard University/OCHA, Report of the Inter-Agency Expert Consultation on Protected Areas (1999), available at www.hsph.harvard.edu/hcpds/report.pdf.

Hayner, Priscilla B. "Fifteen Truth Commissions—1974–1993: A Comparative Study." *Human Rights Quarterly* 16 (1994), p. 597.

Higgins, Rosalyn. "The United Nations Role in Maintaining International Peace: The Lessons of the First Fifty Years." *New York Law School Journal of International and Comparative Law* 16 (1996), p. 135.

Holbrooke, Richard. *To End a War.* New York: Random House, 1998.

Honwana, Alcinda. "Healing for Peace: Traditional Healers and Post-War Reconstruction in Southern Mozambique." In *Religion Health and Suffering,* edited by R. Porter and J. Hinnels. London: Kegan Paul, 1997.

Honwana, Joao. "The United Nations and Mozambique: A Sustainable Peace?" *Lumiar Papers No. 7*. Lisbon: Instituto de Estudos Estrategicos e Internacionais, 1995.

Huband, Mark. *The Liberian Civil War*. London: Frank Cass, 1998.

Hulls, William. *The Two Hague Conferences and Their Contributions to International Law*. Boston: Ginn, 1908.

Human Rights Watch. *Accountability in Namibia: Human Rights and the Transition to Democracy*. New York: Human Rights Watch, 1992.

———. *Angola Unravels: The Rise and Fall of the Lusaka Peace Process*. New York: Human Rights Watch, 1999.

———. *Easy Prey: Children and War in Liberia*. London: Human Rights Watch Children's Project, 1994.

———. *"Leave None to Tell the Story": Genocide in Rwanda*. New York: Human Rights Watch, 1999.

———. *War Without Quarter: Colombia and International Humanitarian Law*. New York: Human Rights Watch, 1998.

Ignatieff, Michael. *The Warrior's Honor: Ethnic War and the Modern Conscience*. London: Vintage, 1999.

International Committee of the Red Cross. *Bibliography of International Humanitarian Law Applicable in Armed Conflicts*, 2d ed. Geneva: ICRC, 1987.

———. *Commentary on the Additional Protocols of 8 June 1977 to the Geneva Conventions of 12 August 1949*. Geneva: ICRC, 1987.

———. "Report on the Protection of War Victims." *International Review of the Red Cross* 296 (1993), p. 391.

International Task Force on the Enforcement of UN Security Council Resolutions. Final Report, *Words to Deeds: Strengthening the UN's Enforcement Capabilities*. New York: United Nations Association of the USA, 1997.

Judah, Tim. *Kosovo: War and Revenge*. New Haven: Yale University Press, 2000.

———. *The Serbs: History, Myth and the Destruction of Yugoslavia*. New Haven: Yale University Press, 1998.

Kalshoven, Frits, and Yves Sanoz (eds.). *Implementation of International Humanitarian Law*. Dordrecht: Nijhoff, 1989.

Katjavivi, Peter H. *A History of Resistance in Namibia*. London: James Currey, 1988.

Kent, Randolph. "Humanitarian Assistance and Inter-Agency Co-operation: Constraints and Prospects in an African Context." *International Journal of Refugee Law—OAU/UNHCR Special Issue* (1995), p. 235.

Korany, Bahgat, and Ali Hillal Dessouki (eds.) *The Foreign Policy of Arab States: The Challenge of Change*, 2d ed. Boulder, CO: Westview Press, 1991.

Kritz, Neil J. (ed.). *Transitional Justice: How Emerging Democracies Reckon with Former Regimes*. Washington, DC: United States Institute of Peace Press, 1995.

Krog, Antji. *Country of My Skull*. Johannesburg: Random House, 1998.

Kuper, Jenny. *International Law Concerning Child Civilians in Armed Conflict*. Oxford: Clarendon Press, 1997.

Laqueur, Walter. *Guerrilla: A Historical and Critical Study*. London: Weidenfeld and Nicolson, 1977.

Lawyers Committee for Human Rights. *Haiti: Learning the Hard Way—The UN/OAS Human Rights Monitoring Operation in Haiti, 1993–1994*. New York: Lawyers Committee for Human Rights, 1995.

———. *Improvising History: A Critical Evaluation of the United Nations Observer Mission in El Salvador*. New York: Lawyers Committee for Human Rights, 1995.

Lee, Roy S.K. (ed.). *The International Criminal Court: The Making of the Rome Statute*. The Hague: Kluwer, 1999.

Leys, Colin, and John Saul. "Liberation Without Democracy? The SWAPO Crisis of 1976." *Journal of Southern African Studies* 20, 1 (1994), p. 134.

Leys, Colin, and John Saul (eds.). *Namibia, the Two-Edged Sword.* London: James Currey, 1995).

Lillich, Richard B. "The Role of the UN Security Council in Protecting Human Rights in Crisis Situations: UN Humanitarian Intervention in the Post–Cold War World." *Tulane Journal of International and Comparative Law* 3 (1995), p. 1.

Lillich, Richard B. (ed.). *Humanitarian Intervention and the United Nations.* Charlottesville: University Press of Virginia, 1973.

Luck, Edward C. *Mixed Messages: American Politics and International Organization, 1919–1999.* Washington, DC: Brookings Institution, 1999.

Luttwak, Edward N. "Give War a Chance." *Foreign Affairs* 78, 4 (July/Aug. 1999), p. 36.

MacAlister-Smith, P. *International Humanitarian Assistance: Disaster Relief Actions in International Law and Organization.* Dordrecht: Nijhoff, 1985.

MacKinnon, Michael G. *The Evolution of U.S. Peacekeeping Under Clinton.* London: Frank Cass, 2000.

Macrae, Joanne, and Anthony B. Zwy. *War and Hunger: Rethinking International Responses to Complex Emergencies.* London: Zed Books/Save the Children, 1995.

Malone, David. *Decision-Making in the UN Security Council: The Case of Haiti, 1990–1997.* Oxford: Clarendon Press, 1998.

Mavrodes, G. "Conventions and the Morality of War." *Philosophy and Public Affairs* 4, 2 (1975), p. 117.

Mayall, James (ed.). *The New Interventionism 1991–1994: United Nations Experience in Cambodia, Former Yugoslavia and Somalia.* Cambridge: Cambridge University Press, 1996.

McCormack, Timothy L.H., and Gerry Simpson (eds.). *The Law of War Crimes: National and International Approaches.* The Hague: Kluwer, 1997.

Melvern, Linda. *The Ultimate Crime: Who Betrayed the UN and Why.* London: Allison & Busby, 1995.

Meron, Theodor. *Human Rights and Humanitarian Norms as Customary Law.* Oxford: Clarendon Press, 1989.

———. "Rape as a Crime Under International Humanitarian Law." *American Journal of International Law* 87 (1993), p. 424.

Meyer, M. (ed.). *Armed Conflict and the New Law: Aspects of the 1977 Geneva Protocols and the 1981 Weapons Convention.* London: British Institute of International and Comparative Law, 1989.

Minear, Larry, Colin Scott, and Thomas G. Weiss. *The News Media, Civil War, and Humanitarian Action.* Boulder, CO: Lynne Rienner Publishers, 1996.

Minow, Martha. *Between Vengeance and Forgiveness: Facing History After Genocide and Mass Violence.* Boston: Beacon Press, 1998.

Minter, William. *Apartheid's Contras: An Inquiry into the Roots of War in Angola and Mozambique.* London: Zed Books, 1994.

Moore, John N. (ed.). *Law and Civil War in the Modern World.* Baltimore: Johns Hopkins University Press, 1974.

Moore, Jonathan. *Hard Choices: Moral Dilemmas in Humanitarian Intervention.* Oxford: Rowman & Littlefield, 1998.

Murphy, Sean D. *Humanitarian Intervention: The United Nations in an Evolving World Order.* Philadelphia: University of Pennsylvania Press, 1996.

Nabulsi, Karma. *Traditions of War: Occupation, Resistance, and the Law.* Oxford: Oxford University Press, 1999.

Naylor, R. T. "The Insurgent Economy: Black Market Operations of Guerrilla Organizations." *Crime, Law and Social Change* 20 (1993), p. 21.

Nicholson, Frances, and Patrick Twomey (eds.). *Refugee Rights and Realities: Evolving International Concepts and Regimes.* Cambridge: Cambridge University Press, 1999.

Nino, Carlos Santiago. *Radical Evil on Trial.* New Haven: Yale University Press, 1996.

O'Neill, William G. "A Humanitarian Practitioner's Guide to International Human Rights Law." Thomas Watson Institute for International Studies, Occasional Paper No. 34 (1999).

———. "Human Rights Monitoring vs. Political Expediency: The Experience of the OAS/UN Mission in Haiti." *Harvard Human Rights Law Journal* 8 (1995), p. 115.

Orentlicher, Diane F. "Settling Accounts: The Duty to Prosecute Human Rights Violations of a Prior Regime." *Yale Law Journal* 100 (1991), p. 2541.

Organization for Security and Cooperation in Europe. *Kosovo/Kosova: As Seen, as Told.* Vienna: OSCE, 1999.

Owen, David. *Balkan Odyssey.* New York: Harcourt Brace, 1995.

Palwankar, U. "Measures Available to States for Fulfilling Their Obligation to Ensure Respect for International Humanitarian Law." *International Review of the Red Cross* 298 (1994), p. 9.

Parsons, Anthony. *From Cold War to Hot Peace: UN Interventions 1947–1994.* London: Michael Joseph, 1995.

Pictet, Jéan. *Development and Principles of International Humanitarian Law.* Dordrecht: Nijhoff, 1985.

———. *The Geneva Conventions of 12 August 1949: Commentary.* Geneva: ICRC, 1960.

Plattner, Denise. "ICRC Neutrality and Neutrality in Humanitarian Assistance." *International Review of the Red Cross* 311 (1996), p. 161.

Prendergast, John. *Frontline Diplomacy: Humanitarian Aid and Conflict in Africa.* Boulder, CO: Lynne Rienner Publishers, 1996.

Prunier, Gérard. *The Rwanda Crisis: History of a Genocide.* New York: Columbia University Press, 1997.

Pugh, Michael, and S. Alex Cunliffe. "The Lead Agency Concept in Humanitarian Assistance: The Case of the UNHCR," *Security Dialogue* 28, 1 (1997), p. 17.

Ratner, Steven R. "New Democracies, Old Atrocities: An Inquiry in International Law." *Georgetown Law Journal* 87 (1999), p. 707.

Reisman, W. Michael. "Legal Responses to Genocide and Other Massive Violations of Human Rights." *Law and Contemporary Problems* 59, 4 (1996), p. 75.

Reno, William. *Warlord Politics and African States.* Boulder, CO: Lynne Rienner Publishers, 1999.

Richards, Paul. *Fighting for the Rain Forest: War, Youth and Resources in Sierra Leone.* Oxford: James Currey, 1996.

Roberts, Adam. *Humanitarian Action in War: Aid Protection and Implementation in a Policy Vacuum.* Adelphi Paper 305. London: International Institute for Strategic Studies, 1996.

———. "Humanitarian War: Military Intervention and Human Rights." *International Affairs* 69 (1993), p. 429.

———. "The Laws of War: Problems of Implementation." *Duke Journal of Comparative and International Law* 6 (1995), p. 11.

Roberts, Adam, and Richard Guelff. *Documents on the Laws of War*, 3d ed. Oxford: Oxford University Press, 2000.

Robertson, Geoffrey. *Crimes Against Humanity: The Struggle for Global Justice.* London: Allen Lane, 1999.

Rodley, Nigel S. (ed.). *To Loose the Bands of Wickedness: International Intervention in Defence of Human Rights.* London: Brassey's, 1992.

Rotberg, Robert I., and Thomas G. Weiss (eds.). *From Massacres to Genocide: The Media, Public Policy, and Humanitarian Crises.* Washington, DC: Brookings Institution, 1996.

Sassòli, Marco, Antoine A. Bouvier, and Laura M. Olson. *How Does Law Protect in War? Cases, Documents, and Teaching Materials on Contemporary Practice in International Humanitarian Law.* Geneva: ICRC, 1999.

Shawcross, William. *Deliver Us from Evil: Peacekeepers, Warlords and a World of Endless Conflict.* New York: Simon & Schuster, 2000.

Silber, Laura, and Alan Little. *Yugoslavia: Death of a Nation.* New York: Penguin, 1997.

Snyder, Louis. *Global Mini-Nationalisms: Autonomy or Independence.* Westport, CT: Greenwood Press, 1982.

Steiner, Henry J., and Philip Alston. *International Human Rights in Context: Law, Politics, Morals.* Oxford: Clarendon Press, 1996.

Stiglmayer, Alexandra (ed.). *Mass Rape: The War Against Women in Bosnia-Herzegovina.* Lincoln: University of Nebraska Press, 1994.

Stremlau, John J. *People in Peril: Human Rights, Humanitarian Action, and Preventing Deadly Conflict.* New York: Carnegie Corporation of New York, 1998.

Sweeney, John P. *Tread Cautiously in Colombia's Civil War.* Backgrounder 1264. Washington, DC: Heritage Foundation, 1999.

Swinarski, C. (ed.). *Studies and Essays on International Humanitarian Law and Red Cross Principles in Honour of Jéan Pictet.* Geneva: ICRC & Martinus Nijhoff Publishers, 1984.

Tesón, Fernando R. *Humanitarian Intervention: An Inquiry into Law and Morality*, 2d ed. Dobbs Ferry, NY: Transnational Publishers, 1997.

Türk, Danilo. "The Dangers of Failed States and a Failed Peace in the Post Cold War Era." *New York University Journal of International Law and Politics* 27 (1995), p. 625.

United Nations. *Millennium Report of the Secretary-General, "We, the Peoples": The Role of the United Nations in the 21st Century.* UN Doc. A/54/2000 (2000).

————. *Report of the Independent Inquiry into the Actions of the United Nations During the 1994 Genocide in Rwanda.* Attached to UN Doc. S/1999/1257 (1999).

————. *Report of the Secretary-General Pursuant to General Assembly Resolution 53/35: The Fall of Srebrenica.* UN Doc. A/54/549 (1999).

————. *Report of the Secretary-General, Renewing the United Nations: A Programme for Reform.* UN Doc. A/51/950 (1997).

————. *Report of the Secretary-General to the Security Council on the Protection of Civilians in Armed Conflict.* UN Doc. S/1999/957 (1999).

————. *The United Nations and Mozambique, 1992–1995.* (Blue Book Series.) New York: UN Department of Public Information, 1995.

United Nations War Crimes Commission. *History of the United Nations War Crime Commission and the Development of the Laws of War.* London: His Majesty's Stationery Office, 1948.

van Bueren, Geraldine. "The International Legal Protection of Children in Armed Conflicts." *International and Comparative Law Quarterly* 43 (1994), p. 809.

Vines, Alex. *Renamo: Terrorism in Mozambique.* London: Centre for Southern African Studies, University of York, and Indiana University Press, 1991.

————. *Peace Postponed: Angola Since the Lusaka Protocol.* London: Catholic Institute for International Relations, 1998.

Walzer, Michael. *Just and Unjust Wars: A Moral Argument with Historical Illustrations,* 2d ed. New York: Basic Books, 1992.

Weiss, Thomas G. "Principles, Politics, and Humanitarian Action." *Ethics & International Affairs* 13 (1999), p. 11.

Weller, Marc. *The Crisis in Kosovo, 1989–1999: From the Dissolution of Yugoslavia to Rambouillet and the Outbreak of Hostilities.* International Documents and Analysis, vol. 1. Linton: Book Systems Plus, 1999.

Wilson, Richard A. "The Sizwe Will Not Go Away: The Truth and Reconciliation Commission, Human Rights and Nation-Building in South Africa." *African Studies* 55, 2 (1996), p. 1.

Woodward, Susan. *Balkan Tragedy: Chaos and Dissolution After the Cold War.* Washington, DC: Brookings Institution, 1995.

Zartman, I. William. *Ripe for Resolution: Conflict and Intervention in Africa.* New York: Oxford University Press, 1989.

Zartman, I. William, and J. Lewis Rasmussen (eds.). *Peacemaking in International Conflict: Methods and Techniques.* Washington: USIP Press, 1997.

The Contributors

Claude Bruderlein is director of the Program on Humanitarian Policy and Conflict Research at Harvard University. From 1990 to 1995, he served with the International Committee of the Red Cross (ICRC) as an ICRC delegate in Iran, Israel and the Occupied Territories, Saudi Arabia, Kuwait, and Yemen. In 1996, he joined the United Nations Department of Humanitarian Affairs in New York as special adviser.

Charles K. Cater joined the International Peace Academy in 1999. He is the coauthor, with Elizabeth Cousens, of the forthcoming Occasional Paper, *Toward Peace in Bosnia: Implementing the Dayton Accords.* He is now a doctoral student in the international relations program at the University of Oxford.

Simon Chesterman is an associate at the International Peace Academy. He has previously worked at the International Criminal Tribunal for Rwanda and the Office for the Coordination of Humanitarian Affairs in the Federal Republic of Yugoslavia. He is the author of *Just War or Just Peace? Humanitarian Intervention and International Law.*

Pierre Gassmann's first mission with the ICRC was in Nigeria (Biafra) in 1968–1969. After a stint in the private sector, he returned to the ICRC and has since served as head of mission in Mozambique, Uganda, Angola, San Salvador, the former Yugoslavia, and Colombia. He has held the post of regional director for Africa, and is presently regional director for Eastern Europe.

Alcinda Honwana is senior lecturer in the Department of Social Anthropology at the University of Cape Town, South Africa. She has done extensive research on the impact of political conflict on children and youth, as well as on local strategies for postwar healing and reconciliation in Mozambique and Angola.

Bruce D. Jones is Special Assistant to the UN Special Coordinator for the Middle East Peace Process. Until summer 2000, he was responsible for strategic coordination policy in the UN Office for the Coordination of Humanitarian Affairs. Prior to this, he was a Hamburg Fellow for the Prevention of Deadly Conflict at Stanford University. His monograph on Rwanda, *"The Best Laid Plans": Peace Making in Rwanda and the Implications of Failure,* is forthcoming.

Guy Lamb is senior researcher with the Centre for Conflict Resolution (CCR), associated with the University of Cape Town, where he manages the project on Peace and Security. He has written extensively on issues of defense and security in southern Africa, and is coeditor of a forthcoming book on the role of the military in state formation and nation-building in southern Africa.

Edward C. Luck is founder and executive director of the Center for the Study of International Organization of the School of Law of New York University and the Woodrow Wilson School of Public and International Affairs of Princeton University. A former president of the United Nations Association of the USA (UNA-USA), he played a key role in the UN reform process from 1995 to 1997. His most recent book is *Mixed Messages: American Politics and International Organization, 1919–1999.*

Karma Nabulsi is a Prize Research Fellow at Nuffield College, Oxford University, as well as a Jean Monnet Fellow at the European University Institute in Florence. She joined the Palestinian movement in 1975, and between 1978 and 1990 was an official in the PLO, working in various capacities in Beirut, New York, Tunis, and London. She is the author of *Traditions of War: Occupation, Resistance, and the Law.*

William G. O'Neill is an international lawyer specializing in human rights, refugee, and humanitarian law. He was the Senior Adviser on Human Rights in the United Nations Mission in Kosovo from August 1999 to March 2000. He has previously served as Chief of the UN Human Rights Field Operation in Rwanda and as Director of the Legal Department of the UN/OAS International Civilian Mission in Haiti (1993–1995).

Navanethem Pillay was the first black woman attorney to be appointed acting judge of the Supreme Court of South Africa. She is the Honorary Chair of Equality Now, an international human rights organization for action on women's rights based in New York. She was elected as judge of the International Criminal Tribunal for Rwanda in May 1995 by the United Nations General Assembly and as president of the tribunal in June 1999.

Adam Roberts has been Montague Burton Professor of International Relations at Oxford University and a fellow of Balliol College since 1986. His books include *Nations in Arms: The Theory and Practice of Territorial Defense, Documents on the Laws of War* (coedited with Richard Guelff), *United Nations, Divided World: The UN's Roles in International Relations* (coedited with Benedict Kingsbury), and *Humanitarian Action in War: Aid, Protection, and Impartiality in a Policy Vacuum.*

Marie-Joëlle Zahar is a postdoctoral fellow at the Munk Centre for International Studies, University of Toronto. Her research focuses on the politics of armed militias and the motivations that bring these groups to the negotiating table, and she has published a number of articles on this topic.

Index

279

About the Book

In World War I, only 5 percent of all casualties were civilian; in World War II, that number was 50 percent; and in conflicts in the 1990s, civilians accounted for up to 90 percent of those killed. Clearly, the 1949 Geneva Convention on the Protection of Civilians, while recognizing the changing face of war, has not succeeded in reversing the trend.

Focusing particularly on the intrastate conflicts that characterized the late twentieth century, this book seeks to expand the tools available to national and international actors endeavoring to protect civilians in times of war. The authors present a range of perspectives on the evolving norms of international humanitarian law and how humanitarian actors can persuade—or compel—belligerents to respect those norms. Their work is a critical step toward limiting suffering in future battles.

Simon Chesterman, associate at the International Peace Academy, is author of *Just War or Just Peace? Humanitarian Intervention and International Law*.